Clogs and Shawls

by

John Cowell

RB
Rossendale Books

Books by John Cowell

The Broken Biscuit

Cracks in the Ceiling

Elephant Grass

An American Journey

Poems of Life

A Compilation of Poems

Poetical Themes

Published by Lulu Enterprises Inc
3101 Hillsborough Street
Suite 2010
Raleigh NC 27607 – 5436
United States of America

Published in paperback 2020
Category Memoirs & Family History
Copyright © John Cowell 2020
ISBN 978-1-71673-019-1

All rights reserved, Copyright under Berne Copyright Convention and Pan American Convention. No part of this book may be reproduced, stored in a retrieval system, or transmitted in any form or by any means, electronic, mechanical, photocopying, recording or otherwise, without prior permission of the author. The author's moral rights have been asserted.

Albion Street, Burnley: our family home

DEDICATION

*Dedicated to my two sons, John and Craig, and
all of my grandchildren.*

INTRODUCTION

The reason why I started to write this book is quite simple. When I was a young boy, my mother used to tell many tales of her own childhood and that of her own parents and grandparents. I was always intrigued with what she had to say and found her tales both fascinating and poignant. The stories remained within me right into my sixties and that's when I decided to write my mother's biography ...... 'THE BROKEN BISCUIT.' Well .... nobody was more surprised than me on how successful the book was. I got letters from all over the world imploring me write another novel. What gave me the most pleasure was the fact that I had brought a little happiness into other people's lives. It was for this reason that I decided to put pen to paper and write this book. It is a mixture of my mother's life and my own.

CHAPTER 1 - EARLY DAYS

Born in Bank Hall, my first day of life,
Given a twin sister ... just like a wife.
In a way it was great but much to my loss,
Right from the start she was to be boss.

These words are from a poem about my life. They are very true but to be fair my twin Mary was only the boss because I allowed her to be so. My mam, Winifred Cowell, had given birth to twins and in the next bed a lady had, nine days previously, given birth to a little baby boy. The lady was called Mrs Cheetham and she named her son Robert. Little did we know then, that although 'Bobby' and I were to have many differences, we would become lifelong friends.

****

I was quite robust with a thick crop of black hair whereas Mary was very delicate and her hair was thin and wispy. On many occasions whilst pushing us in the pram people would stop Mam and make comments:

"Oh the little girl is much bigger than the boy isn't she? My, the little girl has got a lot more hair than the boy hasn't she?" Mam would quietly point out their mistake leaving them a little embarrassed.

In spite of her size, Mary was always the boss, letting me know it in no uncertain terms. But despite pulling my hair and clonking me with her rattle or anything else she could lay her hands on, I took it all in my stride and hardly ever retaliated. To say the least, my life has been both varied and interesting, although at times quite arduous and trying.

I was born in Bank Hall Hospital on April 11th 1939 at 7 o'clock in the morning and my twin sister Mary came into the world 5 hours later at 12 noon. Mam wasn't feeling too well following the births as I was born feet first and Mary was breech, presenting buttocks first. Mam already had two older children, Maureen, who was 4 years and 1 month old, and Jimmy aged 20 months.

Mam wasn't too happy when she'd discovered she was pregnant for the third time. Her unhappiness stemmed from the fact that my dad wasn't the most supportive husband in the world; he much preferred the company of his drinking friends to that of his family, spending most of his time and money in the pub. He had a horse and cart and was a rag and bone man but also dealt in scrap iron, having many good business connections. When business was slack he would go out selling ice-cream and the transport system was a horse and cart. The firm he worked for was Allen's and the depot was on Standish Street. Despite being a shrewd businessman with a flare for making money he had an even greater flare for spending it, especially on his crony boozing friends. He'd freely buy drinks for everyone in the pub, and relished in the popularity that surrounded him. His name was John, but to his family and friends he was better known as 'Jack'. He also, due to his quarrelsome nature, had another nickname around the town pubs ... 'Barney'. He was well liked by all his drinking companions because of his generosity, but it was a different tale when it came to finding some housekeeping money ... sadly, poor Mum had to fight for every penny she got from him.

In her frustration she became angry and raised her head to Heaven crying out, "No ... no I don't want this baby God! I know when I was a young girl I always dreamed of having four children of my own; but that was with the help and support of a loving caring husband. However, Jack thinks more of his so-called friends in the pubs than he does of his own little ones. I can't bear the thought of bringing another baby into this world ... please God understand!"

Well, she got her answer all right ... it was as if God answered, **"Oh, so you don't want this baby do you not Winifred ... well, we'll just have to see about that won't we?"**

A few days later whilst attending the antenatal clinic one of the midwives approached Mam with a smile on her face.

"Well well Mrs Cowell, haven't we got good news for you ... you're having twins!" Mam was flabbergasted.

"Oh dear!" she thought to herself, "That just serves me right doesn't it God ... testing Your infinite wisdom?" After the initial shock she was left with little option but to settle down into some sort of routine. Despite Dad's wanton ways he always seemed to rally round at times like this. He stayed off the beer whilst Mam was in hospital and cared for my two older siblings catering to their every need. When Dad was good ... he was very good.

At the time Mam and Dad lived in a council house at number 36 Dalton Street in the Bleak House Estate ... it was Mam's pride and joy ... she used to call it her sunshine house. She'd only been married five years and had already moved six times. This was the only decent place she'd ever lived in ... two of the previous five were in slum condemned areas with atrocious living conditions. Dalton Street however had a garden, three bedrooms, but most important of all ... a bathroom. An added bonus was that she got on very well with the next-door neighbour, Mrs Alice King. Alice often looked after Maureen and Jimmy whilst Mam took Mary and me to the clinic, as Mary needed sunlight treatment in order to build her up.

My oldest sister, Maureen, was only just turned 4 years old, but was already coming into her own doing little chores around the house, acting like a little mother to her younger siblings. She was a Godsend to Mam. Whilst Mam was still in hospital she helped Dad with the housework and looking after Jimmy. She wasn't very big herself and used to stand at the sink on a wooden box to do the washing up. Maureen recalls standing at the front door when the ambulance arrived. Mam stepped out followed by Dad, who was carrying Mary in one arm and me in the other. When Dad was like this, things were great but it wasn't long before he went back to his errant ways. In the following months Mam struggled on doing everything in her power to raise her young family alone.

****

In the September, when I was just five months old, Germany invaded Poland and three days later the Second World War began. The Government introduced rationing and ration books were issued from specially designated government buildings. Air-raid shelters sprang up all over town in back-yards, schools and workplaces. The voice of Winston Churchill was constantly on the wireless and warnings were plastered on billboards alerting people to the impending danger, preparing them for war.

The Prime Minister, Neville Chamberlain, made an announcement over the wireless, *"Unlike the First World War, this is not just going to be a soldiers' war, it's going to be a people's war too ... every man woman and child will be involved. Most attacks will be at night-time, so be prepared to spend many hours in the air-raid shelters provided in case of air attack."*

****

Despite the war, things didn't change much for Mam. Our Maureen and Jimmy had just got over a bout of whooping cough when Mary and I contracted it. I was quite robust and soon recovered whereas Mary, being so delicate, became seriously ill as the cough developed into croup. My twin sister fought for every breath and certainly would have died but for the constant vigil kept over her by Mam. Mary retched at every mouthful of food and gradually went down to her birth weight. Mam had to stay up night after night painstakingly spoon-feeding her. Mam was exhausted herself and felt she wasn't doing enough and so approached her doctor.

"Dr. Bird," she said, "I feel that I can't cope anymore, could you please take little Mary into hospital so as to take some pressure off me and make things a little easier?"

"I'm sorry Mrs Cowell but I can't do that," he replied, "you see, they won't be able to look after her the same as you, and when she cries they won't always have the time to pick her up and cuddle her like you do. No, they can't do anymore for her there than what you are doing right now."

So the constant vigilance and spoon-feeding carried on … and on … and on, for almost five months. Despite being very weary, Mam never once lost her patience; as a matter of fact, she had a strange wonderful calm about her that transcended from above throughout the whole period. Eventually after five months of agonising torment, Mary started to show signs of improvement.

This was only one of many struggles that Mam endured, but through it all she persevered. Her biggest worry was that her children would be taken into care and separated from each other. She'd heard many bizarre tales of how children were being deported to Australia never to return. She was determined to keep all her little ones together no matter what the cost to herself.

"I want all my children to grow up knowing and loving each another," she would say to herself, "I don't want them scattered to different parts of the globe." She also dreaded the fact that her children, like many others, would be taken into care and then fostered out, becoming skivvies to the more privileged folk.

****

36 Dalton Street was certainly Mam's dream house but alas, her dream was about to be shattered. Because of Dad's drinking habit, Mam was forever short of money and consequently got into arrears with the rent. Despite having four children the Council was very strict and served an eviction order on her. She wrote to them asking for leeway but they were unforgiving ... shortly afterwards the Bailiff's van arrived. Mary and I were in our pram outside and our Maureen was gently rocking it ... Mam was sat on the front step with Jimmy on her knee. The Bailiff's workers were hardened men but this pathetic sight touched them so much that even they couldn't carry out their grim task. Nevertheless, the Council would not relent and served another notice ... Mam, along with her young family, had to go. Dad did the job himself, loading all the furniture onto his cart.

As it happened, there was a family living just across the street from us, the Halsteads. A young 14 year old boy, Walter Halstead, witnessed the whole sorry spectacle and he was moved to tears.

"This can't be true?" he thought to himself. "Surely to goodness the Council can't be throwing Mrs Cowell and her children out onto the street?" During the time spent in Dalton Street, young Walter used to run errands for Mam and he'd become quite attached to her young family. He ran across and tapped Mam on the shoulder.

"What's happening Mrs Cowell, what are they doing with your furniture?"

She could see the concerned look on the young lad's face and tried to reassure him, "It's all right young Walter, don't worry about it ... we'll be all right, you'll see."

He was a very perceptive young lad and, despite her assurance, he sensed the truth. He felt both mad and sad at the same time about the injustice of things, as he'd always looked up to Mam and admired her.

In fact, he'd always had a kind of teenage crush on her because of her long flowing dark hair and other special features. He knew in his heart that something cruel and heartless was happening ... the memory of that terrible day was to remain with him for the rest of his life. He watched as Dad guided off the horse and cart with Mam and us four children perched in between the sparse furniture.

"Good-bye kind lady," he muttered to himself as the cart turned right at the bottom of Dalton Street onto Coal Clough Lane. "Good luck and God bless." Walter didn't know it at the time, but he wasn't to set eyes on that poor family again for another sixty years.

Within the next few months Poor Mam moved another three times, living in appalling cramped conditions. To further complicate things, Dad got his calling up papers and had to report to Litchfield in the Midlands where he enrolled into the Catering Corps. Mam didn't like him being away from home but at least she had a regular allowance from the Army. It wasn't much, but it was there every week without having to fight for it. Like her mother before her, she learned to get by any way she could, including going to the market near to closing time in order to buy produce at knockdown prices. One item she always bought in quantity was broken biscuits, these were the only kind we ever got during our early years; no matter, they tasted just as good as full ones, and we kids never once complained. Another method Mam used to get by was to exchange one particular commodity for another. She was a great believer that sugar was good for sustaining our energy levels, and would often exchange a packet of tea for a two pound bag of Tate & Lyle; hence, we kids became quite accustomed to drinking sweet, weak tea.

Shortly after Dad got called up, Mam realised that she was pregnant once again; our Maureen was only five years and three months old and was already the eldest of four.

A little house on Whitaker Street, where we were living at the time, was already too small for us, and when Mum was offered a bigger one in the same area, she eagerly took it. In early January 1941, when Mam was eight months pregnant, we moved into ... **14 ALBION STREET.** It was to be our home for the next twenty years.

****

Albion Street was situated in the very heart of 'The Weavers' Triangle' ... so called because of the cluster of factories and tall factory chimneys which punctuated the skyline. Burnley, being a very important industrial town, had more factory chimneys than any other town of comparable size in the world; thick dense smoke constantly hung over the town like a shroud. The main industry was cotton, as the damp climate of Burnley was ideal for its production. Day after day the tall chimneys belched out thick smoke and soot, which coated all the buildings and terraced houses in grime. Like many other milltowns, Burnley's Victorian buildings had been built during the Industrial Revolution of the 1800's. As a child, I could never remember living anywhere else other than this over polluted area of town.

The Leeds and Liverpool Canal ran through the length of Burnley and was overlooked on both sides by large cotton mills and weaving sheds. Running parallel on the topside was Trafalgar Street, a main thoroughfare for traffic. The local people always knew Trafalgar Street as simply 'Trafalgar'. Built in close proximity to these dreary mills on the other side of Trafalgar was a labyrinth of cobbled streets that ran up to a railway embankment. Albion Street was the exception, being much longer and steeper than any other street; it continued over a railway via a stone bridge, carrying on for another half mile to the gates of Scott's Park.

Number fourteen was below the railway-bridge in the middle of the terraced block. It had two bedrooms, two downstairs rooms and two cellars. All the rooms were bare without a strip of wallpaper on the walls. The plaster was crumbling and there was evidence of damp everywhere. Still, it was better than some of the hovels we had lived in.

The downstairs living-room was the only room with lighting, an old antiquated gas-lamp that hung from the ceiling. The focal point of the room was a large cast-iron fireplace with a mantelpiece. Pans could be placed on top of and into a built-in-oven with a heavy door. The fire-grate was about fifteen inches off the floor to allow ashes to fall through the grid. On the other side, a water boiler with a hinged lid rested below a shelf on which kitchen utensils were stored. The fireplace may not have been a pretty sight, but once the fire was lit the cast iron framework contained heat and radiated welcome warmth into the living room.

It was a cold draughty house, and the wind would howl up a flight of stone steps from the cellar below. The bare stone flags of the living-room floor didn't help matters either. When Mam looked around the house for the first time she fixed her gaze on a small pot sink that sat on cast-iron legs under the window. Flimsy flea-ridden lace curtains billowed in the draught from a rotting windowsill.

"Well at least I've got running water and a gas geyser," she thought as her eyes wandered around the room. "Thank you God for small mercies!" She opened the backdoor to find a flight of fourteen steep stone steps. Taking up most of the yard space was a large air-raid shelter that housed the lavatory.

"Bloomín éck," she murmured to herself, "I don't fancy going down there on a cold night ... or any other night for that matter." She didn't like the situation very much but being a realist she knew she had little option.

The living room was only small, but Dad had just procured a large ornamental sideboard, which took up most of the space against the back wall. Mam felt quite pleased because the reflection from its enormous mirror added depth to the room and made it feel much cosier.

****

After we had gone to bed our Maureen helped Mam to wash up and tidy the house. She then helped with the ironing, darning socks and other chores. But Mam didn't take her for granted and was eternally grateful, thanking God every single night that Maureen had been her firstborn. At times like this Mam would take stock of her life.

"Well God, it's not much but it's better than not having a roof over our heads. Please shine Thy holy light down onto this humble home and bless all who live in it. Please grant that my unborn baby and all my young ones remain healthy and strong. I ask Thee for guidance to bring my children up in a proper manner and keep them free from evil. Also, if it's not asking too much, please let my husband come to his senses so we may rear our young family together." Unfortunately the latter part of the prayer was not answered ... at least it seemed that way.

Mam had only been in her new home three weeks when she went into labour.

On January 29th 1941 ... **her birthday child, 'Barry' was born.**

Despite Dad not being able to visit her in hospital it was a very special occasion, as it was also Mam's birthday. But even as she cuddled my little brother Barry in her arms she was fretting about us other young ones; our Maureen and Jimmy had gone to stay at grandma's house in Bacup, whereas Mary and I were being cared for on one of the hospital wards.

The following day Mam was quite pleased as she was informed that Dad had been allowed some compassionate leave. He arrived on the ward and our Maureen was with him. As on previous occasions, he picked up our Barry, his newborn son and made a great fuss, appearing to be highly delighted.

He was full of false reassurances and appeared delighted, "By 'eck this is great, three sons and two daughters; this is what life is really about." Then turning to Mam, "Right Win, I swear to you that when this war's over, I'm going to be a changed man, we're going to be a proper little family all cosy and nice together."

But things didn't turn out that way. Our Barry was just about nine months old when Dad was discharged from the army on medical grounds suffering from bronchitis and emphysema; he was only thirty-three, but already, his fast living lifestyle was beginning to catch up on him. On arriving home, he was very poorly and had lost a lot of weight that he could ill afford to, as even in a prime state, he only ever weighed around nine stone. Consequently, he needed a lot of care and attention, which meant even more work for Mam. Still, she took everything in her stride and if the truth be known, she actually enjoyed it because for the first time in her married life Dad actually stayed in; we were all one big happy family together.

Because of Mam's unrelenting love and attention, Dad grew stronger. But sadly as his health improved, he gradually drifted back into his wayward ways. Three little boys and two little girls, enough to make any man happy ... but not Dad. He still preferred the company of the 'yobbos' in the pub to us young ones. A game of cards and a few pints of bitter were more to his taste than helping to raise his family. The promise he'd made in the maternity hospital had gone by the wayside. Still, Mam more than made up for his lack of support, making sure that none of us went short of love.

Time passed by and Mam struggled on, using everything at her disposal to make our home a happy place. Bath time was quite an ordeal in our house. One evening, after our Maureen had just helped to bath Mary and me, she stood us on an old settee. Mary became over excited, laughing and giggling as she jumped up and down on the old battered sofa. However, the merriment turned to tears when she hurt one of her toes on a protruding spring.

"O-oh come here and let me kiss it better," Maureen reassured her. "Bloomin' 'eck what big tears our little Mary ... we're gonna have to get out the mop and bucket!" Then Mary's tears turned to laughter as Maureen pretended she'd hurt her finger on the same spring.

"My Maureen, can I kiss your finger better?" Mary giggled, her pain now forgotten.

"E-eh that's better, you're such a pretty little girl when you laugh. Now lift up your arms while I put on your nightie," smiled Maureen as she dressed Mary in some warm clean clothes that had been draped on a wooden rack, which hung from the ceiling over a warm fire. Mary and I then stood on a moth-eaten pegged rug in front of an old metal fireguard, which protected us from the flames.

Like Mary, Barry was always a delicate child, and in need of constant care and attention. He was forever contracting chest ailments and was to suffer from asthma in his future years.

By now Mary and I were walking and very mischievous. To make matters worse Jimmy was hyperactive and forever demanding Mum's undivided attention.

My earliest distinct memory was when I was barely three years old. I was playing at the bottom of the stairs when I got terrible stomach pains and was violently sick. Mam tried putting me on the potty without a result ... being inexperienced she then aggravated the situation by giving me a dose of working medicine. The next thing I recall was waking up in a hospital cot with about twelve steel clips in my tummy. I'd just had an emergency operation for a burst appendix and by all accounts had nearly died. I couldn't understand what was happening as Dad, Mam and our Maureen were by my cot-side making a real fuss. It turned out that Dad and Maureen had been there all night awaiting my recovery. Mam had just arrived, having had to look after the other children.

I held out my arms beckoning Mam and she picked me up with tears in her eyes, "Oh thank you God ... thank you so much!" she whimpered as she gave me a big hug.

Next it was Maureen's turn, "E-eh my little brother ... come here and let me love you!"

Even Dad picked me up and gave me a gentle hug muttering, "Eh my lad, thank goodness you're all reight ... I thought we were gonna lose thí." I couldn't fully understand what all the fuss was about but, all the same, I enjoyed the attention.

A few days later Dad came and collected me and this too was very memorable ... it was the one and only time that I met my Uncle Ted.

"Right cock, afore we go home I'm gonna take you to see my brother Ted who's on Ward Three." Uncle Ted was very poorly and confined to bed but all the same he gave me a hearty greeting.

"Eh all reight little ún ... by gum, I believe you've been in the wars. Never mind, young fella you don't seem to have come to any harm. Anyroad, come here and let me have a reight look at thí." I was usually apprehensive in these kinds of situations and needed a little friendly persuasion from Dad.

"Go on our John you know who it is don't you ... it's your Uncle Ted, mí brother?" I'd heard Dad talk about his brother Ted but, never having seen him before, I was still guarded. Ted, sensing my wariness, soon put me at ease.

"By éck lad, you've fairly grown since the last time I saw thí. Then again ... you were now't but a babe in arms and now look at thí. Well, d'you know who I am then?" he grinned.

"U-um," I replied through pursed lips, "you're my Uncle Ted."

"Aye that's reight lad. Anyroad, you'll have seen one ó these afore?" he said showing me a flat cap.

"Yeah," I responded with a smile on my face, "it's a 'watta' ... mi daddy has one."

Ted started to laugh, "Good lad ... I can see we're gonna have to watch thí. Anyroad, you might have seen one afore, but not like this ún ... this one's magic!" He then took some sweets from a toffee bag on the top of his locker and dropped them into the cap along with some pennies. My eyes lit up ... I was beginning to like my Uncle Ted. My pleasure increased even more when Ted shouted for one of the more able patients to come to his bedside.

"Will you take this little lad around the ward with this here cap and introduce him to t'other patients ... his name's John and he'd like to meet ém all." Ted handed me the cap saying, "Go on young John ... tha'll be all reight."

I was still feeling edgy as I looked up at this big man wearing pyjamas. With cap in hand I glanced first at Uncle Ted and then Dad as if asking for approval.

"Go on our John, like your Uncle Ted said ... you'll be all reight," he assured me.

As we set off round the ward, Ted remarked on what I had said to him, "A 'watta' ... that's a good ún our Jack ... I've never heard mí cap called that afore."

"Aye our Ted, he's probably heard me callín it a ratter."

"I'll tell thí what ... he's a grand little lad and he certainly seems to be out o' the woods now doesn't he?"

"He does that Ted ... touch wood. It's hard to believe that only a few days ago he freightened the life outa me, I thought he were a goner for sure ... his eyes were rolling about in his head and he were just like a rag doll when I carried him into t'hospital."

In the meanwhile I was happily going around the ward getting the flat cap filled with pennies and sweets. After leaving the last bed I happily made my way back to Dad's side.

"Look what I've got Daddy," I said with a large smile on my face, rubbing my hands in glee.

"By éck cock, you have done well ... you've even got some thre'penny bits in there."

"Aye and think on our Jack," put in Ted, "no borrowing out of it forra drink in the pub."

Dad just gave a cheeky grin.

I left the ward holding Daddy's hand and on reaching the exit I turned and gave Uncle Ted a friendly wave. Sadly, that was the last time I ever saw him for he died shortly afterwards.

****

The next vivid memory, which was to remain with me, and in some ways affect me for life, was the time I spent in the Workhouse with my twin sister Mary and younger brother Barry. Dad had been up to his old tricks again and was serving time in Wakefield Prison whilst Mam was in hospital 'buying' another baby. I remember being shepherded into a barrack type room with some other children by some matronly type women in uniforms, who then started shouting and laying down strict rules. The most horrendous part, as far as I was concerned, was when all of us children were shown a dark eerie cubbyhole leading down some stone steps into pitch darkness. The formidable women then instilled fear into us all by threatening to put us in that awful place should we misbehave. The terrible threats rendered us all passive and afraid.

"Right you little scruff bags," bellowed one of them, "this is the Bogey-hole and if you're bad that's where you'll go!"

Within a few days the inevitable happened ... I got into a fracas with one of the other children. I was dragged to the Bogey-hole by the scruff off my neck with threats of, "Right you little brat ... in you go and the Bogey-man's gonna come and get you!" I screamed incessantly, kicking out at the big woman, but to no avail; she was too strong for me and I finished up in the pitch-darkness terrified and shivering. My fear intensified as I conjured up gory and gruesome images in my mind.

"Let me out of here, it's dark and I'm frikened," I wailed, "I don't want the Bogey-man to get me! Sob sob ... I'm gonna tell mí mummy over you!" I kicked the door and screamed for all my worth but it was useless ... I had to remain in that eerie place for what seemed hours.

Other cruel things happened in the Workhouse but this particular incident left a lasting mark on my impressionable mind, and haunts me to this day. Both Mary and I hated being in that awful place but we had to stay there for two months until Dad was released from prison. We were highly delighted when he came to collect us and greeted him with open arms. On reaching home our joy turned to perplexity when we discovered that there was a new addition to the family.

Mam was in bed in the living-room cradling a little baby girl in her arms ... Barbara had been born. The family was now complete ... Dad, Mum, three little boys and three little girls. This should have been enough to make any man happy, but not Dad ... no, not Dad.

CHAPTER 2 - FAMILY STRUGGLES

The memory of the Workhouse wasn't very pleasant but Mam more than made up for it. I loved nothing more than sitting on her knee around the fireside whilst she told the most enlightening stories about her own upbringing and schooldays in Bacup, a small Lancashire town in the Rossendale Valley. She was a raconteur of the highest order ... her tales were both fascinating and poignant. She told them so explicitly and with such feeling that tears would well up in my eyes ... other times I'd roll about laughing.

Our home was sparse and dire ... the bare stone floors, the one gaslight and just cold water to hand, but after Mam finished telling her tales I would throw my arms around her neck, saying with real concern.

"He-ey Mam, weren't you poor?" Then I'd prompt her to tell more, "Will you tell us agén about your little brother Jimmy who got killed in the pit when he wer' only a lad?"

This was a really sad tale about how my Grandmother had struggled to raise ten children under terrible conditions. They lived in a two-roomed back to earth house, full of rising damp, with stone flag floors.

"There was no lighting," Mam said wistfully, "except from candles or an old paraffin lamp. Water had to be carried in a large bucket from a standpipe near to some communal toilets. U-um, and many a time during the winter months the standpipe was frozen solid so you can imagine what it was like then ... br-rr-r, it makes me shiver to think about it ... it was awful!"

I would often interrupt her tales asking, "Bloomín éck Mam, did you have to share the lavatory with other people?"

"We did that lad and first we had to traipse to the end of the block via a landing and down fifteen stone steps. Another thing, we could only have a bath on Wednesdays because all the neighbours took turns at sharing an old tin bath that hung on the wall outside. Aye, can you imagine carrying buckets of water from the standpipes and then having to heat it over the fire in a large double-handled pan? And also, to keep the fire going we had to lug coal from a cubbyhole that was at the top of the stairs."

"What d'you mean Mam, was the coal place upstairs?" I quizzed her.

"Yes it was, the coal chap used to empty bags of coal down a chute from Todmorden Road."

"Blimey Mam it must o' seemed funny having to go upstairs for the coal."

"Well no it didn't our John, but don't forget we didn't know anything else."

"Yeah all right Mam but it would've seemed funny to me."

The rest of Mum's story went something like this:

Large factories overlooked our small house, casting long shadows, which left it in permanent semi-darkness. There was a constant foisty smell in the air. Because of the dire circumstances my older brother Martin and two baby sisters, Teresa and Nellie, died causing untold sorrow. My younger brother Jimmy was a Godsend to mí mam and thought there was no one else on God's earth like her. He used to help support her in every way possible and especially so during the sorrowful times. He was a likeable lad and a well-known character around Bacup working on the market stalls and selling the 'Evening Telegraph' in the Town Square. Every penny he earned he gave to mi' mam. Tragically, he was killed in a coal mining accident just a few days before his seventeenth birthday. On the day of the funeral hundreds of people lined the streets and followed the horse drawn hearse to Bacup Cemetery. My poor mother didn't have young Jimmy to console her on this occasion; it was terrible... her hair turned snow white overnight following his death.

I was 18 years old at the time and badly affected by my brother's death, which brought back painful memories of the deaths of my other brother and two baby sisters, which were due to the atrocious living conditions. It was awful ... simply awful!"

On other occasions Mam told stories about her own parents' childhood days and those of her grandmother.

I loved the tale of my great grandmother Joanna. Unlike 'Cinderella' it was a 'rags to riches' story in reverse, relating back as far as 1869 to County Mayo in Ireland where Joanna was born.

Joanna Lyons, the daughter of wealthy landowners and staunch Protestants, was just a slip of a girl of seventeen with the world at her feet. Alas, she she fell deeply in love with John Callaghan, an employee on her father's estate and a devout Catholic. When Joanna's father heard about the relationship he adamantly forbade it. However, Joanna and John eloped to England and married, whereupon Joanna's father disinherited her leaving her completely penniless. Consequently, for the first time in her life, Joanna experienced the pangs of poverty. The young couple subsequently had four children, but on writing home to her parents in Ireland, on each occasion, her letter was returned unopened ... she never heard from her parents again! The poverty had disastrous effects on their marriage and John left home taking with him his eldest daughter Mary, who was later adopted and brought up by his relatives.

I interrupted Mam at this point, "Mary ... was that mí granma?"

"Yes that's right, and like you know, she was brought up in Stacksteads by the Tiddy family and raised in the Catholic faith."

"And when she grew up she met mí grandad in Bacup and they got married in a little church in Rawtenstall … is that right Mam?"

"Yes that's right our John … it was called 'St. James the Less'. Anyway, that's enough for one night … it's bedtime now."

"A-ah Mam, just tell us a bit more … please!"

She'd go on a little while longer and then I'd have to go to bed. Lying in-between the bedclothes, I would ponder over the absorbing tales thinking how lucky I was to have such a cosy bed to sleep in.

On occasions Mam would tell tales about the First World War and the appalling conditions in the trenches on the front line. Grandad suffered from chronic bronchitis and was always grumpy, but after listening to his harrowing tales I could well understand why.

"Besides," I would think, "my grandad isn't very well … what with all the gas bombs and having to spend fours years in them cold wet trenches an' all. U-um, I think I'd be grumpy too if I'd had to go through all that lot!"

"Bloomin' 'eck Mam, I hope there's not a war when I grow up," I put in, "I wouldn't like to live in them cold wet trenches."

"No, neither would I our John, my dad said it was like hell on earth! U-um, it wasn't just the war either. When the soldiers returned from that terrible place, the Government had a couldn't-care-less attitude and the men had to face appalling conditions. Mí poor dad came home full of expectations, but he had to pick up the threads of his life unsupported. What made it worse was that he'd been shot through his shoulder and was never able to use it again efficiently. The Government had promised this would be a land fit for heroes, but like many others who'd survived the terrible conditions on the 'Western Front,' he found the country in a state of economic depression. For those who could find work the pay was poor and they had to work in all conditions for a meagre two shillings a day. Many a time Dad came home from work drenched to the skin. Against their pride, many of those heroic men ended up in the Workhouse."

Mother's storytelling totally enthralled me as I sat on her knee listening intently.

"Go on Mam tell me some more ... how did you go on as a little girl at school?" She then went on about the poverty and deprivation of her own childhood.

"Mind you," she would stress, "many other families languished in the same abject poverty." She paused for a moment in deep thought, "He-ey, mí poor mam and dad had nothing ... they didn't stand a chance. By éck our John times were hard, when I think about it; I don't know how we survived at all. Our Katie and I were forever in bother for fighting. We had to stick up for ourselves against girls from better to do families who were constantly attacking us with nasty comments and sarcastic remarks. Even the teachers seemed to look down on us. Mind you, we weren't the only ones ... many other children suffered the same plight as we did, constantly struggling to survive!" At this point Mam paused, a sad expression on her face. "In fact," she stressed, "just like my own family, many children died because of the appalling conditions!" She reflected sadly on one terrible incident pausing for thought, "My best friend, Mary MacDevit, was one of those children ... she was only fourteen when a terrible Tuberculosis epidemic, known in those days as consumption, swept through the town killing her and two of her brothers and sisters. They all died within two months of each other."

"E-eh Mam that were a shame, I bet you missed her."

"I did that lad," she murmured softly, "more than you'll ever know ... it still brings tears to my eyes when I think about her."

"Were you workín in the mill when it happened Mam?"

"That's right our John. In fact, I worked at Ross Mill with your Aunt Katie for about five years. The mill owners were slave drivers and by the time I was nineteen I decided I'd had enough. So I took myself off to London where I became a waitress in a big hotel.

"Bloomin' 'eck Mam, were you not scared o' goin' down London on your own."

"Of course I was scared, in fact I was frightened to death, but I felt as though I had no option. I just had to get away from the humdrum lifestyle in Bacup or die."

"And did you get a job easy Mam?"

"Well I was very lucky because I already had a letter of introduction to a businessman given to me by an old lady called Ginny, whom I used to run errands for when I was a girl. He was a kind gentleman called Mr. Baron, who'd previously lived in Bacup and was related to the old woman. He kindly took me into his household and, after listening to my story, he introduced me to the trade. I'll never forget when he informed me that he'd found me a position in a hotel and a place to stay. I felt so elated and convinced myself that this was the start of a new life"

"Flippin' éck Mam, is that where you met Dad?"

"No son, I worked down London for about eighteen months and then, after a short break back home in Bacup, I took myself off to Morecambe and that's where I met your dad." She pondered again a little before adding, "Yeah, and that's when my troubles really began!"

I giggled at that remark, prompting her to tell me more.

"Well, we had a stormy courtship in Morecambe but I really loved him. I became pregnant with Maureen and, after a lot of consideration, we got married in Lancaster. After that we returned to Burnley, your dad's hometown. Due to your dad's reckless behaviour we lived in atrocious conditions, moving from place to place. We were living in a little room in the Bridge Inn when Maureen was born. We then moved into a condemned house in the Croft Area near to your Aunt Lily's and that's where Jimmy was born. From there we moved up town into Dalton Street on the Bleak House Estate."

"Dalton Street Mum," I interrupted, "isn't that where me and Mary were born?"

"That's right lad, so now you know the rest."

"E-eh Mam," I said throwing my arms around her neck, "weren't it hard for you ... you were so poor!"

I used to lie in bed at night and go over the stories in my head until sleep finally claimed me. I loved all Mam's poignant tales and their fascination remains with me to this day.

****

Just after our fifth birthday, Mary and I went into the infants' class at St. Thomas's School in the care of some mature nuns. I thought it was really funny to see ladies walking about in penguin type robes. Sister Mary Gonzala, an elderly nun, took a shine to me, treating me very kindly. The feeling was mutual and, from the beginning, a genuine friendship was formed between us. She regularly displayed her mark of affection by kindness.

Reflecting back I was a very happy child, but one thing did trouble me ... everytime Dad came home drunk from the pub there were constant rows. During the arguments I would stand at the bottom of the stairs quivering ... even at my young age many thoughts ran through my head.

"Oh please God, don't let Daddy hurt Mummy! Please Jesus mék mí daddy so he's not angry! When I'm a daddy, I'll never get drunk and frighten mí kids." I knew Dad was so very wrong acting the way he did. I used to tell myself that I would never be like that when I grew up.

Dad's behaviour meant that poor Mam had to virtually raise her young family on her own, but she more than made up for his shortcomings. In a sense, she ruled us with a rod of iron and her word was law but she was always kind. She loved us all deeply and would have gladly died for us. She gave each one of us love and affection in abundance and instilled a strict morale code into us. We all accepted this quite naturally and took everything in our stride. The simple values, which she impressed upon us, formed the fundamental bedrock of our lives.

Times were hard and Mam strove to keep food on the table, using every method at her disposal. On market days she'd hang about the stalls at finishing time so as to obtain cut fruit and broken biscuits at knock down prices. Living in abject poverty, even a meal of fish and chips from the 'Chippy' was a luxury she could ill-afford. On some occasions we had to make do with dripping butties or jam and bread.

"Mam, will you make us some magic soldiers?" one or other of us would ask. She'd then spread some margarine onto freshly baked bread and cut it into segments.

"Here you are children, these are little magic soldiers. Now if you shut your eyes and wish, they can be anything you want them to be."

"Oh goodie, mine's gonna be a cream bun," said Barbara excitedly.

"And I'm gonna have a chocolate cake," laughed Barry "yummy yummy!" Mam was always touched by our reaction. She'd look around the table and marvel at our enthusiasm and our fertile imagination.

"Thank you God," she prayed with tears welling up in her eyes, "my little ones have so little and yet they're so happy … they're grateful for every little morsel I give them." She had to smile to herself at the way we really did enjoy the scraps of food. At times like these she felt that, despite her plight, everything was worth it.

By now she had got to know the Trafalgar area quite well knowing where all the shops were and, despite being overprotective towards her children, she generally got on well with the neighbours. She had a few rows but these were usually sorted out and there were generally no hard feelings.

****

Because of the blackout during the war years it became quite dangerous trying to negotiate the outside fourteen stone steps when going to the lavatory. Nevertheless, strict rules by the War Office had to be adhered to. On moonless nights it could be quite daunting, as it would be pitch black on the backstreets. All the same, every evening as dark loomed every household was responsible for making sure that all curtains were securely drawn. Not even the smallest chink of light was permitted to show on the outside. Strict regulations to enforce this were implemented and heavy fines and even imprisonment to anyone infringing the rules.

"Why do we have to be in the dark all the time Mummy," we would ask as we cuddled together around a glowing fire.

"Because during a air raid, even a little chink of light can be seen from as high up as ten thousand feet or more in the night sky "

To help boost people's morale during the blackout, local jokes were printed weekly in the Burnley Express:

One night Mrs Clayton, who lived in one of the many terraced houses, heard a knock on the backdoor. On opening it, there was a rather official looking warden stood there.

"Hello officer, what can I do for thí?"

"Well, I'm here Mrs. Clayton to reprimand you cós you're showing a chink ó light through your curtains."

"Oh I'm sorry officer, I'll shut ém right away and I'll mék sure it don't happen agén."

"Aye all right but think on it doesn't... or I'll have to report thi."

"Righto officer, thank you very much ... bye."

Five minutes later there was another knock on the door and on opening it, Mrs. Clayton was surprised to see the same warden standing there, looking rather embarrassed.

"I'm sorry Mrs. Clayton but could you do me a favour please?"

"Certainly officer, what is it?"

"Well" he stuttered, "could you just open your curtains for a second ... I've put mí torch down somewhere and I can't find mí way outa the backyard!"

Another one which was a favourite of my dad's:

A woman had just bought some fish and chips at the chip shop, and she had a very strong aroma about her.

As she was trying to find her way home by groping her way along the walls of terrace houses, a man knocked her down.

On picking her up, he apologised, "I'm awfully sorry luv ... I thought tha were't door to chippy."

Many jokes like these filled the local newspapers in an effort to keep the people's morale high and the community spirit close knit. But people took everything in their stride, even the daunting times they had to spend in the dark dank air-raid shelters during an air-raid warning. Mam refused to do this, having weighed up the situation from every angle. In the case of threatened attack she would gather us all together ... if we were in bed she would leave us there. Despite being on tenterhooks herself, she always tried to remain calm for our sake.

"But what if a bomb drops onto t'house Mummy?" Jimmy asked anxiously one night, "We'll all be killed!"

"Yes, I know that our Jimmy, but if a bomb landed on th'air-raid shelter we'd be killed anyway."

"What are the air-raid shelters for then?"

"Well, if a bomb landed on the house it wouldn't kill the people in th'air-raid shelter but they could be buried for days on end. They could face a horrible death, much worse than being killed instantly. No, I don't want that for any of my kids ... if they're going to die let it be in the comfort and warmth of their own beds."

"But I don't want to die Mummy!" said Jimmy nervously.

"I know that son, nobody does, but it's the lesser of two evils ... I'm just doing what I think is best under the circumstances. Anyway, don't fret yourself so; it's not going to happen."

****

As a child I found life on Albion Street fascinating. With the entire goings on and the many different characters there was never a dull moment. Nobody had anything much but no matter, the close knit community spirit and the friendliness more than made up for it.

Everyone helped each other and this became apparent if a neighbour was ill. Lots of people would rally round, making meals or doing anything else necessary for the family concerned. Constant round the clock care would be given until the family could once again cope for themselves.

Some neighbours would go to great lengths, putting themselves out on a limb in order to help their fellow-man ... even to the extent of risking their own lives.

One particular incident was when a fire engine roared up Albion Street. It is memorable because the clanging of bells attracted people. The fire engine stopped lower down the street to attend a house-fire at number nine.

At the time, Mrs. Florence Shackleton, whose husband was serving abroad in Egypt, lived next door at number seven. Living at home with her were her two sons, Jimmy and Tom, and her three daughters, Amy, Maud and Sally.

Mrs. Shackleton smelt smoke, which appeared to be seeping through the walls from next door, and went to investigate. To her horror she found the hallway ablaze, making it impossible for anyone to enter or leave the house. Her fears were intensified by the fact that a young couple with a baby girl had recently moved into the house and the child's cradle was in the frontroom.

"Oh my goodness," she gasped, "the baby's trapped in the frontroom!"

Without any thought of injury to herself, she got a stand-chair and smashed the window. Using the same chair as a step up she climbed onto the windowsill and into the smoky room. After fumbling about in the hazy fumes she found the baby lying on an old battered settee. She immediately wrapped the child in her coat and then tried to make her escape. Alas, the floor caved in and she fell through to the cellar below, still protectively clutching the baby to her chest.

Meanwhile, another neighbour had called the Fire Brigade. After dousing the flames the firemen found Florence huddled in a corner of the cellar still cradling the little baby girl in her arms. Both Florence and the child were immediately taken to hospital and treated for smoke inhalation. By the grace of God, neither she nor the baby suffered any major ill effects. However, Mrs. Shackleton did suffer a minor back injury, which was to trouble her in the coming years. She had to wear a plaster cast for quite a long time afterwards.

The incident was the talking point around the neighbourhood but, despite a write-up in the Burnley Express, Mrs. Shackleton never did get the recognition or commendation that she richly deserved.

But overall, things turned out fine and, like anything else, it did have its funny side. A neighbour, Mr Daly, later removed the plaster cast using the only tool he had ... a tin opener! Florence's children kept the plaster cast a long time afterwards as a souvenir and a reminder of their mother's outstanding bravery.

Florence's incident is but a reminder of the resilience, determination and bravery people displayed in those trying times as they all rallied together in friendship and mutual support.

****

Nobody had a television, yet most people were happy. Elderly folk and parents alike sat on their doorsteps and derived sheer pleasure from watching children playing street games. Rounders, skipping, football and many other games were enjoyed by many youngsters on the steep cobbled street. It was also amusing to watch the antics of many different characters, and especially so at weekends, after the pubs had closed. Lots of people, including women, would come tottering over a footbridge at the bottom of Albion Street in a merry state and individuals could easily be identified by their high-pitched voice or the song they were singing. One lady in particular was renowned for her chorus line 'Don't sweetheart me if you don't mean it.'

Jack Bickle, who lived across the street at number twenty-seven, never failed to make the kids laugh. He was partially sighted and wore thick-rimmed spectacles. One afternoon, after a session in the Malakoff Pub, he was tottering from side to side as he staggered up Albion Street and our Maureen and Winnie Clarke found it amusing. He looked really funny, stopping for a breather every few yards, crouching over grasping his knees huffing and puffing.

"Hiya Jack, are you all right?" our Maureen asked.

"Aye all reight cock ... and you?"

"Yeah ... I'm not so bad."

"Good ... that's good," he mumbled. Then after a short pause, "Anyroad, canya tell me cock ... if I keep goin' up here, will I come to Scott's Park?"

"Yeah you will Jack." Winnie chipped in.

To their delight he replied in a drawled out voice, "Oh good, thanks a lot ... I must be on the right street then!"

****

Before the outbreak of war Britain imported two thirds of its food from other countries around the world. But during the hostility, due to ships being sunk by German U-boats in the Atlantic, the government introduced rationing on limited supplies of food such as sugar, meat and tea. People grumbled but, in a way, it was good as it stopped rich people from buying large amounts of rare commodities while poor people starved.

The government introduced many slogans to encourage people during the harsh times:

'DIG FOR VICTORY' could be seen displayed in big letters on large billboards throughout the town.

A popular wartime song:

Dig, dig, dig!
And your muscles will grow big,
Keep on pushing the spade!
Don't mind the worms,
Ignore their squirms,
And when you back aches, laugh with glee
Keep on diggin'
Until we give our foes a wiggin'
Dig, Dig, dig for victory!

The campaign was a great success. People turned flower gardens and lawns into vegetable gardens. Golf courses, rubbish tips, railway embankments and parks were dug over to grow many types of produce. People who didn't have a garden grew lettuce, radish and runner beans in window boxes. Indeed, every effort was made.

As all the vegetables were grown at the same time they couldn't all be eaten at once. There were no freezers and so mothers would bottle up fruit and vegetables in large glass Kilner jars and preserve them for the winter months.

As eggs were in short supply, dried egg powder appeared in the shops. But even this was rationed.

By the spring of 1941, many more ships were sunk. Amongst other commodities, wheat was in short supply. In order to conserve wheat, people were encouraged to cut down on bread and eat more potatoes and vegetables.

As an incentive the Ministry of Food designed two cartoon characters, **POTATOE PETE** and **DOCTOR CARROT,** the children's best friend. The two characters were displayed on various billboards throughout the town and they were very popular amongst young children.

POTATO PETE came up with many recipes including Potato Pie along with a little rhyme:

Potato Pete, Potato Pete,
See him coming down the street,
Shouting his good things to eat,
Get your hot potatoes from Potato Pete.

DOCTOR CARROT, encouraged children to eat carrots to help them see better during the blackout. A regular joke amongst local folk was that carrots must be good for the eye sight as you never see a rabbit wearing glasses. However it is not a myth, as carrots are rich in vitamin A which aids night vision.

BLACK MARKET:

Because of meat rationing and other commodities, life became rather tiresome and this led to people bending the law. Consequently a thriving black market emerged. Almost everyone *knew a man* who could get hold of some scarce item that had fallen off the back of a lorry.

Heavy fines and even imprisonment were imposed on anyone caught dealing in stolen goods. But this didn't put people off and if a special treat happened to come there way they took advantage of it. Harsh penalties were also imposed on anyone picking coal of railway line, but people still did it. A man eager to fend for his family would say, "Take the chance of getting caught or don't pick it and freeze to death."

****

When Dad wasn't out on the beer he was good company in the home and, despite his wanton ways, we all loved him. He had a comical sense of humour and at times could be very funny. One day he was relaxing in the livingroom and had just taken a cat nap in the chair. I kept bombarding him with questions but, being tired, he wasn't in the mood.

"What's the highest mountain in the world Dad?"

"U-um, I'm not too sure about that our John," he yawned.

A couple of minutes later I asked, "What's the largest continent in the world Dad?"

"Sorry lad, I don't know that either."

I asked him several more questions, but each time his answer was always the same.

After receiving all the negative replies I happened to say," You don't mind me asking all these questions do you dad."

He just gave me a cheeky grin and winked joking, "No lad, you'll never learn anything if you don't ask."

CHAPTER 3 - THE CELLAR TOP

One night just a week before my sixth birthday, something happened that affected me badly. Dad arrived home in a paralytic state and as the depressing effects of alcohol reached its peak he caused a right ruction. He was in the most obstreperous of moods and I was witness to a most terrible distressing event.

It was nearly nine o'clock and, like any other evening, Mam was getting us kids ready for bed. Maureen wasn't there, as she'd gone to stay at our grandparents' house in Bacup. Jimmy, Mary I had just been bathed and were sat around the fireside; Barbara, who was now eighteen months old, was sat on Mary's knee. Mam had just lifted Barry out of the dolly tub, and was drying him as he stood on a wooden table. He only had a towel wrapped around his waist and she was about to put his nightshirt on when Dad walked in. We were all surprised to see him, as he was never usually home at that time of night; we were also taken aback, as it was obvious that he was drunk. His hair was disorderly, he was unshaven, his speech was slurred and he was unsteady on his feet. Barry was never Dad's favourite+ by any means and he made no attempt to disguise the fact.

"E-eh, who's a bonny little boy then?" he drawled as he approached Barry reaching out towards him beckoning, "Come on then ... give your daddy a kiss!"

Little Barry shuddered and then turned to Mam clutching at her dress.

"Come on then," Dad repeated drunkenly, "give your daddy a kiss!"

"Leave him alone" rapped Mam, "you're drunk!"

Dad retaliated and sniggered at her, "Oh-h! ... I'm drunk am I? You and your bloody kids, that's all you flamín well care about! Well, I'm telling you now, this bloody kid's gonna gimme a kiss right now, or I'll turn this flamín house upside down." He staggered closer to Barry, who clung still tighter to Mam and she in turn put her arms around him.

"Let go of the little brat!" snarled Dad.

Mam adamantly refused and repeated angrily, "Leave him alone Jack! He doesn't want to kiss you whilst you're in that state." She kept hold of Barry with one arm, whilst trying to fend Dad off with the other.

This riled him even further, making him more aggressive, "You bloody swine you're nówt else!" he growled, then, without further provocation, he fisted her in the face!

Immediately, all my siblings and I started screeching simultaneously, "Oh no Daddy, please! ... Please leave mí mummy alone! Please don't hurt her!" He looked at our appealing faces and appeared to calm down a little.

But he was still in an obstreperous mood and turning once more to little Barry, he asked mockingly, "You don't love your daddy do you?"

Barry was only a frail little lad, but even at his young age he had a mind of his own, he answered, "No I don't!" adding sobbingly, "You're always hitting mí mummy you are."

Dad sniggered, then turned to Mary, who also always spoke her mind, and he asked her the same question.

She replied defiantly, "No I don't love you either ... you're awful and I hate you when you're drunk!"

The same question was asked of Jimmy who replied in a distressed but determined voice, "No I don't ... I love mi mummy better than you!"

"Arrgh!" grunted Dad getting more despondent by the minute, as his ego deflated.

Barbara was whimpering but he couldn't ask her, as she was too young to understand what was going on.

Finally, he turned to me, but this time, he changed the question a little, "And who do you love then, your mummy or your daddy?" I pondered as I looked straight into Daddy's sad eyes, as I could see the hurt there, and actually felt sorry for him.

There were so many different thoughts running through my head all jumbled up together: *How much I loved Daddy when he was sober and how I wished he would never be as he was at this moment. I was very confused for even at my young age, I felt that should I say I didn't love him, then Daddy would stand all alone and sorrowful in his own home. Should I say I did love him, then that would hurt Mum's feelings. Besides that, I knew only too well that all my brothers and sisters really did love Dad but felt that Daddy didn't know that.*

I glanced at Mum knowing that she had done no wrong, then back at Dad. To everyone's surprise, I mumbled warily through tight lips, "I love you Daddy!"

Mam looked rather bewildered and I put my head down in embarrassment. Immediately, as though synchronised, my sister and brothers showed their obvious disapproval by tutting and blowing at me.

Dad intervened by roaring at them, "That'll do you lot, we'll have less of that! Anyroad, whilst we're at it, you can get the three of you up the dancers right now!"

"Leave them alone!" retorted Mam, "They haven't had a drink yet."

Dad growled sarcastically, "O-oh, what a shame, your poor little kids haven't had a drink yet; well, this is one night when they're gonna go to bed without one."

Mam stood defiantly in front of him stating, "Jack, I'm telling you now, my kids are going to have a warm drink before they go to bed … and that's final!"

"O-oh, that's final is it?" he growled becoming angrier still, "I'll show you what's bloody well final!" He approached the fireside where the three offending children were now huddled together and Mary was now holding baby Barbara in her arms. As he approached them, they all shuffled to an alcove close to the cellar top door. To prevent him herding them towards the stairs, Winifred placed herself between the children and the lobby. Then … Dad caught Mam completely off guard as he suddenly opened the cellar top door and pushed each one of the children, including little Barbara, into the darkness.

After shutting the door, he stood with his back placed firmly against it mocking Mam, "Right then, if they won't go to bed, then they can bloody well stop in there for a while."

He hadn't achieved this easily, for the moment Mam realised what he was doing, she'd thumped, scratched and kicked him but to no avail … he'd finally succeeded. The four children were screaming at the top of their voices inside the cellar top, whilst I was quivering with fear in the living room as thoughts of the Bogey-hole in the Workhouse immediately sprang to my mind.

Mam was frantic for the safety of her children and she became quite hysterical screaming, "Jack, get away from that door, it's pitch black in there! If one of the kids fall down those steep steps, they could be killed stone dead."

He knew that little Mary was holding baby Barbara in her arms, and that there wasn't enough room at the top of the cellar for two let alone four, and yet ... he just replied by grinning and mocking her, "You silly woman! Now whatta you gonna do?"

She carried on biting, scratching, thumping and kicking him, but it was useless, he just wouldn't budge. She then resorted to getting down on one knee and pleading with him, "Please Jack! Please I beg you ... let my kids out of there!"

"There you go again," he snorted, "your bloody kids! Always your kids, never mine ... oh no."

But even as he was speaking, he realised that Mam was attempting to pick up a steel poker, which stood in a heavy poker stand on the hearthstone. He immediately bent down grabbing it before she could, then rammed his back once more firmly against the door. During this brief scuffle, the kids tried unsuccessfully to get out and by now they were bawling all the louder.

Now, with the poker in his hand, he teased Mam even more, "Ye-es! Wouldn't you just love to do it?" he mocked looking at the poker.

A look of abject terror spread over Mam's face and the look of horror in her eyes chilled me to the bone.

The taunting went on a little longer and then, for some reason unbeknown to me, Dad did a very strange thing. He turned the poker around in his hand so that he was holding the point ... then handed Mam the handle.

"There you've got it ... are you happy now?"

Instinctively, Mam raised the poker ready to strike replying, "Right Jack, that's it, this has gone far enough; now let my kids out of that cellar top or God forbid ... I will kill you!"

Dad could tell she was in deadly ernest and yet ... he still unwisely chose to mock her, "You silly woman you're nówt else! Whatta you gonna do now?"

She was more in control now, and in deadly earnest, "Jack, I mean it!" she said calmly, "I don't want to do it, but for the last time I'm asking you to let my kids out of the cellar top, or so help me, I'll ...."

He unwisely interrupted her at this point and unbelievingly, he still carried on taunting her, "Go on then ... do it! Cós I'm telling you now ... they're not coming out." Without further ado Mam struck him as hard as she could and the poker caught him right smack in the middle of his forehead. He was quite stunned by the blow and tottered forward a little as though he was going to fall, but then managed to straighten up, remaining on his feet with his back still propped against the door. Blood trickled down his face and he looked very dazed.

By now, Mam had become more frantic than ever and, more in desperation than anything else, she repeated her warning. Dad didn't respond. Whether or not he could hear her didn't seem to matter anymore; all that mattered to her was the safety of her kids. Consequently, she let him have another blow and the poker landed in the exact same spot as before! This time, blood gushed out flowing all down his face and onto his clothes. His forehead was split wide open, and there was a deep gash that ran from the top of his head right down to the bridge of his nose. He automatically put his hands to his head, then started staggering towards the staircase; his hands were crawling along the wall leaving smudges of blood everywhere. On reaching the space at the bottom of the stairs, he stumbled and fell into the passageway onto his back. He was motionless, but his eyes were open, and he was staring up at the ceiling with his head lying in a pool of blood.

Having witnessed the entire episode, I was shaking in my shoes and my jaw was quivering; strangely though, my fear was not for myself but for my daddy. Arguments in the home always affected me in this way, but usually it was my mum whom I feared for.

On seeing Dad fall into the lobby I ran to him and knelt by his side pleading, "Oh Daddy, please don't die! Please! Please! I love you Daddy!"

I knew Dad wasn't dead because I could hear him mumbling; also his arms and fingers were moving a little as though he was trying to say, "I hear you Son."

Meanwhile, my siblings had emerged from the dark cellar top and were crying. On seeing all the smudges of blood on the wall and his dad lying in a pool of blood in the lobby, Jimmy became hysterical yelling, "O-oh, mí daddy's dead ... mí mummy's killed him!"

After consoling him and the others, Mam went to the lobby to see to Dad.

She could see how badly hurt he was and after giving me a cuddle, she reassured me, "Don't fret yourself our John, Mummy's going now to get some help for Daddy."

She then passed by me, and hurried next door to Mrs. King's. Alice, who had heard the rumpus through the wall, came at once to take care of us young ones. Afterwards, Mam went down Albion Street and across Trafalgar to a police telephone box. She first called for an ambulance, then the police stating that she thought she'd killed her husband. Within minutes, there was a police squad car at the front door with two uniformed policemen and two plain-clothed detectives.

On seeing Dad lying there amongst all the blood, one of the detectives asked, "Right, what's happened here then?"

Without hesitation, Mam blurted out, " It's my husband ... I meant to kill him!"

The detective in charge knew Mam from old and tried to correct her, "Now Mrs. Cowell, please don't say that, you don't know what you're saying."

"I meant to kill him!" she stressed adamantly. "My children were in danger, and I thought they were going to be harmed."

"Mrs. Cowell, I don't think you realise the gravity of the situation; you've got to realise that anything you say will be taken down, and used in evidence against you. Up to now, I have heard nothing, but now I have to ask you again ... what happened?"

For the third time, she replied "I meant to kill him! I know he's my husband, but he was going to harm my kids," and that's all she would say.

The detective felt sorry for her and begged her to tell him more, "Please Mrs. Cowell, I implore you ... tell me more!" After a pause, he turned very serious and stressed, "There's a lot more to this than meets the eye isn't there?" Despite his coaxing, Mum refused to change her statement, leaving him rather despondent. He said, "I'm so sorry Mrs. Cowell, but under the circumstances, you leave me no alternative but to place you under arrest."

"Yes, I understand that," she replied "but first, can you please let me make arrangements for my children, I don't want them put into care?"

In the meantime, an ambulance arrived and after administering first aid to Dad they placed him on a stretcher and took him to hospital. Mam made arrangements for us twins and baby Barbara to stay with Mrs. King, whilst Jimmy and Barry were left in the care of Mrs. Bacon, a lady who lived at number eight.

As the police were leading Mam away, all us children were sobbing and pleading with them, "Please don't take Mummy away ... she didn't mean to hurt Daddy!" The expressions on the policemen's faces said it all; it was quite evident they didn't like their job at that moment.

As Mam passed by me, I grabbed hold of her dress and tugged hard at it till she bent down towards me, "I'm sorry Mummy," I sobbed, "I love you as well!"

She embraced me giving me a little peck on my cheek, "Yes ... I know you do my love, now don't you fret yourself so! It's not your fault and Mummy does understand why you said what you did."

The curiosity of the neighbours had been aroused and they were all stood on their doorsteps with prying eyes as Mam was driven away. She was remanded in custody overnight at Burnley Police Station, which was situated at the back of and underneath the Mechanic's Institute Building near to the Town Hall.

The following morning, she was released on bail on the condition that she appeared in court the very next day. Just before leaving the station, she was given the good news that Dad's condition was stable, and that he was going to be all right; nevertheless, the charge against her still stood. The first thing she did on being released was to go to the market to buy some cakes and other luxuries for us kids. On reaching home, she gathered us all together telling us the good news about Daddy.

We were all highly delighted to hear that he was all right, and our delight increased even more when she announced, "Right kids, tonight, we're going to celebrate and have a little party."

Mam savoured the moment as all of us responded spontaneously with cheers of, "Hooray! Hooray!" By the time evening arrived, Maureen had returned from Bacup and she helped Mum to organise things. Two wings were pulled out on the wooden table enlarging it, then all us kids sat around just staring in awe at all the goodies.

"Wow ... we've no need to use our imaginations this time," we thought, "this is the real thing." After the little feast, we all sat around the fireside listening to Maureen and Jimmy telling stories. That night we all went to bed feeling much happier.

The next morning before leaving to attend the court hearing, Mam again had to make arrangements with the neighbours to look after us children.

On arrival at court, the detective in charge approached her and again made a request, "Mrs. Cowell, I beg you once again to change your statement, and tell us exactly what happened. I'm almost certain that if you do, then all charges against you will be dropped." She politely refrained and strolled quietly into the dock. The proceedings started and were not going in her favour, until Dad, who had discharged himself from hospital, was brought into court. His head was swathed in bandages and he was acting as a witness for the prosecution. He was quite sober now and full of remorse and guilt, once again becoming the nice person who everybody loved.

On seeing Mam in the dock, he immediately started shouting, "Get my wife out of there! She's done nothing wrong ... it was all my fault!"

"You mean to say you don't want to prosecute your wife sir?" asked the prosecutor.

"No I don't ... it should be me in the dock, not her!"

Whereupon, the case was dismissed, but Mam was placed on probation for a year.

The following is a quote from the Burnley Express dated April 11th 1945, which incidentally was Mary and my' sixth birthday:

WIFE'S ALLEGED ATTACK ON HUSBAND.

When Winifred Cowell (31) of 14 Albion Street was placed in the dock at Burnley Magistrates Court yesterday to answer a charge of inflicting grievous bodily harm on her husband, John William Cowell, by striking him on the head with an iron bar, the husband, whose head was swathed in bandages immediately rose in court and said, "Excuse me but I am not prosecuting my wife,"

The Clerk "You don't want to take action against your wife?"

"No! It was my fault."

"You have no desire to give evidence against her?"

"No"

Following a conversation with the Chief Constable the Clerk told the bench he would have to ask them to remand the accused in order that he could communicate the information laid on the charge, and the husband's desire not to give evidence to the Director of Public Prosecutions

The presiding magistrate then informed Mrs. Cowell that she would be remanded on bail for 14 days in order that the Clerk could communicate in the meantime with the Director of Public Prosecutions with a view to obtaining his consent to the withdrawal of the proceedings if necessary.

Ironically, there was an article in the same newspaper about ways of celebrating the forthcoming peace and the heading was as follows:

<u>A "PEACE" FESTIVITY OF 1814.</u>

BURNLEY' CELEBRATIONS WERE

THE COUNTRY'S BEST.

The article was about how our ancestors celebrated the end of the Napoleonic wars. It went on to say how Burnley was preparing to commemorate the end of the present hostilities in Europe.

It was ***ironic*** because although the end was in sight in Europe … it still seemed to be ongoing in our house.

CHAPTER 4 - PEACETIME

Mary and I were just turned six years old when the most wonderful thing happened ... **the end of the war!** It was declared over the wireless throughout the country. In the face of defeat Hitler had killed himself and Germany had surrendered. It was a night that was to remain forever in people's minds ... even us children.

We didn't have a wireless in our house but it didn't matter. It soon became apparent by the sound of many excited voices outside our house that something very special had happened. Almost every neighbour was outside chatting to each other on the stone flags or dancing merrily on the cobbles.

"What's up Mummy," asked Barry, "why is everybody holding hands and laughing?"

"E-eh son, they're laughing because they're happy. You see, they've all just had some wonderful news ... the war's over son, the war's over!"

"Does that mean we don't have to be frightened o' being bombed any more Mam?" asked Jimmy.

"That's right lad, we don't have to live in fear anymore ... we'll all be able to sleep safely in our beds at night."

Just then, droves of people came strolling down Albion Street from above the railway-bridge. Young people lined the street 5, 6 and 7 abreast linked up to each other, skipping and dancing as they pranced along. Everyone was elated, cheering and singing as they passed our doorway.

"Come on everybody, get your glad rags on and get yourself down to the Town Hall ... we're all gonna have a right rave up!"

Along with my brothers and sisters, I became very excited, wanting to join in the festivities. My excitement increased more so when Mam and Dad agreed to follow the happy crowd with all the family. I walked briskly along holding Dad and Mary's hand whilst Dad carried Barry on his shoulders. Maureen and Jimmy followed close behind as Mam pushed little Barbara in a pram.

"This is great," I thought as we walked along Trafalgar, "I've never been out with all mí family at the same time before."

"Keep close to each other, we don't want anyone getting lost in this crowd," said Dad as hundreds more flocked from off Patten Street and Gresham Place. On reaching Manchester Road, the crowd swelled to thousands as more people emerged from other districts.

"Bloomin' 'eck," said Mam now becoming quite perturbed, "I've never seen anything like this in my life before." She stopped and expressed her concern to Dad, "Oh I'm sorry Jack but I daren't go any further with the two little ones … I'm frightened that they may get crushed in that crowd. You go ahead with the others, but take care of them mind, and keep a close eye on them!"

"I'll keep an eye on them as well Mam," said Maureen, "don't worry about it … we'll be all right."

"Right Jack," said Mam, "I'll get going now and I'll make a little treat for you when you all get back home."

"Right our Jimmy, you heard what your Mam said," asserted Dad, "you and Maureen stick close by me and I'll hold onto the twins' hands."

During the hustle and bustle even Dad was perturbed and the nearer we got to the Town Hall the more concerned he became. Not daring to go any nearer he stopped by the side of the Canal Tavern on the corner of Finsley Gate.

"All right kids, this is far enough ... I don't want any of you getting' hurt."

"O-oh please Dad, let us go a bit nearer so we can see better," Jimmy, Mary and I pleaded.

"No, you can stay here ... you wouldn't be able to see anything down there anyroad among all that crowd! Anyway, whaddaya moaning at ... if you look across the road you can see all those firemen looking out from the Fire Station windows." Every single window of the Fire Brigade Building was open as the firemen waved banners and cheered loudly.

Hundreds of kids, including Bobby Cheetham and his brothers, who lived on Finsley Gate, scrambled over the steel railings of Brunswick Church and clambered up onto the wide window ledges. Brunswick Church was directly facing the Town Hall on the other side of Manchester Road, giving the children an excellent view. Other kids scurried hither and thither, climbing onto the tops of bus shelters or gas lamps to attain a better position.

"Oh can we go over there Dad with them other kids? Go on Dad ... please!" I pleaded.

He was nearly persuaded but thought better of it, "No, they're a lot bigger than you and things could get a bit rough. Anyroad, it's a long drop inside there ... if you fell off one ó them ledges you could be killed stone dead!"

"Oh go on Dad ... please! Bobby Cheetham's in there and he's only the same age as me," I begged.

"There's now't I can do about that our John, he wouldn't be in there if his dad were about."

"All right then, can we climb up onto one ó them gas-lamps afore any o' t'other kids get here?"

"Aye all reight, I suppose so ... but be careful."

"Yeah!" Jimmy, Mary and I yelled simultaneously, running immediately to the three remaining gas-lamps, and scrambling up onto the crossbars.

I now had a very good view of everything that was going on, I could see right to the bottom of Manchester Road and there wasn't a space available anywhere. I had an excellent view of the Town Hall Clock and was intrigued to see it lit up for the first time in my life. It gave me a wonderful feeling to see crowds of people swaying in harmony as they merrily chanted away. Children perched on their dads' shoulders gazed in wonderment at the colourful spectacle. By now the crowd was as far back as Trafalgar and people were stood shoulder to shoulder on all the adjacent streets. The bulk of the crowd was around the Town Hall and the Mechanics' Institute, awaiting the Mayor's speech. As the Mayor finished speaking the Town Hall Clock started to chime midnight and a strange wonderful silence descended on the place. No sooner had the last chime struck than something spectacular happened. The large crowd erupted spontaneously, breaking into the most festive of moods, holding hands and singing 'Auld Lang Syne' and other sentimental songs. Emotion was running high and everyone started to hug and kiss each other. It was a sight to behold, especially through the impressionable eyes of a child.

"Bloomín éck," I chuckled, "this is better than New Year's Eve … I've never seen ow't like it afore!" I felt a nice warm glow surge through my body as I sensed the feeling of all those happy folk. I glanced over to where Dad was standing with our Maureen. "Good, he's not looking," I mumbled to myself, "I'm gonna go and get a bit closer."

I climbed down the gas-lamp and intermingled with the crowd finally getting right across from the Town Hall. I knew I'd be in bother with Dad, but that was the last thing on my mind … I was determined to join in the festivities. My excitement grew as brass bands appeared out of thin air, playing the wartime songs of Vera Lynn. I laughed heartily when I saw women dancing unashamedly in their nighties while men played mouth organs and clashed dustbin lids together. The thing that intrigued me most was when people formed lines and started to dance the Conga as a musical rhythm reverberated around the place.

"Come on young fellow, do you want to join in?" said a kindly lady, "I'll make sure you're all right." I didn't need asking twice and enjoyed every minute as people danced along Elizabeth Street, Parker Lane, St. James Street, Manchester Road and all the adjacent streets. I was actually witnessing a public expression of joy that the town had rarely seen before. My mind flashed back to the stories Mum had told me about my grandfather returning from the First World War and how Bacup had celebrated in a similar way. I was completely mesmerised by the goings on ... it was a magical event in every sense of the word. I'd only just turned six years old but even at that young age, I sensed in my heart that something very special was happening. It seemed to me that Heaven was rejoicing and God's angels were singing alongside us.

"This is a very special night," I thought, "a moment that will never ever happen again." I knew instinctively that it was nigh impossible to understand the feelings of every single person on that most wonderful of all nights unless you were actually there to witness the event yourself. At that moment the Town Hall Clock struck one o'clock bringing me back to reality.

"O-oh flippin 'eck', is it that time already," I mumbled, "mi' dad'll kill me!" The inducement to stay was great, but I knew I was in enough trouble already. It took me about five minutes to get back to the Canal Tavern as I sidled through the crowds.

"Where the bloody hell have you been," bawled Dad, "we've bín looking all o'er the flamin' place for thí?"

"I'm sorry Dad, I …"

"Never mind you're bleedín sorry," he rapped, clipping me round the lughole, "get back there with t'others and do as you're told in future!" But Dad's anger didn't last long because he was too intent on enjoying the moment himself.

"Righto kids, come on, we'd best get going, your mam'll go mad if we stay out any longer." I wanted to protest but didn't push my luck … I'd got off very lightly so left it at that.

On reaching Trafalgar we could still hear the crowd heartily singing, "Hang out your washing on the Siegfried Line." The merrymaking was still in full swing.

As we passed along Trafalgar there were still many people on the streets listening to their wirelesses and chatting away to each other. The same applied to Albion Street. It was a warm night and it felt as though it was only about nine o'clock. To add to the occasion, Mam had done some baking.

"Righto everybody, I know it's late but you can all have a bun, some broken biscuits and a cup of tea before you go to bed. It's been a very special day today and certainly one to celebrate."

"Hey Mam, does this remind you of when mí grandad came home from the war when you were a little girl?" I enthused.

"It certainly does our John … I was just thinking that before you got home."

On going to bed, Jimmy and I were too excited to sleep.

"Bloomin' 'eck our Jim I reight enjoyed míself … did you?"

"Yeah it were great our John, it's the best night I've ever had. Did you see all them blokes in night shirts dancing with them women in their nighties?"

"Yeah," I giggled, "it wer' really funny weren't it?" We talked a little more before finally dropping off to sleep ... it was certainly a night to remember, giving us something to talk about for a long time to come.

****

In spite of going to bed late I was up early the next morning eager to find out if anything else was going on. Many of the neighbours had already decorated the outside of their houses, draping Union Jacks and bunting from their windows. Within days every street and public building throughout the town was festooned with colourful trimmings and balloons to celebrate the joyous occasion.

One special memory is the first day we returned back to school. I was still in the infants' class and, along with the other children, I was given a large parcel. On opening it I got the surprise of my life.

"O-ooh, look what I've got our Mary," I blurted out excitedly, "a toy car!"

"Yeah and look what they've given me," she replied happily cuddling a very pretty doll.

We were both elated and couldn't wait to get home to show off our new toys. It reminded of an intriguing tale that my mam had told me when I was a child. Mam's tale went as follows:

"I was only six years old and it was the night my dad, returned home from the First World War after serving four tortuous years on the Western Front. My mother had trimmed up our little house with paper chains to make his homecoming special. To make the occasion more memorable Dad had brought home a present for my two siblings and me. He gave me a rag doll, the like of which I'd never seen before, with long plaited golden hair. I couldn't believe it as I stared at the doll in awe. The little doll filled me with sheer delight. I'd never before had a

doll of my own, and I just stared at it in wonderment, marvelling at the happy expression on its face.

'This is really mine,' I thought, 'my very, very own.' It was only a rag doll, but to me, it was the most beautiful dolly in the world and it gave me lots of comfort and joy; for that very reason, I chose to name her just that ... 'Joy'. To me that little dolly was my very own little baby, and I was to keep and treasure it for many years to come right into my adult life. Little Jimmy was also highly delighted because he got a toy clockwork tin car. To make the event even more special, Mam had arranged a welcome-home party for Dad and for the first time in my life ... our little house echoed to the sound of joy and laughter."

"Look what I've got from school Mam!" shouted Mary unable to contain her excitement, "a little dolly and it goes to sleep when I lay her down."

I was just as eager to show Mam my present. "And they've given me a toy car Mummy that I can wind up with a little key. Is it like that little car that mi' grandad brought back from the war for mí Uncle Jimmy?"

She smiled at me as she reminisced a little going back to that night so long ago, "U-um, it does seem rather coincidental ... a doll for me and our Katie and a car for mí little brother Jimmy. Oh, how I loved that doll, it was the most ...."

Her thoughts were interrupted as I tugged at her dress, "Well Mam ... is it like mi' Uncle Jimmy's car?"

Looking at my inquisitive face her eyes welled up as she replied, "It is love, it's very much like it ... I hope you get as much pleasure from it as my little brother did."

"And does my dolly look like yours did Mam?" asked Mary.

"Well no Mary. You see, mine was only a rag dolly whereas yours is more like a real baby."

"But you loved your dolly didn't you Mummy?"

"Oh yes, very much indeed," she replied wistfully.

There was a happy atmosphere in the house, as all my other brothers and sisters got presents too, the best ones that they had ever had.

****

Most people were happy because the stringent restrictions, regarding lights, curfews, and the like, were lifted, but the thing that most delighted me and all the other kids was a street party, which was being organised for us.

"When's our party gonna be Mam ... will it be this Saturday afternoon?"

"No John, it's not till the Saturday after."

"A-ah, why not ... Rowley Street's having theirs this Saturday after the matinee?"

"Look, there's nothing I can do about that... anyroad what difference does it make?"

"U-umph, it doesn't seem fair, them getting theirs first."

"You won't think that the week after when you're having yours will you?"

"No, I suppose not Mam. Anyroad, I'm gonna go round there this Saturday after the picture's finished to see if I can join in."

"Yeah, and fat chance there'll be of doing that our John," she laughed, "there'll probably be loads of other kids with the same idea."

Still, after the Saturday matinee, my mates and I made our way to the bottom of Rowley Street ... we were well aware of the festivities and wanted a slice of the action.

Grown-ups were running the party with two ladies acting as stewards to make sure no stray kids gatecrashed.

"Now you young úns ... thá knows only too well that this party is just for the Rowley Street kids."

None of us said anything, we didn't have to ... the expressions on our faces said it all. With bowed heads and bottom lips clenched under our top teeth, we showed our obvious disappointment.

One of the ladies began to succumb to our abject appeal, "E-eh Lizzie, just look at 'em, how can we leave 'em out ... what dusta think?"

"Aye I suppose tha's reight Nellie ... they do look a pitiful sight don't they?"

To our delight Lizzie invited us to join in, "All reight kids go and join the party and enjoy yourselves; no getting up to any mischief mind!"

Before she'd time to finish ... we all scurried amongst the other excited youngsters. We stopped for a moment, looking in awe at all the food laid out on the tables ... never in our lives had we seen so many goodies ... cakes, mince pies, jam rolls, the lot!

"By éck," I thought, "just look at all the goodies ... u-um, they're real too, no need to pretend this time."

The following week was the time for the Albion Street party and what a party it was. Just like Rowley Street, all the grown-ups waited upon the tables. Never before had the kids seen anything like it on their street. It gave Mam and all the other parents a lot of joy to see all their children so happy. The street echoed to the sound of laughter like never before. I was in my element and to add to my happiness I was given a silver shilling as were all the other children.

The summer of 1945 was very memorable in more ways than one. Everything went great, the weather, the parties and for the grown ups ... V J Day! This was a great excuse for yet another rave up ... not that Dad needed one.

"What's happening Mam," I asked curious as to why all the adults seemed to be scurrying about, "why are all the grown-ups so happy?"

"Ah well our John, there's been another wonderful event … the Japanese have surrendered unconditionally."

I didn't understand the full impact of this but sensed it was good news.

But one thing I did know … Dad was in a very jovial mood as were lots of other men. They celebrated all right, every single pub in Burnley ran dry … there wasn't a drop of beer to be had anywhere.

CHAPTER 5 - JUNIOR SCHOOL

At the age of seven Mary and I moved up from the infants' class in to junior school, under the guidance of my idol ... Miss Quinn. I adored this lady from the first time I set eyes on her, conjuring up romantic images of her in my mind.

"U-um, the beautiful Miss Quinn, she's just like a film star the same as Maureen O'Hara and Susan Hayward." I'd always been fond of Sister Mary Gonzala, but this was different ... much different!

Miss Quinn was very young with dark wavy hair that seemed to bounce about buoyantly with every movement of her head and she had the most beautiful complexion with skin like velvet. Every time she came near me I went all dithery. I was mesmerised and just couldn't take my eyes off her; she had the most pronounced smile ... I was in love for the first time.

"Oh those eyes, those beautiful eyes," I would murmur in a trance "I hope she likes me as much as I like her," I was certainly besotted and used to dream about her.

Besides teaching, one of Miss Quinn's duties was preparing all us pupils for our first 'Confession' and our first 'Holy Communion'.

There was another set of twins in our class: Nora and Teresa O'Sullivan, who were just six days younger than Mary and me. Like us, these two girls were very close but, unlike the Cowells, they were seldom seen apart and even sat next to each other in class. The four of us took our vows of devotion to God very seriously, keeping up with our prayers and going to church every Sunday and on days of obligation.

I enjoyed many aspects of school life and everything was going fine until one day Miss Quinn came out with something that made me quite unhappy. She actually announced to the class that she was shortly to be married and would be leaving the school. I couldn't believe it ... my dream was shattered!

"How can she do this to me?" I thought as she flashed her engagement ring to some of the excited girls, "I always thought she'd wait for me until I'd grown up."

Nevertheless, she did get married, and she left the school ... I never ever saw her again.

At first I felt very sad and still daydreamed about her, but the images I'd conjured up of her gradually diminished.

****

In 1947 nobody had a television set; in fact, only the privileged few had a wireless. Although I was only seven, I used to be fascinated with the sound of voices coming out of these little wooden receivers. I was also a little confused.

"Mam," I would ask, "are there some little people in the back of those boxes?"

"No," she would reply with a smile on her face, "it's something to do with electricity." I wasn't convinced and would peep into the back of one everytime I got the chance. On my way to school I passed a few houses which had a wireless on their window sill. Out of curiosity I used to peer into the back of them. The number of small wires inside the wooden box intrigued me, and also added further to my confusion.

"U-um, I wonder why they call ém wirelesses," I'd ponder, "there's thousands of wires in there?"

Gradually, nearly every household rented one of these contraptions for one shilling and thre'pence a week from Radio Rental. Our home was no exception and a special treat for us on a Saturday night was to sit around the hearth listening to various serials. At other times 'Dick Barton Special Agent' used to keep us all pinned to our seats and we were all enthralled as storyteller, Valentine Teller, recited 'The Man in Black'. Comedy programmes had every one of us in stitches. These included 'Life with the Lyons,' starring Bebe Daniels and Ben Lyons and 'Raise a Laugh,' starring Ted Ray. Another favourite was 'Over the Garden Wall,' with Norman Evans. Amongst the popular comedians were Beryl Reid and Jimmy Clitheroe. Game shows included Wilfred Pickles with his famous catchphrase, 'Give 'em the money Barney!' As Barney was Dad's nickname this particular phrase always created a laugh in our house. Every week people tuned in to listen to new budding talent on the 'Carrole Levis Show'.

Dad always looked forward to the 'Sports Results' at 5pm on Saturday evening, which was always preceded with a special signature tune. This was enjoyed in many homes and of all my mates, Bobby Cheetham, the joker of our pack, was always coming up with riddles passed onto him by his older brothers.

"Which town is connected to the Sports Report?" he asked me one day.

"I haven't a clue Bobby ... which one?"

"Durham," replied Bobby with a smirk on his face.

"I don't get it ... how do you mean, why Durham?"

"Well just listen to the music that's played afore the programme starts. 'Durham durham durham durham ... durham durham durham!"

"Hey, that's a good ún Bobby ... I like it."

The wireless became the main source of amusement second only to going to the pictures. However, picture houses did not open on Sunday afternoons and so many people loved listening to Billy Cotton and his band on the BBC.

He always opened the show by shouting "Wakey-Wakey!" It became commonplace for most families to sit around their living room listening to the various radio programmes.

There were plenty of picture places, at least one in every area of Burnley. The one in the Trafalgar area was the 'Alhambra', but lots of us kids preferred to go to the Temperance, better known as the bug and scratch, which was a little further away in the Croft Area.

Saturday was spending money day and Mam always gave us ninepence each. I always met up with my mates Ronnie Hopkinson, David Whittaker and Kenny Clayton on a Saturday afternoon to go the matinee at the Alhambra. The entrance fee was three pence leaving me with sixpence to spend on goodies. Bags of crisps were three pence each and a tub of ice cream was a staggering six pence. I always bought a bag crisps which left me with enough to buy penny drinks on the way home whereas our Mary always threw caution to the wind and treated herself to an ice-cream.

On the way to the matinee my mates and I would always talk about the previous week's episodes.

"Oh I wonder how Johnny MacBrown's gonna escape from that burning building that he wer' trapped in?" I said.

"I don't know," laughed Ronnie, "but he always seems to manage it somehow doesn't he?"

"Yeah," put in David, "I thought he were a gonna for sure the week afore when he fell into that den o' snakes."

"Hey you never know," said Kenny naively, "he might get killed for real this time." All the rest of us burst out laughing.

"You must be joking Kenny," laughed Ronnie "they wouldn't be able to put any more chapters on then would they?"

"Anyroad, never mind Johnny MacBrown ... what about Flash Gordon and the Clay Men?" said David.

"What about 'em?" I asked.

"Well, d'you think Flash'll be able to rescue Dale Evans from Emperor Ming's clutches afore that dragon eats her?"

"Oh aye easy, just watch ... he'll break its neck with his bare hands." replied Ronnie.

At that we all started laughing and then made our way into the pictures. As foreseen, our heroes performed the miracle of getting out of their predicament, only to finish up in another precarious one, leaving us all guessing until the following week. Other favourite characters were the Lone Ranger and Tonto, Zorro and Hoppalong Cassidy. In between trailers, the cinema always put on a cartoon which would send us into raptures. Lots of the kids loved Mickey Mouse, Donald Duck and Tom and Jerry, but my favourite was 'Mighty Mouse'.

This was also the time and place where many boisterous kids let off steam, especially at halftime. One particular incident caused a bit of a riot. Some lads sneaked upstairs and peered over the balcony. Using peashooters they fired dried peas onto unsuspecting kids below, hitting them on the head, neck or face.

"Ouch!" howled David as a pea stung his left cheek. "Who did that?"

Things settled down a bit and then Ronnie let out a shout, "Ouch, that hurt!" Before long the cinema was in uproar as more cries went up.

"Right, that's it," growled Ronnie as he spotted a lad peering over the balcony, "it's the Whittle Fielders, come on ... let's go get 'em!" David, Kenny, Ronnie and I ran for the doorway leading to the upstairs with a few other lads following. Within a few minutes all hell let loose as we started battling with our fists flailing the air trying to kill each other. The usherettes gradually restored order but not before quite a few blows had been exchanged.

When the matinee had finished it was easy to guess what film had been showing. If it had been Zorro, we would all put our coats around our shoulders to form a cape and fence with each other. One time the showing was the Lone Ranger and Tonto.

"You kimmy savvy?" joked Ronnie.

"Si bien Señor," I replied.

"Bueno, let's go ... vamoose." Ronnie set off along Trafalgar slapping his backside and shouting "Giddy up, giddy up." We all tried to catch him but there was no chance ... our make believe horses hadn't a cat in hell's chance of catching Ronnie's swift footed steed.

One matinee that we all enjoyed was the day of the flood ... and it wasn't on the screen! A water pipe burst in the toilets at the back of the cinema and water flowed down the aisles banking up against the stage. All the kids on the front row were highly delighted as the water got deeper and deeper. Along with some other kids, Ronnie, David and I took off our clogs and socks and started to paddle splashing everybody in sight. This nearly caused a riot. Others floated ice-cream cartons and lollipop sticks on the water pretending they were boats. Many lads started stamping their feet and whistling loudly whilst others hurled missiles through the air hitting girls on the back of their necks. The usherettes couldn't keep all us excited boisterous youngsters under control and the film had to be abandoned. Complimentary tickets were given out for the following week. On the way home, after the matinee finished we always made for Sunderland's Sweet Shop at the bottom of Sandygate, where we could buy penny and ha'penny drinks of Sarsaparilla, Dandelion and Burdock or Lemonade. This is where our Mary came into her own because, having spent all her money, she'd then look on with pleading eyes; Jimmy, Barry or I would buy her a drink.

It so happened there was a little old fellow, who always carried a walking stick. He was a very pleasant gentleman, known to us children simply as **Old Louie.** Every Saturday afternoon after the matinee finished, he was always sat in a garden area facing the sweet-shop. He was forever setting riddles for us kids to solve, and then he'd reward whoever came up with the answer, by giving him or her a few coppers. It wasn't the done thing to accept money from strangers but Old Louie was well known, liked and trusted by everyone.

One time a crowd of us gathered around him waiting for him to give us his weekly riddle. "Right everybody," he muttered like a schoolmaster, "the first ún to tell me twelve coins that mék a shilling gets this here thre'penny bit."

Immediately, there were shouts of, "That's easy ... twelve pennies."

"Whoa, hang on to tha' hosses! I haven't finished yet," stressed the old chappy. "What I was gonna say is that tha caint use any pennies at all."

We all puzzled over it for a while before saying, "No, it can't be done."

Our Jimmy wouldn't be beat though, and after some deep thought he blurted out, "Yeah, I've got it, I've got it!"

"Go on then lad, gimme tha' answer."

Jimmy stuck his chest out replying proudly, "A tanner, a thre'penny bit, two ha'pennies and eight farthings."

"By gum lad, tha's got it," said old Louie looking rather astonished, "hasta heard it afore?"

"No Louie, honest!" It wer' just that ….."

"Not to worry thesen lad, I believes thí; here's tha thre'penny bit, tha' deserves it."

That was it! Jimmy was always generous; back to the sweet shop for another penny drink for himself, and some ha'penny drinks for our Mary, our Barry and me.

****

Besides going to the Saturday matinee at the Alhambra, I also liked to go to the Temperance Monday, Tuesday or Wednesday evening because they put on a mini-series there. My favourite hero was Superman and I couldn't wait for the programme to start. Talk about Johnny MacBrown's escapades; they were nothing compared to Superman's. One week he unwittingly opened a lead-lined box, which his archrival Lex Luthor had sent him. When he opened the box he was immediately exposed to deadly rays from a piece of kryptonite and the serial ended with everyone wondering whether Superman would live or die. I went along the following week with my mate, Bobby Cheetham.

"Bloomín' 'eck," commented Bobby, "I wonder how Superman escapes this week … he wer' dying when we left him!"

"I'll bet thí ow't that Louise Lane comes just in the nick o' time to save him," I said.

"A-ah well, it'll mék a change from him rescuing her won't it?" quipped Bobby. We both laughed and after the film finished the riddles continued.

"How many picture places in Burnley canya think of beginning with the letter 'T'?" asked Bobby.

"Well there's the Temp for a start, then the Tivoli and … u-um!" After quite a bit of deliberation I answered, "Them's th'only two I can think of."

"Oh there's plenty more," sniggered Bobby.

I pondered a while longer before asking, "Go on then I give up … tell me then!"

Bobby burst out laughing, "Well, there's th'Alhambra, th'Empire, th'Empress th'Imperial, th'Odeon ……….!"

"Go on, get out of it you silly sod … I thought you were serious." Both of us burst out laughing together.

The wisecracks weren't just one-sided; there were times when I caught Bobby on the hop.

I'll tell you what it is Bobby," I said one day in the schoolyard, "she's a right old trouble maker is that Annie who lives on Kepple Street isn't she?"

"Annie ... Annie who?" he asked looking puzzled.

I cracked up laughing, "Got yá, it's that Annie Mossity ... ha, ha, ha! Do you get it ... animosity?"

"Annie Mossity'" he mumbled fiddling about with his hair, "I don't get it." And then the penny dropped, "Oh aye, I see what you mean ... animosity ... ha, ha, ha!"

"You must be slipping Bobby, you were a bit slow on the uptake there ... that's not like you."

Not to be beaten Bobby went on, "I'll tell you somét that's funny, there's a little old wonan who lives on Patten Street and she's really confused but comical with it."

"Oh yeah I know who you mean ... it's Mrs Smith who has a little dog called Patch."

"Aye that's reight but have you heard the latest?"

"No Bobby I haven't, but I 'm sure you're gonna tell me." So Bobby carried on:

Mrs. Smith was sat around the fireplace when there was a knock on the door. When she opened the door a policeman was standing there.

"Good morning Madam, would you be Mrs. Smith?" he asked politely.

"That's reight officer ... what can I do for thí?"

"Well," he said pausing for a second, "do you have a little dog called Patch?"

"Ye-es," she replied a little puzzled.

"Well I'm sorry to tell you Mrs. Smith but some of the neighbours have been complaining that Patch has been chasing some young kiddies on a bike."

To the policeman's surprise and bewilderment she answered in all seriousness, "Oh no officer, it couldn't o' bín my Patch. You see ... Patch hasn't got a bike!"

"Ha ha ha!" I cracked up, "That's great Bobby ... I love it!"

I was always on my guard when he was telling a tale thinking there may be a catch to it. And so was our mate Ronnie, but one time he fell for one of Bobby's pranks, hook line and sinker.

Bobby, Ronnie and I were playing in the school yard and Bobby said in a rather sad voice, "Eh Ronnie, have you heard about what happened to mi Mam's cat."

"No Bobby. Why, what happened?"

"Well," he said going into a rather sombre mood, "we had a burst pipe in our house and mi mam had to call in a plumber. It was a lead pipe and to fix it he had to use a blow lamp, but first of all he had to fill it up with petrol."

"I didn't know they used petrol in blowlamps," quipped Ronnie."

"Oh it wasn't like ordinary petrol, it was white and looked like milk and especially because he had it in a small milk bottle."

"Bloomin' 'eck Bobby," Ronnie chipped in, I've never seen petrol that colour."

"No Ronnie, neither had I. But like I said it's only used in plumber's blow torches. Anyway, what happened is the plumber went away for a while to have some dinner and he left the flamin' bottle on the window sill. Well when I saw it I thought it was milk."

"Ha ha!" laughed Ronnie, "Don't say you took a swig?"

No, luckily for me I didn't, but the cat did. I put some on its saucer and it lapped it up."

"Blimey!" gasped Ronnie now intrigued with the tale. "What happened?"

"Well it seemed all right at first and then it made a kind of hissing noise. It stiffened with its tail in the air and it arched its back. I tried to pick it up but it just shrieked and started running in circles all around the room."

"Bloomin' 'eck!" gasped Ronnie, "What happened then?"

"Well I tried mi best to catch it but it wer' just too fast. It then ran into t'other room and started to run in circles again." Bobby paused a little, looked rather sad adding, "It did this for about five minutes and then just collapsed on an old pegged rug in front o' the fireplace and lay their still as anything. I wer' gutted 'cos it wer' mi' own fault"

"Oh no," stressed Ronnie really concerned, "was it dead?"

Bobby put on a really sad face prior to bursting out laughing, "No you silly sod, it had just run out of petrol."

Ronnie just stood there with his mouth agape. I've got to admit that I didn't know what was coming and I too burst out laughing as well. Ronnie took it on the chin and even he laughed. "Good one that Bobby, you got me that time. I'm gonna try and catch somebody else out with it."

****

If any of my mates or I happened to get copped by the local bobby for doing something untoward, we generally got a sharp clip behind the ear and that was the end of it. One time I'll never forget is when my mate Ronnie and I played a prank on two policemen for devilment. We both constantly got up to mischief but on this occasion we definitely overstepped the mark. I was about ten at the time and I'd just acquired a toy plastic knife that had a retractable blade. At the time, it was a very popular toy with all the local kids, especially in the schoolyard. We'd pretend to stab each other, and then stagger about as though we were injured. When the plastic blade was retracted, then let go quickly, it made a distinct clicking sound and sounded just like a flick knife. The incident occurred one evening as Ronnie and I were walking along Trafalgar. As we approached the Co-op Shop there happened to be two policemen stood in the doorway.

As we spotted them the idea of tomfoolery came to us.

"I'll tell thi' what Johnny," quipped Ronnie, "let's act the goat and pretend we haven't seen 'em."

"I know what we can do," I grinned putting my little ploy into action," it'll get 'em really mad."

"What's that then?"

"Right Ronnie, this is the plan. Just as we're going past them two bobbies you pretend to be mad at me and I'll pretend to pull a real flick knife out on you."

"Good idea," replied Ronnie, "that should get 'em goin', let's do it!" It worked all right, too well in fact.

We were just approaching the doorway when Ronnie blurted out loud enough for the two policemen to hear, "I'm tellín' thí Johnny Cowell, if you don't wrap up I'll belt you one!"

"That's what you think," I replied pulling out the toy knife. I let go of the already retracted plastic blade, which made one 'eck of a click!

"Hey!" shouted one of the policemen, "What's going on, what have you got there?"

I immediately put the toy knife behind my back replying, "Oh, it's nówt officer."

"What do you mean, it's nówt? Let me have a look … **now!**" I kept up the pretence a little longer before showing the toy knife to the officer. Then, much to the policeman's displeasure, I burst out laughing.

"Oh, you cheeky young bugger you're nówt else!" he raved as his face turned red with rage. Then, without a second thought, He gave me one hell of a crack about my head that made my ears ring for a week, Ronnie didn't get away with it either, he received the same treatment from the other bobby. Needless to say, the toy knife was confiscated and the prank was never ever repeated. Ronnie and I never told our parents about the episode either, for fear of getting another crack.

****

One day, David, Kenny and I had been playing football on Whittlefield 'Reckory' and we were making our way home along Trafalgar.

As we passed the Alhambra Pictures Kenny commented, "Oh look what's on the pictures ... 'Old Mother Riley's Ghost'."

"Oh I'd love to see that," I commented, "Ronnie saw it t'other night and he told me it were really funny."

"Yeah ... he told me the same," said David.

"It's no good bothering," moaned Kenny, "there's no chance o' that, we're all skint."

"So what," said David, "how about dodging in through the side door from that ginnel which runs down the side o' the factory?"

"Good idea David," there's always somebody coming outa there at half time," I agreed. So all three of us crept down the ginnel and waited patiently. Sure enough, after about ten minutes, some people came out. Nimbly as anything David nipped in the open door with me close behind. We walked tentatively down the middle aisle and then made our way to some seats.

"Where's Kenny?" whispered David.

"I don't know, I thought he wer' behind me until we got here."

"Never mind, it doesn't matter ... he's probably chickened out." Just then the film started and we both settled back to enjoy it. Little did we know that our little scam was about to be discovered. The film was hilarious and we were both laughing heartily when the beam from a torch highlighted us.

"You two lads," rapped the usher, "come out here now!"

"Flippin' 'eck," whispered David, "how the bloomin' 'eck has he found out about us?"

"I dunno, I haven't got a clue," I muttered.

"Right," growled the usher looking at David, "what's your name?"

"David Whittaker."

"And you'll be John Cowell then … right?" he asked shining the torch in my eyes.

I was still trying to figure out how we'd been rumbled, " Yeah that's right … whaddaya want to know for?" I asked arrogantly.

"Because you've both sneaked into the pictures without paying, that's why."

"Oh no we haven't," replied David rather cockily.

"All right then … where's your tickets?" Both of us lied, saying we'd lost them.

"Oh have you now? Well come with me, we'll soon sort this out!"

"We'll be all reight Johnny," whispered David as we were marched upstairs, "he can't prove now't." He couldn't have been more wrong; to our horror, there was a shock awaiting us. Bella Whitaker, David's mother, was stood by the pay-desk in the foyer and she was fuming.

David's face turned three shades paler, "Oh bloomin' 'eck, now I'm forrit … I wonder how she's found out?"

"It must have bín Kenny," I muttered under my breath, "how else could she know?"

"Less o' that whispering you two, this is no laughing matter," rapped Bella. "And as for you," she growled clouting David about the head, "what have I told you about dodging into the pictures ... it's stealing?"

"But Mam we didn't ...!"

Bella cut him short in mid-sentence, "Don't lie on top o' everything else ... you're forrit when you get home as it is. Aye and that goes for you too Johnny Cowell!"

"But I haven't said now't."

"And I don't want any back chat either, you're in trouble as well when you get home. Your mam weren't too happy about having to cough up money she didn't have."

The manager weighed up the situation and could see we were both going to get chastised when we got home.

"Right Mrs Whittaker, I can see that they're both gonna get their come uppence ... if you pay for the tickets, then I am willing to let the matter drop this time. But I can assure you that if it happens again, I'll call the police."

After paying the cashier, Bella got hold of each of us by the scruff of our necks and frog-marched us back home where we were dealt with accordingly.

It turned out that Kenny had spilled the beans but not intentionally. As he was walking up Albion Street our Mary had called across to him.

"Kenny, do you know where our John is, mí mam's bín looking all oe'r the place for him ... we haven't seen him all day?"

"Aye, he's in th'Alhambra pictures watchín 'Old Mother Riley's Ghost' wí David Whittaker."

"What's that," came a loud voice from behind him, "Did I just hear you say our David's in th'Alhambra?" On turning Kenny went grey, he knew he'd put his foot in it when he saw David's mam.

"Well ... I ... I'm not sure, I only think he is," he stuttered trying to get out of it. But it was useless ... Bella was too wily for that.

"You can stop your fibbing young Kenny Clayton ... you're just trying to cover up for 'm now!"

Bella then went to see my mam, who gave her permission to sort it out.

We both got a good hiding'. It was the last time that we dodged in the pictures ... at least for a while anyway.

****

Only the very privileged children had toys. But it didn't seem to bother most kids; they made their own games getting up to all kinds of tomfoolery. This was especially true about our Jimmy ... give him a bag of dried peas and it would keep him occupied for hours on end. He didn't use the peas to fire from a peashooter or a pea-gun. No, he used them for playing his favourite game ...'soldiers'.

He enjoyed nothing more than going upstairs into the back bedroom where he would spread the peas onto the bare wooden floor. He'd put a handful in one corner of the room and a handful in another, finishing with little piles everywhere. By using old newspapers and discarded shoeboxes he'd form little garrisons and impregnable strongholds. He'd take a sheet off the bed and throw it onto the floor in a crumpled heap and the humps and grooves would represent mountains and valleys. Each pile of peas was a regiment of soldiers or a tribe of Indians, and each single file symbolised men on the march.

His incredible imagination did the rest. His games varied between Cowboys and Indians, the North and South American Civil War or the English fighting the Germans. It didn't matter to Jimmy though, whichever armies fought against each other, it was still deadly serious.

If anyone of us walked into the bedroom we had to knock first or woe betide, if we disturbed his concentration, we faced his wrath.

"Right you can come in but watch where you're standing," he'd bellow, "there's a battalion under siege over there and loads of Indians in that corner. Sometimes Barry used to join him and quite enjoyed it but I could never get into the game.

"Our Jimmy's upstairs again Mam playing soldiers with a bag o' dried peas," one or other of us would remark.

"You leave him be, at least it keeps him quiet and out of mischief," she'd reply.

Whether it was raining or brilliant sunshine, Jimmy preferred to stay inside in the back bedroom with his army. Mam didn't mind at all because at least it kept him quiet and she always knew where to find him.

Our Maureen hardly ever got into mischief but even she had her moments. She had a friend called Winnie Clarke, who lived two doors higher up from our house at number 18. Winnie was just two months older than Maureen and they got on really well. So well in fact that Winnie practically lived at number 14 ... she was like one of the family. The young girl was actually called after my mother Winifred.

Ironically, this came about inadvertently because of my dad. Mam was seven months pregnant with our Maureen and, because of Dad's wayward ways, she'd ended up in the Workhouse. Mam was very distressed and felt she couldn't cope but then something very touching happened, which boosted her self-confidence and raised her self-esteem. As it happened, a lady in the next bed, called Maria Clarke, had just had a baby girl. During one of their many talks together, the lady said to Mam, "Do you know something Winifred, I love your friendship and I've decided to call my little girl Winifred after you."

It gave Winifred a nice inner feeling and a ring of confidence. What she didn't realise then, was that the little girl would become like part of her own family and always be known as young Winnie Clark.

One day Maureen and Winifred were upstairs in Winnie's house playing make-believe and other silly games.

"I'm bored," said Winnie, "can we not think of any other game to play?"

"What about Snakes and Ladders or Ludo?" replied Maureen.

"No, I don't mean a boring game Maureen ... I mean something exciting and scary."

"What, like putting sheets o'er our heads and pretending to be ghosts, coming out of that cubbyhole?"

"Hey hang on a minute Maureen, you've just given me an idea."

"Oh yeah, whattaya thinking then?"

"Well, you know how your Jimmy's always playing at soldiers in the back bedroom with them dried peas?"

"Yeah ... go on."

"Well why don't we climb up into the roof space through the manhole that's in the top ó that cubbyhole?"

"U-um, but what's that got to do with our Jimmy?" asked Maureen naively.

"A-ah well I've bín up into the loft space afore and it's possible to crawl right along the street fro' house to house."

"Are you sure Winnie, I didn't think you'd be able to do that?"

"I'm positive; I've done it loads 'o times."

"Aye all right I believe you, but what's that got to do with our Jimmy?"

"Oh come off it Maureen, you're not that thick are you!"

"Hey watch it Winnie!"

"All right, all right, I'm only kidding. Anyroad, we can crawl through the loft space until we get over your back bedroom and we can make howling noises down through the manhole."

"Right, I'm forrit," mused Maureen, "we'll frighten our Jimmy to death!" So off they went first climbing onto a chair and then lifting themselves up through the manhole.

"Bloomin' 'eck Winnie it's dark up here," protested Maureen feeling a bit timid.

"Yeah I know, but there's a bit ó light coming in through the slates and if you leave the manhole cover off we'll manage. But be careful, you'll have to mék sure to keep your weight on these little wooden joists or else you'll go through the ceiling." Both girls negotiated the little trek safely and then they lifted up the manhole cover of number 14.

"Are you ready Maureen?"

"I am that Winnie ... start blowing." They both took a deep breath and then tried hooting like an owl to create a ghostly sound.

"Hey who's that, who's up there?" wailed Jimmy. They stopped blowing for a while but as soon as he went quiet they started again.

"Right," whispered Winnie, "I think he's gone back to his dried peas ... hoo-oo-oo!"

"That's it," bawled Jimmy, "I know somebody's up there 'cos the manhole cover's bín moved!" Once again Maureen and Winnie went deadly quiet. However, their little prank backfired, as they heard Jimmy shouting downstairs.

"Mam, you'd better come up here quick, I think somebody's tryin' to break into t'house through the loft."

"Quick." panicked Maureen, "we'd better get out of here, mí mam's coming!" Young Winnie nimbly scarpered through the roof space but Maureen fled rather clumsily. She was only half way back when she missed her footing and her leg went right through the ceiling of number 16. As it happened Alice King was just making the bed and lots of plaster landed on the top of her head.

"What the Devil's going on," she screeched when she saw a leg dangling from the ceiling. She nearly popped out of her skin when, a minute later, Winnie came waltzing out of the cubbyhole.

"I'm sorry Mrs. King, we were only playing, we didn't mean to break your ceiling."

"Young Winnie Clarke, I should o' known ... you're always geddin' up to mischief. Anyroad, who else is up there with you?"

"My friend Maureen, from next door to you."

"What, you mean young Maureen Cowell?"

"Yes Mrs, King, we wer' only ......"

Alice was furious, cutting in, "Never mind you wer' only ... I don't want to hear any of your flimsy excuses!" She then bellowed loudly, ordering Maureen to come down through the manhole at once. Alice was all fired up ready to tear a strip off Maureen but when she saw her she actually felt sorry for her. Maureen's face was dirty, her dress was torn and she had a big gash in her leg. Instead of scalding her Alice warmed to her.

"Oh young Maureen, just look at the state o' you. Come on we'd best go downstairs and I'll get thí cleaned up afore your mam sees you." She bathed Maureen's leg and put a bandage on it and told her to wash her hands and face.

"All I can do with your dress is brush it down ... I don't know what you're gonna tell your mam though."

"But what about your roof Mrs. King, aren't you gonna tell her about it?"

"No lass, I think you're in enough trouble as it is already without me adding to it."

"But who's gonna mend it for you?"

"Don't worry about that, I'll get onto the landlord and tell him the ceiling collapsed. Not to worry yourself lass, it wer' in a rickety old state and in need of a new one anyroad."

Both girls were eternally grateful to Alice and promised they'd do some shopping for her and other little chores if she were ever stuck.

They never again interrupted our Jimmy's game o' soldiers

****

Jimmy, Barry and I all slept in the front bedroom in a double bed. Barry was always the warmest because he slept in the middle, and as the bed springs sagged Jimmy and I always rolled close to him.

Before getting into bed all three of us would kneel down by the bedside and say our prayers out loud without any embarrassment. All three sets of prayers were different.

My favourite prayer was quite simple and to the point:

"If I should die before I wake,

I pray the Lord my soul to take.

Please God, look after Mam and Dad and all mí brothers and sisters 'cos I want them to go to Heaven as well. Anyroad I'll try and be good tomorrow. And thank you for making Mam happy today. I know she was 'cos she went to bed this afternoon with mi dad, and when they got up I heard Dad say, 'E-eh, that wer' better than arguing weren't it love?'"

Barry's prayers were always more serious, quoting a decade of the 'Rosary', an 'Our Father' and a 'Glory be to the Father' followed by an 'Act of Contrition'.

Jimmy's prayer was short and sweet, *"I'm sorry for being bad today and I promise You I won't put any worms down any o' mí sisters necks tomorrow ... thank you God, Amen."*

After the prayers we'd usually chant a little song in unison to keep the Devil at bay.

'If you don't let him in at the window,
He's sure to come in through the door,
Or through the skylight in the dead of the night,
Or he'll work his way under the floor.'

Once the prayer session was finished we'd then get down to serious business ... 'I spy with my little eye'.

"Righto Barry, you're on first."

"Right ... I spy with my little eye something beginning with 'W'."

"A wall," said Jimmy.

"No, that's not it."

"A window," I said.

"Yeah that's it our John ... you're on now."

"Bloomin' 'eck!" moaned Jimmy. "That was too flippin' easy."

"Oh yeah, if it were that easy ... why didn't you geddit?" I asked. "Anyroad it's my turn now so I spy with my little eye something beginning with 'L'."

Various guesses were made in vain, 'a leg – a latch – a light'.

"We haven't got a light," I said.

"Course we have ... what about the one fro' the candle," smirked Jimmy.

"Yeah all reight, but that's not it anyroad."

Silly guesses followed, 'A lump in the bed' 'a little door' but without success.

"All reight we give in ... what is it?"

"A lion," I said feeling pleased that I'd outsmarted them.

"Whaddaya talkin' about? There's no lions in the flippin' bedroom ... not even a toy one!" protested Jimmy.

"Yeah there is," I gloated, "up there on the ceiling."

"On the ceiling ... whaddaya talkin' about?"

"Well just look up ... can you see all them cracks?"

"Yeah, so what?"

"Well, look at that reight big one above your head and then move your eyes a little to the window. Just at the side o' that piece o' wood that's stickín down you can see a lion's face."

"Oh aye I can but that's cheating … it's not a real one"

"Who said ow't about it being a real one … there's no rule about that."

"Hey I should o' got that," Barry blurted excitedly, "'cos I can see loads o' different things up there in the ceiling. If you look over there you can see a castle, and in this corner there's a woman's face."

True enough, there were so many cracks in the plaster that many different faces, animals or objects could be conjured up. From then on the game of 'I spy' took on a different meaning, becoming much more complicated.

****

Christmas was always the time for exchanging gifts no matter how paltry they were.

It's the thought that counts," Mam would say as we opened our flimsy parcels.

Using all our little scams to raise money, all my brothers and sisters managed to come up with something.

Our enterprising schemes always amused Dad, especially when he got a packet of fags or a tin of tobacco. He was highly delighted one Christmas when I handed him an oxo tin, lined with coloured paper full to the brim with tobacco. He wouldn't have been so pleased if he'd known where it came from.

I'd come up with the idea four months previously in September after seeing a lad picking up discarded cigarette ends from the gutter.

"What are you doing?" I asked him.

"I'm collecting dockers for mí dad," he replied stuffing the butts into a paper bag.

"You don't mean to say he's gonna smoke 'em do you ... not after they've been in everybody else's gob?"

"No ... not like they are now you silly sod! He'll break 'em up first and put all the flakes in his bacco tin so he can roll his own fags later on."

"U-ugh ... that's disgusting! You don't know whose mouths them dog-ends have been in."

"So what ... it doesn't seem to bother mí dad. As long as he's got a smoke that's all he cares about."

As I made my way home I got to thinking. "What a good idea, I'll do that for Dad this Christmas ... it'll save me loads o' money. Yeah, why not ... he'll never know the difference."

I convinced myself and from then on I picked up dock-ends from wherever I could ... the gutter, the pavement and even wastebins. But I was fussy ... I never collected any soggy ones. I acquired an oxo tin and lined the inside with red paper and painted fancy patterns on the outside. By the time December came the tin was full to the brim.

"Great, I've cracked it!" I congratulated myself feeling quite smug. "All I need to do now is buy two packets of cigarette papers to put in the box and find a safe place to hide it." I had a good hiding place underneath some loose floorboards in the front bedroom where I kept my treasured possessions. I felt very smug and couldn't wait for Christmas Day to see Dad's face. As it turned out I didn't have to wait that long.

One night, a few days prior to the event, Dad stayed in and he was fidgety. He hadn't turned over a new leaf, he just didn't have any money to go boozing with ... and worse still, he didn't have any fags either. As the evening passed he became irritable and made it obvious by tutting and blowing.

"For crying out loud Jack!" quipped Mam, "You're like a bear with a sore backside ... why don't you send our John to Wilding's Shop for five Woodbines?"

"Because I've no flamin' money woman!" he rapped. "What have I been trying to tell thí all bloody night?"

"All right, all right ... keep your hair on I'm only trying to help. Surely you've got eightpence ... that's all it'll cost you?"

"Eightpence Woman! It might as well be eight pounds for all I care ... I haven't got a red cent. Anyroad Winnie," he said changing his tone, "you don't happen to have ...?"

"No Jack I haven't," she cut him short, "it's no good asking me I haven't got any money either. And besides, if I had I wouldn't give it to you to squander on fags."

"U-umph," he moaned, "that's typical in'it ... bloody typical. Anyroad I might o' known what the answer would be."

"Well there you go then ... why did you ask in the first place? Anyway, if you're so stuck why don't you get them on the tick until weekend?"

"You're joking, that woman wouldn't let me strap up to thre'pence ... you know what she's like."

"Oh well you'll just have to miss out for once won't you? Anyroad, it'll happen do you good ... your chest has been gurgling like a rusty old engine lately."

"Thank you very much Winnie ... that's all I need," he grunted, growing even rattier.

This is where I stepped in ... their conversation got me to thinking, "U-um, I've been raring to surprise Dad for ages ... why not now? Yeah, why not indeed ... I can't see me getting a better chance than right now?"

So I slipped up to my bedroom, retrieved the gift and excitedly made my way downstairs. As I approached Dad he was sat in the armchair near to the cellar top, looking rather down in the dumps. His gloomy expression changed to one of surprise when I handed him the box.

"What's this then our John," he asked, "it's not my birthday is it?"

"No it's not Dad," I replied smiling, "it doesn't have to be your birthday if I want to surprise you does it? Anyroad, it's actually your Christmas present. I wasn't gonna give it you till next week but I think now's as good a time as any."

"Oh aye, how come ... tha's never given me a prezzie afore Christmas Day before?"

"Aye I know Dad, but I can't bear to see you looking so miserable ... what with having no fags an' all."

"Blimey, does it show that much lad?"

"Yeah it does Dad. Anyroad, I've a feeling that this might buck you up a little."

"By éck cock you've got me all fired up and curious," he blurted out as he eagerly started to rip off the wrapping paper. "I think I like these little surprises," he giggled like a little boy. Within a minute he was sat there with the tin box in his hands.

"Bloomín éck our John you certainly packed it well, there must be twenty elastic bands holding it together."

"Aye I know Dad ... I just wanted to make sure it'd be all right."

"You're not kidding our John," he joked, "you can say that again ... it's like gettin' into Fort Knox."

Finally he opened the box and, much to my delight, he was ecstatic ... all my scheming seemed worthwhile.

"Oh great!" he shouted excitedly when he saw the tobacco tightly packed into the tin along with the cigarette papers. "Just look at this Winnie what our John's bought me."

He gloated as he unfolded a cigarette paper and took a pinch of tobacco. The rapid mood change and the happy expression on Dad's face amused Mam. "Just look at him now," she smiled at me, "he's like a dog with a bone. It doesn't take much does it ... he can't wait to have a fag."

"Too true I can't" laughed Dad, "I'm gasping for a drag and this bacco smells fantastic. "Anyroad our John," he said turning to me, "it's good of you to think of me ... it must have cost you a bomb?"

Luckily I was prepared for this question.

"No Dad it didn't, I only had to buy the fag paper ... I got the bacco for now't."

"For now't," he queried, "how d'you mean ... for now't?"

"Well, what it is" I replied convincingly, "for the last few months I've bín collecting all the dog-ends that you've been leaving in the ashtray ... I didn't think you'd mind."

"Mind? You must be joking! I think you've done great ... what a good idea and enterprising too. Good lad ... I like the way you've used your initiative."

"Thanks Dad ... I'm glad you like it."

"Like it, I love it ... this has made my day." As he took a long drag on the self-made cigarette he mumbled and coughed a little. My heart sank as he pondered for a moment.

"Oh 'eck ... is he gonna catch on?" I thought as he coughed and spluttered yet again, but my concern was unfounded.

"By gum that's grand," he murmured, "but it tastes different somehow. I can't quite put mí finger on it ... u-um, a little stronger perhaps."

"Oh," I spluttered trying to think of something fast, "maybe the bacco has dried out a little in the tin Dad. Happen I should have wrapped it in silver foil?"

"Aye, you're probably right our John. Anyroad I'm not complaining," he sighed in sheer bliss as he took another long drag, "this is great ... thanks a lot cock."

"Thanks a lot!" I thought cringing a little, "He'd bloody well strangle me if he knew the truth."

Despite a feeling of guilt I often giggled when I thought about the incident afterwards. But I never discussed it with anyone for fear of Dad finding out.

****

One meal I always enjoyed was Sunday dinner. Mam always dished it out about five o'clock as a dinner-cum-tea. This suited me fine, as I often played football on Clifton Reckory with my schoolmates and never got home until after six o'clock. One Sunday our Jimmy played as well and when we got home the others had already eaten.

"Sit yourselves down and I'll get your dinner out of the oven," said Mam.

"U-um, it smells good Mam," said Jimmy, "I'm starving ... I could eat a scabby donkey."

"That'll do!" she rapped. "I'll not have you talking like that. Anyway, I hope it's not burned ... don't blame me if it is."

"Don't worry about it Mam," I put in, "I'll scoff the lot ... mí stomach thinks mí throat's bín cut."

We were both heartily scoffing when she placed a small plate on the table containing two pieces of sponge cake ... one piece was noticeably bigger than the other.

"There, I've done a bit of baking," she said, "but make sure you eat your dinner before you have any cake."

My mouth watered at the thought of sinking my teeth into Mam's baking and I was determined to finish my dinner first so that I could take the big piece. That was my intention, but I didn't stand a chance. Jimmy shovelled the food down his throat so fast he almost choked. He'd finished before I was halfway through mine, then smugly pushed his dinner plate to one side and reached for the largest piece of cake; I was fuming!

"Ar-rgh, just like you, you greedy sod!" I moaned. "You always take the biggest piece."

"Stop whining!" he sneered. "You're allús going on about somét."

"Oh aye, that's easy for you to say," I grunted, "so long as you're getting your own way all the time."

"All right then clever clogs … if you'd o' finished first, which piece would you have taken?"

"I'd have taken the smallest piece," I replied with a wry smile on my face.

The smile quickly turned to a pout when he laughed derisively, "Well then … you've now't to moan about have you? Stop your whinging … you've got the smallest piece!"

****

Because of the poverty many youngsters were often hungry. Children of families in need did not have to pay for school dinners and even breakfast was supplied for the more impoverished. This was all very well but there was a stigma attached to free school meals and the children in receipt of these benefits were always on the receiving end of abuse from their peers. Every Monday morning they stood out like sore thumbs when the teacher collected the dinner monies straight after calling the register. During the obligatory head count she would ask the children for their dinner money.

The poorer kids would answer in embarrassment, "Free meals Miss."

The more fortunate ones from better to do families would walk proudly over to the desk and hand over their money and stroll back to their seats, smirking at us on free meals.

"U-um," they'd mutter under their breath, "we pay for ours ... at least we're not beggars like some in this class!" The hackles would rise on the back of my neck but, like others in a similar situation as me, I just had to grin and bear it.

Like children everywhere the kids of Trafalgar played street games and got up to lots of mischief. Whether it be summer or winter they found many inventive games to play. These included skipping, tig, hopscotch, rounders, piggy in the middle, ring-a-ring a roses and many more. One game was to draw a circle near to the house wall and each child would place a coin within the ring. They'd then stand at the kerb and take turns at trying to knock the coins out of the circle with a ball. Each kid took turns by standing at the flag edge, aiming at the chalk ring, and bouncing the ball against the house wall. If a boy or girl happened the drop the ball, it was then somebody else's turn.

One favourite game amongst the boys was playing 'bobbers'. On saying this, Marian Pilkington could play as good as any boy and often challenged me.

"D'you want a game o' bobbers Johnny Cowell?" she asked one day.

"Aye all reight Marian, but I'm not using any of mí iron'ees ... I'm gonna play with mí glass alleys."

"Reighto, I'm not bothered," she replied pulling a glass marble out of her bobber bag.

"Bloomin' 'eck Marian, you've got plenty o' bobbers in your bag today."

She gave a cheeky grin, "Yeah, I've just bín skinning some o' the Derby Street lads ... they can't play bobbers for toffee, it were like takin' candy from a baby, ha, ha, ha!"

"Oh aye, well don't expect any mercy from me, I'm not gonna give thí a start."

She just laughed, "Just throw your bobber Johnny Cowell ... we'll soon see who needs giving a start."

For a while, we played ordinary marbles in the gutter then Marian changed the game. "How about playing nug Johnny, it's better than this game?"

"Go on then, I like playing that as well," I agreed.

For this game we used one of the sunken cobbles in the middle of the street as the nug, which was like a hole in the ground. The idea was to land a marble into the nug, giving that player the opportunity to aim at their opponent's bobber.

Marian was the first to achieve this, "Reight Johnny watch this!" she gloated, skilfully aiming and hitting my bobber full in the face.

"Wow, good shot Marian ... I think we're gonna have to call thí 'Dead Eyed Dick'!"

She laughed answering, "Right, do you still fancy your chances?" We played happily for a couple of hours with neither of us gaining the upper hand, each having the same amount of marbles left, before deciding to call it a day. Marian and I met up many times after that, enjoying the intriguing game. We were both well-matched, sometimes winning sometimes losing. But the outcome didn't matter ... we had a great respect for each other, becoming good friends. Sometimes lads would double up as partners and throw out challenges to other kids. I always partnered up with Marian and, by 'eck, I was onto a winner.

****

Despite the poor living conditions the resilience of most children was evident by their happy and carefree attitude. Much to their credit, hardly anyone ever committed a crime ... burglaries were very few and muggings were unheard of. Our front door was never locked, but nobody would dream of entering without permission. Mind you, if anybody had ever broken into our house it would have been to put something in, as there was never anything of value to steal. This applied to many households, and overall, everybody had respect for other people's property.

Many children were often hungry and would resort to various scams to fill their bellies. One of these was to visit the Fire Station. The large exit doors for the fire engines were situated on Manchester Road. However, the poor kids would stand by a tunnel entrance on Finsley Gate beckoning the firemen.

"Can we have a look at the fire engines mister?" They knew that once inside they could revert to other ruses; often their pleas were rewarded.

One of the crew usually took them under his wing, "Aye all reight cock, come on in ... you can only have five minutes mind." The kids enjoyed looking at the fire engines but their main concern was food.

"U-um yummy yummy, that's a nice smell," one would hint as they passed the canteen. The crew nearly always succumbed to their sorry plight as they talked amongst themselves about the kids.

"He-ey, just look at th'expression on their little faces ... you can't help but feel sorry for 'em canya?"

"Aye, they look like they've had now't to eat for a month."

To the kids' delight they were usually given a meat pie and piece of cake or something like.

"Just look at 'em ...the poor little mites!" one of the men would comment as the kids stuffed every last morsel of food into their mouths. The firemen got used to seeing the same faces but pretended not to notice.

"Right kids, now we don't want to see any of you around here agén for a while ... you've got to give t'others a chance."

Despite the friendly warning some kids visited the station regularly.

****

Mother wasn't the only one to tell tales of her childhood ... Dad did as well. As a child he'd always lived in the Croft Area of town.

"E-eh, I'll tell thí what our John," he would say nostalgically, "everybody wer' poor, but they were good days."

When in this kind of mood I would encourage him to tell a tale, "Oh go on Dad, tell us about when you were a little lad ... please!"

"We-ell, I lived on Pickup Street in the Croft area near the Town Centre. Just round the corner from us were Miller Street and Norton Street. It was at the top of Miller Street in a courtyard that Cece's made their ice-cream. And let me tell you, Cece's ice-cream was absolutely delicious; no other ice-cream in the country came anywhere near it. Mr Cece has his own special recipe, a secret formula handed down from generation to generation and it definitely has a taste all of its own. Now let me get to the point of the story. Every morning you'd see loads of horse and carts pulling away loaded up with ice-cream. Me and mí mates would go round there trying to scrounge a free cornet or anything going before they set off, but there wasn't much chance o' that. To set up, the men used to put th'ice-cream into a metal cylinder and then place that into an even bigger one ... a tub within a tub if you like. The larger outer tub was filled with ice cubes to stop the ice-cream fro' melting."

"Did they ever give you a free ice cream Dad?" I interrupted.

"Not so many times afore they set off lad, but if they'd ow't left at th'end o' the day we stood a good chance. Anyroad, it didn't really matter if they didn't give us one 'cos there was another reason for waiting for 'em to come back."

"How d'you mean Dad?"

"Well, you'll not believe this but here goes. Just afore returning to the depot the ice-cream fella always drove the horse and cart into Boot Street, which had a small gradient. This allowed the back 'o the cart to tilt slightly backwards. The chap then pulled a plug fro' the bottom of the outer cylinder allowing all the melted ice cubes to drain from the drum, into the gutter and down a grate. Now you can believe this or believe it not, but loads o' kids, including girls, would get down on their bellies and sip the ice water."

"What! From the gutter?"

"As I stand here our John that's the Gospel Truth!"

"U-ugh, I wouldn't o' fancied that! Anyroad, what did it taste like?"

"It might seem far-fetched but it's true. And in answer to your question ... it was delicious."

"What, d'you mean to say that you supped it as well Dad?"

"Aye I did that, all the kids did, and so would you o' done. I can't say why but that ice-water had a taste of its own ... it was absolutely delicious! Thinking about it now I can still imagine the taste ... it wer' like nectar. Just like a bear's drawn to honey ... that was us kids."

"U-um, I don't know so much," I mumbled, "maybe. Anyroad like you said Dad, it does seem a bit far-fetched," adding jokingly, "Like a bucket of pee from China, ha, ha, ha!"

"You can laugh all you want our John, but when I wer' a lad people were destitute and lots o' them kids were hungry. Anyroad, let me tell you about 'The Relief'."

"The Relief Dad ... what's The Relief?"

"If you just shut your gob and listen I'll tell you."

"All reight Dad, I'm listening ... I'm listening."

"Well in them days the most needy, especially those with large families, had to apply to 'The Relief'. In earlier days the office was situated in a little narrow sloping ginnel, which ran from off Nicholas Street. The ginnel levelled out and this is where the official in charge would stand on a wooden platform shouting out names from a register." He paused for a little and smiled, "Coincidentally, the official in charge was called 'Mr. Penny'. He was a small man, who always wore a black billycock hat complemented by a black coat and waistcoat from which hung a watch and chain. To complete the outfit he wore pinstripe pants and black leather shoes. At the time the Relief was referred to by the locals as 'The Parish'. People always had an appointed time and would go and stand in the ginnel with t'others and wait for Mr. Penny to call out their names."

"Joe Smith."

"Here."

"Have you been working this week?"

"No."

"Joe would then go through to th'office, sign a chit of paper, and pick up his bit o'money. This was the state of affairs for many years, but later on, the premises were transferred to a large public building on Finsley Gate."

"Is that where the dole office is now Dad, I've seen loads o' people queuing up outside there?"

"Aye it is lad, but anyway let me get on with my tale. The main diet for most people on Relief was fish and chips from the 'Chippy'. Many a barbed comment would be thrown out, 'Aye, thá can allús tell them that's on Relief ... they've bín dragged up fro' the chip chop.'

Young growing lads had big appetites and when sent to the 'Chippy' they'd poke a hole in the paper and pinch a few chips and often drink some of the vinegar. I always did this and mí dad would grumble when I got home. 'The miserable bugger … the bleedin' chips are geddín less and less every time thá goes to that chippy!'"

"Ha, ha, did he ever catch on it were you Dad?"

"No did he 'eck as like … I'd o' got a right old crack around the lug-hole if he had o' done."

"Going back to The Relief Dad … did they hand out the money freely?"

"Did they 'eck as like, you'd to be on the bread line afore you got ow't. Let me tell thí what happened to a mate o' mine who tried to get a new pair ó clogs for his lad Billy."

"Good," I thought as Dad carried on with another tale, "my little scheme to soak up more tales from him has worked."

"Just let me get this right," he said pondering a little, "Little Billy was growing quickly and needed some new clogs. His dad applied for some relief and had to go, with cap in hand, in front of the 'Board of Guardians' to try and get a new pair.

'But there's nothing wrong with this pair,' pointed out one of the indignant guardians presiding on the panel, 'there's still plenty of wear in 'em.'

'Yeah, I know that, but the lad's going through a growing spell and they're hurting his feet.'

Another grim official stroked his chin saying, 'We can't just give clogs out at random, everything's got to be considered … we need to sort out the wheat from the chaff.'

'Whaddaya talkin about,' rapped young Billy's dad losing his patience, 'sort out the wheat from the chaff? We're talking about a young growing lad here, not flamín' wheat growing in a field. Surely a bit o' common sense has to come into it ... the lad'll be crippled if he wears these much longer.'"

"Oh 'eck Dad, did the young lad not get his clogs then?"

"Well yes our John, in this case he did. However, young Billy got his clogs but many others weren't so lucky. Loads o' people were turned away and got now't ... it were just the luck o' the draw. Many o' the poor kids had to mék do and finished up wí crippled feet." He paused for a moment before adding, "Yeah our John, that's the way things were ... everybody wer' poor! Your mam tells you tales about what it wer' like in Bacup when she wer' a lass, but it wer' just the same here in Burnley. People were destitute and lived in small cramped dilapidated back-to-back houses. There were no dustbins and we'd to empty our rubbish into hugh waste disposal bins that were kept at th'end o' the block. Everywhere you went you saw lots o' kids with dirty faces and tousled hair. Mind you, despite their crass existence, people were proud ... you never saw any graffiti on the walls or litter in the streets like you do nowadays. Aye, and the women used to donkey stone their front steps till they gleamed. One old lady used to swill the flags outside her house and she even donkey stoned some o' them. She was a bit eccentric mind and was forever chasing us kids off if we went anywhere near her flags ... we nicknamed her Nellie Silverflags. There's no doubt about it ... despite the poverty and deprivation the streets were a credit to the people who lived there."

I loved it when Dad was in this sort of mood and I certainly took advantage of the situation. I gleaned as much information from him as I could and soaked up many nostalgic memories.

CHAPTER 6 - YOUNGSTERS' ESCAPADES

The summer holiday came and went, and now was the time to go up into Miss Drennan's class. Like children everywhere the kids at St. Thomas's School could be heartless and cruel. Along the way I found myself in many scrapes and despite not being a fighting lad I had to face up to things because we Cowells were constantly singled out in the schoolyard. This stemmed mainly from the fact that Dad was a ragman and he'd also just recently been sent to prison for the second time for handling stolen goods. It became apparent on the first day back at school after the summer holidays that we were in for a lot of abusive comments. At playtime, in the schoolyard, I was the first in the firing line from two lads called Peter Birtwhistle and Paul Whitham.

"Hiya Cowheel ... canya dad fly like your dad?"

"What aya talking about Birtwhistle," I responded.

"Well, he's a bird isn't he ... a jailbird, ha, ha, ha!"

"Yeah, and I bet he's in with all the murderers!" mocked Paul Whitham.

"Get lost!" I retaliated, "he's a better dad than yours anyroad!"

"Oh aye ... you mean when he's not in jail?"

"Don't stand for that our kid," rapped our Jimmy who'd heard the stinging comments from across the playground, "get him thumped!"

"Lay off our Jimmy!" I said trying to play down the situation, "I'll handle it my way."

"Handle it your way," jeered Peter Birtwhistle, "what you really mean is you're scared to death!"

"Don't start somét you can't finish Birtwhistle!" warned Jimmy.

"Why what will you do Cowheel ... put me in a padded cell with your dad?"

"A padded cell," queried Jimmy, "what the flamin' 'eck are you talking about?"

To the amusement of all the other kids Peter Birtwhistle burst out laughing and fired off another insult, "Well your dad'll be in a padded cell won't he ... padded out wí loads o' rags off the rag-cart? Ha, ha, ha!"

Enough said! Jimmy's composure changed from controlled to seething anger.

"You swine!" he screeched, his face red with rage. Fuming, almost frothing at the mouth, he immediately set into the lad with both fists flying.

It wasn't long before lots of kids formed a circle and the loud chanting of. "A fight, a fight!" resounded through the schoolyard.

I could feel the tension building up inside me as the air became more and more charged. Within minutes I too was rolling about the floor fighting Paul Whitham. One of the reasons I didn't like fighting was because I often finished up on the losing end but in this case it was different. My adrenaline was flowing as it always did when I had been goaded into a fight.

"Right Whitham," I thought, "it's either you or me!" I laid into him for all I was worth and didn't stop until he wailed he'd had enough. That was good enough for me ... I was quite happy with the outcome. Whitham never bothered me again after that.

****

Other kids also threw out many hurtful comments, "Hiya Cowheel, hasta bín visiting your dad in jail this weekend ... how did you get there, on the rag-cart?" I never reacted to these offensive remarks unless pushed to the very limit.

Mary, like Jimmy was fiery and she too had many run-ins with the girls. They could be very catty, coming out with similar sly comments but it didn't wear with Mary. Having the same temperament as Jimmy and a natural ability to fight, using her fists like a boy, she soon put them in their place.

At home, we talked about our scrapes in the schoolyard, but Mam never intervened so long as it was amongst children of our own age, and that's how we liked it. One thing though, Mam wouldn't tolerate bullying. It wasn't one-sided either; she'd taught all of us kids never to bully any little ones, and God help us if we did.

Despite all the jeering and insults we still loved Dad dearly and couldn't wait for him to be released from prison. My family and I all eagerly awaited his homecoming and we decided to arrange a special treat for him. Our Maureen was the main instigator and she'd had us rehearsing a little welcome home song for hours on end. . This came about one cold blizzardy day in February 1947 and snow had drifted up to the level of bedroom window sills throughout every street. Dad had been released from Strangeways' Prison at noon and was due home about three o'clock.

But at two o'clock, it started to snow quite heavily and the flakes were as big as leaves sticking as soon as they hit the ground. The wind began to stir up and we could all hear it blowing and whistling down the chimney; just the thought of having to go outside made me shiver. By five o'clock it was quite dark and we all became agitated.

"Oh bloomin' 'eck Mam!" muttered Maureen as she looked out of the window, "Just look at all that snow, I hope mi dad's going to be all right." She was rather anxious, and kept going to the front door to watch out for him coming down the street, but he was nowhere in sight; by now Albion Street was knee deep in snow.

We kids bombarded Mother with questions, "Are you sure it was today he was being released Mam?" "Do you think they might have kept him in a bit longer Mummy?" "Do you think he might be buried in't snow somewhere Mam, and can't get out?"

Even little Barry asked, "You don't think he'll be freezing to death somewhere, do you Mummy?"

"Yes, I'm certain that he's been released today and no, they won't have kept him there any longer, he'd have made sure of that. As for your other questions ... I just don't know what to think. And anyway, it's no good worrying about it because there's nothing we can do except wait. Mind you, we could happen say a little prayer."

"Is he coming home on the bus Mam or the train?" asked Jimmy.

"Most probably on the bus because it's a straight run from Manchester to here; why do you ask?"

"Well, our Barry could be right when he said mí dad might be stuck in the snow 'cos buses are always getting stuck over them their tops when it snows a lot."

"Oh thank you Jimmy, thank you very much, that's all we need. Now listen everybody! Try not to fret yourselves because your dad is a lot more resilient than you think, and even if he is stuck somewhere, he'll be able to take care of himself."

"What does resilient mean Mummy?" asked Barry innocently.

Maureen had to smile to herself as she gave him a little hug, "It just means that Daddy can look after himself our Barry."

"Oh right!" he responded. And then as an afterthought, "But I'm still gonna say a little prayer for him, 'cos God'll help him then, won't he?"

Another hour passed and there was still no sign of Dad. Every one of us became quite despondent and fidgety. Then finally, at half past seven, we heard the front door open followed by the sound of footsteps trudging up the lobby. My eyes were fixated on the living room door and, finally, to my delight he was there. But on seeing him my delight changed to perplexity for he was a sight to behold. He was like a snowman, and an old one at that, with long white bushy eyebrows. His teeth were chattering, and he looked absolutely frozen to the marrow. Striving to catch his breathe he just crouched forward resting his hands on his knees, puffing and panting. Prison life had certainly taken its toll and Dad appeared drawn, and looked every bit of his thirty-nine years. Mother Nature was really catching up on his fast living lifestyle.

He couldn't speak and remained crouched over gasping for breath. After regaining his composure he grunted a little before telling us how the bus had got bogged down in a snowdrift over the moors and he'd had to walk knee deep in snow for three miles.

"Never mind, you're home now all safe and sound and that's all that matters," said Mam.

"Yes, that's right reiterated our Maureen, welcome home Dad." At that we all ran up to him letting him know in no uncertain terms how much we all loved him.

After a warm meal of hot broth and dumplings he settled down in front of the fire and that is when we sang the little song that we had been practising. Our Maureen took charge. To Dad's surprise, Jimmy, Mary Barry and I lined up in single file in front of the fire, and then started marching on the spot in our nightclothes.

Maureen then began to conduct us using a twelve-inch wooden ruler as a baton, leading us as we all started to sing in harmony:

"We're a happy little family, yes we are, yes we are!
We're a happy little family, yes we are.
The reason for the fuss,
Is 'cos Dad is back with us,
We're a happy little family,

Yes we are."

At the end of the first chorus, Barry broke rank, and went up to Dad, giving him a hug ad a kiss saying, "I love you Daddy, and I'm glad you're back home with us." After the warm welcome he went and stood near to the living room door, and then Mary Jimmy and I each did exactly the same each in turn. We formed a single rank file once again, and then started to march up stairs to the second chorus.

"We're a happy little family … yes we are, yes we are!
We're a happy little family … yes we are.
All our sins are all forgiven,
And we're marching up to heaven.
We're a happy little family,
Yes we are, yes we are!"

Dad was very touched by our little welcome home gesture and tears welled up in his eyes. It was a cold wintry night with snowdrifts up to the windowsills and the icy howling wind outside cut through to the bone; but the atmosphere inside our home was warm and glowing. It was certainly a night to remember.

****

Jimmy was forever battling with Michael, Joseph or Kevin Cheetham. One thing though, when two lads were fighting nobody else ever intervened. Also there were strict rules … no kicking, no biting, no pulling hair … everybody strictly adhered to these rules. The two lads would get stuck in, trying to knock three bells out of each other. Still, when the fight finished, they'd shake hands and then play happily together as though nothing had happened.

One thing that bigger lads did in the schoolyard was to constantly tease the younger ones, inciting them to fight. They'd then form a circle around the two fighting youngsters whilst at the same time keeping an eye out for the teacher. The head teacher was the renowned Miss Gordon, a strict disciplinarian, who ruled with a rod of iron.

Bobby Cheetham and I were forever on the end of these incitations and invariably had many battles much to the bigger lads' amusement.

Miss Drennan was very strict and nick-named 'The Battleaxe'. On reflection it should have been 'Battlecane' because she was always wielding it. If anyone misbehaved she would throw a tantrum, which was often followed literally by a piece of chalk or the board duster.

One day though she had the class in raptures. She was a very stout lady and always wore loose fitting dresses. Whilst throwing one of her tantrums, she started to stamp her feet hard on the wooden floor and, to the amusement of all the class, her large bloomers fell to her ankles. She quickly whipped them back up again and ran out of the class in embarrassment. She was the laughing stock of the school for months afterwards.

****

Like all children at the time my real adventures and life forming experiences took place in the world beyond the school gates.

One day I was out with my two mates David and Ronnie and we were making our way to Thompson's Park. On the way there some bicycles in a shop window intrigued me. Before I'd realised it, my two mates were well in front.

On catching them up Ronnie said to me, "Hey look at this, David's found a tanner while you were looking in that window … thre'pence a piece."

"No, tuppence each," I replied, "there's three of us."

"You're joking … you weren't with us when we found it."

"A-ah that's not fair!" I complained. "You knew I wer' coming."

"It méks no difference, we're not splitting it three ways ... we can both buy a thre'penny cornet now when we reach Thompson's Park."

"Please yourself then," I said, "I'm not bothered o'er tuppence. I still think it's unfair though."

I didn't fall out with them about it and we carried on to the park where we stayed for a few hours before making our way home. It was on the return journey that something happened, which made Ronnie and David regret their selfishness. We walked through the town centre and turned into Manchester Road. As we were passing by the Burnley Express Office on Bull Street I once again became interested by the contents in a shop window. Like before, Ronnie and David walked on and they were both well in front before I decided to follow. I'd just set off when three blokes came tottering out of the back alley of the Clockface Hotel. It was obvious that they were merry, as they all had their arms around each other and were staggering about. It became clear by their chatter that they had won some money on the horses.

"All reight young ún, how's it going ... what's the glum face for?" joked one of them as they bumped into me.

"I haven't got a glum face ... it's your fault, you nearly knocked me down," I said cockily.

"E-eh, don't be so serious cock, I wer' only kidding," he laughed. "Anyroad, here's a tanner for upsettin' thí." I was aware that I shouldn't take money from strangers, but seeing as there were three of them I felt safe. Besides, it was broad daylight and there were plenty of people about.

"Hey Burt," quipped one of his mates, "you mean bugger ... is that all you're givin' the young lad after what you've just won?" To my surprise he turned to me and handed me a shilling, "Here you are cock ... go and enjoy thaself."

The third man, being rather more intoxicated than the other two, fumbled through his pockets and pulled out a handful of coins.

"Well lad," he mumbled, "I ain't just come up on t'horses, I've been winning at cards as well ... what dusta think about that?"

"I think you're very lucky," I answered trying my hardest to placate him.

"Ha ha ha!" he laughed merrily, "You're reight about that cock! Anyroad, it's your lucky day too 'cos I'm gonna treat thí as well. Here you are lad ... what dusta think about that?" he chuckled handing me a silver coin!

I couldn't believe my eyes ... there in the palm of my hand was a half-crown piece!

"Wow!" I yelped jumping for joy, "Half a dollar, I've never had this much money in all mí life afore ... mí mam'll be o'er the moon when I tell her!" The three men started laughing, highly amused at my obvious delight.

"Good lad Billy ... you've just méd the young lad's day," said his two mates laughing as they walked off. I gazed at the money in my hand unable to believe my luck.

"I'm rich, I'm rich!" I giggled to myself. "I've never had this much money before ... ever!"

Coming back to reality I chased after Ronnie and David, catching them up on Hammerton Street; I couldn't wait to tell them of my good fortune.

"Give o'er, you lying sod!" retorted Ronnie. "You mean to say they gave you four bob just like that?"

"It's the 'Gospel Truth," I whooped not being able to contain my delight. "Anyroad, you can see for yourselves," I gloated showing them the coins in my open hand.

"All reight I believe you ... are we splitting it three ways 'cos we're all together?"

"No, am I 'eck as like," I replied adamantly, "I would have done if you'd have split that tanner with me earlier on. It wer' you who said I wasn't with you then ... that means that you weren't with me now when this happened."

Both of them reluctantly agreed. I couldn't wait to get home to give most of the money to Mam. The sheer look of surprise and happiness on Mam's face filled me with delight. Also the fact that I kept a shilling to myself, which was a lot of money; in fact, it was more than a week's spending money.

****

The folly of youth blinded us to the many perils, which surrounded us. Playing on the railway was dangerous and strictly forbidden ... anyone caught thereon was liable to prosecution. It had a double track, being part of the main Leeds to London Railway. Nonetheless, this didn't deter many children and both boys and girls frequently used it as a playground for general tomfoolery. The girls would make sandwiches and play happy families, having picnics on the grassy embankment. Being more boisterous, the lads would often spoil their fun by acting silly and sometimes fighting.

One day our Jimmy, Kenny Clayton, David Whittaker, Ronnie Hopkinson and I were frolicking about when another gang of lads came climbing over Patten Street's wall. They were from the King Street area on the other side of the footbridge. The leader of the group, Bernard Aspinall, was the same age as our Jimmy and he was the 'cock' of St. Thomas's School. Bernard and Jimmy didn't get on very well and it wasn't too long before this became apparent.

"All reight Cowheel, hasta been out ragging with your dad lately?" sneered Bernard.

"Get lost Aspin ... get back to scruffy King Street where you belong!" retaliated Jimmy.

"Oh yeah and who's gonna make me then ... you and who's army?"

"Don't be so fly just 'cos you're with your gang!"

"Ha ha ha ha!" roared Bernard, "Don't mék me laugh ... I could take thí on with one arm behind me back Cowheel!" That did it, the veins stuck out in our Jimmy's neck as he seethed with anger. Two seconds later both lads were at it tooth and nail tearing lumps out of each other. Being of similar age and well matched they rolled about the sloping embankment grappling furiously. Consequently, they rolled over and over until they finished up at the side of the railway line. The fighting carried on for a while with neither lad gaining the advantage. First one was on top then the other as they tumbled onto the first set of lines thumping and gouging each other and then stumbled in-between the two gritty railway tracks.

All the lads from both gangs, including me, were enjoying the fight and loud jeering filled the air as we all yelled in frenzy, "Come on Jimmy, you've got him ... you've got him!" "Come on Aspy ... you'll murder him!"

I was as enthusiastic as the others until I saw the signal rise!

"Our Jimmy ... Bernard, stop it quick, there's a train coming!" I shouted at the top of my voice.

All the lads now became agitated shouting similar things, "Come on, stop it ... you'll be killed!" "Be quick, I can hear the train coming!" "Oh flippin' 'eck, I can see the smoke from the train ... tell 'em to give o'er!" The shouting increased as we saw the train coming round the bend, but to no avail ... Jimmy and Bernard carried on trying to rain blows on one another, each refusing to yield. By now I was scared ... I feared for my brother's life and Bernard's too.

"Oh éck," I thought, "they're so intent on fighting they can't hear any of us." Without further ado, I dashed down onto the track. By now Jimmy and Bernard were grappling on the opposite line but still in a precarious position. Bernard was on top and appeared to be getting the best of our Jimmy.

"Stop it Bernard, there's a train coming," I screeched as I tugged at his sleeve, "you're both gonna get killed!" Bernard, who didn't seem to hear me and must have thought I was trying to help my brother, landed out catching me with a solid back hander. By now the train was perilously close but the fight continued. "Blow this for a tale!" I muttered, and made my way to the other embankment clutching my cheek. The other lads watched in horror as the train sped by; it was a goods train and they had to wait in nervous anticipation while twenty wagons passed by. To their surprise and sheer delight the fight was still ongoing. Finally, when both Jimmy and Bernard were totally exhausted, the fight ended. Jimmy was the worse for wear, and on the whole, Bernard was the overall winner ... still, some good came out of it.

"By 'eck Cowheel, that wer' a good scrap weren't it?" said Bernard grinning all over his face. "I've got to put mí hand up ... I didn't think you had it in you."

"Aye all reight, but less o' the Cowheel ... Aspy!"

"Ha, ha, ha!" roared Bernard. Both lads then shook hands, laughing heartily ... and they remained good friends thereafter.

****

The Railway was also used as a shortcut to many of the other adjacent streets. Kenny Clayton and I would run the backyard walls and climb over the railway on our way to the tennis courts where we used to play football; ironically this place was also out of bounds. No matter, lots of us lads in the neighbourhood would congregate on the gritty pitch for our favourite game. We were all keen supporters of Burnley Football Club and as we kicked the ball about on the tennis courts we would each pretend to be one of our heroes from Turf Moor. Mine was Tommy Cummings.

Many a good game of cricket was enjoyed on the back street much to the annoyance of the neighbours. A dustbin made an ideal wicket and an old jersey or coat represented the crease and determined the length of the pitch. The walls on the Albion Street side were only small but those on the Patten Street side were about eight feet high. The idea was to knock the ball past the bowler. If one knocked it over the shallow walls it was counted as four runs; however, if this happened twice … the runs counted but the player was out. On the other hand if it was knocked over one of the high walls the player was out for a score of six.

Other games were also played on the back-street; one of these was wall running. Kids would run on top of the back-yard walls leaping from one to another negotiating the back-yard gates. It was a dangerous thing to do and many of the mothers were concerned. Without realising it they'd shout many a funny comment from the top of the stone steps. "What have I told thi' about running on them walls … if you fall off and break a leg, don't come running home to me!"

I became really fleet footed at this game and challenged others to a race. We'd start from Maggie Astin's house at the bottom of the back-street and the winner was the first to reach the railway embankment. The challenge was that I would run the gauntlet on the walls whilst they ran the cobbles on the back-street.

"One – two – three go!" The fast runners would be slightly in front of me, but on reaching the top of the back-street they had to climb a high railway wall whereas I simply sprang nimbly from the backyard wall and was over the wall onto the grassy verge in a flash.

Another dangerous thing that lads enjoyed was daring each other to walk the length of Albion Street's railway bridge wall which overlooked the railway lines. It was a kind of ritual, which nearly every lad went through for fear of being ridiculed by the others if they chickened out. In comparison to the backyard walls it was quite wide, but it was very frightening to stand up on it ... especially at the highest point over the railway track. I well remember the first and only time I attempted it; I was with my mates Ronnie, David and Kenny Clayton. A few older lads were playing by the bridge and they started to tease us younger ones.

"Come on you lot ... have you passed your test yet? Before you can be a member of any gang you have to walk on top o' the railway bridge from one end to t'other."

"I'll go first," I said wanting to show off in front of my mates, "it should be easy 'cos it's pretty wide." I'd ran along backyard walls since I was a little lad and thought this should be easy. I was a show off but my little act of bravado failed. It didn't seem too bad at first as I set off, as it wasn't too much of a drop to the sloping embankment. However, as I progressed, overlooking the railway lines the sight was too much, I became petrified and sensibly decided to quit. I'd to put up with some sneering remarks but it didn't matter ... my legs were trembling and I knew that there was no way I'd attempt it again.

Then came Kenny's turn! He started the walk in a similar way to me and it soon became apparent that he too was scared. He started to panic and lost his balance, plummeting into tall ferns. Luckily the drop wasn't far, but all the same, he couldn't stop himself from rolling over and over down the steep embankment, finishing up on the railway track. He ended up with a few cuts and bruises but wasn't badly hurt. Nevertheless, much to David and Ronnie's delight, the bigger lads decided that this stunt was too dangerous after all.

"It's all reight you other young úns, there's no need to do it ... we all believe you're brave."

****

Boys were more into football and cricket or playing knock and run. It was nigh impossible to play football on the front street, as the ball kept running down the steep incline and across Trafalgar into the factory yard. And as the tennis courts were out of bounds, the only place available for us to play the game was on Clifton Rectory, which was quite a long way off.

One game that was thoroughly enjoyed and played by both boys and girls on the front street was rounders. But, it was frowned upon by the neighbours, as many a window was broken. If any of my peers happened to break a window, Mam would have to pay part of the cost. This was a constant source of controversy, as many kids would run off after causing damage. Many a neighbour would knock on Mam's door complaining about one of us, demanding recompense.

Her reply was always the same, "Right then, if my child has done it I will pay for the damage, but first of all we must wait until my children come home so that I can ask them about it."

The usual response was something like, "Nay come off it Winnie, they're bound to say it wasn't them aren't they?"

Much to their displeasure she would answer, "My children don't tell me lies ... if they say it wasn't them, then I believe them."

"Oh yeah, they're sure to own up to it aren't they? Umph, some bloomin' hopes!"

"Like I said, 'my children don't tell me lies,' if one of them has broken your window I will know the truth and you will get your money." Occasionally, during the conversation, one of us would appear on the scene and Mam would ask outright.

"Right, "This gentleman here says that you have broken his

window ... is this true?"

If the child was innocent, the reply was always a definite, "No Mam, it wasn't me ... honest!"

This usually left the neighbour feeling rather disconcerted and unhappy about the affair. Nevertheless, if the child was guilty of the offence, Mam always knew, as his or her head would drop with a quiet murmur of 'ye-es' dribbling through tightly pursed lips. This was the normal course of events and all the neighbours learnt that they would get a fair response if any of us had done anything untoward. As we got bigger, Mam would make us pay part towards the cost if we had been doing something we shouldn't.

Taking everything into account, play areas where we could play peacefully were almost non existent. This meant that many of us kids had to make our own amusement, which in turn meant we got up to mischief. The canal was known to us local kids as 'the Cut' and it became a popular place for swimming and other escapades. Many a lad went home to face a good hiding with his clothes drenched after falling in off a makeshift wooden raft.

Another play area was a derelict piece of land, which was enclosed by high stone walls and bounded by Trafalgar, Dent Row and the Manchester Road Railway Station Paddock. Inside were the remains of demolished houses and cobbled streets; stored therein were lots of long wooden telegraph poles. It was designated as G.P.O. private land, but despite the forbidding 'KEEP OUT' signs, it was a favourite haunt for many kids. Yes indeed, it was a place for gang huts, hide and seek and general tomfoolery. If a person of authority like a warden, policeman or whoever came along, one or other of us kids was sure to spot him, and alert the rest of us. It was very rare for anyone ever to get caught, as there were so many different escape routes over the high walls by scampering over the stacked logs.

****

The back-street wasn't the healthiest environment in the world … with foul smelling backyards and dustbin ashes strewn all over the place. My two brothers and I had the job of keeping our backyard and cellar clean. I was cleaning the cellar one-day when I heard a lad's voice shouting down the coal-chute from off the front street.

"Hey, is there any chance o' giving us our ball back?"

"Righto then … whereabouts is it?" I asked.

"It's gone down the space in front of your cellar window … I can see it on the stone ledge." The ledge was about two feet wide.

"Aye OK, just hang on a minute … I'll have to climb up forrit." On climbing on to the ledge the ball was there, but I also spotted a penny. As I picked up the coin something occurred to me.

"That penny must o' fallen down here when kids have been trying to knock coins outa the chalk circle. U-um, if there's one coin down here, there may be more." After throwing them their ball back I cleared away a few cobwebs and then got down to cleaning the ledge. "Bloomin' 'eck, some o' this muck must have been here since t'house was built," I thought. But my efforts were rewarded … to my delight I found two shillings and thre'pence in pennies, ha'pennies, thre'penny bits and a tanner.

"Great!" I thought chuffed with myself, which got me to thinking. "I'll ask Mrs King next door if she wants her cellar cleaning … there may be some money on her ledge as well. U-um, even if there isn't I can charge a bob for doing the job." I got the job and sure enough there were some more green mouldy coins amidst the dirt. Mind you, there weren't as much … about one shilling and thre'pence.

"Still," I murmured to myself, "counting the shilling payment, that's two and thre'pence. That's not bad … not bad at all."

From then on I set up quite a nice little scheme for myself, asking the neighbours on either side of the street if they wanted their cellars cleaning.

I knew my little scam would only be short-lived, but I was quite happy as I said to myself, "You've gotta make hay whilst the sun shines."

I only found thre'pence in one of the cellars, but still smiled as I mused to myself, "Oh never mind ... 'Every little helps,' the old lady said as she wee'd in the sea."

****

Even as a young lad, I realised there was a lot of ill-feeling between Mam and Dad's sisters. As a youngster I wasn't too sure where the blame lay, but the truth became abundantly clear when I tried visiting my aunts on my travels. At each home I always received the same cold reception. One time I went to my Aunt Beatie's house.

"Oh what do you want ... we haven't time for the likes o' you?" Other sneering remarks were made as though I wasn't even there, "U-umph, I can't do with scruffy kids ... just look at the holes in his socks and look at his pants ... I don't think they've ever seen a wash tub."

"Yeah, he looks like he could do with a good meal and I don't think his hair's ever seen a brush or comb."

Then came the crunch that I wouldn't tolerate, "I hope he doesn't bring any nits into this house." **That did it!** I was only nine but the implied criticism of my mam was too much and I was having none of it!

"Hey, don't call mí mam like that," I retaliated angrily, "she's better than you are and she looks after us better than your brother does!"

"Watch your lip you cheeky young beggar you're now't else ... speak when you're spoken to!"

"I'm not being cheeky and I'm not a beggar, it's you who's being rude ... calling mí mam names."

"Right, that's it, wait till we see your dad ... then you'll be forrit!" Beatie rapped. You won't be so cocky then."

"I'm not bothered, you can tell him what you want ... anyroad, I'll tell him myself what you've bín saying about mí mam."   At this they realised that I'd fully understood everything they'd been talking about, and so tried playing down the situation.

"Now come on our John, don't take on so, we didn't really mean anything wrong. Anyroad, sit yourself down lad and have a nice piece o' cake and a glass o' pop." But it was too late, the damage was done ... they'd run down mí mam and I didn't want any more to do with them.

"No thank you, I don't want anything off you. Anyroad, I'm not your John and I don't want to be. I'm going now and I won't come back to your house ever again."

Beatie tried making amends, "Now come on lad, let's be friends ... we don't want this to get out of hand do we?"

"Don't fret yourself Aunt Beatie, I won't say anything to mí mam ... I wouldn't want to hurt her feelings, she's been hurt enough by you lot already. I won't ever come here again but I'll still talk to you if I see you in the street," I said respectfully adding food for thought, "that's the way mí mam has brought us up." At that, I turned and left; sadly I never ever went there again.

Another time I went to Blackpool with our Barry and Barbara. I'd scrimped and saved every bit of spending money until I had enough to go to Blackpool on the train ... it was a dream of mine to see this magical place. I'd heard tales from Dad that his eldest sister, my Aunt Annie, had a large hotel in the heart of town.   I'd planned for ages to go there on my own and I was determined to do so. I didn't mention it to Mam because I was afraid she wouldn't let me go. Still, my younger brother Barry and sister Barbara got wind of my plan and pestered me to take them along.

"But I've only got enough money to pay for mí fare and a butty when I get there," I said trying my best to put them off.

"Oh go on our John," pleaded Barry, "we won't need to buy anything when we get there 'cos we'll be able to go to Aunt Annie's hotel and she'll give us somét to eat."

"U-um, I suppose you're right, but I still don't have enough to buy your train tickets." As it happened our Jimmy was listening and he always had a little put to one side from doing odd jobs and errands for the neighbours. Despite his fiery temper he was generous to a fault and regularly treated his younger siblings to a penny drink at the toffee shop. On this occasion he went a bit further and gave us enough to buy two more return tickets. It was all he had but he wasn't bothered.

"Oh it's reight," he said, "I can always mék some more money collecting jam jars and taking bottles back to the Labour Club."

"But what about you," I asked, "don't you want to come?"

"No I'll be all reight playing soldiers upstairs with mí dried peas," he answered quite unconcerned, "I'd rather do that than ow't else."

"Right, thanks our kid, "I said turning to Barry and Barbara, "Come on then you two, we'd best get going afore mí mam gets home."

We caught the train all right landing in Blackpool about one o'clock. After asking directions we finally arrived at Aunt Annie's hotel about two hours later. It was the first time in my life I'd ever seen her and so I wasn't too sure what to expect. On knocking on the door we were received by a maid who showed us into the hallway. Within a minute Aunt Annie made herself known to us and she wasn't very pleased. It was obvious by the stern look on her face that she felt put out by our sudden appearance.

"What the flippin' 'eck do you think you're playing at," she barked, "don't you realise I have a busy schedule ... I haven't got time to mess about with you lot!"

"So this is my Aunt Annie is it?" I thought to myself. "U-um, she's not what I thought she'd be like."

She interrupted my thoughts by asking bluntly, "Anyroad, what does your mother think she's playing at sending you over here without letting me know?"

"Mí mam doesn't know we're here," I replied indignantly, "it was my idea to bring mí brother and sister."

"Oh was it now? Well you can bloomin' well turn round now and take 'em back to where you came from!"

"Come on," I said to Barry and Barbara who were both showing their obvious disappointment, "let's go, we're not staying where we're not wanted."

"But I'm hungry!" groaned Barbara, "I haven't had anything to eat since breakfast and I only had some cornflakes then."

"So am I," Barry said rubbing his tummy, "and I'm thirsty as well!"

"Listen here both of you, I'm hungry as well," I moaned loud enough for Aunt Annie to hear, "but it makes no difference ... we'll make do till we get back home."

"All right that'll do," put in Aunt Annie, "you can stop for ten minutes. I'll make you a cup o' tea and some biscuits, but then you'll have to go. Like I said afore ... I haven't time to mess about with you!"

I felt like telling her to shove it but I demurred for Barry and Barbara's sake. After our little snack we made our way to North Station and caught the five o'clock train back to Burnley. That was my first recollection of Aunt Annie and Blackpool ... we never went to her hotel again. On arriving home Mam scolded us for going without her consent and then asked how we'd gone on. She was obviously displeased at the outcome. Inevitably this added further friction to the relationship between her and Dad's sisters. Dad tried to play down the situation pointing out that Annie was right in some respects.

"Bloomn' 'eck Winnie, you've got to see it from her point of view," he stressed, "she's got a business to run and you must admit she didn't know they were coming."

"Never mind that!" she snapped, "I know it must have been inconvenient for her but for crying out loud Jack she could have made them some dinner before they set off back home."

"Ar-rgh, you've no idea what it's like to run a business," he moaned, "our Annie …..!"

"Never mind your Annie," she cut in, "you always side with your sisters no matter what! Can't you just see our side of things for once in your life? Bloomin' 'eck Jack she knew they'd travelled all that way … couldn't she have offered them the hand of friendship?"

"Well," he responded mellowing a little, "maybe she should have made 'em a meal, I'll go along with that."

"There's no maybe about it," Mam barked, "it's the first time your Annie's ever seen any of 'em … surely she could have gone out of her way under the circumstances!"

"Yeah, I suppose you're right," he mumbled not wanting to get into an argument about it.

"Oh 'eck," I murmured feeling guilty, "I hope I haven't created more ill-feeling between Mam and Dad's sisters."

****

The final incident that determined my way of thinking was when I went to a Christmas party at my Aunt Lily's house. Aunt Lily was stone deaf following a childhood illness. This was the first time I'd ever been invited whereas my cousins had been there many times. In spite of wanting to go to the party I was a little tentative, as I wondered what sort of reception I would get. When I reached the house a few of my cousins were already there in the front room frolicking about. I felt a bit out of place but when they started playing Monopoly I became intrigued. I'd never seen this game before and found it much more interesting than snakes and ladders. When I saw the banker dealing out the fake money I asked if I could join in.

"No, it's too late ... we've already started," grunted one of them." I didn't know how to play the game but I knew this wasn't true.

"No you haven't ... nobody's shook a dice yet," I protested.

"Aye all reight then," moaned another one of them, "you can join in but no spoiling our fun!"

The game got under way and the activity started to build up. Before long I got excited, becoming a little boisterous and an argument ensued between us. Aunt Lily came stomping into the room because of the noise. Without asking what the quarrel was about she clouted me around the earhole.

"Now that'll do," she rapped, "behave yourself and let the others play properly ... they were invited here before you!" I wasn't hurt physically, but that remark finally convinced me that neither my siblings nor I were welcome there.

"That's it," I muttered to myself, "I'm not stopping where I'm not wanted!" Without further ado I went to the lobby and started to put on my coat.

"And where do you think you're going then?" asked Aunt Lily, annoyed at me.

"I'm going home Aunt Lil; I don't want to stop at your party."

"Don't be so touchy," she bawled, "now get your coat off and get back in there and enjoy yourself."

"U-um, some hopes," I muttered under my breath.

"What's that you just said?" she rapped, "Look at me when you're talking to me ... you know I'm deaf!"

I was aware of her affliction and I felt sorry for her but, in my mind, that didn't excuse her for what she'd just said and done.

"No, I'm sorry Aunt Lil, I'm going home ... I don't want to stay any longer." She tried to stop me leaving but to no avail ... I was determined to go and go I did.

As I walked home past the cotton mills I reflected on the situation and what I was going to tell Mam. Once again I didn't want to cause Mam further grief or widen the chasm, which already existed between her and her sisters-in-law.

"No," I thought to myself. "there's enough animosity between them without me making it worse."

"Hello our John," said Mam on seeing me, "what are you doing home so soon from the party?"

Being discreet I told a white lie, "I felt a bit sick Mam and I just wanted to come home ... anyroad, there were loads o' mince pies and you know I don't like them." Mind you, I suffered for it ... by teatime I was absolutely starving. To make matters worse I got a right rollicking later when Dad got home.

"You ungrateful little wimp you're now't else ... that's the last time you ever get invited to any parties. Our Lily told me how you turned your nose up at everything they offered you, you faddy little bugger. Anyroad, what have you got to say for yourself?"

"Now't Dad ... I just didn't want anything."

"Oh you didn't want anything did you not? Well just cop this for good measure," he growled giving me another clout across the head.

Still, I wasn't for telling the true story ... I didn't want Mam hurting anymore.

A few days later when I was out with Dad on the rag-cart we happened to be in the Croft Area.

"Right our John we'll just call at our Lily's for a sandwich and a brew. Aye, and while we're there you can apologise for upsetting her t'other day."

"But Dad, I ...!"

"No buts lad ... you'll do as you're told!"

I reluctantly followed Dad into Aunt Lily's house but adamantly refused to eat or drink anything.

"All right you awkward little sod, maybe you don't want ow't but there's one thing for sure," bellowed Dad, "you're gonna apologise to your Aunt Lily afore we leave this house!"

I resolutely stood my ground ... I just put my head down, hunched up my shoulders and said nothing. Dad raised his hand to hit me again but then Aunt Lily intervened.

"No Jack, don't hit him ... it doesn't matter, let it go!" It wasn't so much what she'd said as the way she'd said it ... Dad sensed there was more to it than meets the eye.

"What's up our Lily ... is there something you haven't told me?"

"No no, it's just that I don't want to get the lad into trouble."

"It's a bit late for that ... now just tell me again exactly what happened."

"Well they were all arguing in t'other room, so I went in and clouted him."

"Aye, and what were they arguing about?"

"Well I don't know," she replied nervously, "I never asked."

"Hey hang on a minute ... did you clout any o' t'other kids?"

"Well no, I ..."

"Oh come off it our Lily," he intervened, "I'm beginning to see our John's side o' things now ... no wonder he left the flamin' party!"

Turning to me he asked, "Right lad, now you can give me your version of events."

Reluctantly I told him what had happened.

"Right our Lily," quipped Dad, "I wanted our John to apologise to you, but now I think shoe's on t'other foot."

"It doesn't matter Dad ... honest!" I tried to protest.

"Aye it does lad," he stressed, "and I think I owe thí an apology too for clouting you the way I did," He then made it clear that he understood my mode of thinking. "By 'eck lad I'll tell thí what it is ... I'm proud o' you, trying to keep it all from your mam an' all." Talking to me like this, Dad made me feel good, a feeling which was enhanced when he added, "I'm sorry for clouting you our John and to make amends I'm gonna give you a tanner today instead of thre'pence."

My eye's lit up, and even more so when my Aunt Lily came in with some cream buns and a glass of pop. From that moment I grew rather fond of Aunt Lily.

On the way home Dad mentioned it once more, "You acted very wise for your years our John to keep it from your mam, and I think it's best left that way." We were both in agreement about that.

****

There were a few occasions when Dad laid off the beer and stayed at home with the family. When he was like this he had a vibrant personality and we all loved him dearly.

If only he'd been like this all the time, things would have been great. Alas, this was not to be and despite his many blessings, he still unwisely preferred the company of his boozing cronies to that of his family and gradually slipped back into his wily ways. It really was a shame, he was quite clever and astute in many ways, yet so foolish in others; he had a real flair for making money, but an even greater one for spending it. When he was flush, he always had many so-called friends around him, he didn't think twice about buying drinks around the pub. Nonetheless, it was a different tale when it came to finding some housekeeping money; this was the main cause of many household rows.

His boozing continued and sadly, we kids never saw much of him, when we did it was often after being woken up by him shouting from the bottom of the stairs in a drunken state, "Winnie! Whe-er-e's my supper?" This would cause ructions, but all the same, it was a regular occurrence. Many a time, he'd just fall asleep in the chair, remaining there till the early hours, and wake up shivering as daylight dawned.

During many of the rows, he often threw out slanderous remarks like, "Aye, none o' the flamin' kids are mine anyroad!" However, this came to an abrupt end due to a particular incident when our Maureen was about fourteen. One evening she was getting ready to go out, when he made a comment about what she was wearing, telling her to change. She became defiant, refusing point blank, so he started to assert his authority.

At this point, she came out with something that left him completely deflated, "Why should I? You can't tell me what to do," adding the killer blow, "you're not my dad anyroad!"

I happened to be near Dad and his face went a deathly white, he could have been knocked over with a feather. For the first time in his life he was absolutely speechless and just stood there with his mouth agape. At first, he had mixed feelings ranging from anger and astonishment, hurt, to complete frustration.

After the initial shock, he managed to splutter, "You what ... what did you just say?"

"You heard what I said!" she muttered rather sheepishly through clenched teeth and quivering lips, "You're forever telling mí mam that you're not mí dad, and that goes for all my brothers and sisters as well."

Dad was absolutely shocked, and it wasn't only because of what she'd just said either; it was the way in which she had expressed herself. She'd never spoken to him in this manner before … it took him completely by surprise. In that instance, he realised the error of his ways, what a terrible mistake he'd made saying those awful things and so tried to make amends, "Oh, our Maureen, please don't say that! Of course I'm your dad … and that goes for all mí other kids as well." There was a little pause, then he said, "So think on love … you won't ever say that to me again will you? Please!"

"That's all very well Dad," she relented as she could now see the hurt in his eyes, "but why do you keep saying those terrible things to Mum?"

"Come here love and give your dad a hug and I'll try and explain" he answered somewhat nonplussed. He then embraced her saying, "It's because I'm stupid, and when I've had a drink, I say stupid things I don't really mean."

"But why Dad? I don't understand why you want to hurt Mum so much, don't you love her anymore?"

"Yes I do love, in fact … very much so, but like I said, I do and say stupid things when I'm drunk. You know the old saying don't you … you always hurt the one you love?"

"Oh, I don't know what to think Dad, it's all right you saying that but it's still not very nice for Mum is it? Anyway, there's something else whilst we're at it, our Jimmy and the others keep asking what you mean when you say those things to mí mum."

With these words, he put his head in his hands, "Oh my God! What have I done … how stupid can I get?"

At that point, Maureen started to reassure him, "Look Dad, don't fret about it 'cos we all know you're our real dad, and we all love you, but you've got to promise me that you'll never ever say that to Mum again."

He looked at her pretty face, replying in the most sincere way, "Yes our Maureen, I promise with all my heart … never again! Never! Never! Never! And that's one promise that your dad's gonna keep."

"Thanks Dad, but whilst we're on the subject, may I ask you just one more favour?"

"You certainly can love, what is it?"

"Well, it's just that you're not the only one who keeps saying it … your sisters do as well."

He screwed his face up a little at that remark, "U-um, I see your point. Don't worry your pretty little head about it any more, I'll sort it … I'll definitely sort it."

True to his word, those hurtful remarks never ever passed his lips again. It's just a pity that our Maureen didn't get him to promise to give up boozing at the same time.

****

During my time at St Thomas' School I wrote a poem for Mam on 'Mother's Day':

MUM

You've been there right from the start,
Doing everything with the kindest heart.
You teach us the difference from right and wrong,
2Though on occasions, you have to be strong.
Although our home is small and dire,
You make sure there's always a cosy fire.
Despite conditions caused from above,
Our home is always filled with love.
For Sunday dinner you try to please,
With potatoes, cabbage, meat and peas.
Every night you teach us to pray,
And now it is my time to say.
Of all the mothers put to the test,
From all of them you are the best.
When I grow up and a father I be,
I'd like to think I'll be as good as thee.

CHAPTER 7 - MSS GORDON

Time passed by and then came the day we all dreaded ... moving into Miss. Gordon's class. She was the renowned 'Dragon Lady' a reputation handed down to us by our older peers. She had a short boyish crop of dark straight hair streaked with grey, giving it a salt and pepper effect. Her pointed nose and ruddy complexion blended with her little beady eyes, giving her a wizened look. Despite being about five foot four tall with a slender frame she was still a daunting figure as she peered frosty faced over her jam jar spectacles. Her shrill piercing voice made it clear from the start, that she would not tolerate any nonsense whatsoever. However, it must be said she was given good reason to assert her authority on the very first day.

We were all stood by our assigned desks awaiting the command to sit down. I was stood in between Ronnie Hopkinson and Bobby Cheetham.

"Bloomin' 'eck Johnny," whispered Ronnie, "it doesn't look like we'll get away wi much in this class does it?"

"Aye I think you could be right there Ronnie," I muttered through the side of my mouth for fear of being heard.

"See who dares to stand longest after she's tel't us all to sit down," dared Ronnie adding, "pass it on to Bobby." Feeling edgy, I nudged Bobby giving him the message, this time using the other side of my mouth.

"You what?" replied Bobby, "I can't hear thi." Just then the chalk duster came flying through the air hitting Bobby on his left cheek.

Miss Gordon's autocratic manner had now changed to anger, "You insolent boy, come out here this minute ... what have I just said about talking in class?"

"But Miss, I ..."

"Never mind excuses ... come out here now!"

Bobby made his way to the front of the class but not before glaring at me, teething "I'll get thí for this Cowheel ... it's your fault!"

"Right then," bellowed Miss. Gordon, "what's your name?"

Bobby gave her a bemused look answering, "But Miss, you know my name ... I was in Miss Drennan's class last year."

"Don't be impertinent boy ... just answer the question!"

"Bobby Cheetham," said Bobby through tight lips.

Bobby Cheetham what?" she asked indignantly.

He paused a little before replying, "Bobby Cheetham nothing else ... I haven't got another name."

"U-umph, you stupid boy ... how do you address me then?"

"Oh by 'Miss Gordon' Miss."

"Right then, now I'll ask you again ... what's your name?"

By now Bobby had got the message, "Bobby Cheetham Miss," he replied with a smile, feeling pleased with himself.

"And you can take that smirk off your face; I won't tolerate that sort of nonsense in my class."

Once again Bobby tried protesting, "But Miss ..."

His pleas fell onto deaf ears as she deftly picked up the bamboo cane; she was determined to use Bobby as an example to stamp her authority on the class. She swished the cane a couple of times before ordering Bobby to hold out his hand. He tentatively held it out but nervously kept drawing it back.

"Keep it still boy," she rapped, "or you'll receive two instead of one!" Bobby's face winced and turned a distinct red as the cane came down on the four fingers of his left hand.

As he returned to his seat he clamped his bottom lip with his top teeth and curled up his top lip hissing, "Right Cowheel ... in the schoolyard at playtime!"

This was just one of our many squabbles and, as we grappled with each other, we were caught by one of the nuns and had to report to Miss Gordon. We both walked sheepishly into the classroom, and on seeing us she was furious ... especially with Bobby.

"Well well," she pointed out, "it's you again you impudent boy! Obviously one stroke of the cane was not sufficient to make you behave properly ... this time my boy you're going to get one on each hand!"

Bobby knew it was hopeless to protest but then I jumped to his defence, "But Miss, it wasn't his fault ... I started it." I wasn't being heroic ... the way I saw it, I was going to get the cane anyway; besides, Bobby had already had the cane on my behalf.

"Oh yes, and what happened then?" she rapped.

"Well I jumped on his back and he was only tryín to get me off."

"Right," she said turning to Bobby, "under the circumstances you can go but mark my word boy, anymore fighting and you're for it ... understand?"

"Yes Miss, it won't happen again, I promise," muttered Bobby backing out of the classroom. I had to stay and I got the same punishment that Bobby had received earlier ... just one stroke of the cane but it was enough to bring tears to my eyes.

Bobby and I became bosom friends thereafter, getting up to all kinds of mischief ... neither of us ever becoming a favourite of Miss Gordon. Albeit, despite getting the cane on a few occasions, I became quite fond of the headmistress.

This came about during the reading session. Every afternoon we all had to read quietly to ourselves for about an hour. At the time I was reading a story about Saint George and the Dragon and I loved it. Whereas most of the other children hated this lesson, I actually looked forward to it. Once I got my nose stuck into the book I became completely enthralled. Miss Gordon noticed how engrossed I was and to my embarrassment she sang out my praises to the class.

One day she actually peered over my shoulder commenting, "I'm very pleased with you John Cowell, your reading skills have come on a treat. Mind you, you must take after your mother … she's a wonderful writer."

"U-um," I thought, "I might have been chastised on a few occasions, but only when I deserved it … she might be strict but at least she's fair. Yeah, she encourages me with my reading and sums and she praises me when I do well. Perhaps she has a soft spot for me … anyroad, no matter what t'others think, I like her."

Because of her strict discipline most pupils didn't like her … hence, her nick-name Dragon Lady. And because of her strict ruling on fighting she was forever sending for my mam because of the constant brawls that my brothers and sisters got into. Despite this, Miss Gordon, had a bit of a soft spot for Mam because she could see how hard she was struggling to bring up six of us under extremely difficult circumstances, also what a good caring mother she was. There were many times when Mam couldn't get to the school to talk over the situation, but on these occasions, she would always send a note with one of us.

One day after a discussion, Miss Gordon turned to Mam and asked, "Mrs Cowell, could I just ask where you learned to write?"

"Certainly," Miss Gordon she replied, "I did all my learning at St. Mary's School in Bacup when I was a young girl, why do you ask?"

"Well it's just that you always write an excellent letter, expressing yourself in the most explicit way," adding, "have you had a further education?"

"No I'm afraid not Miss Gordon, you see, due to my family and other circumstances, I've never had the opportunity. It's just that I've always loved reading, and I seem to have a natural flair for writing."

"You certainly do" replied Miss Gordon, who then came out with something that took Mam by surprise. "Mrs Cowell, have you ever thought of writing your autobiography? I think it would make wonderful reading."

After some thought, Mam replied, "Yes Miss Gordon, perhaps it would, but I couldn't do that, as there are too many hurtful things that I wouldn't like to come to light, and not just for me but for my children's sake as well."

"Yes, I can quite understand your feelings about that Mrs Cowell; it just seems a shame to let such a wonderful story go untold."

Mam was touched by the head mistress' comments but, all the same, she wouldn't change her mind.

Well, that was it ... the end of a great story before it ever began.

Miss Gordon did send for Mam on other occasions and one time it caused quite a lot of concern. The head mistress pointed out that although Maureen was quite bright, she was struggling with her reading and writing skills. "I'm sorry to tell you this Mrs Cowell, but I'm quite perturbed, as I feel that she is capable of doing much better."

"Thank you very much Miss Gordon for bringing it to my attention. I've got to agree with you on this topic because I feel the same way; I promise you that from now on, I'll take her in hand. If you could arrange some homework for her, I'll help her any way I can and I'll make sure that she keeps at it."

This Mam did, every evening when the rest of us were in bed, she'd sit with our Maureen, going over things endlessly. Maureen complained bitterly, but no matter ... she had to read a couple of short chapters from her schoolbooks or write a short essay or letter. But as time progressed, Maureen was eternally grateful, as she eventually became quite fluent and proficient. Miss Gordon was very pleased with her progress, so on one of Mam's visits, she complemented her on the achievement.

"Mrs Cowell, I am really pleased with Maureen's progress, it is plain to see that she is now much more competent. Although she is still a little way behind schedule, I feel confident that she will soon catch up. I'd also like to congratulate you; you must have the patience of Job, because it's obvious that you must have spent countless hours with her."

Mam felt a little embarrassed, just replying, "Well, u-um ... it's my duty isn't it; she's my child?"

"Yes that's all right Mrs Cowell, but you've got all the other little ones to think about as well, it simply amazes me how you do it."

"Ah well, what it is Miss. Gordon, my children are my life, and nothing on this earth is more important to me. They're good kids, and each one of them is so unique in his or her way, and they give me so much love and joy. I can't really say why I love them so much ... I just do."

Miss Gordon smiled at her replying, "You just did Mrs Cowell ... you just did."

****

The first hour of each day was taken up by religious instruction, which entailed reciting passages from the Catechism parrot fashion. The twins, Nora and Teresa, were always well versed in these matters as were certain other members of the class. But lots of boys would be bored, mumbling under their breath making a mockery of the recitals and especially 'Decades of the Rosary'.

"*Hail Mary full of grace,*

Wore broken clogs and fell on her face!"

The girls, being much more serious, would reprimand them.

One girl happened to say to Bobby, "A-ah, that's a great big sin, you'll have to go to confession on Saturday and confess to Father Hartley what you've bín saying."

"E-eh ther's no need for that," Bobby teased, "I'll just say three 'Hail Mary's', an 'Our Father' and an 'Act of Contrition' afore I go to bed toníte ... I'll be all reight then."

"I'm gonna tell Miss Gordon over you ... then you're forrit," she responded.

"Please yoursel you tell tale tit," he mocked followed by,

"*'Tell tale tit,*

Your tounge'll split,

And all the little dogs'll have a little bit."

"Oh shurrup you!" she snapped, "I'm not bothered what you call me."

"Woo-oo, temper temper, mind your halo doesn't slip!" Bobby sneered. "Anyroad, if I went to confession that's all the priest would tell me to say."

"A-ah, you're bad you are ... you'll go to hell for ever and ever!"

The girl's efforts were fruitless ... Bobby just jeered, "Yeah yeah yeah ... and I suppose you'll go to Heaven on a broomstick."

****

I liked arithmetic but found one aspect of it quite difficult ... multiplication using double figures or more. Miss Gordon introduced this new topic, but despite going over it several times I couldn't grasp the fundamentals of it. One day I was really struggling with a problem and turned to Bobby Cheetham, who was sat next to me.

"I'll never do this Bobby, I don't get it ... how do you multiply 45 by 23?" Bobby had grasped it very quickly and eagerly showed me the method.

"Well just put the 23 under the 45 like you would if you were adding up."

"Yeah, I know that ... but then what?"

"It's easy; first you multiply the 5 by the 3 ... what's that?"

"That's 15 ... now what?"

"Well just write down 5 and put the 1 up onto the line next to the 4."

"Yeah ... go on."

"Multiply the 4 by 3 and then add the 1 that you've put onto the line ... that méks it 135."

"Right, I can get that far but I don't know what to do next."

"Oh that's easy," replied Bobby feeling pleased with himself, "just multiply the 45 by the 2, which comes to 90. You then place the 90 under the 135, but this time you have to move the number one step o'er to the left so that the 0 is underneath the 3, and the 9 is underneath the 1."

"Aye, and then what?" I asked still nonplussed.

"Well, this is the easy part; all you have to do now is add up both o' them numbers and you've got the answer."

On doing this, it clicked ... I too had now grasped it.

"Great Bobby, I've got it ... the penny's dropped at last." It was strange that Miss Gordon with all her knowledge and expertise had not been able to get through to me whereas a bit of friendliness from my mate did the trick.

****

Around this time I started to get interested in girls. The local 'Sweetheart' of St. Thomas's was a girl called Sally Kelly. At the time there was a song that went:

'Oh ... the boys are all mad about Nelly,
The daughter of Officer Kelly,
And it's all day long they bring'
Flowers all dripping with dew,
So ... let's join in the chorus of Ne-el-ly Kelly,
I...I ... lo-ove you!'

All the boys would chant the song in unison, replacing the name Nelly with ... 'Sally'.

As it happened there was another girl in the school with the same surname ... 'Moya Kelly'.

On first setting eyes on Moya, I was smitten ... all thoughts of Miss Quinn quickly vanished, this was the real thing. Moya was a little younger than me and, like Miss Quinn, she had the most gorgeous dark hair with natural waves. I so much wanted to talk to her in the schoolyard during playtime, but I was too shy and could never get up the courage.

Alas, the nearest I ever came to being her boyfriend was at the Saturday Matinee at the 'Temp' ... better known as 'The Bug and Scratch'. We were sat next to each other watching 'Flash Gordon and the Clay Men' and I bought her a bag of crisps spending my last thre'pence. But my little ploy didn't work ... she wasn't interested; it was as though I didn't exist. Ironically, Moya started to go out with my friend shortly after that ... Bobby Cheetham.

"Mind you," I kept telling myself, "Bobby has got the advantage over me 'cos he lives on Finsley Gate the same as Moya."

Poor me, what a shame ... the first two loves of my life, both unrequited.

****

Mam was always waiting at home for us all when we came in from school and would have a warm meal ready. Doing a part-time cleaning job for a wealthy lady fitted in well with her busy timetable. Tea was usually served about 5pm. Extensions on the wooden table would be pulled out, ensuring a place for everyone. Meals were sparse but Mam knew that we'd all had at least one good meal … the school dinner. One fad she had … she always brewed up in a large teapot putting in plenty of sugar. She strongly believed that sugar was good for keeping our energy levels high. Sugar was on ration but no matter, Mam often sent me across to a neighbour's house with a packet of Brook Bond tea to be exchanged for a two-pound bag of Tate and Lyle sugar. I remember thinking that Mam was getting the better bargain. "Bloomin' 'eck," I would say to myself, "a big packet of sugar for a small packet of tea." The teapot didn't blend in well with the drinking vessels … jam-jars, some still with a golliwog label on them.

"Oh, I'm fed up o' drinking outa jam-jars," our Mary would complain, "when I get bigger and have some money I'm gonna go down town and buy some proper cups."

I didn't like milk in my tea … so the boiling water was forever cracking the jam-jars and also, I kept burning my mouth on the rim of the hot glass.

Maureen's complaint was different again due to one of Mam's fads, "Oh no Mum … you've gone and put a load o' Senna pods in the teapot again!"

"Hey, never you mind about that, get it drunk," Mam would reply, "it's good for keeping your bowels open."

"Keeping 'em open," quipped our Jimmy, "by 'eck Mam, you put in so many senna pods … we should have cleanest bowels in Burnley."

"No, I'm sorry Mam," Maureen would protest, "I can't drink it with Senna pods in'it ... I can't stand the smell, never mind the taste."

****

Another craze amongst the lads was collecting fag cards in the schoolyard and around the streets. These were only discarded cigarette packets but no matter, a lad was never happier than when he had a handful. Most of us kids were poor and we never had any money. Still, we could always swap fag cards for other stuff from more fortunate lads. Park Drive, Woodbine, Player's Navy Cut and Capstan Full Strength packets were very common, whereas Rough Rider and Passing Cloud were much rarer and therefore more collectable. The most sought after card by all and sundry was a Royalty and every lad wanted to add this precious commodity to his collection.

The fag cards were found under seats in the pictures, on buses or even in the gutter. The Ribble Garage was situated on Trafalgar close to Gresham Place and there were some large waste bins just inside the main entrance. Lads would forage through these bins finding many of the common fag cards and sometimes if they were lucky ...a 'Miss Blanche'!

Lads could be seen playing 'faggies' on every street corner. A card would be stood up against the wall and two boys would kneel down on the flag edge and alternately flick cards at it. Many cards would finish up on the floor and the boy who knocked down the target would happily scoop up the lot. Mind you, lads wouldn't play with rare fag cards, as these were far more valuable and were used as a form of collateral, readily exchangeable for other commodities.

I became very skilful at the game and so never went short of tuck. However, there was one lad, Jack Lofthouse, who was even better at the game than I was. Jack didn't go to St. Thomas's School but he lived on Rowley Street just below the Railway. I would spend many hours on

Rowley Street trying to triumph over Jack but I nearly always ended up the loser. Jack was older than me and a bit of a tearaway, but I liked him and looked up to him … we frequently got into mischief, often doing very dangerous things.

Many a time I would be walking along Trafalgar and I'd hear a voice shout, "All reight Cowheel, how d'you fancy your chances today?" On turning it would be Jack.

"Aye, all reight Lofty … but less o' the Cowheel!"

"Aye and less o' the Lofty afore I clips thí round the lug'ole!"

It was all friendly rivalry and we both took it in good part. Mind you, as well as being a good fag packet player, Jack was also a very good fighter … not many lads would tangle with him.

During one session I lost about fifty cards to Jack and was feeling rather dejected.

"Well, what can yá expect?" teased Jack, "You Albion Street wallies don't stand a cat in hell's chance playin' against us Rowley Street kids."

"Don't kid yourself … I'll win some more at school tomorrow and I'll be back here after I've had mí tea," I responded.

"Oh aye, and where are you gonna get some fag packets from to play with in the first place?"

"Don't worry Lofty … I'll think o' somét."

Some kids would go to any lengths and risk life and limb to obtain rare fag cards and Jack was one of these. Being a few years older he tended to lead me into mischief and I would follow enthusiastically. On this particular day, as I was walking off rather disheartened after my heavy loss, he shouted after me.

"How would you like a sack full o' brand new fag cards John … aye, and rare ones at that?"

"Oh yeah, sure Lofty… and what's the catch?"

"No catch, I've been told there's thousands of 'em just waiting to be picked up in the Paper Mill."

"Aye, I believe so," I replied, my spirit rekindled, "there's bín tales going round the school yard about it."

"Well, whaddaya say ... are you gam' o' what?"

"What now?"

"Aye, why not, it'll be goin' dark in about half an hour ... we should be able to sneak in th'back way along the Swift River?"

"Aye, all reight Jack, but have you got ow't to carry 'em in?"

"Yeah, I think there's a couple o' sacks in't coal 'ole."

"Just one thing Jack ...before we go you've got to agree to split everything fifty-fifty when we get back."

"Yeah all reight, fair enough I promise thí... come on then, let's go!"

Off we set towards a railway viaduct, which ran by the side of Ashfield Road. We stealthily made our way past Clifton Lodge, a polluted waterhole, by the side of the Paper Mill and via an old ginny track until we reached some steel railings overlooking the Swift River. Both being quite nimble, we easily scaled the railings and climbed down a steep wall until we were on a narrow cobbled bank at one side of the fast flowing river. By now it was quite dark but the moon emitted a little light. We scrambled along cautiously keeping near to a high stone wall until we finally reached the mill. There were two entrances into the building ... a natural way across a bridge from the factory yard or by scaling the bridge from the far side of the Swift River, which lay directly under the main entrance. To avoid being seen by workmen we took the latter path. To reach the entrance we both had to climb a slimy wall and over some more steel railings. Once inside the mill we dived for cover behind a large stack of paper bales. There were books, comics, magazines and lots of other things but we were only interested in one-thing ...fag packets. We'd routed through various bales for about twenty minutes then Jack let out a shout of sheer delight.

"Quick John, come here ... see what I've found!" I couldn't believe it ... there were stacks of 'Airmail' cigarette cards all in pristine condition.

"Bloomin' 'eck Jack, what a good do ... them's one o' the rarest fag packets and they're all brand spanking new!"

"Sh-shh, be quiet afore anybody hears thí! Anyroad, hold one o' them sacks open so I can fill it up." Within minutes we'd filled both sacks and were on our way back along the bank of the Swift River.

For the next few days Jack and I were the envy of our schoolmates ... we certainly didn't go short of tuck for a while after that.

On one occasion, when raiding the mill, it had been raining and the Swift River had risen flooding the banks to within a foot of the wall. Not to be beaten, Jack and I stealthily made our way along slippery cobbles and managed to gain entrance to the mill. Whilst we were inside filling the sacks we heard footsteps, so we both dived for cover behind some large bales. Two men came and started moving some of the bales about. Two hours passed before we got the chance to escape, making our way to the bridge. However, there was a shock awaiting us; the heavens had opened up and the river had now overflowed its banks. We couldn't just walk over the bridge to the other side, as the office and the watchman's hut were there in the main yard.

"We'll have to crawl across that pipe John, it's th'only way outa here," suggested Jack. On looking down I could see a steel pipe about twelve inches in diameter, which ran alongside the bridge, spanning the river.

"Flippin' 'eck Jack, I hope I don't fall off … I know I'm a good swimmer but I don't fancy goin' in that water."

"Arg-gh, you'll be all reight … anyroad, we don't have much option do we?"

After climbing down we both inched across the pipe on our bellies finally reaching the other side where there was a narrow ginnel, which led onto Ashfield road.

"What a good do," said Jack … "let's go!" We ran off as fast as our legs would carry us and didn't stop till we reached Trafalgar.

We went back to the Paper Mill a few times after that but our little escapades came to a temporary halt because lots of other lads started to do the same thing. Consequently, the mill owners got wind of what was going on and took preventative measures, putting up barbed wire on top of the bridge and around the pipe. But Jack wasn't to be put off; he'd had a taste of the good life and wanted more. Come what may he was determined to find another way into the mill.

Consequently, he came up with a scheme, which was fraught with danger. I was with our Jimmy at the time.

"I don't know about you John," said Jack, "but I'm gonna raid the Paper Mill again toníte."

"But how are you gonna do that Jack … we only tried last week and you know we couldn't get past that barbed wire."

"Yeah, I know that but I've fathomed out another way o' gettín in there."

"Aye, and how's that then?" I asked.

"Well, we can get in there by side o' the lodge and o'er the roof."

"O'er the roof … you must be joking!" I panicked. "To get into the main part o' the mill we'll have to cross from one roof to t'other over a steel girder and there's shredding machines below it. And anyroad, what do you mean … we can get in there?"

"Well you'll be coming with me won't yá?"

"No, will I bloomin' 'eck as like ... no way!"

"Oh come on, what's up withee ... we've shinned o'er that pipe that runs o'er the Swift River loads o' times?"

"Yeah, I know we have but that ain't nowhere near as high as that girder and there's no flippin' shredders underneath it."

"Please yourself, but you'll not get any fag packets off me if you don't come."

"I'll come with thí if you want Jack," interrupted our Jimmy, "our John's freightened to death of his own shadow."

"Whaddaya talking about?" I grunted becoming slightly annoyed, "I've raided the papermill loads o' times more than you have."

"Oh aye but you've never gone o'er the roof afore have you?"

I thought about it for a minute before greed got the better of me. I couldn't bear the thought of our Jimmy out-doing me so I foolishly agreed to go with them.

We made our way to Clifton Lodge prior to scaling the factory wall. The roof was constructed like a saw blade similar to the ones on a cotton mill with north facing lights. We had to jump from one set of sloping slates to another. Then came the dangerous part ... crossing over the girder, which was about nine inches wide and eighteen inches deep. The gap in-between the buildings was only six feet across but when I looked down, I could see a glass roof with paper shredding machines underneath ... it was terrifying! I was used to racing along the backyard walls at breakneck speed and jumping over garden gates but this was different ... much different. My heart sank, thumping wildly and I temporarily froze on the spot. But it didn't seem to bother our Jimmy or Jack as they balanced across the girder like trapeze artists. I had come this far and didn't like backing out for fear of ridicule. I knew I was being foolish but I eventually got up the nerve and followed them cautiously, straddling the steel girder on my backside gripping the top flange tightly.

On entering the building through a skylight we found ourselves in a different part of the mill.

"You look o'er yonder Johnny while me and Jimmy rout through these here bales," said Jack. "Give us a shout if you find anything."

"Reighto Jack but keep your voice down, somebody might hear you."

I tentatively made my way across the floor and climbed in amongst a mountainous stack of bales. I was still reeling from the effects of crossing over on the girder and my hands shook nervously as I fumbled about looking for any signs of fag packets. The shaking stopped however when I noticed a silver object that seemed to be beckoning me.

"It can't be what I think it is," I thought as a feeling of excitement passed down my spine, "surely it's not a Royalty?"

But to my sheer delight it was. It was a Royalty, exactly what the name implies ... 'The king of all cards' ... the most prestigious and sought after card ever. I couldn't believe my eyes as I stared at the sacred card in the palm of my hand, unblemished in mint condition. I pinched myself to make sure I wasn't dreaming. I just couldn't believe my luck. Coming back to reality I realised that where there was one Royalty there may be more. I eagerly rummaged deeper into the bale. My excitement grew to fever pitch as I found another fifteen. I just couldn't put them into the sack; I put them in my pocket.

"There's no way I'm sharing these wí Jack and our Jimmy," I thought as greed once again overtook me, "these are mine!" I convinced myself that I wasn't doing anything wrong. "Yeah, fair do's," I smirked, "finders ... keepers."

Besides the Royalties there were lots of other rare cards.

"Jack ... Jimmy," I shouted forgetting the advice I'd previously given Jack, "come over here quick there's millions o' good úns in these bales.

"Flamin' 'eck I don't believe it," blurted Jack, "let's get our bags filled and get out of here quick!" Filling the sacks was the easy part ... the hard bit was going back the way we'd come, but this time burdened down with the loot.

This proved even more difficult than I'd anticipated because when we climbed back onto the roof through the skylight it was dark and had been raining. Hence, the slates were slippy, leaving us no option but to make our way back from bay to bay by sliding down the slates on our backsides. By the time we reached the girder our pants were soaking wet. But now came the precarious task of crossing over the steel support, which was also slippy underfoot from the downpour.

A shiver went down my spine as I knelt down onto my hands and knees and grasped the top flange of the reinforced steel joist. The building was now lit up and as I looked down I could see men working the shredding machines below me, making every nerve in my body tremble. As I cautiously edged inch by inch across the fearful divide, Jack became impatient.

"Come on Johnny you soft bugger ... get a move on, we want to get out of here!"

I didn't answer ... I was too scared. In fact, I momentarily froze with fear. Our Jimmy joined in with Jack, throwing out similar remarks until I gradually reached the other side. I paused a moment then sighed with relief for the very thought of falling through the glass roof to a horrible death made the hackles on my neck stand out like the quills of a porcupine.

Jack was the next to follow, but unlike me, he made it seem easy. Despite the damp he fearlessly walked across the divide without any bother.

Then came our Jimmy's turn! He was almost across when our little scam nearly ended in disaster! He stumbled a little and on trying to regain his balance he dropped his sack.

"Blast it!" he cursed, "All that work for now't!" Nevertheless, on looking down he could see that the sack was lying on top of the glass roof. It was only about two feet down, so he decided to try and retrieve it.

"Come on our Jimmy, leave it, it's not worth it!" I pleaded becoming agitated.

"No way … I didn't come here for now't; I'm not leaving without them faggies."

"It doesn't matter Jimmy, there's enough in my sack for both of us," I pleaded all the more, "just leave ém, it's too dangerous." My plea fell on to deaf ears … Jimmy was fearless. He got down and placed his foot on the bottom flange of the girder, and then, holding on with one hand, he tried reaching out with the other. But no matter how he tried he just couldn't reach the sack … it eluded him by about six inches.

"Can ya find me a stick with a nail in'it our John … I'd be able to hook it if I had one?"

"Oh sure Jimmy … there's bloomin' hundreds of 'em lying about up here."

"All reight don't get fly … just have a look about, there might be somét." I looked but to no avail … we had no option but to leave the sack where it was.

"Bloomin' 'eck I could bloody well kick myself," Jimmy kept repeating as we made our way home, "I'm a dopey swine aren't I?"

"Never mind Jimmy, look on bright side," said Jack, "we've still got plenty o' rare fag packets and a good tale to tell all our mates."

"Aye we have haven't we and ….?" Jimmy suddenly stopped in mid-sentence and cracked up into a fit of laughter.

"What are you laughing at Jimmy … what's up?" I asked puzzled.

Jimmy couldn't stop chuckling, "Well it's just struck me, and I think it's really funny. Whatta them fellas in the papermill gonna think when they see that sack o' fag packets on top o' the glass roof?" He roared with laughter again, "They'll be wondering for ever an' a day how the hell it got up there!"

Jack and I laughed along with him, "Yeah, you're reight there Jimmy," said Jack, "eh, it's bín a good night an'it?"

All three of us were happy. Needless to say, we never raided the Paper Mill again … at least I didn't. In all probability, Jack or our Jimmy went back with some gadget or other to retrieve the sack of fag cards. Anyway I wasn't bothered … I still had my secret treasure … the precious Royalties.

I was a bit of a show off and like Jack said … it was a good yarn to tell in the schoolyard. After I'd finished telling my tale Bobby Cheetham laughed and as usual came out with a funny comment, which raised a few laughs.

"Bloomin' 'eck Johnny … I'll bet you were cut up about losing them faggies … ha ha!"

Somebody else went a bit further than that. There was a small notice board in the cloakroom area and at playtime quite a few girls had gathered around it and were laughing hysterically.

"Whatta they laughing about?" asked Bobby

"I don't know," I answered, "let's go and have a look." Other lads, whose curiosity had been aroused, came along too.

Bobby was the first to look at the board and immediately roared with laughter as did the other lads when they saw it. I just smiled at first but then even I had to laugh ... not quite as robust as the others, as the joke was on me. But I had to admit ... I saw the funny side.

Somebody had written on the notice board:

<u>SPECIAL OFFER.</u>
Chopped Cowheel
3 fag packets per 1lb.
Can be obtained from the Papermill.

I never did find out who the culprit was but I strongly suspect it was Bobby.

****

I was always the outdoor type and loved camping along with my mates Ronnie Hopkinson and Kenny Clayton. We often went to Hurstwood, a popular picnic area on the outskirts of Burnley, and pitched our tent down by the riverside. We only had a small tent and a make-do ground sheet but this didn't put us off. We'd usually set off Saturday afternoon and return back home Sunday evening. One weekend our Barry asked if he could come along with us.

"U-um, I don't know our Barry ... what about your asthma?"

"Oh I'll be all right ... I haven't had an attack for ages."

"Yeah I know that, but don't forget it gets really cold at night in a tent."

"Oh come on our John, let me come ... I've never been camping afore."

"Aye all reight then, but you'll have to get stuck in like the rest of us."

Barry's eyes displayed his obvious delight, "Great, I'll just go and tell mí mam so she knows where I am."

Before setting off on our little adventure I handed him a rucksack, "Here, you can carry that for starters and don't forget what I said about keeping up with th'rest of us." So off we went arriving at our campsite around 2 o'clock. It was a clear day with brilliant sunshine and the temperature was in the 80's.

"I'm going for a swim," said Ronnie, "is anybody else coming?"

"I'm gam'," replied Kenny, "especially near that little waterfall where the water's deeper."

"Me too," I said, "how about you our Barry?"

"Yeah, why not … I'd love to." For the next two hours we splashed about in the running water thoroughly enjoying ourselves.

"Hey this is great," yelled Barry as he doused his head under the waterfall, "have we any soap so I can wash mí hair?"

"Whaddaya going on about? It's not the bloomin' 'Ritz'?" joked Ronnie. All four of us laughed … we were having a great time. Afterwards, we got down to the nitty-gritty of making something to eat. This is where Barry came into his own, collecting some kindling, with which he got a fire going. He was also more adept than the rest of us when it came to cooking.

"Hey, your Barry's doing all reight John," said Ronnie, "we'll have to let him come with us again sometime."

Later on we all got settled around the fire and laughed the night away. Taking everything into account it had been a really good day. We felt like cowboys out on the range after a day's round up.

"Reight lads, time for a bit of shuteye," quipped Kenny in his best cowboy accent, "another day on the range tomorrow."

"We'll all have to kip together our Barry," I said, "you can sleep in the middle wí Kenny … it'll be warmer."

"Aye all reight our John, I couldn't care less where I sleep ... I've really enjoyed misel' today, it's bín really good."

We talked a little while longer before gradually drifting off. Everything was fine until about 4 o'clock in the morning. Barry woke me, tugging at my shirtsleeve. At first I couldn't make out what he was trying to say, but then I realised that my younger brother was struggling for his breath.

"I ... I ... ca-n't bre-athe our John, I ... ca-n't ...!"

At that moment I realised the gravity of the situation. I'd seen Barry like this many times before and knew that I had to do something quickly. I wasn't versed in First Aid but knew instinctively that I had to get Barry sat upright to help his breathing.

"Right our Barry," I reassured him, "whatever you do don't panic ... I'll get you home somehow!" After helping him to get dressed I decided we had no option but to make the long walk home. By now Ronnie and Kenny were stirring and I told them what was happening.

"There's now't any of you can do about it so you may as well go back to sleep ... I'll see you when I get back." The sun was just coming up as Barry and I stepped outside the tent and the early morning dew was glistening on the grass.

"Put this around your shoulders our kid," I said, draping a blanket around him. Barry offered no resistance, he was only too grateful. Besides, by this time he could hardly speak.

"Come on our Barry, we'd best get going ... we've a long trek back." It took about one hour to reach the village of Worsethorne and another ninety minutes to reach the outskirts of Burnley. It was about 7 o'clock as we passed Turf Moor Football ground, when I heard a voice from behind us.

"And where do you two think you're going at this time o' the morning dressed like that?" someone growled in a deep gruff voice. I turned to see a rather stern looking policeman, whose face was full of suspicion.

"We're going home ... mí brother's not so well, and he needs help." I answered.

"Oh yeah sure ... and where would home be then?" After explaining the situation, the constable became very sympathetic to our plight.

"Right lads, come with me and I'll get thí sorted out." At that, he went to the nearest police telephone box and within minutes there was a police squad car on the scene.

"Right lads, we'd best get thí up to t'hospital right away."

"Oh it doesn't matter officer ... if you take us home mí mam'll know what to do," I said.

"U-um, I don't know about that ... it'd be going against mí better judgement."

"Honest officer, it'll be all right," I assured him, "mí mam's done it loads o' times afore!"

So the policeman took us home to Albion Street, but he insisted on staying until he could see that everything was all right. It didn't take long ... Mam was ever so efficient, giving Barry the necessary medication and nursing care. Within minutes he was feeling much better as his breathing became easier.

Mam, who was always so correct in her speech, then spoke in a way which surprised me, "Righto lad, get this warm drink inside thí and then get thásel upstairs into a warm bed afore tha' catches tha' death o' cold ... tha'll be as reet as rain afore dinner time."

"Bloomin' 'eck Mam," I chuckled, "I've never heard you talk like that afore ... it sounds really funny coming from you."

"Yeah, well I'm tired aren't I? Anyway it just goes to show that anything rubs off after a while doesn't it?"

Mam then turned to the policeman, "Thank you officer for all your help, I'm very grateful ... I don't know what we would do without the police force."

"Think nothing of it madam," he said touching his helmet, "I'm only too glad to be of service and happy that the young lad's all right. Anyroad, now that things are in order I'll be on my way."

I was happy now knowing that our Barry was all right and I felt rather peckish. I had some cornflakes, a fry up and a nice pot of tea before setting off back to my camping buddies.

"Where are you going our John," Mam asked, "surely you're not going back to Hurstwood are you?"

"I sure am Mam ... I told Ronnie and Kenny I'd be back to let them know how we went on."

"Aye go on then, on your way ... there's no stopping you," she muttered.

Well, that was the end of another little escapade. Barry recovered all right and over the years he did go camping again. But that was with organised groups like the Police Youth Club and others like it ... never again with me!

****

One Saturday night I happened to stay in the house with Barry listening to music on the wireless.

"Oh I'd love to be able to play a musical instrument," he commented, "especially the piano."

"Hey do you know something our Barry, so would I. It's something I've wanted to do ever since I was a kid."

"Oh yeah? Well I know a lad who goes for piano lessons to a woman's house on Coal Clough Lane. He's been going there for about two years now and he's a really good player. He told me she's a regular piano player at the Keighley Green Club for all the club turns."

"Right Barry, get to know what number she lives at and we'll go and see if she'll teach us."

The next day Barry got to know the lady's address and we both paid her a visit. She was a rather posh looking lady in her fifties and her house was luxurious. Her blondish hair with tints of grey was tied up in a bun at the back and she wore gold rimmed glasses. She was definitely the school teacher type. She became a little reluctant after asking us if we had any experience of playing the piano to which our answer was, "No."

But she relented somewhat when our Barry put on the little boy lost act, "Oh please Miss, I've always wanted to play the piano and I've been told you're the best teacher there is."

This abject appeal and especially the flattery seemed to catch her attention. Oh all right," she answered, "against my better judgement I will take you both on, but only on the condition that you both work very hard and you don't miss any lessons. She then gave us our appointed times and told us it would cost half a crown per lesson. It was a lot of money to us, but to be fair she said if we both came at once she would only charge us for one person.

"It's still a lot of money," said our Barry on the way home, how are we going to afford it?"

"Well one things for sure Barry," I said, "mi' poor mam can't help us."

"Not to worry our John, we'll just have to run a few more errands for the neighbours and try and find more milk bottles to take back to the shop."

"You're right there. Anyroad, if we haven't got enough I'm sure our Jimmy will help us out, he's always got a bob or two in the bank."

Anyway, things turned out all right. By the time our appointment arrived we had enough money to pay for our first lesson. The hour was spent going up and down the scales and learning notes. She versed us in two set lines of five, upon which notes were placed, which were called treble and base clefs. When the session was over she gave us some music sheets and for homework we had to practice the notes placed on either lines or spaces within each clef.

"Don't forget," she reminded us before we left, "just think of a face for the notes in the spaces of the treble clef, F A C E. And for the lines in the treble clef just think of the simple sentence - 'Every Good Boy Deserves Favour' - E G B D F." We also had to remember the notes of the base clef. These were not as easy to learn\, but were not too complicated.

By the time of our next lesson, Barry and I were quite pleased with ourselves as we practised with each other and both felt confident that we were doing well. She was quite pleased with our progress and once again she had us practising up and down the scales. This went on for four weeks and each week she gave us more homework to do and we carried on in the same vein. But on the fifth week she pointed out that our theory was coming on well but our actual playing was not improving at all.

She then asked the question," Do you mind telling me how much time you are practising on the piano while you are at home?

"Piano at home?" our Barry replied quite innocently. "But we haven't got a piano in our house Miss."

Well the look of surprise on her face said it all. Blood drained from her face as it turned a pale shade of green and her mouth was agape. She momentarily seemed to stop breathing as she barely gasped out in a high pitched squeaky voice, "Yo-ou-u haven't got a pia a n-oo?"

"Oh 'eck our John," muttered Barry, "I don't think she's very pleased."

"You can say that again," I mumbled through tight lips, "I think this is the end of our piano lessons."

I was right too. After recovering her composure she quietly dismissed us telling us never to venture near her place again. To this day I still can't play the piano.

****

In spite of our poor surroundings, Mam brought us all up with good morals and was constantly correcting us on our misdemeanours. It is true to say that none of us. including our Jimmy, ever used bad language of any kind or took the Lord's name in vain. Another fad she had was to constantly correct us on our grammar, she didn't even like us using slang words, which we did all the time. A prime example that springs to mind was that she invariably corrected us on was the difference between 'teaching' and 'learning'.

For example: one night after tea she asked me, "And what have you been doing at school today our John?"

"Oh the teacher's bin learning us sums Mam."

"No, that's wrong," she responded, "she's been teaching you, you're the one who's being taught."

Mind you, it did have its funny side like the day when she came home to find some sugar spilt onto the floor. Five of us were sat around the table.

Barry was the nearest to hand, so she asked him, "Who's done this then?"

To her dismay he looked up at her replying, "Not me Mam, I haven't done nówt."

"No Barry, "she corrected him, "you haven't done anything."

Much to our delight, Barry innocently replied, "Yes Mam, I know, that's what I just said."

One colloquial expression that was commonly used and readily understood by all and sundry in the schoolyard and around town involved the word **Agate.** Whether or not it was used in Bacup as in Burnley is uncertain. But one thing for sure is that it used to confuse and displease Mam immensely, as one or other of us was constantly saying, "He was agate," or "They were "agate," etc.

Our Jimmy came home from school one day and he'd been fighting. When Mam asked him what the fight was about, he replied quite naturally, "It wasn't my fault Mam 'cos a lad in the school yard was agate, 'Your dad's a rag chap Cowheel,' and then he was agate that I was stupid!"

"Jimmy, what do you mean by he was agate?" asked Mam.

"Well he kept calling me names didn't he?"

At this point, she became a little irritated, "Well yes, I gathered that, but why don't you just say that instead of agate? A gate is what hangs on a backyard wall or a farmer's field; do you understand what I'm trying to say?"

"Yes all right Mam."

It seemed a bit pointless though, as Mam discovered to her bewilderment on asking him, "And what did you say back to him that caused the fight?"

Quite excitably he replied, "Oh straight away Mam, I was agate …..!"

Despite the frustration though, she sometimes had to smile to herself when one of us innocently came out with a funny expression or excuse.

One incident that made me laugh was when our Barbara was about four years old. Mam was rummaging through a bottom drawer for something when she came across a banana that must have been there for quite a while, as it was black, squashed and horrible. She knew Barbara was the culprit as my little sister was forever hiding sweets and the like in a secret hideaway.

"Barbara!" she shouted, "come here ... what's this?"

On reaching the sideboard Barbara asked, "What Mummy, what do you want?"

"Just look at this," rapped Mam, "it's disgusting! What have I told you about hiding things in the drawers?"

To Mam's surprise and amusement, after glancing into the drawer, Barbara just shrugged her shoulders, nodded her head, and in all innocence replied, "No Mummy, that's not my banana ... mine's a yellow one....!"

I burst out laughing and it definitely brought a smile to Mam's face.

Mam was always a good story teller and many of her intriguing tales held me spellbound. Some of them even helped us with our studies. I was in the house one day when our Jimmy came home from school feeling rather disgruntled and he complained bitterly to Mam. "Bloomin' 'eck!" he moaned, "We've been having a boring history lesson today all about the American Civil War," adding, "Why can't they teach us something to do with our own country?"

"But it is to do with our country," put in Mum, "and especially so a cotton town like Burnley."

"How do you mean Mam," asked Jimmy becoming curious, "how could something that happened in America affect Burnley?"

"Good question Jimmy," she replied pleased with his enthusiasm. "I'll try my best to explain it to you. Let's see, where do I start? In the two decades from 1840 to 1860 the cotton trade was booming in Burnley. As a result many factories were built alongside the Leeds and Liverpool Canal as were many streets of terraced houses for the mill workers just like the one we live in. Market trade for woven cotton was expanding rapidly; and they couldn't produce it fast enough. Gradually though over a spate of time, the traders had huge stockpiles in their warehouses that they couldn't sell; hence, panic started to set in amongst the wealthy mill owners. A unique situation arose because the market was flooded with finished cotton goods, causing the price to collapse, while at the same time the demand for raw cotton fell. The greedy businessmen were facing financial ruin but, luckily for them, fate took a hand. They were let off the hook when the American Civil War broke out. The effects of the war caused a devastating depression in the Lancashire textile industry. But to the mill owners it was a blessing in disguise, as now the cotton products, which they had been unable to sell, could now be sold at highly inflated prices. Blockage of shipping lanes and lack of import caused the price of cotton to rise by several hundred percent. Despite the plight for every cotton worker, the wealthy merchants were in their element as it actually made them extremely rich men."

"But Mam," Jimmy intervened, "if they became very rich men, why did they call it a cotton famine?"

"Ah well, just like what happens all over the world today, the rich got richer but the poor people got poorer. Although it was good for the wealthy, it had devastating consequences on the working class. Raw materials could not be had and this inflated prices even more. Many mills had to shut down and thousands of workers were laid off, subsequently leading to **The Great Cotton Famine**. This was also known as **The Cotton Panic.** Countless families had to live in sordid squalid conditions on starvation rations, many resorted to begging whilst others died of malnutrition and related diseases. The only person to profit, other than the mill owner, was the pawnbroker. Factories no longer bought quantities of raw cotton to process which caused vast unemployment throughout the cotton trade. Workers in

North West Lancashire went from being the most prosperous in Britain to the most impoverished. Do you want me to go on Jimmy, there's more?"

"Yes please Mam," he replied, "you make it sound much more interesting than when the teachers tell it," adding, "how did the poor people survive then?"

"Well, because of the devastating situation, the government had to set up local relief committees in cotton towns like Burnley and Bacup where food, clothes and coal tickets were issued. Governing bodies appealed for money both locally and nationally. The destitute applied for relief under the, 'Poor Laws' act through the. 'The Poor Laws' Union'. Local relief committees experimented with soup kitchens, and direct aid. In 1862, sewing lessons and industrial classes were organised by local churches, and huge attendances triggered off a Poor Law payment. Despite the setting up of these help centres the poor people only got the bare necessities and still lived in lamentable heart breaking conditions. This state of affairs lasted for four harrowing years throughout the duration of the war."

"Oh what happened then Mam, did everything get back to normal back here in Burnley when the war finished?"

"Well, yes and no our Jimmy. You see after the civil war, cotton was gradually restored and many mills prospered and became larger. On saying that, because of the depression, some towns had diversified from cotton to other industries and many other operatives had emigrated."

"Thank you Mam," said Jimmy, "I enjoyed that much better than the lesson I had in class."

"Yes and I enjoyed it too Mam," I broke in, "I've been listening to what you've just told our Jimmy, and you made it sound really interesting."

There's no doubt about it," Jimmy said as Mother left the room, "Mam really does tell a good tale, she absolutely brings everything to life "

"You're right there our Jimmy," I agreed, "she's a fantastic storyteller, I love listening to her tales."

****

I never had any money, but armed with a few fag packets I was always assured of some tuck. One of my mates, Desmond Lee, always came to school with sixpence, which was enough to buy a packet of dates at the corner shop on Whittham Street. I loved this exotic fruit and would gladly exchange ten faggies for a handful, feeling quite confident that I would soon replace my little stack.

Mind you, even though I was skilful at the game I didn't always win, as some of the other lads were very competitive. One of these was Tommy Neville and he generally gave me a good run for my faggies. However, one day, lady luck was on my side … I couldn't go wrong. By the end of playtime I'd skinned Tommy of every fag packet he had.

Feeling rather despondent, Tommy tried wrangling with me, "Come on Cowheel, and lend us a few fag cards and gimme a chance to win a few back."

"You must be joking Nev … I'd be playing for mí own faggies!" I noticed the dejected look on his face and remembered how I'd felt when Jack Lofthouse had skinned me. "I'll tell thí what Nev … have you ow't to swap?"

"Aye all reight Cowheel," he replied fumbling in his pocket, "how about this?"

I couldn't believe it, there in Tommy's hand was a little white mouse. Wham … instantly I was interested!

"Right Nev … how many faggies forrit?"

Tommy was a crafty so and so and he immediately noticed my enthusiasm, "Well you can have it for sixty fag cards but I want some rare ones as well."

I realised my impetuousness had cost me, so I went into the haggling mode, "I'll tell thí what Nev, I'll give you fifty forrit and that includes twenty brand new Airmail."

Tommy couldn't resist and so the deal was made ... I was now the proud owner of a little white mouse.

I couldn't wait to get home to show my brothers and sisters, "Don't tell mí mam," I said, "she'll go mad if she thinks there's a mouse in t'house." Mary became quite excited as she saw the little mouse run along my arm.

"Oh can I have it our kid ... I promise you I'll look after it."

"No way!" I responded, "I want to keep it for mysel' ... I'll have loads o' fun with it. Anyroad, I'll be able to look after it better than you ... I've already got it a little cage to sleep in."

Mary tried her best to get round me but to no avail. Nonetheless, she'd made her mind up to have the little mouse, and have it she would ... at least for a little while anyway.

Next morning I couldn't wait to go to school to show off my new pet. But to my horror, when I went to pick it up, the cage door was open ... it had gone!

"Hey who's got mí mouse," I yelled, "somebody's whipped it?" My mind flashed back to the previous day, "Come on our Mary, you've got it haven't you?"

"Have I 'eck as like," she snorted, "the bloomin' cat'll have etn'it!"

"Oh don't say that, it can't have," I spluttered anxiously, "I put the cage reight on top o' the sideboard afore I went to bed last night."

"Well that's no good is it you silly sod ... the cat can easily climb up there!"

"Oh no!" I thought feeling really deflated at losing the little creature, and bad for being so thoughtless as to let it come to harm. My self-esteem was to return later that day when I realised that Mary had conned me. She had taken my pet and, after putting it in a shoebox, had hidden it in a safe place. Being crafty she'd sewn a pocket with a buttonhole to the inside of her blouse. After placing the little mouse therein she made her way to school.

She was the centre of attention amongst the girls in the schoolyard as she let the mouse run from the palm of her hand, up the sleeve of her cardigan and out onto her neck. She was fearless of the little thing whilst most of the girls screeched loudly as it scurried along.

I paid no attention as the girls were in another section of the schoolyard and they were forever screeching about something or other.. All the same, Mary's little scam came to light shortly after entering the classroom.

Half way through Catechism the lesson was disrupted by giggling from the girls' corner. The mouse had got out of the pocket and was once again running within Mary's clothing. Being a show-off, Mary pulled funny faces and exaggerated her shoulder movements. This caused uproar, making the girls laugh hysterically.

Miss Gordon restored order by bringing the bamboo cane crashing down onto the desk and bellowing loudly, "Quiet!" Silence descended on the class immediately as a semblance of order was restored. "Mary Cowell, what are you playing at?" rapped Miss Gordon. "What's going on?"

"Nothing Miss," replied Mary putting on the 'Miss Innocent' act, "I've just got an itchy back and I'm trying to scratch it." By now the mouse had run down her sleeve and she had it grasped firmly in her hand. It was obvious to Miss Gordon that Mary was holding something.

"Never mind nothing, come out here at once and show me what you've got in your hand ... I won't have you disrupting the class!"

Under the circumstances most girls would have been wetting themselves but Mary, although anxious, was actually pleased.

"Oh 'eck I'm dead," she muttered under her breath as she made her way gingerly towards the headmistress, "she'll kill me when she finds out what I've got." But her anxiety was offset by the thought that she'd look good in front of her classmates.

"Right Mary Cowell," said Miss Gordon sternly, "I'll ask you just one more time ... what have you got in your hand?"

Mary bent her head as she felt Miss Gordon's eyes boring down into her but still remained defiant. Looking up from her furrowed eyebrows she made a gesture by a barely perceptible movement of her shoulders.

She then repeated, "Nothing Miss. ... I haven't got anything!"

It was plain to see that Miss Gordon was fast losing her patience as her voice raised a decibel, "You impudent stupid girl ... now open your hand this minute!"

Mary chuckled involuntarily, unable to suppress a giggle.

"You insolent girl ... open your hand I say!" snarled Miss Gordon now completely losing her patience.

Mary said no more, but amusing thoughts went through her head, "Right Miss. Gordon, you asked for it ... on your head be it!" By placing her left hand over her right and cupping them together, she managed to take hold of the little mouse's tail in between her right thumb and forefinger. Then to the delight of the class she held out her arm dangling the little mouse in front of the headmistress. It was now Miss Gordon's turn to let out an ear-splitting yell as she dropped the Catechism to the floor.

"A-ar-rgh," she screamed, backing away from Mary, "get away from me and take that horrible creature out of my classroom this minute you awful little girl!"

Mary, amused by the look of horror on Miss Gordon's face, prolonged the situation by letting go of the mouse's tail, allowing it to land on the headmistress's desk. As it scurried along the desktop, Miss Gordon stiffened and backed up against the blackboard with outstretched arms and open fingers.

Hardly able to speak, she pleaded through gritted teeth, "O-oh catch it quick and take the nasty thing away!" The tiny mouse seemed to sense her fear as it crouched at the end of the desk sniffing the air with its nostrils and looking up at her with its little red eyes. The movements of its whiskers were enough to make Miss Gordon freeze as though she was being held up at gunpoint.

Mary was enjoying the moment and more so because, by now, the classroom was in raptures … she had become a celebrity. She purposely fumbled, allowing the little mouse a final dash across the desktop before picking it up.

"Right, have you got it now?" asked Miss Gordon sighing with relief.

"Yes Miss, it's here …"

"No no, don't show me … just take the horrible thing away out of my sight and don't come back until you've got rid of it!" Mary happily took her leave, sniggering as she passed by my desk.

"I'll get you for this," I mouthed through clenched teeth, "I'm warning thí … you'd best look after mí mouse or I'll murder you!"

She wasn't bothered, just the opposite in fact … she was able to skive off school for the rest of the morning to take the mouse home.

"Great!" she muttered to herself, "I've got outa doin' the Catechism and a boring arithmetic lesson."

However she didn't get away with it scot-free; she had to return to school that afternoon to face the wrath of Miss Gordon ... and also mine.

CHAPTER 8 - THE 11+ EXAMINATION

The final year at St. Thomas's was in Miss M Gordon's class ... she was the niece of Miss Gordon. My favourite lesson was mental arithmetic. One morning Miss M Gordon handed out slips of paper with the numbers one to twenty printed on them.

Tapping her desk with a ruler she addressed the class, "Right everybody, I'm going to give you some problems, which I want you to work out in your head. I won't be writing anything down on the blackboard so listen carefully. Once you've figured out the answer, write it down against the appropriate number."

"Please Miss, can we have some scrap paper to work it out?" asked Ronnie.

"No Ronald, that's the whole point of the exercise. You have to work it out in your head and just write down the answer ... that's why it's called mental arithmetic."

"Bloomín éck, that'll be hard won't it Miss?"

"Try not to worry about it," she reassured him, "I'll start off with easy questions and gradually build up to harder ones. Now get your pens ready." You could have heard a pin drop as all the class waited in trepidation. "Right first question ... 7 times 3 take away 11."

"U-um that's easy," I thought as I wrote 10 against the first number.

"Number two ... 18 take away 7, then multiply by 7."

Once again I found it quite easy. Mind you, the problems became more difficult when objects were involved.

"If you bought 3 pounds of apples at 5d a pound and a loaf of bread for 4d ... how much change would you have left out of 2 shillings?"

"That's one and thre'pence for t'apples," I thought, "plus 4d for t'loaf ... that's 1s/7d. Ték that away fro' the two bob ... yeah, 5d." I chuckled a little to myself, "U-um, I think I'm gonna like this here mental arithmetic."

I did appear to have a natural ability at this topic nearly always attaining a 20-20 score but our Mary, who sat just in front of me, really struggled, obtaining very poor marks. On the other hand, she was very good at English, both composition and grammar, whereas I found these subjects very difficult. When it came to filling in choice words to spaces in a sentence I was hopeless. For example:

I WENT -- THE PICTURES WITH MY --- FRIENDS BUT WE ARRIVED --- LATE.

The choice words of course were: TO, TOO, and TWO.

The way I saw it ... the space in between 'WENT' and 'THE' was smaller than the other two spaces so that must be TO. But now I couldn't fathom out which of the other two words to use because the spaces appeared the same and both TWO and TOO were three letter words. I had no alternative but to make a wild guess at it. Consequently, I came up with many wrong answers whereas Mary always fared very well.

So be it, Mary and I got our heads together in order to solve the problem.

"Right our Mary, when it's mental arithmetic I'll give you the answers and when it's English grammar you can give 'em to me." Subsequently, during various tests, a lot of whispering went on from one desk to another. Other times I craned my neck to see what she had written on a scrap of paper.

Our little scam worked, both of us attaining better marks in our weaker subjects. However, it worked so well, we ended up being too clever for our own good ... Miss M Gordon saw through our little ploy and made an example of us in front of the whole class.

Unaware of what was to come, I swelled with pride as she announced, "Very good John Cowell, your English marks have greatly improved this week." But I was quickly deflated by her next remark, "It seems strange, in fact miraculous, that Mary's marks in mental arithmetic have also suddenly improved." At this, all the class started laughing.

"Stop that ... stop it at once!" she rapped. "This is no laughing matter, I won't tolerate cheating in my class ... is that understood?" Both Mary and I were ordered to the front of the class where we received a severe whacking on each hand. We were then separated, each having to sit at opposite sides of the class.

Bobby Cheetham immediately took advantage of the incident and made a joke out of it, and I had to admit it was a good one. It went as follows:

One day after a mental arithmetic test, Miss M Gordon addressed Mary and said, "Mary Cowell, you've been copying of your John."

"Oh no I haven't," replied Mary defiantly."

"Oh yes you have and I can prove it." said Miss Gordon glaring at Mary.

Mary, still feeling rebellious retorted, "How can you?"

To her dismay, Miss M Gordon answered, I've got two papers in front of me, one is John's and the other is yours. It seems strange to me that all the answers are the same except to question number seventeen."

"Well doesn't that prove that I have been copying," answered Mary feeling quite cocky.

"Oh but it does Mary Cowell," said Miss M Gordon asserting her authority. "In fact, very much so."

"How does it?"Mary mumbled in bated breathe.

Much to the delight of the class, Miss M Gordon responded, "Because for the answer to question number seventeeen your John has put I don't know, and on your paper you've put, 'Neither do I!'"

****

My English grammar gradually improved but mental arithmetic remained my favourite subject.

Bobby remained the comedian, but I obtained a puzzle book and would set little problems for my friends during playtime.

I had a favourite conundrum and one day I asked Ronnie to solve it:

"If a man an' half earned a guinea an' half in a day an' half ... how much money would one man earn in a day?"

"But you can't have half a man," smirked Ronnie.

"All right a man and a boy if you like ... come on Ronnie, stop muckín about, you know what I mean."

"Yeah, I know what you mean all reight ... I wer' only kidding. Anyroad it's easy ... a guinea."

"No that's not it, you're wrong."

"Whaddaya talkín about ... it must be. If a man and half earns a guinea and half then a man must earn a guinea."

"Yeah, he earns a guinea all right, but in a day and half ... I said how much does he earn in a day."

"Oh aye, I see what you mean." He thought about it for a while and made a few stabs at it before saying, "All right then, I give up ... how much?"

"Fourteen shillings."

"Fourteen shillings ... how the flippin' 'eck do you mék that out?"

"Well, do you agree that a man earns a guinea in a day and half?"

"Yeah"

"Right then, there's three half days in a day and half ... do you agree on that?"

"U-um ... go on."

"Well, all we have to do now is divide 21 shillings by 3, which gives us 7 shillings. This means that if he earns 7shillings in half a day, then he must earn 14 shillings in a full day."

"Aye all reight clever clogs, you've proved your point. Now I've got a riddle for thí ... Are you ready?"

"Yeah all right ... go on then." I said.

"Right, I've got a photograph here of one person. Now listen to what I'm gonna say and then you have to tell me what relation this person is to me."

"Right Ronnie I'm listening ... fire away."

"Reighto, here goes …. *'Brothers and sisters have I none, but this man's father is my father's son.'* Now like I said afore ... what relation is this person to me?"

I pondered for a while before answering, "It's you, yourself."

"No. No it's not," replied Ronnie with a smirk.

"It has to be cós you've no brothers and sisters and you said *'my father's son'*."

Yeah, but I didn't say this man is my father's son ... I said this man's father is my father's son."

Bloomin' 'eck Ronnie the mind boggles tryin' to work that one out ... who is it then?"

"Well it's a bit complicated," gloated Ronnie, "but here goes. I have no brothers and sisters so I'm definitely my father's son ... are you with it so far?"

Yeah righto ... carry on."

"So according to the riddle I am this mans father ... therefore the man in the photo is my son."

"Oh aye, is that right?" I said jokingly, "Well all I can say Ronnie is you don't look that old!"

"Ha ha, very funny!"

That is what life was like in the schoolyard. We all liked to crack jokes, but at the end of the day exams had to be passed and it was in this final year at St. Thomas' that we had to prepare ourselves for the 'Eleven Plus' prior to moving up into 'Senior School'. It was Miss M Gordon's responsibility to encourage us with our studying. Nevertheless, hardly anyone took it seriously and the frolicking and tomfoolery continued.

****

I had many friends but my best pal was Ronnie Hopkinson. In some ways this caused me a problem, as I had a speech impediment, not being able to pronounce my 'R's at all.

This gave rise to further jeering in the school yard, as he I forever shouting, "Wonnie," across the playground. Ronnie happened to be the fastest runner in the school, which created a big laugh in the classroom one day, as I blurted out, "I think Wonnie is a weally good wunner.

But it wasn't just at school, I also got ridiculed by my own brothers and sisters, when I came out with remarks like, "I'm just goin' wound to Wonnie's to play out!" Mam became rather concerned and spent many hours trying to correct my impediment without success. Finally she arranged for me to have sessions with a speech therapist and I had to attend every Thursday afternoon for a two hour session.

****

Sunday ... the day of rest. Dad made sure we all went to church in the morning and would have a hearty breakfast of bacon, egg, beans and fried bread waiting for us on our return.

Jimmy was always ravenous, "Pass me the brown sauce will you ... I love bacon butties wi' loads of HP on 'em," he would say impatient to gobble up all that was laid before him

Mam was usually allowed a lie-in but she always knew what the sermon at mass was each week. To keep us on our toes she would ask one of us at random what the Gospel was about ... this particular morning she asked Barry.

"Oh it was about a man having two sons and one went away for a long time without telling anybody where he was going."

"Oh yes Barry, go on ... tell me more."

"Oh well, to tell you the truth Mum I didn't get it 'cos, instead of being mad at him, when he got back home, his dad killed a cow and then they had a big party. The other son, who'd been there all the time, was mad 'cos he said his dad had never ever done ow't like that for him."

"That's very good our Barry," said Mam, "you've more or less got the gist of the story ... I'll just enlighten you a little." She then went on to explain the meaning of the parable.

Mary was always on her guard in case Mam asked her questions because many a time she'd skive off church, pocketing the collection money for a penny drink later on in the week.

"A-ah, that's a really big sin our Mary!" Barry would say seriously. "If you die before going to confession next Saturday you'll go to hell!"

"Oh yeah our Barry, and even if I go to confession ... d'you think I'm gonna tell the priest I kept his flippin' penny ... no chance!"

She was crafty ... so as not to be caught out by Mam's probing questions she always covered her tracks, asking one or other of us what the sermon had been about. One Sunday morning, shortly after the mouse incident, I dropped her right in it.

"What was the sermon about this morning our John?" she quizzed me the moment I got home from church.

"Oh it was about the 'Master' giving each of his three servants a bag of gold to look after whilst he went away on business. The first two servants invested the gold well and were praised on the Master's return. But the third servant got told off 'cos he'd buried his gold in the ground."

"Yeah, I know the one," said Mary highly delighted, "I'll be all right now if Mam asks me." Little did she know that the sermon had been 'The feeding of the five-thousand'!

Mary fell for it hook, line and sinker. When the truth came to light she got a right good hiding. Mam also dragged her to the priest's house making her own up to everything.

"There were no need for that our John," she moaned bitterly afterwards, "you got me into a load o' trouble."

"Well it serves you right our Mary," I scoffed, "I were only getting' mí own back o'er mí mouse!"

One thing that everyone looked forward to on Sunday morning was reading the 'News of the World' newspaper. Mam liked doing the crossword and used to send it away every week in the hope of winning a thousand pounds. She never did but one time won a writing competition for an article she wrote about a poor lonely old lady who had a very bad skin complaint and whose only companion was a very old dog. The title of the story was 'The loneliest person'. The prize, a prestigious television set fully licensed and maintained free for five years, didn't go to Mam but to the old lady who the story was about. This pleased Mam, for it made her happy to have been able to bring some happiness into the little old lady's life.

Dad was more into the football results and league tables … and of course reading the many scandals that filled the pages.

However, he got the shock of his life one morning when Mary asked out of the blue, "Mam ... what does intimate mean?"

"You what!" Dad bawled out nearly falling out off his chair, "Whattaya doing reading that paper?"

"Well you read it Dad ... why can't I?"

"Never mind, 'why can't I' you cheeky young bugger ... give it me here right now and don't let me catch thí reading it again!"

****

Mam was always loving and fair, treating us all in the same way. On saying this, she was also strict and her word was law ... if she asked one of us to do something, it had to be done. Being fair she tried to share the chores and errands equally amongst us. No matter, she didn't always get it right as in my case.

"Oh 'eck we've run out of bread," she said, "just run on to Dick Smith's and get a loaf our John."

"A-ah Mam, I went this morning ... it's our Barry's turn!"

"Oh you went this morning did you ... well I've just asked you to go again so you can bloomín' well go again right now!"

"U-ump, flippin' 'eck, it's not fair," I complained bitterly.

"Oh it's not fair is it not? If you give me any back chat I'll make you go again every time we need something for the rest of the week."

I knew better than to argue further ... she never made idle threats and certainly meant what she said ... so I did as she bid.

A constant nuisance was the gas mantle. It hung very low from the ceiling and was forever being broken by someone's head, creating a great long flame. It also got broke many times by sudden gusts of wind created by the back door slamming as someone opened the front door. This meant switching off the gas fitting, leaving the house in darkness except for the light emitted from the fire. The mantles only cost pennies but Mam never had enough money to keep any spares.

"Nip round to Nora's back door our Jimmy for a new mantle and be quick about it," Mam asked him one day. He was too wily to grumble and just took the money muttering one or two things under his breath. Meanwhile the house was in darkness as we awaited his return.

One chore we all hated was emptying the slop buckets from each bedroom. These had to be carried from upstairs, through the living room and into the cellar via the stone steps and then emptied down the lavatory. Many a time they would be almost full to the brim, with the contents swishing about and spilling all over the place.

"Right our Mary," Mum would shout, "mop that lot up with some disinfectant." A daily ritual in our house for whoever happened to be closest to the mop and bucket.

It wasn't very nice having to use a bucket but it was the lesser of two evils. Having to go to the lavatory in the middle of the night and sit in the dark dank air raid shelter was enough to put the willies up the hardiest of men. The thought of having to go downstairs and then down the outside stone steps into that cold dark dank place was, to say the least ... frightening!

It wasn't only during the night either. In winter, as the nights drew in, the girls would be frightened of venturing out into the dark. One evening Mary complained she was too scared to go to the lavatory.

"Oh I daren't go down there on my own ... will somebody stand on guard at the top o' the steps for me?"

"You'll be all right," said Mam, "I'll get one of the lads to watch out for you."

"Oh but what about the light Mam ... it's pitch black in that shelter?"

"You'll just have to roll up part of the Burnley Express and use it as a torch."

"It's too windy Mam ... everytime I do that it always blows out before I get there."

"Not if you go through cellar it won't."

"O-oh no Mam, you know I'm scared to death o' that cellar ... it's even darker than th'airaid shelter!"

"All right, I'll go to the bottom of the cellar steps with you and our John can stand at the top of the outside steps."

"Flamin' 'eck," I whined, "nobody ever does it for me!"

"That'll do our John!" warned Mam.

By the time Mary got to the lavatory the paper was almost burnt through and she moaned that the flame was dwindling.

"You'll have to use some of the lavvy paper that's hung on the nail our kid," I shouted, "that's what I do!"

****

In our school, there were one or two children from better off families, but on the whole, most were from poor backgrounds. One thing, perhaps more memorable than any other, was that it was still very much the age of the clogs. Clogs were worn by almost every schoolchild and adult alike; my family and I were no exception to the rule. Clogs may have looked and sounded cumbersome, but were in fact very comfortable; they kept us dry shod in rain and snow alike and were far superior to most other types of footwear. However, there was a definite stigma attached to them for they were associated with poverty. Perhaps this was because a clogger's fund had been set up for the distribution of clogs to poor families and people in need, especially so at Christmas time. Whatever the reason, people of the upper class used to look down with contempt on anyone wearing clogs.

Girls mainly wore rubber soles and heels, but the lads preferred irons, so they could make sparks fly by kicking the ground; they liked the sound of them better too. Being a bit of a tomboy, our Mary was an exception to the rule, preferring irons so she too could make sparks along with the lads. The sparking was much more effective when the clogs had just been re-ironed. It's a far cry nowadays in schoolyards to what it was like in the 1940's, as then the clanging of clogs was so distinctive as we children played on a concrete surface. This was especially so as we lined up in single file before marching into class to the sound of a bell with our clogs going clip clop, clip clop!

When it was snowing, the snow used to build up solid in between the irons, much to our delight, this would make us two to three inches taller. Sadly though, it had to be taken off by briskly kicking our feet against the school wall before entering the classroom.

At playtime, competitions were held to see who could make the most sparks in one dash across the schoolyard. The idea was to kick the ground whilst on the run as many times as possible, but it didn't count if sparks were not made. Most of us kids used to kick with our natural foot about once every third stride. This is where our Jimmy came into his own as he became quite expert, managing to strike effectively every time on his right foot. This obviously made him quite happy, but Mam wasn't too pleased as it meant a lot more trips to the clogger's.

Every district had a clogger's shop and the one on Trafalgar was near to Derby Street. I had to make regular visits to have my clogs re-ironed and I found it an enlightening experience. Dozens of steel bars hung from the ceiling and each one contained many different sizes of irons. I would sit on a wooden bench alongside other lads awaiting my turn, while the clogger worked busily away on the other side of a counter. He always wore a long leather apron and it intrigued me to watch him skillfully working away with nails in his mouth, using special tools doing everything from de-nailing, soling and heeling, to making a complete new pair of clogs. He worked on a special type of anvil called a last; his main tools were a special claw hammer, pincers, files and a very sharp knife with a curved blade for cutting leather.

Clogs were shod many times before their use was finished and, when the time came for a new pair, the clogger took every precaution to ensure they were comfortable and a good fit. When I had a new pair made, he first measured my feet and then picked a correct wooden sole to match up to a leather upper. The wooden sole, which felt very comfortable, must have been specially prepared to make it weatherproof, as it rarely ever cracked or split.

There was a well-known saying that wearing clogs was good for strengthening the ankles and legs; this certainly proved true in my family as we all had good strong straight legs. They were also said to be good for health reasons and renowned for warding off colds and other ailments. This certainly rang true in our Barry's case; it certainly helped contain his asthma.

It was still the age of the knocker-up, but in our house, we didn't need one. The reason for this was that from six o'clock onwards, I could hear the constant clattering of clogs walking down Albion Street, and I could even determine what time it was by the different sounds.

For example, at six o'clock some colliers would come clip-clopping by our house in their steel bottomed clogs. It was a comforting sound as I knew I could just turn over in my comfy bed for a while longer. About an hour later, just before seven o'clock, there would be a cacophony of clog sounds as many weavers scurried down the cobbled street making their way to the weaving sheds. A little later, Joe Smithson, who lived above the railway bridge, had a bad limp and he made a most distinctive sound.

"Oh 'flippin' eck," I'd moan to myself on hearing him, "it's time to get up for school!"

****

Every July during Wake's weeks Dad used to put his horse Peggy out to pasture in a small field. He really did have a way with horses and was a great believer that they needed a break just like humans. At the end of the fortnight he would go and collect her and she would come running happily to the fence as soon as she saw him. One particular morning he asked Barry and me to go with him to give him a hand.

"How come Dad, you've never asked us to come before?" I asked.

"Ah well this time she's in the field with two other horses, so she won't be as keen to lose her freedom."

"Oh right Dad, but can we ride her back to the stable?" said Barry.

He agreed and so the three of us set off. As soon as we reached the field, Dad gave a loud whistle. Peggy lifted her head and saw him all right, but instead of coming like she usually did she bolted off in the opposite direction.

"There, what did I tell you, I knew what she'd do," he said pointing to the far side of the field, "it's always the same in a situation like this. Can you see them other horses that she's with o'er in yon corner?"

"Aye I can Dad," said Barry, "and they seem to be really enjoying themselves."

"You're reight there lad, they've got used to their freedom in th'open air."

"E-eh, just look at 'em frolicking about, kicking their hind legs into th'air Dad," I chuckled, amused by their playfulness.

"Yeah, she's enjoying herself all reight," put in Dad, "but I'm afraid her playtime's o'er ... it's time now to go in there and collect her." This wasn't so easy ... as soon as we approached Peggy, all three horses set off at the gallop.

"Right lads, there's only one thing for it now," said Dad.

"What's that Dad?" asked Barry.

"Well, take these two sticks and go and stand in't middle o' the field where I tell you."

"Oh 'eck, I've a feeling I'm not going to like this our John," said Barry.

"No, me neither," I replied.

Dad could see the concerned look on our faces, "Don't fret about it, you get over to that end of the field our Barry and you stand in that patch o'er yonder our John."

"Oh aye, and what do we do then?" I asked.

"Well, I'm gonna approach the horses and when they start running towards you, I want you both to start waving them sticks about and drive 'em into that far corner where the field narrows a bit. When they're there we'll all close in on 'em and I'll do the rest."

"You must be joking Dad ... they'll trample on us!" I protested.

"No they won't, trust me ... if you do what I say I'll have Peggy in no time." After reassuring us Dad walked towards the horses and as soon as he got near to them they set off at the gallop again. The moment I saw them heading my way I took flight and bolted for the nearest fence.

Dad was furious and really bawled me out, "Why didn't you do what I told you and stand your ground like our Barry did?"

"'Cos I was freightened 'o gettin' trampled on Dad, them blooming horses were galloping straight at me!"

"Come on lad, like I said ... they'll not run thí down. Trust me I know all about horses."

"Yeah, you know that Dad and I know it ... but do those flamin' horses know it?" I said quivering from head to toe.

"Look our John listen to me, I've dealt with horses all mí life ... I wouldn't let you do it if I thought you'd get hurt."

"All right Dad, I'll do it but I'm telling you now ... I'm scared!"

"You'll be all reight lad, you'll be all reight ... don't worry about it."

This time I did stand my ground ... I was shaking like a leaf but I held out. As the horses thundered towards me I could feel the thud of their hoofs pounding the ground. After a few moments I had reached the point of no return ... it was too late to run, they were almost upon me! With no alternative left I started to wave the stick in the air and Barry did the same from where he was standing. To my amazement and relief, the horses did exactly as Dad had said they would. They headed for the confined space in the corner where Dad was waiting and he did the rest. Within minutes he had the bridal on Peggy and quietly guided her out of the field.

"Bloomin' 'eck Dad, I've got to put mí hand up, you wer' right ... but it wer' still scary."

"I can imagine it were our John. I've got to admit there was one point there when I saw them galloping towards you that I got a little bit concerned myself!"

"Oh thank you very much Dad ... now you tell me!"

"Anyroad lads you did yourselves proud, thanks a lot. You can take turns now at riding Peggy back to the stable ... you've earned it."

As I rode Peggy from the field she proudly raised her head and whinnied as though saying goodbye to her comrades.

****

Every Good Friday a festival was held down 'Pendle Bottoms' and Dad would go there with his horse and trap to sell buggy rides to the excited children. One year, Jimmy and I asked if we could go with him.

"Aye, you can if you want but don't expect any free rides."

"Whattaya mean Dad? We're talking about helping you so that you can go for a drink in the pub."

"Oh aye, there's a fat chance o' that, I'm hoping to be busy all day. Anyroad, you can come if you want but think on what I said."

It was a pleasant sunny day and we arrived there about 10 am. Already crowds of people were beginning to emerge on the scene. Dad set up his pitch outside the pub and it wasn't long before a few kids were queuing up for a ride. The trap seated eight children and by midday, Dad had done about eight trips.

"Right lads," he said, "I'm going in the pub now for a drink ... I'm dying o' thirst."

"That's all right," I said, "I'll ték over while you're in there." Dad had no qualms about this, as he knew I could handle Peggy, so he handed over the reins to me.

"Aye all reight then, but I'll keep slipping out now and agén to check on things and to collect the brass."

"You'll be all right there Dad," said Jimmy, "I'll look after the money whilst John téks care of t'horse."

That was it; both Jimmy and I thoroughly enjoyed the rest of the afternoon. After a while Jimmy took the reins, letting me handle the money. Every now and then Dad kept popping out of the pub to bring us both a glass of lemonade each and to keep check. Each time Jimmy handed him a handful of money.

"Bloomin' 'eck," he said with a big grin on his face, "I should have thought o' this afore shouldn't I ... what a good do!" Nonetheless, he was still aware that Peggy needed a rest and so ordered us to stop for a 45-minute break. After the interval lots of kids were queuing up around the buggy again raring to go, clamouring for more. Things carried on much as before and we took handfuls of money. At the end of the day everybody had enjoyed it. To make it even better, Dad gave Jimmy and me half a crown each.

****

One morning I looked out of the front bedroom window and to my surprise there was a lorry parked straight facing on the other side of the street. As I poked my head out of the window I saw a man delivering bundles of wood from door to door.

"That's funny," I thought, "I'm sure I saw a child's head move behind the steering wheel in the cab." Sure enough, at that moment, a little lad's head bobbed up in the driver's seat and then the horn started to blast.

"Bloomin' 'eck!" I spluttered, "That's dangerous, leaving a little lad in the wagon on his own ... I'd best go and check it." I scampered downstairs but as I got to the lobby I could see through the open door that the wagon was moving slowly.

"Bloody hell, the little lad must have taken t'hand-break off!" I panicked.

I raced through the lobby but by the time I'd reached outside the wagon was careering out of control down the steep street. All I could do was watch in horror hoping that the young boy would be all right. The wagon careered in a straight line until it hit the flatness of Trafalgar where it veered left and crashed into a factory wall taking part of the factory gates with it. Luckily, there were no other kids playing on the street and it didn't collide with any traffic on the main thoroughfare. I was the first to arrive on the spot and to my delight the little boy was no worse for wear, albeit a little shaken up.

Tears rolled down the youngster's cheeks, "Sniff sniff ... mí daddy'll kill me for brekkin' his wagon!" he sobbed.

"Don't worry about it cock." I reassured him knowing that his dad would be only too pleased that he was all right, "I think he'll let you off this time. Mind thí, you'll have to promise not to mess about in any big wagons agén."

I was quite touched by the young lad's reply, "Oh I promise thí ... I won't e'er do it agén 'mister' ... honest!"

****

Trafalgar was a very poor area, yet, most people appeared happy. Despite living in deprivation and having to endure appalling conditions the resilience and fortitude of the people were second to none. Throughout the wretched situation the inhabitants rallied together when the situation demanded it and the community spirit was very close knit. During these austere times one shopkeeper profited more than any other … the pawnbroker. Various pawnbrokers's shops established themselves in different areas of the town. Consequently, there was one on Trafalgar at the corner of Lord Street near to the Alhambra Picture House. One Monday morning Mam was broke and she asked me to take some oddments to the pawnshop. One of the neighbours, Mrs Thompson, who happened to be in the house, stopped me before I got to the front door and started to talk to me in a broad Lancashire dialect.

"E-eh I'm glad I've copped thí lad," she whispered, "dusta think thá cúd ték a few items to th'pop shop for me while tha's at it?"

"Yeah, course I will Mrs Thompson," I replied politely.

"Reight cock, wilta just come with me o'er to my house to collect 'em?"

"Yeah righto."

On reaching her house she handed me some items. "Here you are lad," she said cautiously handing me a gold watch and chain, "now think on thá doesn't mention this to anyone … mí husband'd kill me if he found out 'cos it's a family heirloom. The reason I daren't go myself is I'm freightened of anybody seeing me."

"Yeah I understand Mrs Thompson and I promise you," I said crossing my heart, "I won't tell a soul."

"Good," she muttered routing through her purse, "ther's a tanner here for your trouble. Mind thí, I want you to barter wí yon fellow in that pop shop and get as much as thá can."

"Leave it with me Mrs. Thompson, I've bín there a few times and I have a good idea on the goin' rate."

"Aye I know thá has Johnny Cowell, some of the neighbours have telt mí about thí."

"U-um what a good do," I chuckled to myself as I left the house, "a tanner just for going to t'other end o' Trafalgar."

When I reached the shop there were already two elderly chaps and a woman inside, all three skint, wanting to pawn various items.

"How much wilta give me for poppin' this," asked the first man handing over a brown paper parcel, which contained a pinstriped suit.

"After scrutinising the suit the pawnbroker answered with a straight face, "Well, the most I can let you have is eleven shillings … I'm being generous mind!"

"Eleven bob? Tha's being generous all reight," sniggerd the bloke, "on th'reight bloody side!"

"Well that's my offer … take it or leave it."

"Aye all reight I'll ték it but first … what will it cost me to redeem it?"

"That depends sir … do you want it hung or wrapped?"

"How dusta mean … hung or wrapped?" asked the fellow scratching his head.

"Well if you want it hung on a coat hanger and placed in a wardrobe, so as to keep it nice and trim, the pledge price is one and thre'pence for the first three months and a tanner for any other month after that."

"Oh aye, and what's the other method then?"

"Well then I'll just put it under the counter wrapped as it is now amongst some other parcels," said the pawnbroker stressing, "where it may become a little crumpled."

"Never mind about it getting crumpled ... what will the pledge cost me?"

"Well, that'll be a shilling for the first three months and thre'pence a month thereafter."

"A bob!" he moaned, "that's daylight robbery!"

"That's my charge sir," the pawnbroker replied smugly, "and like I said before ... take it or leave it!"

"I'll ték it, I'll ték it ... I don't have much option do I?"

"Thank you sir," the pawnbroker smiled. He took the parcel, placed it under the counter and gave the poor man his money along with a redemption ticket.

The woman, a thin faced lady in her late forties and wearing a dark shawl over her shoulders, handed over a small gold ring.

"How much dusta think thá could let me have for this?" she mumbled with bated breath. Once again the pawnbroker scrutinised the gold ring, this time using an eyepiece, which fitted snugly into his right eye.

After what seemed an age he answered with the same smugness as he had done with his previous customer, "U-um, the best I can do for you is five shillings and sixpence."

"Five and six," she cried out, "but that's my wedding ring, I've had it for nearly twenty-five years ... it's worth a lot more than that!"

"It may be worth more than that to you dear for sentimental reasons, but this is a business I'm running ... not a charity. Anyway, that's my price ... take it .....!"

"I know," she cut in sharply, "ték it or leave it! Cut the yuk and just give mí the money and mí ticket!"

The next gentleman was treated in much the same manner as he pawned a brand new pair of boots that he'd probably just procured from a mail order catalogue.

Then came my turn.

"Right," he said after going through the same rigmarole, "fifteen shillings for the watch and chain."

"Fifteen bob ... you must be joking!" I echoed, "It's worth a lot more than that and you know it ... you've got some for sale in the window for three quid and they're not as good as this one."

"That's my price, take ....!"

"All reight," I bluffed, "I'll leave it and ték it to that pop shop on Parliament Street!"

Even though I was only a young lad he took me seriously because I'd frequented the shop quite a lot of late.

"Go on then, twenty-one shillings, but that's definitely my last offer."

"U-um," I thought, "a guinea, that seems about right. Yeah righto," I agreed handing him the watch and chain. I then went into the bartering mode for my mam's articles.

On getting back to Mrs Thompson's house she greeted me cheerfully as I handed her the money along with the ticket.

"Eh tha's a grand lad Johnny Cowell ... y'wanna a cuppa tay?"

"Oh yes please Mrs Thompson ... thank you very much."

"And I suppose tha'd like a piece o' cake to go with it eh seeing as tha's a growing lad?" She paused for a moment looking at me with her wizened eyes, then asked, "Anyroad, wilta do me a favour young Johnny Cowell?"

"Yeah course I will Mrs. Thompsom ... what is it?"

"Well, I'd like thí to hold on to this ticket for me for chance mí husband finds it. He'd murder me if he thought I'd popped ow't ... y'know what I mean lad."

"But how will you be able to redeem it?" I asked rather naively.

"Not to worry thysel' lad; if thá comes across here after school on Friday I'll have enough money for thí to get it back for me. And don't fret thysel; I'll give thí another tanner for your trouble."

"Righto Mrs. Thompson, I'll do it for you, but thre'pence'll be enough."

"Tha's on Johnny Cowell, tha's on ... let this be our little secret!" Sure enough, true to her word she redeemed the watch and chain the following Friday. But it wasn't long before she required my services again. In fact, after that I made many more trips to and from the pawnbroker's with that gold watch and chain. A friendship developed between Mrs Thompson and me and our little secret remained safe over the years. I liked this lady and it wasn't just the thre'pence ... she always came out with a cup of tea and biscuits. I also liked the different funny expressions that she used to come out with. One day she reminisced a little about her life.

"E-eh dusta know lad, I might not have much money but I still count mí blessings. When I'm feeling down in the dumps I just thinks o' poor Nellie Higgins and her family who live across the back ... poor woman, she's as poor as a church mouse! Aye mí heart goes out to her, especially when I sees them lads of hers with their breeches arse hangin' out ... e-eh, the poor little mites! I've seen her many o' time traipsing down them stone steps to't petty wí now't on her feet ... she can't even afford a decent pair o' clogs. Aye, and ther's plenty more in th'same boat as her. I might be poor but my Alf's a good husband, who works every hour that God sends. It wer' only t'other day that I got onto him and I were agate that he's doing too much but he won't ték any notice o' me. Mind thí, we're still living fro' hand to mouth but it don't matter 'cos we more than mék up forrit with all't love we show each other."

It was obvious by the way she carried on that she was a God-fearing woman.

"Mind thí, I don't take ow't for granted. I might not go to church every Sunday but I allús puts misel' in God's hands afore I go to sleep. I thank Him every níte for givin' me mí health and strength to look after misel' and for having a good husband. Once I've done that I drops off to sleep 'cos ther's now't nobody can do about it." She paused for a moment before adding, "E-eh lad ... if I didn't have God in mí life I don't know what I'd do."

"Where does Alf work," I asked becoming intrigued with her tales.

"Oh, he's a tackler in one o' weaving sheds and a bloomin' good ún at that. He works his socks off to keep them looms runnin'. He were only agate last níte, 'I've gotta keep 'em runnin' lúv ... them weavers are on piece work and the more they earn, the more I earn.' He don't mék much but, bless him ... he comes homes Friday dinnertime and tips up every penny."

I had to smile to myself as amusing thoughts ran through my head, "That's where I come in all ready willing and able to carry out my little service."

"Aye, and that's when I call upon thee lad to redeem mí goods fro' th'pop shop," she said as if reading my thoughts.

"What time does Alf start work?" I asked. I actually knew the answer to this because of all the weavers that passed by my bedroom window every morning. But the reason for my question was because I wanted to glean even more fascinating tales from this interesting woman.

"He starts at seven o'clock lad, but he doesn't need to leave t'house till five to seven 'cos he only has to mek his way to Thompson's mill. Mind thí, he gets up at six o'clock when Joe Fletcher, the knocker-up, taps on the window with his long stick."

"But you don't need a knocker up Mrs. Thompson," I queried, "there's always a few colliers coming down the street at that time making their way to the pit."

"Aye I'm aware o' that but Alf allús says that thá can't rely on that. He wer' only agate t'other day, 'What if they didn't turn out one day … I'd be in a reight stúk if I were late for work. Anyroad thá can allús rely on old Joe Fletcher … he's the best knocker-up in Burnley.' There wer' now't I could say about that wer' they lad?"

"No I suppose not," I responded, "but one thing puzzles me Mrs Thompson … Joe Fletcher must have to knock the miners up at five o'clock or even sooner?"

"Yeah that's reight lad," she said nodding her head in agreement.

"Well, what I'd like to know is … who knocks Joe Fletcher up; I've always wondered who gets the knocker-upper up?"

"Go on y'daft ha'porth!" she responded with a hearty laugh.

"Righto Mrs Thompson," I said after draining the last drop of tea, "I'll be on my way now. Thank you very much for the brew … I'll see you on Monday if you need me."

Mrs Thompson's sense of humour and special qualities intrigued me and I liked the way she went about tackling life's problems. A particular incident that springs to mind involved the local window cleaner.

One day after returning from the pawnbroker's she asked me to sit down. "Here you are young Johnny Cowell," she said handing me a brew and one of her scrumptious scones, "get this down your neck, tha' deserves it."

As usual she was very pleasant but I could sense that she was bothered over something … she wasn't her usual bubbly self. I couldn't put my finger on it, but I felt that something was amiss and so I broached the subject with her. "Is something wrong Mrs Thompsom, you seem to be a little down in the dumps today?"

"By 'eck John lad," she responded with a smile, "does it show that much?"

"Not really, it's just that you don't seem quite as chirpy as you usually do."

"By gum lad, you're very perceptive, tha' misses nowt." She paused for a moment and then a smile came to her face, "To tell the truth there is some't that bin' bothering me, but I don't want to burden thi' with mi troubles."

"Oh that's all right Mrs Thompson," I replied curiously, I don't mind ... honest!"

"Aye all reight lad, I'll tell thi' what it is ... it's that bloomin' window cleaner o' mine."

"Oh 'eck, has something happened to him?"

"No lad, no such luck," she joked, "nowt's happened to him ... it's what he's bin' up to what's bothering me."

"Why, what's he done?"

"Oh," she said shrugging her shoulders and gritting her teeth a little," it's not so much what he's done, it's more about what he's not bin doin'."

My curiosity was aroused now more than ever and I prodded a little more. "Not been doing Mrs Thompsom, how do you mean?"

"Well I've a sneaky feeling that he's bin robbin' me for ages. Ya see, I go down town every Thursday afternoon to do the buying in and that's when he comes to clean mi windows."

"Oh aye ... and don't you think he's been cleanin' yours then?"

"Tha's on the right track lad ... he's bin cleanin' mi downstairs' windows, but I'm bloomin' sure he doesn't allus do the downstairs' ones." Her face tensed a little betraying a tinge of anger, "I think the lazy swine's bin too idle to set up his ladder and climb it."

"It's not like you to let things slide," I enthused, "have you tackled him about it?"

"No, not yet," she replied pouting her lips, "but I'm gonna do when he comes to collect his brass. As a matter of fact I'm expecting him anytime now."

She'd hardly finished speaking when there was a knock on the front door followed by footsteps in the lobby. A moment later the window cleaner entered the living room to collect his money.

Mrs Thompsom didn't mess about and got straight to the point, "I'm only givin' thi' half pay this week," she grimaced pointing a finger at him, "'cos tha's never cleaned the upstairs' windows"

"Now that'll do Mrs Thompson!" he rapped arrogantly. "Are you callin' me a thief?"

"I'm not callin' thi' a thief, but I'm tellin' thi straight ... tha's ne'er cleaned 'em!"

"And I'm tellin' thi' straight that I have ... and I want mi brass!"

"All reight then ... if you've cleaned 'em, how come there's still some marks on the window that wer' there afore I went down town."

"Now come off it, don't try that game on me!" he scoffed, "With all the smoke and grime from the factory chimneys around here and the smoke from the trains ... them marks could've bin made since I left."

Mrs Thompsom argued her point a while longer, but to no avail... He wouldn't be swayed and insisted that she pay up the full amount. She was deflated with the situation, but reluctantly handed him the money. By the look on her face it was obvious that she wasn't happy about it. After he left the house, she didn't dwell on it too much, but muttered something under her breathe about catching him out.

Turning to me with a smile on her face she said, "Take heed John lad ... that fella's a rogue and one o' these days he's gonna get his comeuppance."

True to her word she did catch him out and fortunately I was there to witness the amusing event ... it was a joy to behold to see this lady in action. It was about two months later when she put her little plan into action.

Once again I was in her house enjoying all the fringe benefits after a routine trip to the pawnbroker's. "I'm glad tha's here young Johnny Cowell," she said with a mischievous glint in her eyes, "do you remember me tacklin' the window cleaner t'other week about not cleanin' mi upstairs windows?"

"I do that Mrs Thompson. How could I forget it ...you certainly didn't mince words with him."

"Ah well, what it is lad ... I'm gonna tackle him agen today about the same thing. The reason I'm tellin' thi' is because I want you as a witness."

"But Mrs Thompson, when you tackled him about it before, it didn't seem to make any difference."

"Aye, I know that lad, but this time it'll be different ... just you wait and see. Anyroad, he should be here any minute now, but when he comes in I don't want thi' to say a word. Just keep your lug'oles open and say nowt, and happen tha'll learn somet. He thinks he's the best window cleaner in't Northern Union, but I'm gonna knock him down a peg or two."

"U-um, this should be interesting," I thought wondering what she was up to. I was half way through my brew when there was a knock on the front door.

"Hey up," she whispered, here he comes ... action stations. Now don't forget what I just telt thi'."

"Don't worry about that, I'm going to enjoy this," I giggled to myself as the window cleaner's footsteps got closer. He entered the living room in his usual glib manner.

"Good afternoon Mrs Thomsom," he quipped, "a nice day isn't it?"

"Aye it is that," she smiled followed by, "I suppose tha's come for tha brass?"

"Of course I've come for mi money," he grunted cockily, "I've cleaned your windows so now I want payin',"

"Oh tha's cleaned mi windows hasta? Well I'm tellin' thi' streight you robbin' bugger ... tha's ne'er cleaned the one's upstairs!"

At that remark I got to thinking she was going down the same path as before, but I couldn't have been more wrong."

"Now that'll do, don't start that again ... we've gone o'er this ground afore."

"Aye we have and we're goin' o'er it agen cos I'm tellin' thi' to tha face ... tha's ne'er cleaned 'em!"

"And I'm tellin' thi' I have," he snarled becoming agitated, "now give me mi money."

Mrs Thompson stood firm and didn't flinch at all, "So you want your brass dusta?" she asked with a wry smile on her face.

"Of course I want mi bloody brass, he replied rather nonplussed. "What the flamin' 'eck d'you think I'm here for?"

All reight then," she said as her smile changed to a snigger, "if tha wants tha brass, then put your blasted ladder up agen mi window sill."

"Whattaya talkin' about"? he stammered uneasily.

"Aye you might well ask," she sniggered. I'll tell thi' what I'm talkin' about. On Thursday afternoon afore I went down town I put your money in an envelope with your name on it and left it up there on the sill for you to pick up." She pondered momentarily before coolly saying, "And dusta know somet, it's still sat up there like a cheese at for'pence. Now what've you got to say about that you robbin' swine?"

Realising the game was up he just stood there aghast. He didn't say anything at first then started to splutter, "Oh aye that's reight, I remember now ... I was just gonna ...."

"Never mind what you were just gonna do," she rapped cutting him short," lying through your teeth to worm your way out of it won't help thi' now ... tha's not as clever as tha thinks. In fact tha's neither use nor ornament ... tha's bin rumbled." Her voice lowered somewhat in tone but then she became more serious. "Tha's bin pullin' the wool o'er mi eyes for long enough ... aye and probably many other poor folk too. Well I'm tellin' thi now that your little scam stops here. Tha's got the audacity to walk into mi house as bold as brass and demand pennies that we've had to work our fingers to the bone for. Now what I'd like to know is what have you got to say for thasel'?"

He just stood there twiddling his thumbs and said nothing.

"Right, just as I thought ... tha's got nowt to say. Well now I'm gonna tell thi' a thing or two. First of all tha can clean all mi windows for the next two months for nowt. If tha refuses I'll tell all the neighbours on the street what tha's bin up to. And whilst I'm at it I'm in two minds to report thi' to the cop shop ... I don't think they'd look upon it too lightly do you?"

Having no choice he went about the task set before him under the watchful eye of Mrs Thompsom. She didn't sack him. In fact he was to remain her window cleaner for many years to come, but he never again got up to any of his old scams. On many an occasion after that Mrs Thompson and I had many a laugh about it over a brew and biscuits.

Mrs. Thompson wasn't my only customer; lots of other neighbours, who were in a similar predicament to her, got in touch with me and were only too willing to use my services. The pawnbroker got used to my haggling ways and so I always got the going rate for my customers.

Mr Jenkins, a retired weaver who lived on his own in dire circumstances, stopped me one day.

"Young Johnny Cowell, wilta ték these to th'pop shop for me to see if thá can get ow't forrém?" he asked handing me a pair of well-worn shoes that he'd highly polished.

"Well I'll see what I can do for you Mr Jenkins but I can't promise anything."

The pawnbroker must have been in a good mood that day because he actually offered two shillings. Mr Jenkins was delighted … it was enough to get him a bite to eat.

"Eh thank you very much cock … here's tuppence for your trouble!"

"No it doesn't matter Mr Jenkins … I were goin' there anyroad for somebody else," It was a white lie but what else could I do … I didn't have the heart to take that two-pence off him. "No," I thought as I left his house, "the poor bloke looks like he hasn't got two ha'pennies to rub together." As it turned out I got an even better deal for him later on.

"Johnny Cowell, canya redeem mí shoes for me?" he asked about a week later.

"Yeah course I can Mr Jenkins," I said taking the redemption ticket from his hand.

I handed over the ticket to the pawnbroker and he disappeared into the back of the shop. After what seemed an age he came back to the counter scratching his head.

"I can't seem to find them," he said, "the ticket must have fallen off the box and I think it's got mixed up with a load of others that have never been redeemed."

"Oh 'eck!" I answered acting naïvely, "What can we do about it then?"

"Well can you nip round the counter and come into the back of the shop to see if you can spot them?" It was the first time I'd ever been invited to go through into this mysterious room and what a surprise I got ... it was like Aladdin's cave. At the back of the shop there were lots of tea chests filled with children's toys, including dolls of all shapes and sizes. One doll was lying about on the floor like a discarded marionette. There was wooden shelving all around the room from floor to ceiling and each shelf was cram packed full with little parcels. Three large sideboards with large drawers took up most of the floor space. In one corner there was a tall stack of boxes full of shoes.

"They must be amongst that lot," muttered the pawnbroker, "there's nowhere else they can be."

"None of these have any tickets on 'em," I queried, "how come?"

"Ah well, they've all gone past their redemption date ... so they'll be going on sale when I've time to sort 'em out."

"That'll do me," I chuckled inwardly taking all my will power to suppress a giggle. I knew Mr Jenkins took size nines and I didn't think for one minute that he'd object to getting back a better pair of shoes than the one's he'd pawned. After routing through the boxes for a short time I came across a pair that had hardly been worn. "Great," I thought, "he'll be dead chuffed wí these."

But that was the easy part ... convincing the pawnbroker that these were Mr Jenkin's shoes was slightly more difficult.

"No it couldn't have been these, they're nearly brand new, " he said, "I'd have allowed more than two bob for them."

"Maybe not but they were very similar to these," I insisted.

"Aye, as maybe but you still can't have them. I'll tell you what, go in the back room again and have another look."

"Yeah reighto," I agreed making my way through to the stockpile, "but we'll have to sort something out 'cos Mr Jenkins needs 'em for tonight." Unbeknown to the pawnbroker I'd already spotted Mr Jenkin's shoes but I was all geared up to get him this quality pair. "Besides," I said to myself, "it'll mék a nice change from the bloomin' pawnbroker profiteering off somebody's back." After about ten minutes I reminded the shopkeeper again that Mr Jenkins needed the shoes immediately.

Reluctantly, after a few grunts and groans, he agreed to the transaction. "Aye all right, I don't like it but I don't seem to have much option."

"Superb," I gloated as I ran along Trafalgar, "Mr Jenkins'll be o'er the moon with these!"

"By gum lad tha's done well," he said highly delighted, "I've never had a pair o'shoes of this quality afore."

The funny part about it was that he pawned them a few times after that and got an average of half a crown each time!"

****

Nearly all the Burnley Cotton Mills ground to a halt during the Wakes' Weeks, which always fell on the first two weeks in July. Lots of people lugged their heavy suitcases and headed for Blackpool for a well-earned rest. This was yet, another ideal opportunity to make some brass. Our Jimmy, Barry and I would make our way to the Central Railway Station and await returning holiday-makers with our make do trolleys offering to carry large suitcases for a nominal fee.

The weekend coincided with the time that the funfair came to town. Lots of local kids would eagerly make their way to the allotted ground behind the Odeon Picture House wanting to try out all the different rides. One particular Saturday night our Barry came home from the fairground with his friend, Walter Baxendale. Barry was looking rather worse for wear as he had a black eye and a swollen nose.

"What the flamin' 'eck happened to you our Barry," I asked rather concerned, "have you been fighting?"

"You can say that again" replied Walter enthusiastically, "but you'll never guess where."

"It's all right Walter," put in Barry, "I can still talk, I'll tell our John miself."

His tale went as follows:

Barry and Walter were stood outside the boxing booth when a gang of rowdy youths started throwing out insults. One of them was called Bernard Spedding, who happened to do a bit of boxing for the Central Youth Club and he was forever picking on Barry at school. Barry was never a fighting lad and wouldn't be drawn into an argument, but then, Bernard did something that Barry wouldn't wear at all ...... he started to throw out insults about Dad's rag-cart and him being a prison bird. Barry threw all caution to the wind and within seconds both lads were fighting. But the fight didn't last long, as some fellows broke it up; one of these was a fairground worker in charge of the boxing booth.

"Naythén you young úns, if you want to fight tha can do it in the boxing ring, and tha can make half a crown for thasén while tha's at it."

"Oh yeah, and what do we have to do forrit then?" asked Bernard enthusiastically.

"Just three, three minute rounds that's all, how about it?"

A little snigger came to Bernard's face as he turned to Barry, asking, "I'm gam', how about you Cowheel?"

Barry wasn't too keen on the idea but didn't like losing face, so reluctantly agreed. The proprietor wasn't slow to seize his opportunity; he immediately invited the two lads onto a platform outside the boxing booth and announced the forthcoming event to the passing crowd.

"Roll up ladies and gentlemen; we've got something special on here tonight, two shows for the price o' one. These here two young lads are gonna spar against each other afore t'other boxers perform."

It worked like a treat and before long he'd attracted lots of paying customers.

Barry felt very nervous as he stripped to the waist and especially when he glanced across the ring to Bernard's corner. The two lads were as different as could be. Bernard was actually an inch shorter than Barry but very well built with rippling muscles, whereas Barry was skinny and frail looking. The crowd actually started laughing at the stark contrast between the two lads.

The fight got underway and it didn't take very long for Bernard's expertise to show. During the first round Barry sustained a busted nose and hardly landed a blow in return. The second round started in a similar way, but Barry refused to yield in spite of a cut lip and a black eye. Although he wasn't a fighter, he wouldn't give up because he felt he was in the right. Despite being in control of the fight, Bernard's enthusiasm started to wain because of Barry's unrelenting fightback.

The third round began and Barry's determination paid off; he managed to land a telling blow busting Bernard's nose. By now the crowd was going mad, roaring loudly for the underdog; this became more apparent when Barry landed another blow on Bernard's nose, causing blood to trickle down his face. At the end of the bout, there *was no mistaking that Bernard was the overall winner but this didn't bother Barry; the fact that he had stood his ground and given something in return was more important to him than anything else. The crowd showed their appreciation by applauding loudly and the gaffer gave both Barry and Barnard an extra shilling for putting on a good show.*

I was quite impressed by the incident and felt very proud of my little brother. A good thing that came out of it was that the two lads became good friends thereafter.

****

The weeks passed quickly and before we knew it, it was time to go back to school. The ordeal, that some kids dreaded, finally arrived … the eleven plus examination! Miss M Gordon was kept very busy in the classroom preparing us all for this important event. Only the chosen few took the exam seriously, as most of us took it for granted that we'd be going to St. Mary's Senior School the next term as our older peers had done before us. On the morning of the test I went into the examination room feeling quite relaxed because I wasn't bothered one way or the other whether I passed or not.

"There's one thing for sure," I told myself, "I certainly don't want to go to the Grammar School."

We all sat down at our appointed desks where the papers had already been carefully laid face down. The headmistress, Miss Gordon, gave out all the routine instructions on what to do during the test. Miss M Gordon, along with two nuns, overlooked the proceedings making sure everyone adhered to the rules.

"Right everybody," Miss Gordon announced, "The morning test that you have to undertake is your arithmetic paper. If you need anything at all during the test, whether it is paper or anything else, then you must hold your hand up and someone will attend to your needs. The same applies if you want to go to the toilet ... understand?"

"Yes Miss Gordon," drawled the entire class.

"Right then," she advised in a soothing voice not usually attributed to her, "you can turn your papers over now and I'll give you five minutes to scrutinise them before you get down to writing."

On reading the paper I was a little surprised to find the questions quite easy and I'd soon finished with plenty of time to check my answers. Mind you, I found the afternoon paper much more difficult ... then again, English never was my favourite subject.

"Oh well," I thought, "I'll just have to make a stab at some o' the questions and guess what the answers are!"

Then came the day of reckoning ... the results!"

"Right children," said Miss Gordon, "first of all I'm going to read out all the names of those who have passed for Grammar School." No one was surprised to hear certain names called out but then came the roll call for those who'd passed for Towneley Technical High School. This time a few eyebrows were raised ... including mine.

"I'm pleased to say that three boys have passed for Towneley," she announced, "Alan Carter, Alan Green and," she faltered for a second before announcing, "John Cowell!"

"Whoo-oh," went up a mocking chorus around the class, "who's a clever boy then?"

"That'll do!" rapped Miss M Gordon restoring a semblance of order.

"I can't blame 'em for taking the mickey," I mumbled to myself, "I'd have done the same if Ronnie or Bobby had passed."

"Bloomin' 'eck our John, haven't you done well," said our Mary, "mi mam won't half be pleased."

"Aye I suppose so our kid, but I'm not sure I am ... I want to go to St. Mary's with all mí mates."

When I got home Mam knew about it because Mary had already told her.

"Well I'm right proud of you our John; we've finally got a scholar in the family."

"Thank's Mam, but all the same, if you don't mind, I'd rather go to St. Mary's."

"That's up to you lad, it's your life. I've got to say though that you'll have far more opportunities to improve your education if you go to Towneley."

"I'm not bothered about that Mam 'cos I want to go working down the pit when I leave school."

"Oh don't say that," interrupted my older sister Maureen all excited for me, "you'll never get this opportunity again our John ... you must go to Towneley, it's got a really good reputation."

I tried telling her how I felt but Maureen wouldn't listen ... she was really enthusiastic about Towneley and anxious for my future prospects.

"But our Maureen," I protested, "I want to ….."

"I know what you're going to say our John ... you want to be with your mates but believe me our kid they wont stay with you all your life. Please go to Towneley our John because if you don't like it you can always pack it in later on and go to St. Mary's. I'll tell you what ... you've got six weeks off school now so promise me you'll think about it."

"Aye all right our Maureen I promise." I knew she was sincere, only wanting what she thought was best for me. She'd always cared for me, along with my other brothers and sisters, always having our best interests at heart. I wasn't sure what to do but I knew she was making sense ... so I eventually succumbed to her wishes.

Typical weaving shed around the turn of the century

Ruins of Clocktower Mill after being destroyed by fire

Looking along Trafalgar from Sandygate Junction.
Note the Victorian gas lamp outside the Waterloo public house.

St.Thomas's School

Tom Howarth's chemists, Trafalgar

Patten Street and Gresham Place, from Albion Street railway bridge

The Mitre looking along Trafalgar

Rowley Street and Whitaker Street from Albion Street railway bridge

Burnley Town Hall Clock

Looking along Trafalgar from The Mitre

Canal footpath showing Watt's Clock

Trafalgar shops from the corner of Whitaker Street

Brunswick Church which was directly facing the Town Hall. Notice the wide window ledges that the children climbed onto in order to obtain a good view during the peace celebrations.

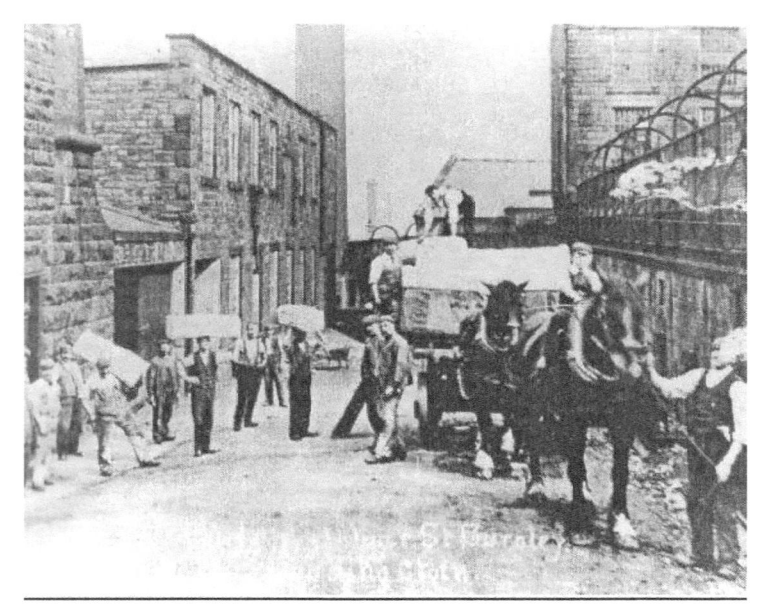

Trafalgar Shed yard around the turn of the century. Note the iron foot-bridge on the right.

View of Burnley from Watt's Clock. Note some of Burnley's many factory chimneys. Note also the church spire on the far right. This was only demolished in 1998.

The Mitre Junction about the turn of the century

Trafalgar shops viewed from Sandygate Junction

Looking down Albion Street from Picadilly Road

Demolition of 14 Albion Street and others in the same block

Looking up Albion Street

Burnley Market Hall – the source of broken biscuits

Albion Street. Note the Victorian gas-lamp ouside number 14. At the bottom of the street the police telephone box is clearly visible at the side of the foot-bridge.

The canal footbridge in the distance with Watt's Clock behind it

Barbara outside 14 Albion Street, looking down the street. Behind her you can see Trafalgar Mill.

Family photograph: my uncle Jimmy is sat on my grandmother Mary's knee, Winifred is sat on the chair with my aunt Katie standing behind. Can be dated as Jimmy was born one month before the start of World War One.

Family photo taken at niece's wedding.
Back row, from left to right: Barry, John, Barabara & Jimmy.
Front row, from left to right: Mary, Winifred & Maureen.

Barbara's wedding day. The two page boys in kilts at the front were Mary's sons.

Winifred at the age of 84 in her garden

Winifred's mother and father: Matthew & Mary. Matthew served in WW1 this photo shows him in his Home Guard uniform during WW2

Jack and Winifred in their courting days

Mr & Mrs Davis sat on their doorstep at No 12 Albion Street. John aged 11 years old and little Ann.

Barry holding one of his pigeons. Note the air-raid shelter in the background.

CHAPTER 9 - TOWNELEY

I can well remember the first morning I set off for Towneley School dressed in a school uniform. Our Maureen was full of pride as I donned my maroon blazer with a badge depicting Towneley Park Gates, short grey pants, black shoes and a school cap.

"Go on our John," she enthused, "you can do it, I know you can."

"U-umph, I don't know so much our Maureen," I said nervously, "I wish I were going to St Mary's with all mí mates."

"Oh I know how you feel our John but you've a lot more chance of doing well at Towneley than St Mary's and your prospects future are much better."

"Aye I suppose you're right ... I only wish I had as much confidence as you do our kid."

I walked down Albion Street full of foreboding ... I didn't fancy the prospect of facing the unknown. As I reached Maggie Astin's house I glanced back over my shoulder to see Maureen eagerly waving me off.

"You'll be all right our John," she shouted cheerfully trying to reassure me, "you can do it ... I've got loads o' faith in you."

When I reached the school my worst fears were confirmed ... I felt totally out of place. It had a much stricter regime than St Thomas's and everything about it seemed regimental. Even the school bell was triggered off by an electrical system unlike the traditional hand ringing bell at St Thomas's. As it rang we all lined up in single files and then systematically marched into a large assembly hall. All the schoolmasters were sat on a stage behind a long wooden table with the headmaster, Mr Lancaster, sat in the middle of the group. It reminded me a film, 'Goodbye Mr Chips,' I'd watched as a child starring Robert Donat and Greer Garson. After formalities were dispensed with, Mr Lancaster gave a long speech, which left no doubt in my mind that he wouldn't tolerate any nonsense.

It wasn't the regimental aspect that bothered me as much as the fact that I had no friends to relate to. Also, everywhere I went the other pupils seemed to tower above me ... I felt quite small and intimidated. After the initial ceremony we were allocated our form teacher and classroom. All first year students were graded A B or C according to their exam results ... I was graded B and I felt happier about this.

"U-um, at least I don't have to compete with the brainy ones," I mumbled to myself.

Another thing that made me unhappy was that the word soon spread amongst my peers that my dad was a ragman and that he'd been to prison.

"Oh no," I thought, "I'm gonna have to go through all the same rigmarole that I went through at St Thomas's, and this time without the support of my brothers and sisters." Some lads were all right but others were bullyboys, especially with me being so little. Just like at junior school I got into many fights and, sadly, I lost most of them. Still, I gave a good account of myself so gradually the taunting began to dwindle.

I gradually made a new friend called Peter Neary, who lived in the Able Street area on the other side of town to Trafalgar. We became bosom buddies and this helped me to settle down a little. But, I still longed to be with all my other mates at St Mary's.

One teacher I liked was the Art teacher Mr Barton. But the irony of it was that I missed a lot of his classes because I had to attend the speech training clinic every Thursday afternoon. I'd attended the clinic for two years now and, although the lady in charge of my training was very kind with infinite patience, it was slow progress. This remained a constant worry to Mam."

My impediment had got into many scrapes at St. Thomas's School and the problem seemed to have followed me to Towneley. One incident that I won't forget in a hurry concerned a big well toned lad called Steven, who was a good footballer. As it happened he had the same affliction as me. It caused a ruction one day as we were getting dressed in the pavilion after a game of football.

"That were a good game John," said Stephen, "I weally enjoyed it … did you?"

"Yeah I did," I replied, "it wer' weally good."

Without any warning he took a swing at me and called me a 'fly little git'! I immediately reacted but got the worst of it because he wasn't just a good footballer … he was a good fighter too. Luckily for me the fight was stopped by one of the teachers.

"What's going on here?" bawled the sport's master as he towered over us, "I won't allow fighting in my class. Now tell me … what started it?"

"Well Sir," stammered Steven, "he was in the wong … he was taking the mickey out o' me 'cos I can't pronounce my R's wite."

A little smile crept to the corner of the teacher's mouth. He was aware of my affliction and obviously found the situation rather funny.

"Oh … u-um, I see," he muttered not really knowing what to say, "I think Steven there is something you ought to know."

After being informed Steven was a little embarrassed but then he saw the funny side and started to laugh. He held out his hand and apologised. I was only too glad to accept his apology; I didn't fancy being on the wrong side of this strapping lad. We both ended up laughing and were on friendly terms thereafter; it was good to have made another friend.

The speech training sessions continued throughout all my first year at Towneley. Each session lasted for a full hour and the lady therapist employed many different methods to improve my speech.

One of these was to place an inflated balloon in between both our faces. "Now put your lips up against the balloon John," she would say, "and I'll do the same and make some funny sounds so that you can feel the vibrations." One of these sounds was the strong trilling Scottish' 'r-r-r-r-r,' sound rolling the r's from the back of her throat followed by the sentence, "I ran the rugged rascals around the rugged rocks."

I couldn't get my tongue around these guttural sounds at all and, when asked to repeat the test, it always came out as " 'w-w-w-w-w,' and I wan the wugged wascals awound the wugged rocks."

The sessions went on like this for almost three years until one day I finally managed to make the 'r-r-r-r-r' trilling sound. It wasn't very good at first but the kind lady further encouraged me, "That's it John, you've got it ... all you need to do now is practise." From then on it was uphill all the way. My confidence grew and, much to my delight and also my mother's, I never again ever had any trouble pronouncing my Rs. The dedicated training of the speech therapist had its desired effect. In fact, to this day, due to the specific training, I probably pronounce my 'R's better than most folk.

****

During my four years at Towneley School I hardly grew and was the smallest in the class and still wore short pants. Because of my size I got nicknamed 'Bimbo', a popular song in the charts at the time sung by Jim Reeves.

We had lots of homework to do at Towneley but because Dad didn't help in this aspect I became very unsettled; rather than encourage me to study he did the opposite. Night after night he made his disapproval quite clear as I tried to do my homework on the end of the sideboard.

"What are you doing cluttering up the house with all them books our John," he rapped, "what have I told thí about bringing schoolwork into t'house? You should do that at school before you come home."

"But Dad," I protested, "I can't … we're not allowed. Anyroad, all mí classmates get homework that they've got to do at home."

"I'm not bothered about anybody else, I don't want thí' to bring any into this house."

"Bloomin' 'eck Dad, I'm struggling with French as it is … I'll get in bother if I don't hand it in tomorrow."

"French," he yelled, "what d'you need to learn a foreign language for anyroad, you're never gonna use it?"

I constantly tried to get my point across but to no avail. Things didn't change much and this affected my studies; consequently I lost interest and this became apparent in my results.

The French teacher was called Mr Fox and he wasn't very impressed with me. But it was understandable as my results were appalling … in the Christmas exams I got a paltry three-percent. He was also the geography teacher and I didn't fare any better in this topic. I think Dad's attitude rubbed off onto me, the way I saw it … I would never leave Burnley, so what was the point of learning a foreign language or the whereabouts of this or that particular country. Mr Fox's displeasure was self-evident as he severely scolded me in front of the entire class on numerous occasions. Even as a lad though, I readily understood why he felt like he did towards me because the way I saw it, my poor results were reflecting back on him.

Looking back over the years I can honestly say that the four years I spent at Towneley School were the saddest years of my life. I didn't let it affect my free time but for most of my school hours I was completely miserable with a cloud looming over my head. It wasn't just that I missed my old mates or the barbed comments from my new peers and the fact that my own father was unsupportive of me. No, it went much deeper than that ... my education suffered terribly. Because of my slow progress, some of the school masters were very cruel to me mentally and the main culprit was the deputy headmaster, Mr Redhead.

As the years passed my results didn't improve. It wasn't only in French and geography that I faired badly at either; my favourite subject suffered too ... mathematics. I couldn't understand why other lads in the class, who I knew were no better than me at this subject, got much higher marks than I did for their homework. I didn't realise that their parents must have been encouraging them, and maybe helping them with their studies. The maths teacher, Mr Redhead, really took me to task because of my poor marks and constantly ridiculed me in front of the class. Compared to Mr Redhead, Mr Fox was a gentleman. Within five or so minutes of entering Mr Redhead's classroom, he would make a beeline for me and the tormenting would begin. Certain lads would get him going on how Burnley Football Club had faired the previous weekend. Although I knew of players like Tommy Cummings I wasn't all that interested in how the team was fairing in the league and I hardly knew the names of other players. He'd ask me questions like, "How did Burnley go on Saturday - Who scored the goals - Who are they playing next week?" When I couldn't answer he'd ridicule me in front of the class, much to the pleasure of my peers. I'd mention that I wasn't in his class to learn about football but he'd just scoff and say something like, "Well what would you like to talk to me about because you're certainly useless at Mathematics. It's no wonder that all the lads nicknamed you Bimbo... it suits you." This created an immediate reaction from my class mates rendering me into a submissive state. He seemed to derive sheer pleasure out of taunting me. Consequently, much to his shame, I never learned anything in his class. One particular incident that has remained with me throughout my entire life (I am now eighty one years of age) occurred after I found a set of field gauges on my way to school. I didn't know what it was, but to me it looked like a small pen-knife. The difference was that when I tried opening the blades, some were very flimsy, almost as thin as paper. I didn't realise the fragile blades, for want of another name, were used for checking and adjusting the timing set-up on a car. I didn't think any more about it and just put the object into my pocket. My big mistake was placing it on my desk after entering Mr Redhead's class. After settling down he made his usual beeline for me, but on this occasion he took on a different format.

"What's this," he sneered as he picked up the set of field gauges, "what have we here then?"

"I don't know what it is sir," I answered, "I think it's some sort of pen-knife."

"Pen-knife!" he scoffed. "You know very well what it is you little thief! Now where did you get it?"

"I'm not a thief sir, I found it on Parliament Street on my way to school this morning and I don't know what it is."

"Found it, that's a good one!" he scoffed all the more, bearing down onto me. "The next thing you'll be telling me is you found it on your dad's rag cart." To my cost this remark had all my classmates in stitches as they roared in bouts of laughter. They couldn't contain themselves much to the delight of Mr Redhead. He got a great kick out of thinking he was a comedian at my expense. That was bad enough but, to add insult to injury, he came out with another cruel cutting comment. "The way you're going lad, you'll probably end up in prison like your dad!"

Despite feeling both humiliated and intimidated, I managed to mumble under bated breath, "My dad's better than you are. Any road, I'm going to report you."

I didn't think he'd heard me, but he had, *"You're going to report me are you, you stupid insolent boy!* You need a lesson in manners, now get out of my sight," he roared in a vile contemptuous voice, "and go and stand in the corridor 'til the end of the lesson and I'll deal with you later."

In embarrassment I slunk out of the classroom with my head bowed. I stood all alone in the corridor feeling totally dejected. During my loneliness I pondered on what had gone on in the classroom and how I'd threatened to report him. I was in the right but my confidence was at rock bottom. "Would the headmaster, Mr Lancaster, take my word against the word of the highly respected deputy headmaster, Mr Redhead?" I knew that there were plenty of witnesses to back up my story, but felt that none of my classmates would be over keen to support me. Still, I was determined to carry out my threat. After what seemed an age the lesson ended and the lads started to file out of class. I stood my ground expecting to hear a lot of jeering and barbed comments, but this didn't happen. In fact, it was just the opposite. Most of the lads patted me on the shoulder saying," Alright John, see you later in the schoolyard."

One lad especially assured me I'd be alright and that was Bram Etherington.

As it turned out, after I'd left the classroom, Mr Redhead, must have realised he'd overstepped the mark and was troubled with afterthought. Or should I say he was frightened to death of getting into trouble. He called me back into class and didn't actually apologise for what he'd said and done but he handed me back the set of field gauges.

"Here you are," he said, "you can have these back. I've been thinking about it and maybe you are telling the truth. Anyway, I've decided to give you the benefit of the doubt."

I didn't reply, I couldn't be bothered. He was actually acting as though it was me who was in the wrong and he was letting it go this time. I found out later from a Bram Etherington that, after I'd left the classroom, he'd gone into a rather quiet mode. Also he'd addressed the class and told them not to pick on me because of my home conditions. What he was really doing was covering his backside in case of any repercussion. On being dismissed I decided to let the matter drop, as I knew it could cause me more hassle in the future. But the thought did go through my head that this was a man whom I was supposed to look upon as my mentor, a person to look up to, respect and gain knowledge from. No matter what he thought about my background, my mother had always taught me to act respectfully to grown ups and especially so to teachers, doctors and the like. But now, as far as I was concerned, I'd lost all respect for this man. Hence, sadly to say, for the remaining time of my schooling my mathematics skills did not improve at all.

Ironically, in my adult life I became very good at mathematics as my natural abilities surfaced. Also as far as foreign languages are concerned I attended Preston University and became fluent in Spanish and also obtained GCSE level in French. And Mr Fox would also like to know that I have since visited many countries all over the world and my geography skills have improved dramatically.

****

One thing that I did like at Towneley was that it had a great big gymnasium geared up with wall bars, vaulting horses, balance beams, climbing ropes and other equipment.

The teacher in charge of physical training was called Mr Saul. He wasn't very tall and had a slim physique. But, despite his appearance he was in peak condition. He could easily walk the length of the gymnasium on his hands and he excelled on every piece of apparatus in the large hall. He quite impressed me with his vigour and enthusiasm in everything he did.

"He's only small," I thought to myself, "but it doesn't seem to bother him ... he really looks like he can handle himself."

Mr Saul was a pleasant easy-going man but asserted his authority and instilled discipline into the class when necessary. This became evident one day when a very big lad refused to do as he was told and started getting stroppy. However, it didn't last long; Mr Saul sorted him out in no time at all and put him in his place.

I liked this man and from then on took a definite interest in gymnastics. And, like my mentor, I became very skilful at walking on my hands.

****

Despite being singled out by many kids at Towneley I still loved going out on the rag-cart with Dad, and especially looking after Peggy, our horse. So during the school holidays I spent most of my leisure time with Dad.

"Come along with me our John," he'd say, "and I'll teach you the tricks o' the trade ... you're better off learning the ropes from an early age. Aye, you never know, you'll be able to ték o'er from me when I'm past it."

However, Dad had an ulterior motive. Every morning he'd send me off to the stable to feed Peggy and muck out the stable. The first thing I did was to feed Peggy and fill her water trough. When she'd finished I'd put on her bridle and bit, then lead her outside where she could graze in a small compound. Meanwhile I mucked out the stable and put all the manure onto a compost heap at the side of the stable. I then scattered fresh straw onto the stone cobbled floor to make Peggy comfortable. I actually found the job quite interesting and all the more so, as there were many garden allotments round about; consequently, lots of people would come for manure to use as fertilizer for their crops. For this small service, I charged between thrépence and sixpence per bag, which was on top of what my dad gave me; everything went towards my spending money.

If Dad happened to be working I'd dress Peggy in all her working regalia: bridle and bit, blinkers, collar with harness, breeching, girth and crupper before finally attaching her to the cart. I'd then jump on board, take to the reins and proudly drive her home. This suited Dad fine, as it gave him ample time to have a brew and a bite to eat before setting off for work.

Consequently, he always showed his approval, "Eh thanks cock, you're a grand lad and doing a great job."

However, Mam wasn't so approving, "Never mind he's doing a great job Jack!" she'd snap at him. "What you really mean is he's giving you another hour in bed!"

But Mam!" I always protested, "I like going with Dad on the cart and I love looking after Peggy ... honest!" It was true; I was never prouder than when I was driving the cart through the streets or riding Peggy bareback when taking her to the blacksmith's to be re-shod. I felt like my favourite characters, Hoppalong Cassidy, Johnny MacBrown or Roy Rogers as Peggy trotted along. And besides, I had an ulterior motive; I liked to show off in front of my mates.

Dad mainly dealt in scrap-iron, but he sometimes went out 'ragging' and this could be quite lucrative too. As he guided Peggy through the back-streets of the many terraced houses he would shout in a drawled out voice, "Rag-bone ... rag-bone, any old rags for donkey stones!"

Often people would come to the backyard gate and hand over a bundle of rags and other items. It was my job to hand out a white stone or yellow stone, whichever they preferred. Others would simply leave the bundle on the backyard wall and I would exchange these for a donkey stone. I always left them a white stone unless they'd specifically left a note requesting a yellow one.

One day a funny incident happened. It was a nice sunny day and we were working the back-streets of Trafalgar. Being a show-off I felt quite chuffed as Dad let me steer Peggy through the many cobbled streets. I loved taking charge of the horse and cart, but even more so in my neck o' the woods.

"Stop at the next back-street in between the Ribble Garage and Gresham Place our John," said Dad, "we'll start here."

"Whoa Peggy ... that's a good girl!" I said exaggerating my voice so as to draw attention to myself from two passing lads.

"Right our John," mumbled Dad as he backed Peggy up the back-street, "get the bag o' donkey stones and let's get cracking! "Rag-bone ... rag-bone ....!"

He usually backed the cart about halfway up the back-street but on this occasion he couldn't, as some workmen had had dug deep trenches and there were heaps of stone cobbles, clay and rubble scattered about.

"Watch out Dad," I warned him as he guided Peggy up narrow passageway, "there's great big hole in the back-street and there's a load of stone cobbles all over the place."

"Aye I know, I can see 'em ... I'm not blind yet thá knows. Anyroad, don't hang about our John; pick up them bundles o' rags and leave 'em a donkey stone." There were three bundles of rags, some old dresses and two donkey jackets. By the time we got back to the cart we had a sack full of rags.

"Get another sack from the back o' the cart our John," said Dad, "and sort out the woollens from t'other rags."

"Why's that Dad?"

"Why? Because I get paid a lot more for woollens than I do for cotton rags ... that's why?" he rapped impatiently.

"All reight Dad ... I only asked, I'll know in't future."

"That'll do ... I want none of your lip!"

We carried on working the back-streets of Patten Street, Albion Street, Rowley Street and Whitaker Street. We didn't stop for a brew at our house because Mam didn't approve; she didn't like the stigma attached to the rag-cart. By the time we'd reached Sandygate there was a mountainous heap of rags loaded on the cart.

"U-um, we've done well our John," grinned Dad feeling pleased with himself, "we might as well make tracks for Reader's Rag-shop down Sandygate."

We were just turning right at Sandygate Junction by the side of Sandygate Youth Club when we heard some blokes shouting frantically from the other side of the road.

"What the bloody hell aya playin' at?" bellowed one in an angry voice." Tha's gone and nicked our jackets!"

As it happened they were council workers, replacing damaged drains on Gresham Place back-street.

"Oh 'eck," I thought, "them donkey jackets musta been theirs!"

"Flamin' emma man!" exclaimed one of the men. "We'd only been away two minutes having a brew ... what the bloody hell d'you think you're playin' at?"

Luckily, Dad sorted it out amicably. After explaining what had happened we had a good laugh about it. Mind you, Dad wasn't too happy about having to unload half the cart to get to the right sack.

"Never mind eh," he laughed afterwards, "it's still bín a good day our John."

"Yeah it has Dad," I agreed, "and it'll be a good tale to tell t'others when we get home."

There were many funny incidents like this whilst working with Dad and that's why I liked it. I also enjoyed going with him to the many weaving sheds where he made deals with the different managers to collect scrap-iron.

But there was one aspect of it that I didn't like. It was after he'd weighed in the scrap-iron and collected his money. Just around the corner from Reeder's Scrap-yard was Dad's favourite pub ... the Salford Hotel. Ironically, Peggy would go into automatic pilot ... without being prompted she'd trot merrily away the short distance and always stop abruptly outside the pub.

"Oh no Dad," I moaned, "you're not going in there again are you ... you'll be ages?"

"Off course I am, it looks like Peggy needs a break." he joked.

"Oh aye, any excuse Dad. But promise you won't be a long time."

"Eh cock, don't knock it!" he replied critically. "This is where I mék a few o' mi' deals... lots o' them factory owners go in here and I've got to keep 'em buttered up an' sweet. Like I keep tellin' you our John ... you've got to speculate to accumulate."

"Speculate to accumulate Dad?" I replied. "That's your favourite saying, but I can't see how it works in this pub."

"Whaddaya talkin' about lad ... how do you mean?"

"Well, everytime I peep in through the door you seem to be throwing your money away buying drinks all around the pub for a load o' boozers."

"See, there you go again, you don't know what you're talkin' about ... I have a lot of good connections in there."

"All right Dad, maybe some of 'em are mill owners who you make deals with, but most of 'em are just plain boozers."

"Aye that may be so, but I've got to appear generous to keep up appearances ... d'you know what I mean?"

"Yeah all reight Dad, but if you can spend so freely on them ... how come it always causes ructions at home when mí mam asks you for some housekeeping money?"

"All reight our John, that'll do!" he rapped. "You're geddin' a bit near to the bone now ... I don't want any cheek off thí."

"U-um, all right Dad ... but promise you won't be so long this time."

"Yeah, right lad ... I promise, I promise."

Promise or not, he was full of false assurances. He meant what he said when he said it ... but I knew that once he got inside the pub he would take some shifting.

Consequently, I prepared myself for a long wait. I hated it but I had nobody to blame but myself, it was my own fault ... I always went with Dad of my own choosing. On the other hand, Peggy loved the respite she got from these hold-ups. During these situations I stroked her forehead and talked to her for hours on end.

"Yeah Peggy, you enjoy it when we get here don't you? Aye," I'd laugh, "you know where to come all right when we leave Reeder's Scrapyard."

"Whinne-ey," she'd respond nodding her head as if she understood every word I was saying. I became very fond of her and her of me ... especially with me feeding and looking after her. Even so, Dad was her favourite and she made it quite clear by whinnying happily the moment he came out of the pub.

I could always tell whether Dad had made a good deal by the look on his face. This particular day he came out of the pub sporting a broad smile.

"What did I tell thí lad, I've just méd a cracking deal with one o' them boozers as you put it. It'll ték me two days next week to pick up all the scrap-iron from his mill. And," he said chuckling to himself, "I got it for a song. Like I said afore our John, it's not what you know in business, it's who you know ... it's what you call wheels within wheels. So think on ... don't knock it in't future."

"Yeah reighto Dad," I replied having to agree with him, "I put mí hand up."

Nonetheless, most days he'd come staggering out of the pub hardly able to stand up.

"Oh no," I'd grumble to myself, "it looks like I'm gonna have to ték him home again before I drive Peggy back to the stable." I'd help him onto the cart and then take him as far as the bottom of Albion Street. I always dropped him outside the Trafalgar Pub and pointed him in the right direction. This gave him a little time to sober up as he tottered up the steep incline. Once he'd reached Maggie Astin's house I'd jump onto the cart and head for the stable. Mind you, I'm sure that Peggy could have made it home on her own ... she certainly knew the way. On the way back to the stable she never failed to make me laugh. To reach the stable yard she had to pull the cart up a short steep cobbled street, which ran from Marlborough Street to Rumley Road. When she got to within fifty yards of the short street she'd pick up momentum to almost galloping speed to give herself a good run up the steep incline. Once she had reached the level on Rumley Road she would then settle back to a gentle walk.

"Ha ha," I would laugh, "you're a clever horse Peggy ...you certainly knew what wer' coming."

****

One fine sunny day, during school holidays, I was about to set off for the stable when our Mary asked if she could come with me.

"You can if you want our Mary but it's not all fun and games, and it can be quite hard and mucky."

"That's all right," she replied, "I'm not frightened of hard work and a bit of muck; I'd still like to come if I can."

"Yeah right, fair enough, let's go then."

When we reached the stable, Mary wanted to feed Peggy. I agreed but first gave her a few basic instructions, "Before you actually go up to the trough our kid, just talk to Peggy and pat her a little to let her know you're there and especially if you approach her on her left blind side."

Mary was fearless and soon got the hang of it, tending to Peggy's needs, whilst I did the mucking out.

"You're doin' all right our Mary," I remarked, "Peggy seems to like you."

"She does doesn't she," replied Mary as she gently brushed Peggy's mane." Animals can sense when somebody likes 'em."

"They can that, that's for sure," I agreed as I forked some manure into a wheelbarrow. "Anyway our kid, when you've finished groomin' her, can you take her outside so she can browse in the sunshine."

Peggy was idly grazing in the paddock when a gang of unruly boys and girls came into the grounds and began making abusive remarks,

"Oh it's the rag tatters," shouted one of them and they all started jeering.

To Mary it was tantamount to a declaration of war and she was raving; her eyes narrowed and her fists clenched.

I remained calm though, reassuring her, "Take no notice of 'em our kid, they come round here regularly, ignore 'em and they'll go away."

It may well have been good advice but Mary was having none of it, she instinctively retaliated, "You bloomin' cowards you're nowt else!" she shrieked. "It's easy to be like that when there's a lot of you, you wouldn't be so brave if it was one onto one would you?"

"Oh bloomin' 'eck," I thought, "that's done it," as I knew only too well that one of the girls was notorious for fighting.

The girl, who was quite well built and slightly taller than Mary, stepped forward asking, "Oh you fancy your chances do you … how about having a go at me then?"

"What, just you and me, or will all your mates join in as well?" Mary responded.

The girl weighed Mary up and down, and started laughing.

She looked back at her friends, who in turn started yelling, "Go on Nellie, get stuck into her, you'll murder her!"

I was on guard but wasn't over concerned because although the girl was bigger than our Mary in body, I knew she wouldn't match up to her in spirit. I also knew that in spite of being outnumbered, it wasn't the done thing for friends to join in when it was a straight one to one fight. Sure enough the fight started but from the outset, it was clear that Mary had the upper hand, there was no contest; they didn't even roll on the floor. Mary fought like a boy lashing out with her fists. After being knocked to the ground a couple of times, and receiving a busted nose, the girl gave up.

But it wasn't the end of the saga, because then one of the lads began to taunt me, "All right pal, so your sister's a good fighter; but it looks to me like she's gotta fight your battles as well!"

I quietly backed off, refusing to be drawn in, "I don't want any truck with you, I think it's best that you all go now."

Some hopes, for having just seen one fight, the unruly crowd was now all fired up and raring to see another; so they all started jeering, encouraging their mate on.

By now, Mary was getting riled up again and she prompted me to retaliate, "Go on our kid, you're a good fighter, you can take him on easy."

I still tried to play the situation down, "That's not the point our Mary, I just don't want to fight."

But I had little choice in the matter, as the lad pounced on me knocking me to the ground. However, even though I didn't want to fight I was quite prepared and on my guard. We rolled about on the floor for a little while but being quite nimble and strong with lots of stamina, I soon overpowered the lad. Despite what had gone on though, I didn't want to hurt him, so merely held him in a vice like head-lock; nevertheless, the boy, not wanting to lose face in front of his friends, kept struggling and striking out. I sensed that this could go on indefinitely and so I dragged him over to the horse trough and dipped his head in it. This didn't work either, as it infuriated the lad even more.

Still, I was in control and quietly whispered into his ear, "Right pal, this has gone far enough, I'm telling you now, if you don't give up, then the next time it won't be the water trough that I'll dunk you in ... it'll be the horse muck!" He still refused to back down but as I dragged him closer to the compost heap, it became obvious that he was onto a loser, so he reluctantly gave up.

"All right, all right," he blurted, "fair enough I give in, you win!" After that, we both shook hands and that was the end of it.

Whilst the crowd were commiserating amongst themselves one of them asked me, "Hey pal, is that your horse then?"

"Yeah it is, why?"

"Well, I was just wondering, is there any chance o' givin' us a ride?"

I was unsure but Mary didn't miss a trick, "Come on our John, why not ... at thrépence a time?"

"Hey you're right there our Mary ... why not?"

Before we knew it, there were plenty of kids shouting, "Yeah, I want a ride as well!" Because of all the noise and goings on, many other kids had gathered around and they too eagerly took up the same cry, **"I want a ride as well!"**

Mary, being a right little organiser took command, "Look everybody, you can all have a go but you'll have to form a queue." She took charge of collecting the money whilst I took the reins and guided the paying passengers around the paddock. Thrépence a time for just two rides around the yard with all the kids yelling for more; what a day, what a killing; even Peggy enjoyed it. It would have been even better but for being stopped by a rather big rough looking bloke, who was in charge of the stables.

I was just leading Peggy off when I heard the bloke bellowing in Lancashire twang, "What the flamin' 'eck's goin' on here, and what the bloody hell atta doing wí that hós?"

"It's nowt to do with you," retorted our Mary, "it's mi' dad's horse."

"Oh it's nowt to do wí me is it not? I'll giv' thí it's tha dad's hós; get the bugger back in stable now afore I kicks tha' arses for thí!"

I informed Mary that the bloke really was in charge of the stables, so we reluctantly had to do as we were told.

Never mind, look on the bright side our Mary," I laughed, "we haven't done too badly have we?"

She chuckled, "Aye, you're right there our John, it's bín a great day an'it?"

The rather large man watched over us until we'd put Peggy back in the stable, and after locking the stable door he bellowed, "Now ged outa here and don't come back I'm warnin' thí! Aye, and don't think I won't tell tha' dad 'cos I bloody well will!"

But we weren't bothered about that, as we happily walked home with our pockets bulging with money.

Dad did get to know about the incident but he wasn't too concerned; in fact, quite the opposite, he rather enjoyed the tale we had to tell and the way we'd used our initiative.

"I'm not bothered about you giving the kids a ride," he said, "cós at least it gave Peggy a bit of exercise, and I'm sure that she would have enjoyed it too; I'm only mad that I didn't think o' doing it myself."

****

Another thing I enjoyed was swimming. Dad had taken me to the Central Swimming Baths at a very early age and I'd taken to the water from the word go. Mary was also a great swimmer and swam for the town team, but she couldn't beat me ... if she could have I'd never have lived it down.

One particular incident sticks out in my mind. It was a scorcher of a day with brilliant sunshine. Loads of little kids were on the front street, poking fingers into gas-tar in-between the stone cobbles. I was pondering on how I used to do exactly the same thing when I was a little lad.

"U-um," I smiled, "many's the time I've had a good hiding for doin' that."

Just then Jack Lofthouse interrupted my thoughts shouting from the bottom of the street, "All reight Johnny, it's a crackin' day to go for a swim ... what d'you think?"

"You're not kidding Jack," I replied enthusiastically, "I'd love to go swimmin' but I aint got any trunks."

"What do we need trunks for ... how about goin' swimmin' in that water tank on the top o' Trafalgar Mill?"

"U-um I don't know Jack, we'd be in real bother if we got caught up there."

"Oh come on ... don't be so bloomin' soft. Anyroad, when has that ever stopped us from doing ow't afore?"

I never could resist Jack's persuasive ways and anyway, the thought of the cool water beckoned me, "Aye all reight then," I shouted down the street, "I'm gam' if you are."

So off we went. The first part, getting into the loft space of the mill, was easy ... we'd done it many times before just for the fun of it. The second stage was much more difficult and dangerous, having to scramble up onto the roof, and then climb a steel ladder, which was fixed to the stone walls of a tall square tower. But on reaching the top our reward was great. The tank was full and the water just invited us to jump in. Both of us stripped down to our pants and dived in. We both thoroughly enjoyed ourselves floating about on our backs, soaking up the afternoon sun. By now we had become complacent, all fear of being discovered forgotten; we actually got cocky and that was our undoing. We both climbed up onto the Trafalgar side of the water tank and started to show off by shouting down at passing lads.

"Hey down there ... why don't you come up here for a swim, it's bloomin' great!" It didn't take long for a crowd of eager lads to gather below and start shouting excitedly back up at us.

As it happened, a lady was just coming out of the Co-op shop and she was horrified to see our legs dangling over the sides of the tall tower. Without hesitation she crossed over Trafalgar, went to a police telephone box at the side of the footbridge, and called for the Fire Brigade.

Within minutes the Brigade arrived and a telescopic ladder was soon in action reaching up towards us. Jack attempted to climb back down the steel ladder but a fireman bellowed up to him through a loudspeaker warning him not to do so.

By now the crowd had swollen, including lots of adults. All the attention we were receiving from the cheering kids made Jack and me feel good ... even important. However, our pleasure was short-lived ... we were both taken to the Police Station where we got severely reprimanded. That wasn't the end of the matter either ... we both got a good hiding when we got back home. It didn't put us off though; in our future years, Jack and I enjoyed many more escapades together.

****

Like me, most of the local kids enjoyed swimming. Many would go to Gannow, North Street or Padiham Baths where they had diving boards. In the summer months we frequented Nelson Open Air Swimming Pool. Other favourite places were Hacking Boat Ferry, near Whalley and the 'Sheepdip' near to Hapton Valley Colliery. This was a deep basin in the riverbed overlooked by a high rock. Kids dived off a high rock into the murky depths just missing underwater rocks by inches. Our Mary was a right daredevil regularly doing the dangerous stunt to show off to her mates; but this came to an abrupt halt one day when a lad was badly hurt needing about thirty stitches to a deep gash in his forehead.

Despite warnings, many kids would go for a dip in the Leeds and Liverpool Canal, known locally as the 'Cut' and come out of the over-polluted water stinking of factory waste or decomposing dead dogs.

Water always had a strange attraction, drawing kids to it whether for swimming or fishing. Around Burnley, official outdoor swimming places were non-existent. This was the main reason why kids chose to swim in the Cut, the Sheep-dip, the mill towers and other murky places. One notorious place was Lowerhouse Lodge. It was a dangerous place where many a child had drowned, but this didn't deter the kids. They wanted to swim and swim they would despite the consequences.

Another murky place, in fact downright filthy, was Clifton Lodge. But this didn't put children off … all they were interested in was enjoying themselves. A rubbish tip surrounded the lodge where lots of kids would forage for fag packets and comics. They didn't often swim in this dirty water but many would venture onto it using make-do rafts or anything else floatable.

One day our Jimmy and his mate Victor Thompson made a raft from an old backyard gate, which they'd re-enforced with old wooden joists from a demolition site. As they set off for the lodge carrying the make do raft they saw me on Trafalgar and invited me along.

"D'you want to come with us our kid?" asked Jimmy. "We're gonna sail this on Clifton Lodge?" Unwittingly I went along, trusting them both implicitly. Mam had just bought me a new pair of pants.

"Now think on our John," she'd warned me, "make sure you change your pants before you go playing out." When Jimmy and Victor asked me to join them, it never entered my mind to get changed.

On reaching the lodge we launched the makeshift raft and then attempted to board it. Victor was the first to embark and I followed. It became evident that it wouldn't take any more weight, as it floated precariously on top of the water. We'd attached a long rope to the raft and Jimmy's task was to pull us into the shore in case of any trouble. To cast off Victor shoved against the bank with a pole creating a pushing motion, moving the raft outwards into the lodge. We thoroughly enjoyed ourselves, but then came the time to be pulled back to the shore.

"All reight Jimmy," bellowed Victor, "we've had enough now ... pull us back in!"

"Reighto Vic, here goes." Without further ado, he picked up the rope and started pulling.

"Whoa, hang on a bit Jimmy ... the ropes got tangled under one o' the joists!" shouted Victor.

Jimmy didn't hear or at least he didn't seem to ... he just kept on pulling. The raft started to tilt a little and both of us tried shifting our weight to rectify it. This added to the problem, causing the raft to tilt to the other side. Victor lost his balance and plunged into the filthy water and I went tumbling in after him. There wasn't any danger of drowning as we were both good swimmers ... but that wasn't the problem.

"Oh no," I moaned on reaching the bank, "mi mam'll go mad when I get home ... I've ruined mí best pants!"

Victor, concerned that he too would be in bother, conjured up a story.

"Listen John, if we go home like this we're forrit ... we'll both get a good hidin'. But if we say that you fell in and I dived in to rescue you, we might get away with it."

"I can't see that Vic … mi mam's not daft and she knows I'm a good swimmer."

"Yeah I know, but if I say that I thought you'd hurt yourself and you were struggling … she might believe that."

"Aye all right," I agreed, "I suppose owt's worth trying."

I didn't have a lot of confidence in our scam, but to my surprise it worked. Both parents fell for it … in fact, Victor was treated like a hero. His dad even thought of going to the Burnley Express for a write up and some kind of commendation. It's just as well that the truth never came to light; we'd have both got a commendation all right … right around the lug-hole!

****

One day I did something very stupid that almost cost me my life, and all because of a silly dare. Many a lad had done it before me and, being cocksure that I could easily do it, I accepted the challenge … *to swim through the Gannow Tunnel.*

"It's only about a quarter of a mile," I thought, "I should be able to swim that far. Yeah why not … I can easily swim thirty-six-lengths of the Gannow Baths so I should be able to make it through the tunnel without any trouble."

In order to carry out the swim, two lads needed to stand on guard, one at each end of the tunnel to ward off any barges. I dived into the murky water and set off into the darkness of the grimy tunnel full of confidence. It was a scorcher of a day but what I hadn't taken into account was the temperature of the water inside the tunnel … it was absolutely freezing. After about two hundred yards I was chilled to the bone and began to realise my foolishness … the little speck of light ahead was much smaller than the one behind me.

"Oh blow this for a tale, I'm going back … sod the bet," I muttered to myself. Then suddenly I became frightened aware now of my predicament and the danger I was in. Bizarre thoughts started to go through my head, "What if a barge comes through ... that's my lot. Oh I hope there's no rats in here ... I never gave it a thought before I set off."

Then to make matters worse ... I got cramp. I tried swimming back towards the light but had to stop and cling onto the nicks in between the large stones forming the tunnel sides. There was a small lip jutting out but it was nigh impossible to cling onto it, as it was full of slime, making it slippy.

"I'll have to rest," I thought, "I'll stand on the bottom." That didn't work either because the water was too deep. In my stricken state I swallowed some water almost choking. In a way this brought me to my senses making me take control of the situation.

"Come on John lad, you can do it," I encouraged myself, "don't panic whatever you do!" I then added a little prayer, "*Please God, help me in my plight, let me get out of this tunnel and I promise You I'll never do ow't like this ever again.*"

I couldn't swim properly but I managed to float on my back and moved slowly along by paddling with my hands. Eventually, after what seemed like hours, I made it through the tunnel and back to safety. Luckily I was none the worse for my experience albeit a lot wiser ... I never ever attempted the foolish escapade again.

****

Bonfire night was one time the neighbourhood kids looked forward to. The main priority for lads was collecting wood for the fire. We were all determined to have the best bonfire in the district and went to great lengths collecting wood from wherever we could. Many a time we'd finish up fighting with the kids from King Street after raiding their stockpile of wood, or vice- versa. Some of us used old rusty saws to cut branches from trees in Piccadilly Gardens, and if we were lucky we obtained some logs from a timber yard on Stanley Street.

One aspect we enjoyed was the run up to bonfire night, as this gave us the opportunity to go singing from door to door and earn some money to buy fireworks. Another way to make money was to take out a Guy Fawke's and stand outside shops or pubs.

On one occasion Barbara, Barry and Rose Clarke wanted to do this but they didn't have a guy.

"I'll tell you what Barbara," said Rose, "you dress up in some old clothes and me and Barry'll go with you."

"Yeah all right," Barbara agreed, "but I'm not gonna walk through the Town Centre in tatty clothes."

"It doesn't matter," said Barry, "we've no need to go down town … we can stand outside that photographer's window at th'end of Trafalgar on't corner of Manchester Road."

"Good idea," said Rose, "there's loads o' people around there all the time."

Off they went and were faring quite well and made about 2 shillings in just a short time.

"This is great," enthused Rose, "we'll be rich if we stay here for another hour."

However, their little scheme came to an end when they were told to move on by a passing policeman.

"Come on you two young úns, you can't stay here blockin' the pavement," he said, "take your guy and be on your way." He got the shock of his life when Barbara got up and started following them.

"That wer' great weren't it," quipped Rose, "did you see the look on that bobby's face?"

"Yeah, it wer' really funny," laughed Barry, "I can't wait to get home to tell t'others."

But it was a different story and not so funny when David Whittaker, Kenny Clayton and I decided to do the same.

"You're best dressing up Kenny, you'll mék the best guy," said David. "Whaddaya think John?"

"Hey never mind I'll mék the best guy," rapped Kenny, "why don't one of you do it?"

"No, David's right Kenny," I said, "you'll definitely be the best."

After a bit of deliberation Kenny agreed but with conditions, "Aye all reight, I suppose so ... but we're splitting th'money three ways."

"Oh yeah," replied David, "that's only fair."

So after out little discussion Kenny got dressed up in a load of rags and really looked the part.

"Bloomin' 'eck Kenny you look great," said David, "especially with all that straw stickin' out o' that rag cap. Come on, let's get going ... we should mék a bomb!" Sure enough, Kenny raised a few eyebrows from passers-by as we walked along Trafalgar.

"Reighto Kenny," said David handing him a mask, "now for the final touch ... afore you sit down put this on."

That did it; I burst out laughing, "E-eh, I'll tell thí what Kenny ... you're the best guy I've ever seen!"

It didn't take long before the pennies started rolling in as grown-ups commented on what a good job we had made of our guy. Everything was going great until three teenage bullyboys interfered. They were big lads, about seventeen years of age, all dressed up to go dancing. I spotted them first coming down Manchester Road.

"Keep still Kenny, ther's three men comin'," I mumbled, "they're just walking past th'Education Office now."

As they drew closer David approached them, "Please have yá got a penny for the guy mister?"

"A penny for the bleedin' guy," snarled the first one, "how about givin' me somét for a pint you cheeky little swine!" Then something very sinister happened!

"How about a bit o' football practice," joked the second one, "let's see if we can kick the flamin' guy's head off?" Without further coaxing he took a run and kicked poor Kenny in the face. Another one was going to do the same until he saw Kenny stand up, crying.

"Flamin' Nora, it's not a guy," said one of them panic-stricken, "it's a real lad!" On realising their mistake, rather than care for the young boy, the cowardly youths went scampering down Manchester Road. Luckily, Kenny wasn't badly injured but he had a cut lip and a great big bruise on his right cheek. It wasn't funny at the time, but we had a good laugh about it later.

Finally on bonfire night there was always a friendly rivalry between the Cowell's bonfire and the Wilkinson's further up the back-street. And, as the night drew to a close, both parties would congregate together on an air-raid shelter telling ghost stories whilst eating roast potatoes from the bonfire.

"Eh, that were a good night weren't it?" we would all agree. It's great is bonfire night ... roll on next year."

****

I never stayed in bed late and usually got up before any of the others. The first thing I did was light the fire. Scraping the fire-grate, allowing the hot ashes to fall through and then gathering them up on a shovel, created a lot of dust. The best way to get the fire started was to use a metal blower, which was placed across the opening of the fireplace, creating a sucking effect from the chimney. We didn't have one so I'd stand the shovel on the fire-grate and then place a sheet of newspaper over it, which had the same effect as a blower. This was a tricky job because I had to be very vigilant; otherwise the newspaper would catch fire. Once the fire got going, the old cast-iron fireplace retained and radiated heat into the room making it nice and cosy. Coal was the main fuel for keeping the fire burning but it was on ration and also expensive. To subsidise it many people queued for hours on end at the gas depot on Parker Lane for cinders. Cinders only cost sixpence a bag but despite the price many folk couldn't afford it and were reduced to picking coal off the railway. This was strictly against the law but it was the lesser of two evils … be law abiding and cold or a law-breaker and warm. It was often the topic of conversation:

"Bloomín éck Burt, aya not freightened o' geddin' caught on the railway … you're forrit if thá gets nicked?"

"Aye, course I am, but what choice have I got … I either pick the coal or we freeze to death in our house!"

I made a small truck from a discarded crate and some old pram wheels, which came in handy for carrying a bag of cinders. It worked out great which got me to thinking, "U-um, I'll ask Mrs. King and some o' t'other neighbours if they want any cinders bringing. Yeah why not … it'll be a bit of extra brass." Before long I had a few willing customers.

Despite the long queues, I only used to carry one bag at a time. The reason for this was because the first half of the return journey was uphill. It wasn't too bad pushing it up Finsley Gate, but once I turned a corner into Manchester Road the gradient became much steeper. I always had a rest outside the Canal Tavern before pushing it over the steepest part … a Canal Bridge. One day, on this part of the journey, something happened. Young Rose Clarke, who lived at number 18, two doors higher up than I did on Albion Street, was attempting to carry two bags of cinders at once on an old makeshift trolley. Consequently, it had broken down.

"Bloomin' 'eck Rose, what are you tryin' to do … kill yourself o' what?"

"Ha, ha," she sneered, 'it's not bloomin' funny Johnny Cowell … I've bín here for ages."

"Yeah I can believe it, I'm surprised you've got this far."

"Oh well," replied Rose, "a bloke shoved it to here for me, but when it broke down he had to go."

"Broken down, the flamin' trolley's comín apart… who made it anyroad?"

"Mí dad made it … anyway, what difference does it make, are you gonna help me o' what?"

"Yeah all reight Rose but we'll have to unload the cinders off your trolley first and try to mend it. I have some rope on mí truck that may do the trick." The axles had buckled on Rose's truck but by using the rope I managed to hold it together a little better.

"I'll tell you what I'll do Rose, I'll just load one o' the bags on it for now and shove it o'er the bridge as far as Trafalgar and then come back for t'other."

"But somebody might pinch it if you leave it unattended."

"Maybe, but have you got a better idea?" Rose just shrugged her shoulders implying she hadn't.

"Right then, just guard t'other bag and mí truck while I push it up there." When I got back we both set off pushing our own load but poor Rose had to give up.

"I'm sorry Johnny; I can't push it up this steep part o'er the bridge."

"All reight Rose I'll give you a lift, but how the bloomin' 'eck did you hope to shove it with two bags on it?"

"I don't know… but mí dad said I had to fetch two."

"Your flippin' Dad! That's not fair ...why didn't he come and fetch 'em himself?"

"Well he said that t'other kids have to do it ... why shouldn't I."

"Oh yeah, lots of t'other kids do it, but mostly lads ... it's bloomin' hard work. Just hang on till I've shoved my truck o'er the bridge and then I'll come back for yours." Once we'd reached Trafalgar we placed the other bag on top of Rose's trolley and set off again. The going was much easier now as if was slightly downhill. All was going well until we reached the main doors of the Ribble Garage.

"Oh no," groaned Rose, "mi' trolley's collapsed again!"

"Not to worry Rose, we're nearly home," I said, "I'll just tie the rope a bit tighter." On attempting to do this I realised it was hopeless. "It's no good Rose, the axle's broken completely in half."

"Oh 'eck, what am I gonna do now?" she moaned.

To make matters worse a bloke came out of the Ribble Garage shouting, "What the flamin' 'eck's going on here? Get them bleeding bags outa the way now ... there's a bus waiting to leave!"

"All reight, keep your hair on, we haven't done it on purpose," I barked.

"Hey, I don't want any lip either or I'll clip thí round the lug'ole ... just get 'em out o' the road!"

"Oh blow this for a tale" I moaned, "I look well getting shouted at when I'm trying to help you Rose. I'll tell you what ... I'll get home wí my bag o' cinders and I'll tell your dad to come and collect yours."

"But he'll go mad if he has to come out," said Rose.

"Well he's no right to; he should have fetched 'em himself in't first place ... especially when he wanted two bags."

It turned out better for Rose in the long run because, although her dad roasted her, she didn't have to fetch any more cinders after that. As for me, as soon as I'd had a bite to eat I set off for another load.

****

Of all my brothers and sisters, our Jimmy was the canniest of us all when it came to making money and saving it. Even in his early teens, he always had some stashed away in the post office; he even kept a little hidden in a secret place under the floorboards in the back bedroom. Unbeknown to him though, everybody in the house knew about it, but no one would touch it, as it wasn't theirs. He engaged in all the same scams as I did but he also had a paper round. With the money he saved, he started up quite an enterprising scheme amongst some of the neighbours. There were about six people on the street, who used to borrow a little money off him on a Saturday, and then pay him back with interest on the following Wednesday or Thursday depending just when they got paid or cashed in their allowance. Each one on average borrowed five shillings and would repay six shillings; this meant that after five weeks, they were actually borrowing their own money. Still, they didn't seem to mind and were only too glad to have Jimmy at their disposal. Mam always encouraged us to use our initiative but in this case, she wasn't very happy, as it put her in mind of Blakey, a moneylender. In the past, when we were in our infancy, she'd actually taken out a small loan with the unscrupulous businessman and found herself in deep trouble as the debt escalated. Hence, she showed her displeasure by having a word with both Jimmy and the borrowers, telling them of her disapproval. Still, the would be victims, as Mam put it, made it quite clear that they didn't mind and were only too glad of the service. Hence, Jimmy always had plenty of money. but to be fair, he was never mean, and he would indulge us younger brothers and sisters with little treats now and again.

It was a scorcher of a day with brilliant sunshine. Jimmy was now sixteen; he'd seen an advert in the paper for a weekend ice-cream man and he asked me if I fancied having a go with him. I went along with the idea, so Jimmy applied for and got the job. It wasn't the same firm that Dad had worked for but the transport system was still a horse and cart; on arriving at the depot there were a few carts just leaving. Jimmy thought that they might think it suspicious if two young lads went in together, so he asked me to wait a little way off and arranged to pick me up later. I waited patiently about two hundred yards down the road, then, sure enough, after about twenty minutes, Jimmy came along driving the cart.

"Would you believe it," he said as I climbed aboard, "they've told me that I can only sell ice-cream in the Trafalgar area? Aye, and they stressed that I must keep to my own patch, as other areas are already covered." I was actually pleased about this, as I wanted to show off to my friends. As we made our way towards Trafalgar, a few people flagged us down but the horse was quite boisterous and hard to handle. Every time Jimmy stopped the cart to serve anyone, it kept trotting off; he just couldn't control it. It was funny really because on a couple of occasions just as someone wanted serving, the horse set off of it's own accord leaving Jimmy quite frustrated; turning to the would be customer, saying, " Oh I'm very sorry but we've sold out."

As I was used to handling Peggy, I suggested taking over, but at first Jimmy was too pig-headed, as he didn't want to lose face. Nevertheless, after a while he saw the sense of it and handed me the reins; it worked out a lot better, so we made our way to Trafalgar.

Unlike Dad who could sell ice-cream to Eskimos, Jimmy and I were struggling. Customers in the impoverished area were scarce on the ground and after about two hours, we'd only just about taken the top off the six gallons.

Jimmy was fast losing his patience, "Umph," he grunted, "this is no bloomin' good is it? Come on our John, I've had enough, I'm taking the flamin' thing back."

We'd just set off when I had an idea, "Hang on a minute our Jimmy! Why don't we make our way to the Prairie Fields where Dad used to go, we're bound to sell a lot of ice-cream there?"

"Because like I've told you our John, I'm not allowed, they gave me strict instructions not to encroach onto anybody else's patch."

"Yeah, so what ... when has that ever stopped you doin' things afore?"

"Hey, it's all right for you!" he snapped, "It's me who has to face the consequences."

"Yeah all right, I agree with you there our Jim but let's put it another way ... are you thinking of doing this job again after today?"

"You must be jokin'! Why?"

"Well then, in that case, you've nówt to lose have you?"

He paused for thought before agreeing with me, "Good thinkin' our John, why didn't I think ' that? Right then get the horse turned around and let's get up to't Prairie now and make some brass!"

We arrived at the Prairie at about one o'clock but didn't actually go onto the field. Jimmy asked me to stop the cart on Colne Road near to the entrance gates where lots of people were coming and going.

"Right John, we're pitching here, it looks as good a spot as any ... I don't think we'll have any trouble selling ice-cream here."

He was dead right; within an hour, we'd sold about half of the stock. Things were going great until other angry ice-cream men, who had been alerted to our presence, confronted our Jimmy.

They were furious, one rather burly looking chap approached the cart shouting, "What the bloody hell d'you think you're playin' at, this is our flamin' patch?" Jimmy didn't take any notice; he let it go in one ear and out the other and carried on serving. "Are you deaf o' what," retorted the bloke, "o' just plain bloody thick?"

"Thick am I?" Jimmy replied sarcastically. "At least I'm selling ice-cream!"

"That's it!" rapped the bloke as he grabbed the horse's reins and started to lead it off.

Jimmy went mad, and even though he was a lot smaller than the bloke, he fronted up to him. To the surprise of all the customers, he jumped off the cart with the ice-cream spoon still in his hand and threatened to ram it down the man's throat. The bloke, being much stronger, grabbed Jimmy, pinned him against the cart and threatened to banjo him.

But luckily for Jimmy, two fellows who were waiting to be served intervened, "Hey mate, what the bloody hell d'you think you're playin' at? He's only a lad; pick on somebody your own size!"

The bloke released Jimmy under protest but warned him, "All right you clever little bugger, you think you're getting away with it don't you? You know bloody well that you're not supposed to be round here," adding, "Where is your flamin' patch anyroad?"

"All right, we shouldn't be here," replied Jimmy defiantly, "but why should you have the best spot anyroad? Besides, ther's plenty of people around here for everybody. I'll move but not for another hour, that should still leave you plenty of time to sell your ice-cream." The bloke was fuming, "Right!" he warned, "I'm going to report you to your gaffer to make sure it don't happen again."

"Please yourself mate, I couldn't care less!" replied Jimmy, knowing only too well that it was his last time anyway.

Consequently, Jimmy carried on serving, but within half an hour or so, a police squad car pulled up and two uniformed policemen got out and approached the cart. Both Jimmy and I were surprised to see them, as we didn't think we'd overstepped the mark that much; however, it was nothing to do with the fracas or being on somebody else's patch. The policemen were a little surprised to see two young lads in charge of the cart, but after explanations, they advised Jimmy that Colne Road was a no-parking area and that he would have to move on. It was a pity really, as there were still lots of people around, given another hour, we'd have easily sold up. As it happened, there was still had about two gallons left.

"Ah well never mind our kid, we haven't done too badly have we?" said Jimmy. "Let's call it a day and make our way back to the depot shall we?" On our way back, we decided to take a short cut through Stoneyholme, which, like Trafalgar, was an impoverished area of town. We were going down Burns Street when a small boy flagged us down. On stopping the cart, the young lad asked, "Please Mister, cudda have a penny ice-cream?"

The cheapest one was thrépence, so Jimmy answered, "I'm sorry cock but we don't have any penny ones."

The look on the little lad's face said it all; his bottom lip dropped as he muttered, "Oh, it's not fair! I never get an ice-cream."

Jimmy looked at me and I couldn't help but grin. He then turned to the little boy saying, "Oh all right cock, give me your penny, it'll only be a little one mind!" He scooped a little ice-cream into a cornet, then paused for a moment before saying, "Oh what the 'eck!" Digging deep into the canister, he then gave the little lad the biggest ice-cream he'd ever seen.

By now, lots of other kids had gathered around the cart, their excitement was aroused when the little lad, who couldn't believe his luck, let out one hell of a shout, "Hey look everybody at my ice-cream what I got for a penny!"

That was it, all the kids clustered around the cart eagerly shouting, "Here Mister! I've got a penny as well … cud I have a big ice-cream like him?"

Once again, Jimmy looked at me, commenting, "Oh bloomin' 'eck our kid ... I've started something here haven't I?"

He didn't get much help there, as I found it really funny and couldn't help laughing. "You've done it this time our kid ... how you gonna get out o' this one?"

"I'm not sure, but I can't help thinkin' that it doesn't seem fair to give one without t'other. What do you think our John, don't they remind you of when we were kids and could never afford an ice-cream?"

"I know exactly how you feel our Jimmy and I know what I'd like to do but I can't really say because at end o' the day, you've the responsibility of the cart, and you'll have to face the consequences."

"Oh sod it!" he exclaimed, "In for a penny, in for a pound!" He then turned to the crowd of children and to their delight he announced, "Righto kids, get your pennies ready, this is your lucky day!" He started dishing out ice-creams to boys and girls alike, and thoroughly enjoyed himself; he even gave treats to some kids who had no money at all. Needless to say, it didn't take very long to sell up. Before going back to the depot, Jimmy cashed up, but first, he took his wages out of the money.

"How come you're doing that our Jim?" I asked.

"I'm taking what's due to me because Dad forewarned me that if there's any money short, it'd be stopped out o' my wages."

On arriving back at base, the boss had heard all about the Prairie episode and was extremely annoyed; but his mood changed when Jimmy told him he'd sold out. Nonetheless, he became outraged again after the money had been handed over.

"What the bloody hell do you call this ... the takings are way down?"

"Oh well they will be because I've already taken my wages outa them," replied Jimmy quite unconcerned.

"What flamin' wages?" he rapped, "I would have docked most o' them anyway for what's missing."

"Yeah, I thought you might;" Jimmy replied casually, "that's why I took 'em first"

"You cheeky young bugger!" he barked, adding, "Anyway, all I can say is you must have been selling bloomin' big portions."

"Oh yeah, maybe I was, but don't forget that this is the first time that I've ever gone out sellin' ice-cream."

"Yes," replied the bloke angrily, "and the bloomin' last as far as I'm concerned!"

Jimmy and I went home in good spirits; it wasn't simply the money either; just remembering the looks of happiness on those little kids' faces made us both feel really good.

****

My youngest sister Barbara was different again from all my other siblings. Whether it was because of a promise that Mam made when Barbara was born or because she was the youngest is not clear, but one thing for certain is that Barbara was rather spoilt. She tended to get away with many things that Mam would usually go mad at. It went on like this until she was ten years old but it came to an abrupt end when she did the unforgivable ... she actually stole something from the house.

It happened in 1953 just before Queen Elizabeth's Coronation; by then, Barbara was in the top class at St. Thomas's. Every year the school held a charity-raising event when the teachers gave each child a donation card that contained twelve small squares. The collection was for the St. Joseph's Penny Collection Fund. The idea was to ask someone to prick a square on the card and then kindly donate a penny.

On completion of the card, it was handed over to the teacher along with one shilling. It was only pennies, but filling in the card was no easy task, as there was always a lot of competition from many other children wanting to fill in theirs.

Enthusiasm would reach fever pitch, as running in conjunction with the fund raising was a visitation by the Bishop of Salford to all Catholic schools. After the visit, the local convent always held a Bishop's Party, and anyone who had sold three cards or more was automatically invited. It was an unfair rule really, as it meant that the more privileged children from well to do families never had any trouble achieving their goal, whereas it was nigh impossible for many from lower class families. Subsequently, every year it was always the same boys and girls who attended the party.

Barbara wasn't having any of it; come what may, she was determined to go to the festivities. What made it worse in her eyes was that she had a friend called Rita, who had three older working brothers, and they all used to spoil her. As Rita always had plenty of money, it didn't present a problem for her to fill in the charity cards, which meant that she was always amongst the privileged ones invited to the party. On the other hand, Barbara was struggling as she went from door to door with little success. As the deadline got closer, it became apparent that she was not going to reach her target.

Meanwhile, back at home, Mam had left half a crown on the end of the sideboard for the clubman. It was a weekly routine, as she bought clothes for us children from a club; it was a loan which she had to repay back at so much a week.

Barbara happened to come home at dinnertime one particular day, and there was nobody else in the house. As she looked at a shiny new half a crown just sitting there, thoughts of the party flashed through her mind. She didn't succumb to temptation straight away but the longer she was in the house on her own, the more her wanton thoughts got the better of her. Before leaving the house, she picked up the silver coin, put it in her pocket and made her way to school. She'd already collected one shilling and sixpence, which meant that she was still left with a shilling after handing over the three full cards. Call it fate or whatever, that shilling was to be her undoing; but for it, her misdemeanour may never have come to light. It was almost the end of May and Princess Elizabeth was about to be crowned Queen the following week and people throughout the town were preparing for the occasion. Being patriotic, many young girls were wearing red, white and blue multi-coloured hair ribbons. The fact that her friend Rita had always been able to spend so freely had created resentment within Barbara and she became rather envious. The shilling seemed to burn a hole in her pocket, as she too wanted to be as popular as Rita. The ribbons cost tuppence each, but no matter, she invited five of her school friends to join her and bought each one a ribbon and one for herself. This was her moment of glory but also her downfall. Still, her little peccadillo did not come to light immediately.

Back in the house, the missing money was not noticed until a week later when the clubman came around collecting again and he pointed out to Mam that two weeks money was due.

This caused quite a stir, as Mam insisted he'd been paid, "I beg to differ Mr Thorpe," she affirmed, "but I left the money as per usual on the end of the sideboard inside the book."

"Oh the book was there Mrs Cowell, but I can assure you that there was no money inside it."

"Hey now just wait a minute Mr Thorpe! I can definitely remember putting it inside the book before I left the house because it was my last half a crown."

"I can't argue with you about that Mrs Cowell, all I know is that the book was there, but there was definitely no money inside it."

"I can't believe this," she muttered, "was there anybody in the house at all when you came?"

"No I'm afraid not; not a soul," he insisted and then went on to say, "Look Winifred, I know this looks bad and it puts me in a bit of a predicament, but surely you know me from old. I've been coming here to your house for many years now and I understand your plight only too well, and I would much rather help you than hinder you."

Mam knew he was sincere, so apologised for placing him in an awkward position, "Yes I know you would Mr Thorpe and I'm sorry if I've caused any embarrassment … it's just that I don't know what to think, I've absolutely no idea what's happened to the half a crown."

She had to leave it at that but, no matter; she was determined to get to the bottom of things. Dad was the obvious suspect, as she just couldn't visualise or bear the thought of any other member of the family taking it. In spite of her suspicions though, she had a deep inner feeling that he wasn't the one responsible.

All the same, she questioned him about it but he threw a tantrum and started to yell at her, "What the bloody hell do you take me for woman? You know flamin' well that I haven't done ówt like that ever since our Maureen was born, so I'm tellin' thi' now, don't come it! Anyway, have you asked all the kids about it?"

She had to admit that she hadn't, so he suggested asking each one of us as we came in. This she did but each of us in turn emphatically denied it; almost everyone came up with the same answer. "Umph no Mam, not me, I wouldn't ever steal anything, you know that."

Even Barbara's answer was convincing, "Oh no Mummy, not me, you've always taught us never to steal anything."

Mam racked her brains but she couldn't come up with an answer. She felt so frustrated because never before had she been faced with this sort of situation where suspicion was thrown onto the entire family. She knew that she couldn't pinpoint the culprit, and as she had no idea where the money had gone, she had no alternative but to let the matter drop.

So Barbara got away with it, she even went to the Bishop's Party. Even then, Mam didn't suspect her, as she knew that Barbara had collected quite a lot of money before the disappearance of the half a crown. Also, Barbara had been crafty, covering her tracks by scrounging pennies here and there from her brothers and sisters, making folk believe that this is where some of the donated money came from. Three weeks passed, Barbara was by now feeling quite smug to think she had outwitted Mam and all the rest of us. Little did she know though that fate was now taking a hand in things … her theft was about to be discovered.

Mam went shopping down town and she caught a bus at the bottom of Albion Street. As she sat down she met Rita's mother Emily, who was already on board.

They were exchanging greetings when Emily came out with something which made Mam's heart turn cold, "All right Winnie, I believe you've found out what happened to that half a crown then?" It wasn't so much what Emily said that made Mam cringe, as the fact that she knew that she was about to learn the truth. But the most bizarre thought that made her tremble was that an outsider knew of it; it made her blood run cold.

Accordingly, Mam reacted rather coolly to the question, "And what do you know about the half a crown then Emily, may I ask?"

"Ah well, our Rita mentioned something about it, and she said that your Barbara had been buying ribbons for some school girls just before the Coronation."

Mam could feel her blood boiling but didn't answer; she just waited until Emily got off the bus, and then followed her. Rightly or wrongly, she then fell out with Emily, accusing her of spoiling her own daughter Rita and turning Barbara into a thief.

After the exchange of words, Mam was rather distraught and decided to make her way back home. On arriving back at the house, Dad, our Maureen and I were sat by the fireside having a pot of tea, and we were all surprised to see her back so soon. During the conversation that followed, Maureen made herself scarce, slipping out of the house so as to forewarn Barbara, who she met on the canal footbridge as she was coming home from school. But in spite of the warning, Barbara wasn't for owning up, she swore blind to Maureen that it wasn't her.

"Listen to me our Barbara," Maureen tried to tell her, "mí mother knows because Rita's mother, Emily, has told her everything; even that you spent some of the money buying ribbons for your school-friends."

Still, Barbara wasn't for coming clean, fervently protesting her innocence, "It wasn't me our Maureen ... honest!"

"Look our Barbara, I'm saying no more except that on your own head be it, if you tell Mam lies on top of everything else you're really asking for it; she's fuming as it is and she'll bloomin' well kill you if you make it worse than it already is."

Barbara dragged her feet as she walked up Albion Street as she was really wary at the daunting prospect of facing Mam. Nevertheless, despite Maureen's advice she chose to lie, defiantly pleading her innocence.

But it was a fruitless effort, Mam was having none of it and really tore a strip off her, "Right then! So that's your answer is it? Well Barbara, all I can say is you're not only a thief, you're a liar as well; I'm going to ask you just one more time ... **did you take that half a crown?"**

Barbara was quivering but still refused to own up and resolutely stood her ground.

Despite lying through her teeth, Mam knew she was guilty, and reverted to another line of attack, "Right Barbara, get your coat on right now 'cos I'm taking you to the police station, and I'll let them sort you out!" she rapped. "And tomorrow morning I'm going to the school and I'm going to show you up in front of all your class mates."

"Oh no Mam please don't do that, I promise I won't ever do it again ... honest!"

"What's that you just said?" asked Mam, "You won't do what again?"

That was it; Barbara knew it was pointless to carry on lying, and so resorted to other tactics. She started to cry, "Oh Mam, I'm sorry! I promise I won't do anything like it ever again."

"You sneaky little swine you're nówt else!" Mam screeched, "You've watched us turn this house upside down looking for that half a crown and you've even pretended to look for it yourself. The worst thing though is that you cast suspicion on all your brothers and sisters even as they were trying to help you get to that blasted party!"

Then for the first time in her life, Barbara got a good hiding and sent straight to bed; she was also grounded for a fortnight. But that wasn't the end of the saga because for at least two years after the event, she got loads of ribbing from her brothers and sisters. Poor Barbara really did get punished because if anything got lost or even misplaced after that, she got the blame!

"Oh our Barbara's been about, she'll have taken it," one or the other of us would say. Consequently, Barbara learned her lesson, never ever stealing anything again and continued to be a valued and much loved member of our family.

****

It was 1953. Our Maureen was now eighteen and actually engaged to be married to a young local lad called Bill Howley, whom she'd been courting for over two years. Bill was a reserved lad and very shy, but in spite of this, he got on well with everyone in our home and we really brought him out of his shell. He had no brothers or sisters of his own, therefore number fourteen Albion Street was entirely different to what he'd always been used to. He had an endearing sense of humour and was readily accepted as part of the family. He got on well with Mam too, despite the fact that she laid down strict ground rules, one being that all the courting was done from the house. She made it quite clear that Maureen always had to be picked up from her home and escorted back there at a reasonable hour. On Saturday nights the young couple regularly went dancing at the Weaver's Institute on Charlotte Street or the Empress Ballroom and went to the pictures once a week. But most evenings were usually spent in our home getting to know the family. There were no airs and graces put on and Bill had to take things as he found them. Nearly every night was wash night, so there was always plenty of activity in the house, as Mam set on the gas boiler and got out the dolly-tub and posser. Nonetheless, he didn't seem to mind; on the contrary, he seemed to enjoy the stark contrast to his own home. His personality began to blossom and he loved to crack jokes as he turned the handle of the wringing machine prior to Maureen hanging clothes on a wooden rack above the fire.

Bill may have been a very naïve young man as far as the outside world was concerned but his horizons were certainly broadened in our house. Everything was open and above board, the fact that Dad was a rag and bone man and had been in prison was not hidden from Bill. To his credit he didn't mind; he loved Maureen and that's all that mattered to him. It was just as well because one evening, his love was really put to the test. He was in the house with my family when Dad walked in with a cardboard box containing a dozen bottles of whisky. The first thing he did was to put it behind a rocking chair that was placed near to the cellar top.

"Oh no Jack," Mam complained bitterly, "You're not up to your old tricks again are you?"

"Oh come on Winnie, I couldn't let these go, I got them for a song," he grinned.

"I don't flamin' well care if you got them given, I don't want them in my house."

"Oh just for once, why don't you relax and let your hair down?" He gave her a cheeky grin, jesting, "I'll pour you a nice tot if you want one love."

"You'll do no such thing; you can take them back to wherever you got them from." There wasn't much chance of that, so an exchange of words took place for about twenty minutes only to be interrupted by a loud knocking on the front door. Our Maureen answered it and on returning to the living room, her face was ashen.

"There are two men at the door Mam," she stuttered nervously, "and they say they're police officers and they want to have a word with Dad."

"Oh my God!" Mam exclaimed anxiously, "now we're for it."

On going to the door one of the men said, "Good evening Mrs Cowell, is your husband in please?"

"He is; why do you ask?"

"Well we have reason to believe that he is in possession of some stolen goods and we have a warrant here to search your property."

"Stolen goods; and what would they be then?" she enquired shaking in her shoes.

"Well, a warehouse was broken into a few nights ago and a shipment of whisky was stolen."

"Oh I see, and just what has that got to do with my husband?"

The detective in charge gave a little smirk saying, "We have our sources Mrs Cowell; now if you don't mind, can we come in please?" She wasn't happy about it but knew she had no option. On reaching the living room, everything appeared normal, Jack was still sat in the rocking chair behind which the whisky was hidden, Bill and Maureen were sat on the sofa and the rest of us were sat around the table.

"Hello Barney," one of the detectives sneered sarcastically, "you know why we're here don't you?"

Mam was afraid that Jack might trip himself up so forewarned him by blurting out before he could answer, "Someone's broke into a warehouse Jack and stole some whisky and they think you've got something to do with it."

"Oh yes, I know all about that ... it happened last week didn't it?"

"And how would you know that Barney?" asked the detective in charge.

"Oh come off it, everybody knows, it's common knowledge around the pubs down town."

"Aye maybe," mumbled the officer rather disgruntled by Dad's reply, "but all the same, we have reason to believe that you have purchased some of it and we intend to search this house."

"Please yourself, I've nothing to hide; search where you like," he replied quite coolly. He may have looked cool but he was trembling inside, as he knew if they charged him he could go to jail for five years this time. The two policemen thoroughly searched the upstairs and the parlour using their flashlights, but only glanced around the living-room with everything appearing so normal. Throughout all this procedure, Bill couldn't believe what was happening.

"Right Barney," said the detective in charge, "we can't find anything but we still have our suspicions and we'll be keeping an eye on you."

"Yeah righto, please yourself," he replied still remaining calm. Mam saw them both to the door saying, "Right officers, goodnight, I hope you find the ones responsible."

"Right, thank you Mrs Cowell, sorry for any inconvenience caused."

"That's all right, you're only doing your job officer." With that, she quietly shut the door, gritted her teeth, took a deep breath and then stormed back into the living room. "Jack," she screeched, "if you ever put us in that kind of predicament again, so help me, I'll swing for you!"

"Shush," he whispered with a grin on his face, "keep your voice down … make sure they're well away from the house before you start." Dad had a way with him and despite being furious about what he'd just put them through Mam was unable to suppress a smile.

"By 'eck Jack, you could get away with bloomin' murder and that's the Gospel Truth," she said.

"Eh that's better love, I like it when you smile, it really lights up your face. Now how about having that drink 'cos I'm telling you straight, I'm having one, my nerves are shattered." Turning to Bill he asked, "How about thee lad, would you like a little one?"

"I think I'll just try one at that, I don't usually drink but after that episode my nerves are a little on edge as well." At that, we all had a good laugh.

Then came the happy day when the young couple got married on the 18th of July 1953. It may have been a happy day for the young couple, but there was a tinge of sadness in our house that morning as our Maureen put on her wedding gown. Emotions were running high and very mixed. The thought that she was leaving the family home never to return got me all choked up, it seemed unbelievable.

"Eh our Maureen," I spluttered with welled up eyes, "I'm goin' to miss you."

"Yes and I'm going to miss you as well our John," she replied giving me a hug. "But don't forget, I'm not going all that far. You can come around to my house for a brew and a piece of cake any time you want. Each of my brothers and sisters in turn gave her a big hug, even Jimmy had tears in his eyes at the thought of his big sister leaving.

She reassured everyone as she had done me, "Don't worry about it, I'll always be close at hand so that you can come and visit me whenever you want, and I'll come and see you all regularly."

She was married in Christ the King Church and the reception took place at the Mitre Hotel. True to her word, she always kept in touch, and there was always a hearty welcome for us all at her new home on Napier Street. I tried as hard as I could to put on a brave face but it never seemed the same again in our home now that our Maureen had gone.

****

In my final year at Towneley School I had hardly grown and the nick-name Bimbo stuck. Because of my size and the way I handled horses Dad mentioned that I would make a good jockey.

"Aye maybe I would Dad but I want to go workin' down the pit." I replied unconvinced.

"Workin' down the pit! You don't know what you're lettin' yourself in for lad … you'd be a lot better off training to be a jockey."

"Aye, maybe I would Dad… I'll have to think about it."

I did think about it and I became quite keen on the idea but then, when I broached the subject with Dad he just brushed the scheme aside as fruitless."

"But Dad," I stressed, "it wer' your idea in the first place."

"Yeah, I know it wer' but I've had second thoughts about it, you're only little our John but I think you're a bit too stocky … you need to be quite slim to be a jockey."

"P-ph!" I pouted, "Thanks a lot Dad … first you build me up and now you shoot me down in flames."

"Sorry lad, I don't want you geddin' your hopes built up … that's why I'm tellin' you."

That was all very well but my hopes had been raised. I hadn't been enthusiastic at first but the more I'd thought about it the more the idea appealed to me, and I was determined to do something about it. I felt let down and being frustrated I went about it in the wrong way.

"It's not fair," I moaned to myself, "nobody takes me serious, even the careers' teacher scoffed at me when I told him what I wanted to do."

I brooded on it for a little while and then decided to play truant. I knew there were some stables over in Gisburn, a little village a few miles on the other side of Nelson.

"U-um," I thought, "if I ask the headmaster for a day off to apply for a job he'll probably think I'm stupid. But he'll think differently if I get the job."

The next morning I left the house as though I was making my way to school but instead of catching the Towneley bus I caught one heading for Nelson. From there I hitch-hiked it the rest of the way to Gisburn, a small village way out in the countryside. I visited a riding stable but it wasn't geared up to training apprentice jockeys and the owner appeared very suspicious of me. He was a rather smart well-built country gentleman, wearing a deerstalker hat and he sported a typical handlebar moustache. He asked me what I wanted in a very posh voice but his manner was offensive.

"Now come on boy, what do you take me for," he barked after listening to me, "what do you really want?"

"What do you mean?" I queried. "I want to be a jockey like I've just told you."

"Go on, get off this property before I throw you off!" he growled pointing to the gate.

"All reight, I'm going," I grunted, "keep your hair on ... I didn't want the job anyroad."

"That'll do ... I don't want any cheek you scruffy urchin or I'll wallop you! And shut the gate behind you!"

I didn't give any more backchat, as he really was a big bloke and aggressive with it.

But I couldn't resist saying sarcastically as I closed the gate, "Thank you for your hospitality."

"Go on, get away you little runt," he rapped, "and don't let me see you around here again!"

I was rather disappointed as I made my way to Nelson on the back of an open-back wagon but I didn't dwell on it too long.

"A-ah well John lad," I mused, "it looks like you're going down the pit after all."

That was the beginning and the end of my career as a jockey. But the incident was not finished as I found out to my displeasure the next day when I attended school. Mr Lancaster, the headmaster, summoned me to his study and asked me why I had not attended school the previous day. I didn't have a letter from Mam excusing me, as I hadn't dared to ask her. I'd been on the verge of asking her to write one for me before leaving for school but I'd had second thoughts about it.

"No, she'll bloomin' kill me if I tell her where I went," I thought, "and there's no chance of her giving me an excuse-me-note. I don't have an option … I'll have to take my chances without one." On reflection I should have told her rather than face the wrath of Mr Lancaster.

"You what!" he bawled when I told him what had happened. "You mean to say you were playing truant?"

"We-ell no not really," I stammered nervously, "I - I didn't think I were … I - - - I thought ………!"

"Never mind what you thought!" he roared cutting me off in mid-sentence, "You were absent without permission and that's truancy in my book!"

"But Mr. Lancaster, I - - - I ……..!"

He cut me short again, "I don't want any excuses," he snarled now yielding a bamboo cane in his hand, "you've broken one of the cardinal rules of the school … now bend over that chair and grab hold of the bottom rail!"

"But Sir, I - - -I ………!"

"Bend over that chair now!"

What happened next was to remain with me for the rest of my life.

I reluctantly crouched over the chair just half bending and fidgeting about.

"Bend over I say," he growled through clenched teeth, "and clutch the bottom rail!"

"Oh well," I thought, "I might as well get it over with … I've had the cane afore."

I may have psychologically prepared myself, but I wasn't prepared for the excruciating pain I felt as the cane landed hard and heavy on my buttocks.

"O-o-oh-h!" I screeched as I danced around clutching my backside with both hands. My wailing had no effect on the headmaster.

"Bend over the chair!" he ordered unmoved- by my reaction.

For the second time I tentatively bent over.

"Get hold of that bottom rail!" he repeated in an icy voice.

Once again the bamboo cane came crashing down onto my rear end with an almighty force, landing in the exact same spot.

"O-o-oh-h!" I screeched again as I danced on the spot. He was still unmoved.

"Bend over that chair!" he repeated in a cool and calculated voice as if he was beginning to enjoy himself.

"But sir," I pleaded, "Please … please … it won't happen ………..!"

"No, it won't happen again … not in my school!" he rapped as he uncharacteristically betrayed his impatience by gently tapping the palm of his left hand with the cane. "Now do what I say … get over that chair!"

"Who-o-ose!" sounded the cane as it came down once more onto my throbbing buttocks. I'd received many a whacking from the schoolmasters but I had never felt pain like this in my life before. By now the tears were streaming down my face.

"Get over that chair," came the dreaded order, "and grab hold of the bottom rail!"

"I can't take another," I whimpered pleadingly, "please sir ... please don't cane me again!"

"**Get over that chair now you insolent boy**!" he demanded completely devoid of compassion.

For the fourth time the fearsome cane struck home in the same spot inflicting the most agonising sickly pain.

"I can't take any more, I just can't," I thought to myself as nausea started to overcome me, "and anyway, I don't think it's fair ... I don't think I've done anything so bad as to warrant this."

I tried to stem the flow of tears and just looked at him with pleading eyes. I didn't utter another word, as I felt it would only fall onto deaf ears. I stood there quiet and ashen faced and felt as though my spirit was broken. I felt the blood drain from my face and the room about me became a blur. He weighed me up for a while as he looked at my ashen face and sensed that I couldnt take anymore.

"Please God ... no more," I sobbed inwardly, "please God don't let him hit me again!"

My silent prayer was answered. "Right boy," he rapped, "now go and sit in that chair facing my desk!" I did as I was ordered and sat tentatively down on the wooden seat in a completely passive state. After seating himself down opposite me he began to give me a lecture.

"Right John Cowell," he said sternly, "I'm not going to beat about the bush because you've gone right down in my estimation." He picked up a file, which was lying on the desk in front of him. "Do you know what this is?" he asked me.

"No sir I replied meekly."

"This is your personal file and it's ironic really because I was only looking through it at the beginning of the week and I've been in touch with a factory enquiring about a job that, in my opinion, would suit you fine."

"Oh thank you sir," I muttered with bated breath.

"Don't thank me boy," he said soberly, "because after this incidence I've lost complete trust in your reliability."

"But sir!"

"Quiet! Speak when you're spoken to and listen to what I have to say. When you leave this room I am going to contact the firm again and cancel the application. No, I don't think I can entrust you with the job, I no longer have confidence in you … my reputation and that of the school is at stake here."

I asked him what the job was but he wouldn't tell me.

"You don't deserve to know," he replied coldly as he placed my file back into the drawer of his desk, "let that be part of your punishment."

I felt deep down that all was not fair. "Right Mr. Lancaster," I thought, "I've always respected you because even though you're strict, I always found you to be fair. But now I see you in a different light. You've already punished me once, why punish me a second time? You should have either taken the job opportunity away from me or caned me …but not both." I didn't voice my opinion, as I felt vulnerable and afraid that I might receive more of what I'd just had.

"So what are you thinking of doing now," he asked interrupting my thoughts, "have you looked for anything?"

"Yes sir," I replied grudgingly, "I've applied to Bank Hall Colliery and they informed me I can start after the Easter holidays if I pass the medical."

"Oh yes … and what was all that nonsense about training to be a jockey then?"

"I don't know sir," I mumbled. I really wanted to say that he wouldn't have thought it was nonsense if I'd got the job.

"Right, on your way," he said pointing to the door, "and let this be a lesson to you."

I left the room feeling rather dejected. I'd never been happy at Towneley but this incident made me want to leave the school as quick as I could.

"Yes, it's been a lesson all right Mr. Lancaster," I mumbled to myself as I walked along the corridor, "more than you'll ever know … I'll think twice before owning up to anything ever again, especially to you." My mind flashed back over the four years I'd spent at the school and the unfairness of it all. "Just let me get away from here," I thought, "the coalmines can't be any worse than this."

To this day I often wonder what the job might have been.

CHAPTER 10 - THE YOUNG MINER

April 1954 was the year I had longed for ... I was fifteen and it was time to leave school. On my first day as a trainee miner I strutted off down Albion Street with my bait box under my arm full of enthusiasm, reflecting on the time that my Uncle Jimmy had done the same all those years ago in Bacup. In spite of Mam's tales of the terrible accident and young Jimmy's death, I wasn't to be put off. I'd always fancied working down the mine since being a small boy and this was my big day.

Mum was obviously concerned but I reassured her, "Don't worry Mam, everything will be all right ... you'll see."

Prior to entering the coal mining industry, I had to undergo a vigorous sixteen weeks course along with a lot of other young lads. I reported to Bank-Hall colliery to commence my training. Bank Hall was the main pit in the Burnley area and by far the biggest. I, along with other enthusiastic youngsters, couldn't wait to venture onto a new phase in my life. The sixteen weeks training was divided into two sections, which meant studying eight weeks at college and working eight weeks down the mine. Consequently, the course was arranged so that we alternated weekly between college and pit. To my disappointment, my first week was to be spent at college.

"Oh Bloomin' 'eck," I moaned, "back to school already, I thought I'd left that behind me."

I envied the lads who were chosen to spend their first working week down the coalmine. But then again, common sense prevailed. "Ah never mind, it'll be my turn next week ... I'll just have to grin and bear it." With that in mind I made my way to the college. It was a small building in the Croft Area of town situated near to Parker Lane. I found myself in a classroom of twenty-five lads from poor backgrounds. I soon settled down, as I already knew some of them, one was Bobby Cheetham and another Freddy Man, who lived on Trafalgar. Everyone was as disgruntled as me about the situation, but as we were all in the same boat, or classroom if you like, we accepted our plight. I was still only four feet nine inches tall and the smallest in the group. Certain bullyboys in the class were inclined to pick on me and taunt me, but this was short-lived … they soon found out that despite my size I could handle myself. Mind you, my friend Freddy Man, who was seventeen, was a really strong lad and tended to take me under his wing. Another seventeen year old lad picked on me a lot and I was no match for him. Freddy, who didn't like what he saw, stepped in on my behalf and soon sorted him out.

With hardly any effort he got hold of the lad by the throat and pinned him up against a wall, "What have I told thí about pickin' on John?" he growled. "If you don't leave him alone I'll rip your head off!"

"Bloody Hell Fred, you can't be stickin' up for that little brat all the time," grimaced the lad, "you're not his flamin' chaperone!"

"No, maybe not but you're older and much bigger than he is so leave him be … right!" The lad knew better than to mess about with Fred, so that was the end of the matter.

After that little escapade things settled down and most of us became quite friendly with each other.

****

On the second week I was very excited, as I knew I would be working at the pit. Once again I reported to the reception area at Bank-Hall where I met up with the same group of lads I'd been in class with the previous week.

We were all given overalls, boots, kneepads, a belt and a safety helmet, which had a special fitting to hold a miner's lamp. Being so small and kitted out like a miner, I looked quite funny. We were split up into groups of five, each group being supervised by an ex-coal-face worker.

Before we set foot on the pit top our team leader addressed us, "Right lads … lets get one thing straight from the start … I'm the 'gaffa' and if you do ówt wrong you'll answer to me … understand?"

He was a mean looking man with blue scars on his faces, a legacy of working on the coalface.

There was no opposition as we all answered in unity, "Yeah … righto."

One group cheered loudly when they were informed they were going down Bank-Hall. Three other groups were sent to other local pits, Hapton Valley, Clifton and Reedley. Our group wasn't quite so happy because we had been chosen to work on the pit-top. I was in this group and sorely disappointed … my day of going underground seemed to be eluding me.

"Still, not to worry John," said Bobby Cheetham nudging me, "our day will come."

The first thing I noticed was how large the tubs were … in fact they were more like railway wagons.

"Blooming' 'eck!" I commented. "What are those … I thought tubs were a lot smaller than that?"

"Eh they're not called tubs young fella," replied the gaffa, "they're mine-cars … we stopped usin' tubs a while back now. Mind you, they still use tubs at a lot o' the smaller pits."

The day was not altogether fruitless; we worked ardently, filling large mine-cars with wooden props, bricks, girders and other materials which were needed by the colliers underground. In between time, the boss explained the workings of the pit and the importance of keeping supplies going.

On Tuesday we were taken to Clifton Pit on the back of a NCB coal wagon, but yet again I didn't get to go down the mine. This time I had to work in the screens where coal was separated from shale. Rubble was conveyed onto large steel shaker pans with holes in them sieving the slack from the cobs. The pans were not fully efficient and it was my job along with my mates to lift large lumps of shale and place them onto another pan. It was a heavy job, so by the end of the shift I was quite tired.

Finally the day came when I got to go down the mine. It was quite daunting because there had been a lot of scaremongering from the more experienced colliers.

"D'you know lad," they'd quip, "it's 500 yards to the bottom o' the pit … that's about 3 times deeper than t'height o' Blackpool Tower? Aye and the bloomin' cage drops like a stone till you're nearly at the bottom. Mind you … there's now't to worry about 'cos it only takes about three seconds."

On reaching the cage I had butterflies in my stomach but didn't like backing out for fear of being ridiculed. Sure enough, the cage did drop very fast leaving my stomach in my mouth. Still, after the first initial shock it wasn't so bad thereafter … in fact, I looked forward to the thrill of it.

Once underground there were lots of long winding tunnels about ten foot high running throughout the mine. To reach some of the coalfaces we had to walk about two miles through these tunnels. The nearer we got to the coalfaces the dustier it got. During my training I worked at various pits in the area, including Copy, Reedley and Huncoat. At many of the smaller mines they didn't have mine cars and the typical tub was still in use.

In order to cut down absenteeism the wage was calculated on a bonus system. My daily pay was 11shilings and 1penny. If I completed

5 days I received an extra day's pay making my gross pay – £3-6s-6d. I couldn't wait to receive my first wage packet, but when I did I got quite a shock. My total stoppages, including the insurance stamp, were a staggering 5 shillings ... leaving a paltry net pay of £3-1s-6d.

After tipping up to Mam she gave me 10 shillings spending money and we came to an agreement that should I work overtime I would share the extra with her.

The first thing I did on receiving my 10 shillings was to go straight down to Fitzpatrick's bike shop and buy myself a bike on hire purchase. It cost £15-15shillings and I had to put down 9shillings as a deposit and pay 9shillings a week for 34 weeks. However, by doing extra part-time jobs I managed to pay off the debt in 20 weeks.

****

The 16 weeks training period soon passed and then I went to the pit of my choice ... Thorney-Bank Colliery in Hapton. Mam gave me a shout at 5-45am and after a hearty breakfast I left home at 6-15am to catch the Accrington bus close to the Mitre Junction. Just as I was leaving the house Mam gave our Mary a shout as she was now working at Barden Mill as a weaver.

Unlike Bank-Hall with a typical shaft, Thorney-Bank was a drift mine. The entrance was via a big tunnel at the mouth of the mine which inserted itself into Hameldon Hill. The pit top was like a railway siding with about four sets of railway lines with points, enabling carriages to interchange. Being a modern pit Thorney-Bank was equipped with mine-cars similar to the ones at Bank-Hall. These were connected together in the same way as railway wagons and pulled along by a locomotive engine, commonly known as the 'Loco'. As the mine-cars came out of the pit full of coal and shale they were, each in turn, shunted over a turntable which automatically tipped the contents via a large steel chute onto a conveyer belt. The belt ran steeply up to a very large screening plant, which was much more sophisticated than the one at Clifton Colliery.

At the new pit I was allocated a clean locker and a dirty locker. Shower units separated the two sections and it was forbidden, after coming out of the pit, to return to the clean section before having a shower. Once kitted out in my working gear I made my way to the lamp-room. Along with two of my mates I stood out like a new pin from the more mature colliers who were strapping special batteries to their belts and fixing miner's lamps into their helmets. A rather stout official looking man approached us trainees and started giving us a few facts. "Right you young úns …right from start I want to point out who I am and just what my job is. My name's George Riley and I'm the safety officer and I want to make it quite clear from the word go that I won't stand for any monkey business of any kind. If I catch any of you riding conveyor belts, jumping onto the back of any of the moving mine-cars or anything else untoward, it'll be instant dismissal … understand?"

"Yeah we understand," muttered all three of us, not having much choice.

The safety officer then turned his attention to me.

"What's your name then young fella and what made you come working at the pit then?"

"John Cowell and I'm here because I've always wanted to work down a mine since I was a little boy."

"A little boy … you're not much bigger than a little boy now," he grunted.

That irritated me … even more so because many of the miners burst out laughing, including my two mates. I was fuming!

"He might well be my gaffa," I thought, "but that doesn't give him the right to take the mickey outa me." I paused for a minute before replying, "Excuse me … you may well be the Safety Officer but I think you're out of order ... how would you like it if I started making personal comments about your belly?"

"Well you cheeky young bugger you're now't else and on your first day!" he rapped.

"Serves you right George," laughed one of the colliers, "you asked for that ... give the young lad credit for stickin' up for himself." The Safety Officer frowned a little but luckily he didn't hold it against me.

"Right John, there's two checks here," he said reasserting his authority, "now listen whilst I explain what they're for." Firstly he handed me a triangular metal check with the number 200 stamped on it. "This is your personal number," he stressed, "and you must keep this particular check on your person at all times whilst in the pit for identification purposes." He then handed over a round disc with the same number stamped on it, "This one is for job allocation which will be explained more thoroughly once you get into the pit."

After the instructions I was taken to another room and introduced to a mature collier. The man's name was John William Worseley and throughout his working life his nickname had always been 'John Bill.' When starting at a new pit it was customary to be supervised for the first four weeks by an experienced collier. In my case my destiny was to be under the scrutiny of John William Worseley.

"Naythen John Bill," said the safety officer, this here young lad's gonna be under your supervision for the next twenty working days so think on you show him the ropes and teach him properly."

"Yeah reighto George ... leave the young lad wí me, I'll take him under mí wing."

"Aye, think on you do and no teachin' him any wrong things eh?" At that George Riley handed a slip of paper to the collier, "Take special care o' this John Bill ... it's an authorisation slip giving you full responsibility o'er the young lad."

Whilst reading the slip of paper John Bill paused for a minute then burst out laughing, "I don't believe it," he said chuckling all the more, "I don't believe it."

"Come on John Bill," quipped one of the other colliers, "let us all in on the joke.'"

"Well, all the years that I've worked here I've been labelled wí the nickname 'John Bill' ... I feel as if I've just become a dad."

"How d'you mean ... what's so funny?" enthused more colliers, now crowding around, all wanting to be in on the joke.

"Well believe it o' not ... this little fellow is called John William Cowell."

At that quite a lot of colliers started laughing, "Eh bloody hell ... you mean to say we've got a little John Bill now!"

I didn't know whether to be mad or pleased ... at least I seemed to be accepted. One thing for sure ... the nick-name 'Little John Bill' was to stick with me throughout my working life at Thorney-Bank.

After the initiation, my overlooker, John Bill senior, guided me to the entrance of the mine. The tunnel was about ten-feet high and ten-feet across and the roof was supported by steel girder type rings ... these were placed about four-feet apart throughout the length of the tunnel. Unlike Bank-Hall it wasn't dusty but there was a lot of water seeping in from the hillside above. Running throughout the tunnel was a single rail track laid on wooden sleepers about three-feet apart. The men had no trouble straddling the sleepers but with my short legs I found myself jumping from sleeper to sleeper rather then walking. After about half a mile I heard the sound of the loco.

"Get yourself into one o' these here cubbyholes young John Bill afore you get run o'er," shouted one of the miners.

As it happened there were cubbyholes about every hundred yards just for this kind of situation. We all waited patiently whilst the loco passed dragging about twelve mine-cars. After walking approximately a mile we arrived at a very large cave-like opening, which was about two hundred yards long, twenty-feet high and twenty-feet wide. It was unsupported, as it had been driven through solid rock. The single-track line opened up to a double track and this is where lots of empty mine-cars were shunted about and exchanged for full ones. This large expansion was known as the 'Landing' and it was here where many job allocations took place. Being a main section of the pit, it was well lit up. It was also the place where all materials, which had been carried on the mine-cars, were unloaded and stacked prior to being transported to different coalfaces. The firemen's station was also situated here; it was literally the nucleus of the pit. The firemen, who acted as underground foremen, planned the day's activities and were responsible for the day to day running of the pit. The Landing was also the main loading point where mine-cars were filled with coal by conveyor belts running from various coalfaces.

A few firemen gathered at the Landing and each one was in charge of a coalface. I watched with interest as colliers handed over their round metal tags, then made their way through adjacent tunnels to their respective coalface. After the dispersion of all the colliers the firemen then allocated jobs to the remaining pit workers.

"Reight young John Bill, afore we start," said my senior, "I'll take you to the firemen's cabin to explain how things work." When we got there a fireman was just hanging the round discs on special designated hooks. "Naythen lad can you tell me what he's doing that for?"

"Well I think it's something to do with the allocation o' the men," I replied, "George Riley said something like that."

"Very good lad," interrupted one of the firemen, "but do you realise the importance of it?"

"Well it's so that you can tell what each individual is doing and where he's working ...I've heard that every hook represents a job."

"Aye you're reight there but there's somét else that's really important ... it's so we can pinpoint where everybody is. And not only that but, before you knock off at th'end o' the shift you have to pick up your check from here."

"Why do you have to do that then?" I enquired.

"Good question cock," said the fireman impressed by my enthusiasm. "Well, it serves two purposes. One - nobody can leave the pit without me knowing about it, and two – when you leave the mine you've to hand your check o'er to the lamp-chap in the lamproom, who then books your time and also knows you're out of the pit. Having to check out like this has a safety aspect attached to it."

"How's that then?" I asked naively.

"Well, if somebody happened to get hurt while working on his own and he couldn't move we'd know something was wrong 'cos his check would still be hanging here at th'end o' the shift ... we'd then send out a search party to go an' look for him."

"U-mm what a good idea ... simple but effective," I replied.

Turning his attention more closely to me, the fireman started to weigh me up, "By 'eck lad, you're only a little ún for workin' down the pit." Then stroking his chin he added. "U-umph, I can't see you being much use as a tackle lad, but I suppose you'll be all right working on a belt end." That did it! During the 16 weeks training I'd noticed men tending conveyor belt ends and shivered at the thought of how boring it must be to just sit there all day with nothing else to do except watch in case the main belt stopped.

Once again I was on the defensive, "Excuse me, I might only be small but I'm very strong and I'm not frightened of hard work. Besides ... I want to be a tackle lad."

"Blimey, that's tellin' me," he responded a little taken aback, "I can see young fellow from th'onset that you'll stick up for yourself. All reight, fair enough ... you'll get your chance."

Turning back to John Bill senior the fireman more or less repeated the same words that the safety officer had said, "Right John Bill, ték young John Bill under your wing and show him the ropes."

After handing over our checks I set off with my overlooker for number 4 coalface. As we strolled along he pointed out various aspects of the mine to me.

I asked him why the men in charge were called firemen.

"A-ah well, one o' the firemen's job is to fire the coal by packing pre-drilled holes on the coalface with explosives and then using special detonators. They also carry a special lamp on their belts called a 'Davey Lamp', which they use for testing for firedamp, a very explosive gas. They've got to do this test every time afore they fire the coal in case there's bín a build up o' gas ... otherwise there could be an explosion. In th'olden days they used to keep canaries down the pit in a cage and they'd flake over at slightest sign of any gas."

"He-ey, that wer' a shame weren't it ...the poor birds?" I quipped.

"Poor birds mí arse ... that wer' better than the colliers coppin' it weren't it?"

"Yeah I suppose so, but I still think it wer' a shame. Anyroad ... how does the Davey Lamp work then?"

"Good question lad. Well for a start a very clever bloke by the name o' Davey invented it. It's a very special lamp as it actually has a naked flame. You know only too well by what they taught thí in training school that no naked flame, matches or anything inflammable can be brought into the pit. Well, the Davey Lamp is so well designed that the flame is rendered harmless. The naked flame is encased in such a way by special thick glass and gauze that it cannot come in contact with the gas. When testing for gas the fireman turns out his own cap lamp and then turns down the naked flame of the Davey Lamp so there's just a small flame. The lamp is then slowly lifted to the roof of the coal-face and if there's any gas lingering about the flame turns blue."

"U-um, that's clever," I said, "very interesting."

We carried on walking deeper into the mine along a meandering tunnel. A conveyor belt ran throughout the length of the tunnel and running alongside it was a small steel track on which small four wheeled bogies ran. These bogies were like trolleys only much bigger and had flanged wheels like those of a train. Tackle lads used them for carrying timber, props, girders, bricks, blocks and other materials to the coalface. The tunnel was constructed similar to the entrance drift but was a lot smaller and much wetter.

"By 'eck," I commented, "this is a flippin' wet tunnel in'it?"

"Naythen John Bill, let's get one thing straight fro' word go," rapped John Bill, "we don't call 'em tunnels when they're running fro' the coalface ... we call 'em 'gates'. Aye and this one is the top gate and there's another running parallel to it on't lower side o' coalface called the bottom gate."

"Oh reighto, I'll remember that."

We eventually reached the coalface, which to my surprise was only about two-foot six-inches high. Running from the face and spilling coal onto the conveyor belt was a scraper chain. This was a conveyor system but instead of a rubber belt it was made up of steel link chains, which ran on top of and underneath, specially designed straight steel pans. The belt attendant was there to stop the scraper chain in case the main conveyor belt stopped.

"Right young John Bill," my overseer stressed, "there's something else you've gotta know. By law, until you're eighteen years old, you're not allowed within 30 yards of the coalface unless accompanied by someone of authority. I'm warning you now 'cos if the fireman or the safety officer catches thí, you're forrít and could be sacked."

As it happened there were two tackle lads throwing some props onto the face for the colliers.

"What about them then?" I asked. "They're not eighteen."

"Aye you're reight there lad but I'm tellin' you they're takin' a risk and they could be down the road if they're caught. Anyroad, it's up to you what you do once you've finished your 20 days wí me"

I pondered for a moment before asking, "U-um, it seems strange to me ... how come they take the risk of being sacked then?"

"A-ah, that's easy lad ... you see, all the colliers encourage 'em to bring tackle right up to the face 'cos it saves them a lot o' hard work. Just look back along the gate and you'll see that the steel track ends about 50 yards short o' the face ... that's a hell of a long way for colliers to hump the tackle."

"Yeah, fair do's, but it's also a long way for the tackle lads to hump it as well," I said looking puzzled. "If they're only allowed within 30 yards of the face why don't they just leave the tackle there?"

"You're catching on quick young John Bill. Well, what it is ... for this service the colliers give the lads some 'pey-brass' at th'end o' the week,"

At this my ears pricked up, "Pey-brass ... what's pey-brass?"

"Well, on payday, after picking up their own wage packets, them two young lads'll wait outside the cashier's office for the colliers to pick up their pay. This is the time of reckoning ... each collier gives 'em half a dollar tip for their loyal services."

"Half a dollar!" I gasped getting more interested by the minute, "And how many colliers work on the face?"

"Let's see, on average there's about twelve ... yeah, that's about reight, twelve."

My brain started to tick over ... the thought of pey-brass gripped my imagination. In a flash I'd worked it out, "30 shillings split two ways ... 15 shillings each – u-um, not bad ... not bad at all." Now more than ever ... I wanted to be a tackle lad.

During my 20 days training I did various jobs with my overseer and once a week we had to attend a belt-end. I hated this aspect of the job but it didn't seem as bad when there were two of us because I had someone to talk to. Not many lads liked doing belt-end work and the firemen were aware of this. Being fair, they shared the task between the lads so that each one in turn attended a belt-end on average about once a week.

On the second week after handing over our checks to the fireman John Bill senior was told to go to the Bluebird.

"Oh no, not the 'Dreaded Bluebird'," he blurted out.

"Go on, get yourself up there and stop your moaning!" quipped the fireman.

Some colliers laughed and made comments, "Don't forget to take your compass with you John Bill." "Keep a sharp eye on that young fellow ... mind you don't lose him in them old workings." "Cor blimey, rather thee than me John Bill!"

I wondered what was going on ... especially when one bloke tapped me on the shoulder saying. "Eh, God bless thí ... you're such a young lad, try not to take it too hard!"

"Come on John Bill what's the joke?" I asked becoming a little agitated.

"It's no joke lad ... we're goin' to the 'Dreaded Bluebird.' And believe you me it hasn't got its fearful reputation for nothing. I've got to admit young ún … this is one time when I'm glad I've got a trainee with me."

"Oh come off it, you're trying to wind me up … you're havin' me on," I insisted.

"Have it your way lad, you'll see … you'll see."

After leaving the Landing we walked some distance along number 4 gate, then turned left and went through two air-lock doors. On the other side of these was another tunnel but it was only two-feet high.

"Reight lad," quipped my senior, "this type of tunnel is called a heading and this particular one is about 500 yards long and leads to a maze o' similar ones. We'll have a minute here 'cos we've a few headings to go through afore we reach the Bluebird and it's no fun walkin' under the low … it's back-breaking."

John Bill was right … it was too low to walk under even when crouched over. I kept catching my back on the roof and had to revert to scrambling on my knees on all fours. I wasn't too concerned about this, as I was quite fit, but what did concern me was the chilliness of the place. As we progressed deeper into the mine the more eerie it got. After the first 500 yards we came to a T Junction and another heading. This one had a very large scraper chain running throughout its length.

"Naythen young John Bill, if you crawled left for about a thousand yards you'd arrive at number 2 face. We're going right for the same distance until we come to th'end o' this here scraper. As you may have noticed, this scraper is much bigger than any o' t'other scrapers that you've seen already … this is the Bluebird."

I glanced left and the light from my lamp zoomed into the distance until it faded into oblivion. I then glanced right with the same effect. We had to climb over the scraper and crawl along the other side of it.

"I'll tell thí what John Bill," I commented, "it's bloomin' draughty and cold 'round here in'it?"

"Aye, that's because this is a main airway for ventilating the coalface an' all t'other gates. And in answer to your question, the wind's much stronger 'cos were under the low. Anyway, let's go … we've got a bit of a trék ahead of us yet!"

Finally we arrived at our place of work. Talk about eerie, ghostly or whatever, it was enough to put the shivers up the hardiest of men. The scraper emptied its contents onto a conveyor belt that went off in another direction through another heading into pitch darkness. Just a few yards on the other side of the belt were the openings to at least five other headings, which veered off in various directions. All the openings were blocked off with strong sacking sheeting.

"If you're ever tending to this belt on your own young John Bill," said my carer, "don't ever go foraging in any o' them headings o'er yonder 'cos they lead into a labyrinth of old workings and you could easily get lost. Besides, ther's no ventilation beyond them sacking curtains and there could be gas hanging about."

"You must be joking!" I quivered, "Go foraging in there; it gives me the shivers just to look at 'em."

John Bill didn't make things easier. He then went on to tell me some scaremongering tales that had spread throughout the pit about ghostly figures wandering about the old workings. I wasn't one for believing in ghosts or evil spirits but this was a frightening awesome place even though there were two of us.

My thoughts were interrupted as the conveyor belt started, "Reight lad, push that button o'er there and get the Bluebird going." said John Bill Senior. Within ten minutes the large scraper was full of coal, feeding its contents onto the conveyor belt. During the procedure lots of spillage accumulated and some started to back track under the bottom side of the Bluebird. "Reight lad, get hold o' that shovel and make sure you stop them scuftings fro' cloggin' up the scraper chain."

"What's scuftings?" I asked.

"Oh it's just another name for loose coal ... you'll soon get used to it being called that, especially on the coalface."

The day passed very slowly, minutes seemed like hours ... we never saw another soul until a young lad, who was taking over for the afternoon shift relieved us.

"All reight lads," he greeted us," you can go now you lucky sods."

"Bloomin' 'eck," I thought, "I'd hate to be in his shoes." The very thought made me shiver ... I couldn't wait to leave the place.

****

The twenty days soon passed ... now I was on my own. It soon became apparent that the nickname 'Young John Bill' was to stick. No matter where I went working in the mine, this was my label. It wasn't just the colliers either; from the firemen to all the pit top workers ... even the safety officer, George Riley, referred to me in this way.

As I progressed I got my chance to tackle drag, but I also spent many shifts attending belt ends and hated it. However, I took it in my stride knowing that it was only fair that I should take my turn along with other lads. Then came the dreaded day when I was told to go on the Bluebird. A cold shiver went through me at the thought of having to crawl through all those isolated headings alone. I knew it was no good protesting, as someone had to do it and today was my turn. I reluctantly handed over my check then slunk off despondently. I made my way through the two air-lock doors and crawled warily through the heading as far as the T-junction. After climbing over the large scraper chain I hesitated for a moment, paralysed with fear, not daring to go any further into the eerie darkness. I gradually built up some courage but every few yards I kept peering over my shoulder, imagining that someone or something was behind me. I eventually arrived at my base and set the Bluebird in motion. For a while I just sat there frozen to the spot, as my gaze was drawn to the maze of old workings.

My mind started wandering as I imagined all different kinds of things, "What's that creaky noise? Who's there? What's that moving?" Just to make matters worse an odd rat would scurry from under the conveyor belt across my path.

That awesome place wasn't just chilly in the frightening sense but also temperature wise. I started shivering and my teeth began to chatter … I really was scared. Even the droning of the Bluebird's engine and the clanking of the thick chain seemed to make a weird sound.

"Oh blow this for a tale," I muttered to myself after pondering for what seemed an age, "I'll have to do something to take mí mind off them old workings." I grabbed hold of the shovel and started shovelling the scuftings for all I was worth. This helped a little for I felt warmer but the eerieness remained.

After what seemed an eternity the conveyor belt stopped so I switched off the Bluebird.

"Oh thank goodness, it must be bait time," I thought, "John Bill told me the belt would stop for half an hour then. Mind, it feels like I've done two shifts already." I'd just taken a bite out of a jam butty when I became aware of the stillness of the place … it was so quiet you could literally hear a pin drop.

"Oh flippin' 'eck," I mumbled, "it's more eerie now than when scraper was droning away." Just then I heard a creaking sound. I felt the hair rise on the back of my neck as a chill ran down my spine.

"Who's that ... who's there?" I shouted trembling. My lamp shone into the pitch darkness but I could see nothing untoward. "It must have bín a cob o' coal falling off the belt or maybe a rat ... or maybe my imagination working overtime." I reassured myself.

As I settled down to finish my bait, I was taking a slurp of coffee from my flask when there was another creaking sound. This time I knew for certain that it wasn't my imagination. All the same, when I peered along the heading everything was motionless; I could see nothing. Not being able to weigh up what was happening I became even more un-nerved as lots of bizzarre thoughts ran through my head.

"I'm not usually nervous like this," I mumbled to myself, "but this bloomin' place is enough to give anybody the creeps. I know bloody well now why nobody likes looking after this belt-end." My mumbling was interrupted as a minute piece of coal struck my helmet.

"All right, that's it!" I shouted, "Come on out whoever you are ... I know there's somebody there." Nobody answered so I climbed over the other side of the belt and started to crawl down the heading. I'd gone about 30 yards when a glint of light was reflected back at me from the glass of a miner's lamp. My heart skipped a beat as I spotted two bodies lying flat out on their bellies by the side of the belt. After getting over the initial shock, I shouted, "All reight, come on, you can get up now ... the games up, I've seen thí!"

When they realised they'd been spotted, two lads turned on their cap lamps and burst out laughing. "Eh, that got you going din'it John Bill ... you looked freightened to death?"

"Too true I was bloody freightened ... so would you o' bín if it had happened to thí, I retaliated. "Anyroad, how did you get here with no lights without making a noise?" I asked.

"Oh that was easy ... we crept up on you whilst the belt was still running and we used the light from your own lamp to guide us here."

They went on to tell me how it was a kind of ritual to do it to every trainee on their first stint on the Bluebird and we all ended up having a good laugh about it. I wasn't bothered in the least … I was only too glad of their company as they joined me for bait-time. After they'd left it still seemed a daunting place, but somehow it didn't appear quite so eerie anymore.

This was my first solo experience on the Bluebird but not my last. Other lads tried to play the same prank on me but I was wise to their game. They'd sneak up on me in the same manner making similar eerie ghostlike sounds. On realising that someone was there, I would turn the tables on them. I would settle myself down in a comfortable safe position then switch off my cap lamp. The roles were now reversed. Without lights they were in a much more precarious position than I was. It wasn't long before they had to switch on their lights and the laugh was now on them. I enjoyed these little pranks because it relieved the boredom and also made me a lot of friends. When I was tackle running I actually played the same prank on new unsuspecting trainees with the same effect.

****

The mine worked on a 3-shift system: days, afternoons, known as back-shift, and nights. The day shift was 7am till 2-30pm, the back-shift from 2-15pm till 9-45pm and the night shift from 11pm till 6-30am … all three shifts had a half-hour break for bait-time.

By law, no one could work on nights until they were 16 years old: however, they could still work the afternoon shift. After working at the mine for two months I was approached by the Safety Officer, George Riley.

"Reight John Bill, as from next Monday I want thí to come in on the back shift and from then on, you'll be alternating weekly from afternoons to days."

Each fireman had his own team of men and each team worked the 3-shift system alternating weekly from days to back-shift to nights. This meant that I would work with one team for two weeks and then change over to another, as the colliers progressed onto nights and I progressed back onto days. Consequently, after leaving one team, it would be another four weeks before I met up with them again and so on.

Little did I know that I was to spend some very unhappy times during the next few months. Of the three teams, two of the firemen were very fair and I got my share of tackle running, but the third ... he was different altogether. This particular fireman was referred to as G T and for some reason, from the word go; he took an instant dislike to me and made my life unbearable. On my first day under him, he told me to go on the Bluebird. I frowned and he took note. The following day, he ordered me to attend the Bluebird again.

"But I went on there yesterday," I protested, it's somebody else's turn today."

"Oh did you now?" he snarled. "Well you can bloody well get your arse up there again today you cheeky little swine!"

I protested again but to no avail, "Hey that's not fair ... you know that we all take turns!"

"Oh we all take turns do we?" he scoffed. "Well I'm the gaffa 'round here and I'll tell thí just one more time you little rat ... move your arse or I'll kick it the all way to the flamín Bluebird!"

I wasn't happy about it and felt like walking out of the pit but I knew that wouldn't help my case. I was left with little alternative but to make my way to the Bluebird full of foreboding. What made matters worse was that some of the other young lads mocked me ... they were highly delighted at not having to go on the dreaded scraper themselves. Every day that week and the following week on the back-shift, I was ordered to attend the Bluebird ... I was extremely unhappy. G T seemed to derive a sadistic pleasure from sending me to the Bluebird. He put me in mind of the deputy headmaster, Mr Redhead back at Towneley School. However, some good came of it ... I became much more acquainted with the place ... it didn't seem quite so eerie and I wasn't scared anymore. I overcame my fear, realising that I had to do something about it in order to save my sanity.

"Blow this for a tale!" I mumbled to myself one day. "I've got to do somét to alter things around here or I'll go round the bend. U-um, for a start, if I'm gonna be coming here on a regular basis I might as well have a bit o' comfort." I achieved this by using everything at my disposal. "I need to build a den o' somét to ward off the cold draughts." I pondered for a little then came up with an idea. Looking towards the old workings my brain started to tick over, "Yeah that's it ... there's bound to be some materials in there that I can use." The thought of it made me feel very uneasy but I wasn't to be put off. "Sod it! In for a penny ... in for a pound! Anything's better than having to put up with these conditions."

As I approached the old workings I could feel the hackles on my neck standing on end, but I was determined to carry out my plan. I wasn't foolish enough to venture far into the disused workings because I remembered the warning that my overseer, John Bill Worseley had given me not to go beyond the sacking sheeting because there could be lingering gas in the old tunnels. All the same, as I shone my light beyond the old sheeting into the darkness, I could see that just a few yards inside there were a few mouldy wooden props and some rolls of sacking lying about. Quick as a flash I nipped in there, got what I wanted and was out again. I got a roll of sacking and four wooden props.

"This sacking is used for diverting the airflow around the pit," I told myself, "so it should be good enough to ward off the cold." Within a short time I'd erected the four props into a square formation and fixed some sacking around them. "This is great," I grinned as the set up formed a nice cosy cubbyhole. There was plenty of sacking left over which I used to make a comfortable seating arrangement.

"U-um, not bad," I thought rather pleased with myself, "it's like home from home."

Taking everything into account things were better, but I still didn't like the situation. I didn't realise it at the time but there was a lot more agro to come!

For the entire two weeks, G T revelled in sending me to the Bluebird every day deriving pleasure from both my misery, and from making the other young lads laugh. The sense of power that he held over me seemed to boost his ego ... I was beginning to despise him. Time passed slowly but gradually the second Friday of the afternoon shift arrived.

I sat there reflecting on things, "Thank goodness, this is my last working day under G T ... at least for another 4 weeks anyroad." Sure enough, the following Monday morning I was working with another team. The fireman treated me like any other lad and I got my fair share of tackle running. However, the next four weeks passed very quickly and before I knew it, it was Sunday evening.

"Oh no," I moaned to myself, "I'll be workin' under G T tomorrow." The very thought of it made me feel agitated. And so I mentioned it to Dad.

"Get him bloody well reported our John ... he's not allowed to treat you like that. ... it's victimisation."

"Aye I know that Dad but it's not as easy as that ... I've got to try and sort it out another way. You never know, I might be going on about nothing 'cos he might treat me different this time. Anyroad, if he does send me on the Bluebird I'll act like I'm not bothered ... I'll pretend to be happy about it."

"That's the idea lad ... don't let the bastard grind you down!"

"Right Dad, you're on ... I'll not let him get to me."

No such luck, things didn't go to plan! I'd only just arrived at the pit and was getting changed in the shower room when I heard G T's mocking voice from behind me.

"Aye, look who we've got here! How you going on young John Bill you little rat-bag ... I hope you're lookin' forw'd to the Bluebird." His face lit up with sheer delight when a few lads started laughing.

I tried to contain my frustration but realised it was useless trying to reason with this sort of fellow, "Get lost!" I growled, "You're now't but a bullyboy ... I'm gonna report thí."

"Ha, ha!" G T just laughed, "Report me ... do what you want you little gít, but you're still going on't Bluebird!"

I did complain to the union chap but was told there was nothing he could do about it. I became very demoralised, having to put up with the ridicule and more so ... the Bluebird. I felt like packing the job in.

"Why should I for the likes of him?" I groaned, "I won't let the bastard grind me down!" Everyday that week I had to attend the dreaded scraper; and the thought of working under G T the following week on the back-shift spoiled my weekend. But then, on Sunday night I had a brainwave.

"I know what I'll do, tomorrow," I said to myself, "I'll go in on the morning shift instead o' the back-shift ... yeah, why not, nobody'll know difference." The more I thought about it the more convinced I became.

So I did it and everything went smoothly ... I even got to tackle drag. However, this was the easy part ... the hard part was getting out of the pit undetected by G T. I knew that at 2-15pm, each fireman would be stood at the Landing organising his workforce. The shift passed quickly and by 2pm I had to think of something.

"I've already picked up my round disc so that's not a problem," I said to myself as I made my way to the Landing, "but getting by G T is a different matter ... I'll try to blend in with t'other colliers leaving the pit."

When I reached the Landing, my luck was in. To my delight there were about fifteen full mine-cars waiting to be connected to the loco. "Great," I mused, "I'll be able to sneak out behind them and make my way to th'exit tunnel." I warily made my way forward from mine-car to mine-car inwardly congratulating myself on outwitting my foe.

Unfortunately, my little ruse did not come off. Unbeknown to me, G T was onto my little scheme and watching out for me like a hawk. Prior to entering the mine, he'd noticed that I wasn't amongst the afternoon crew. On checking with the lamp-chap he'd discovered that I was already in the pit. After weighing up the situation he'd fathomed out exactly what had happened and, he was absolutely fuming.

When I reached the last mine-car I paused a little before making a dash over the last few yards to the safety of the dark tunnel. But alas, G T was waiting behind the mine-car and he grabbed me as soon as I made my move. He was a strong man and literally lifted me off my feet and pinned me up against the rock-face wall. My pit helmet fell off and dangled by the wire of my cap lamp.

"You little bastard John Bill!" he growled curling up his lips, "so you thought you could gedda way with it did you? I'm tellin' thi' now you little gít ... you'd best come in on the back-shift tomorrow or you're sacked! Aye and don't just take my word forrit you little rat 'cos I've had a word wi' the manager about it and he backs me up!" I struggled and tried kicking out but couldn't get out of his grasp ... he was too powerful.

I couldn't move but protested in the only way I could by shouting, "Get your bloody filthy hands off me, you're the bastard not me! And I'm tellin' thí ... if you ever get hold o' me again I'll bloody well kill you when I get bigger!"

G T just laughed mockingly and started shaking me, "When you get bigger you little swine ... just look at thí, you're now't but a little wimp ... ther's now't about thí!"

I felt intimidated by this thug and tears welled up in my eyes. My body shook in trepidation, but still, I resolutely stood my ground.

"Yeah, you think you're a big man tacklin' a little ún like me don't you? Well, I think you're now't but a bloody coward!" I looked defiantly into his eyes adding, "And you're wrong, I will get bigger and I'll remember this day for the rest o' my life ... so you'd better watch out!"

G T clenched his fist and the venom showed in his eyes, "I've a good mind to fist thí right now you little gít ...you wouldn't be so bloody fly then would you?"

"Yeah, why don' you then ... you weak knee'd bastard!" I taunted actually willing him to hit me. "At least you'd be off mí back ... you'd be goin' down the road then instead o' me!"

At this point a passing collier interrupted us, "Whoa, hang on a minute G T! What do you think you're lakin' at ... you're goin' a bit o'er top wí young John Bill aren't you?"

G T had no option but to release me, but as he did so he sneered sarcastically, "Right, you can go now you little bastard but you'd best remember to come in on the back-shift tomorrow ... you'll be needed on the Bluebird!"

My lips tightened, but I still couldn't resist saying defiantly, "Right, I'll be here ... now get your bloody dirty hands off me and you'd better not touch me ever again!" I then added contemptuously so as to get his back up, "Anyroad, I noticed you never answered that collier back ... mind, he was as big as you wasn't he you bloody coward?" Then just to rub salt in his wounds I added, "At least this is one day that I don't have to work under your stinking authority." I was once again actually trying to incite him to hit me ... I didn't fancy it but it seemed worth it at the time.

G T glared at me and then just walked off snarling obscenities under his breath. I started to walk out of the pit singing a happy song loud enough for him to hear.

Reluctantly, I made my way to work next day. The scoffing started even before I entered the pit.

I was just putting on my cap-lamp when G T approached me, "Aye, if it isn't young John Bill! Have you brought plenty o' bait with you to share with the rats on't Bluebird?" I felt my blood boiling as I noticed the sheer look of satisfaction in his evil eyes.

I found it unbearable but then I got to thinking, "Blow this for a tale, why should I let him think I'm bothered?" From then on, rather than show my disappointment, I actually expressed my delight when handing over my check.

"Oh great! Another cushy shift on the Bluebird ... I didn't feel in the mood for tackle running today," I would say cheerfully, adding "it's money for old rope working down't pit in'it?"

I could fair see G T's mind ticking over and sensed what he was thinking, "Does the little swine really like working on the the Bluebird or what?"

I added food for thought by whistling merrily as I made my way to the Bluebird. Even the lads got to thinking that I actually enjoyed it, but I wouldn't let onto them ... no way!

Over the next few months this was the way of things and although I felt better in some respects, I still hated working on the Bluebird.

Time passed and one day I was tackle running for another team ... Jerry Dawson was the fireman in charge. I had worked very hard this particular shift carrying tackle for the colliers and was sat down in the Landing having my bait when Jerry approached me.

"I'll tell thí what it is young John Bill ... you're only little but, by 'eck, you're a bloody good tackle lad ... I only wish you wer' on my team all the time."

I didn't need any prompting, "Oh I'd love that and I'm sixteen tomorrow, so I'll be able to rotate onto nights with you as well."

Jerry pondered for a moment, replying "Right lad, I'll see what I can do ... I'll see the manager about it first thing tomorrow and fix things up."

I couldn't contain my excitement, blurting out, "Oh great, fantastic ... that's the best news I've had since coming to the pit!"

"Whoa, hang on a bit young John Bill, don't build your hopes up ... it's not in the bag yet! One thing I do promise you though ... I'll try my best."

At that moment, I knew how Mam must have felt on her first day in London all those years ago when Mr. Baron had agreed to find her a job in a hotel.

True to his word, Jerry did speak to the manager and the request was granted. I was highly delighted ... it was a great birthday present. What made things better still was that two lads in Jerry's team didn't like tackle running and actually preferred belt-end work. From then on I became a permanent tackle runner and I loved every minute of it. I also derived lots of satisfaction from the fact that I would never again have to work under G T.

Before the week ended something else happened that added to my delight. Jerry asked me if I would like to work some overtime.

"John Bill, how would you like to start your first night shift on Sunday ... you'll get paid double time?"

"Sunday night," I enquired, "but I thought that the pit was shut down then?"

"No, not exactly John Bill ... it's not a working shift but even so every face throughout the pit has to be inspected in case there's been a build up o' gas."

"Oh right, but excuse me for being a bit thick ... where do I come in?"

"Ah well John Bill," replied Jerry, "you see ... nobody, no matter who they are, is allowed to go into the pit on his own in case ow't happens to him. All you have to do is to give me some backing and moral support ... a kind of partner if you like." I remembered what John Bill Worseley had told me.

"Do you mean that I'll be able to go onto all the coalfaces with you?" I asked eagerly.

Jerry's reply left me in no doubt as to how he felt about this, "Aye, that's reight lad but only because you're with me. You know the ruling on this so let's get one thing straight from the word go. I think you're a good worker and that's why I've picked you for my team, but make no bones about it ... if I ever catch you on the coalface without proper authorisation I'll have thí in front o' the manager afore you can blink ... understand?"

That's the way Jerry was ... strict but fair and that's the way I liked it. I enjoyed the shift, as we toured every face in the mine including those in the lower mountain seam. The lower mountain faces went much deeper into the pit and we had to walk about half a mile down a steep 1 in 4 incline to reach them. It was quite a daunting experience because the lower bed faces were only 18 inches high.

Next morning, after the shift was finished, I was having a shower and felt absolutely great. The reason was twofold: one - I'd just completed a double pay shift and two - I couldn't wait for the morning shift workers to arrive ... G T's team. I purposely waited in the shower until I saw G T coming and then I stood there briskly drying myself, exaggerating my movements so as to be noticed. My little ruse worked a treat. It was great to see the look of astonishment on G T's face when he spotted me.

"Hey, what are you playing at you little rat!" he rapped. "Have you swapped shifts again?"

I just stood there grinning defiantly, "And wouldn't you like to know?" I replied with a wry smile.

"I'm warning you, you fly little swine, if you have ... you're for the sack!"

I grinned all the more, "Oh haven't you heard? I'm on Jerry Dawson's team now" stressing, "yeah, and permanently at that!"

"You lying little rat ... I'll have you for this!"

"Please yourself!" I said not being able to suppress the giggles. "Eh bloomin' 'eck, I'm surprised you haven't heard about it ... has nobody told you?" I felt absolutely great as I noticed his bottom lip quiver and tighten. I grinned all the more as a nervous twitch on his right cheek betrayed his frustration. At that moment, Jerry happened to be passing.

"Hey Jerry," growled G T, "is it true you've taken this bloody little wimp onto your team?"

Jerry, who'd noted the mocking tone in G T's voice and the angry look on his face, answered quite coolly, "Yeah, that's right G T, he's the best little tackle runner in the pit ... I'm surprised you didn't snap him up afore I did."

The look on G T's face said it all ... my victory was complete. All the grief that he'd given me was now in the past and at this moment everything seemed worthwhile. As I left the shower room to catch the bus home I was the happiest lad in Burnley.

I never ever again went on the Bluebird.

Ironically, shortly after, G T left Thorney Bank Pit to go working in some gold mine in South Africa.

****

CHAPTER 11 - LEISURE TIME

During my free time I loved nothing better than going to Sandygate Youth Club, which stood at the junction of Trafalgar Street and Sandygate, and what a club it was. It was an ideal place for teenagers to congregate in the evenings and on Sunday afternoons, as it had many facilities including table-tennis, snooker, dancing and even held a special physical training night, which included weightlifting. Three lads from Trafalgar took a great interest in weightlifting and carried off a few trophies in the Lancashire championships. Two of them, Terry Carter and John Topping, lived on Bedford Street, and the other one, Billy O'Connell, lived in the local Barber's shop near the corner of Sandygate. All three were highly competitive and did exceptionally well in their chosen sport.

Some lads took up boxing under the expert eye of Derek Clarke, an ex-boxer. Derek Gallagher, a well-built lad, was really keen on this sport and fared very well.

"Bloomin' 'eck!" I remember thinking as I watched him sparring fiercely in the ring, "I wouldn't fancy doing three rounds wí Derek."

I will never forget the one and only time I ventured into the ring. My opponent was called Les Holroyd and he was about the same age as me.

"How do you fancy sparring three rounds with me?" he asked me one day.

He was the same height as me but not quite as stocky.

"Yeah why not," I replied feeling cock sure that I could easily beat him. That was my undoing. Unbeknown to me Les had done a bit of boxing and he certainly taught me a lesson. He was a left-hander, better known in boxing circles as a southpaw, and therefore led with his right hand. I couldn't get through his defence at all and everytime I tried to land a punch, his right-fist seemed to jab forward catching me time and time again on my nose. Those three three-minute rounds were the longest minutes of my life ... I was certainly outclassed and ... that was the first and last time I ventured into a boxing ring.

The youth club also had a splendid football team. Martin Grogan, a regular team player, was renowned for his footballing skills and was a prolific goal-scorer for the club. Being a great player, he was an automatic team choice. I enjoyed playing football too but with names like Derek Duerden, Frank Neville, Billy Bibby, Roy Swift and other talented players, I was never good enough to gain a regular team place and usually participated as a reserve. One game in particular, which I watched from the sidelines, is very memorable for obvious reasons. Sandygate Youth Club played the Boys' Brigade and won 53-0, a record that stands to this day. Roy Swift created another record which earned him a place in the 'Guinness Book of Records'... he actually scored 27 goals. The amusing thing was, Jack Preston the opposing goalkeeper, finished up getting an award for his performance. Jack received his unenviable award from Sam Bartram, Charlton Athletic's goalkeeper during a televised edition of 'Sport's Round Up'. All the members of Sandygate Youth Club were glued to their television sets that night as the famous goalkeeper presented Jack with a leather football.

As Sam Bartram handed over the football he asked jokingly, "Well lad, what do you think about letting in 53 goals?"

"Well it could have been a lot more," Jack replied cheekily, "cós I made a few good saves!"

"Aye, I suppose it could Lad," laughed Sam, "I suppose it could."

Life was like this, everybody accepted things in good spirits.

In the youth club we learned how to bop prior to going dancing in places like the Empress Ballroom, the Arcadians' under the Roxy or the

Nelson Imperial. Les Harrison and Brenda Taylor merrily bopped the night away and good they were too. Like many other couples they complemented each other and a courtship began.

Alan Billington, the club leader, came up with many ideas, which generated lots of healthy competition between the club members, creating a good atmosphere.

I was quite a good table tennis player but never good enough to get into the first team. The 'A' team consisted of George Wilton, Brian Bunting, Jazz Wilkinson and Ralph Foster; all four were masters at the game and, as a team, they won every trophy in sight. Still, I was content to be picked for the 'B' team alongside Granville Town, Derek Ratcliffe and Alan Carter. I had just turned sixteen and all four of us were of a similar age.

Derek and I became very friendly and spent many happy hours competing against each other at the club and we also used to frequent Ken Stanley's Table Tennis Hall. One Sunday night we had a longer session than usual because, being well-matched, neither of us could gain the upper hand.

I'll never forget our parting words as I set off for home along Trafalgar and Derek made his way in the opposite direction towards Lord Street.

"Eh, I'll tell you what John," said Derek excitedly, "that wer' a bloomin' good session o' table tennis weren't it?"

"It was that Derek, I can't wait till next Sunday to give you another good whopping."

"Whaddaya talking about," he quizzed, "are you not coming down the club tomorrow night?"

"No, I can't Derek, I'm on the flamin' backshift this week," I complained, "so I won't be gettin' home till nearly eleven o'clock every night."

"Oh bloomin' 'eck John, just when we were getting into our stride. Still, never mind ... I'll see you next Sunday. But there'll be now't for you 'cos you'll be a bit stale not being able to practice for a week."

"Yeah, sure Derek, just you wait and see," I joked, "anyroad, I'll see you later ... so long."

"Don't forget what I said Johnny," shouted Derek after walking about twenty yards, "there'll be now't for thí next Sunday ... ha, ha, ha!"

I just laughed and waved in acknowledgement unaware that this was to be my last conversation with him. The next evening when I got home after completing my afternoon shift, Dad was in the house.

"All reight Dad ... have you had a good day?" I asked cheerfully.

"I have our John," he answered solemnly, "but there's one young lad, who lives on Lord Street, who hasn't. Poor lad's been killed at th'end of Trafalgar at the corner o' Manchester Road."

"He-ey Dad ... what happened?" I asked.

"Well, from what I can gather, he was delivering some meat on a butcher's bike and was run over by a coal wagon!"

"A young lad, a butcher's bike ... lives on Lord Street," I thought ... the horrible truth started to dawn on me! "Oh no Dad ... they didn't call him Derek Ratcliffe did they?"

"Aye our John they did ...why, do you know him?"

I didn't have to answer; it must have been obvious by the expression on my face ... I couldn't believe what I'd just heard.

Dad noticed the shocked look and tried to comfort me, "E-eh, I'm really sorry our John, I didn't realise he was a friend of yours."

"Yeah Dad, he's the lad I kept talking about every night last week when I came home from the youth club." Dad was very sympathetic and tried his best to comfort me but, all the same, I still felt really upset. Young Derek was buried from his own home a few days later.

For the first time in my life I was badly affected by death and in a state of shock ... sadly, it was not to be the last.

****

I never played snooker much at Sandygate Youth Club but I did like the occasional Jive. The Rock 'n' Roll era had arrived and interest reached fever pitch as films such as 'Love Me Tender,' 'Loving You,' 'Jailhouse Rock,' and King Creole,' starring Elvis Presley, were shown at the local cinemas. A time that all teenagers were to remember was when the film, 'Rock Around The Clock' starring Bill Haley and the Comets, was shown at the Empire Theatre. When Bill Haley started to sing 'Rock Around The Clock,' lots of teenagers got up and started to bop in the aisles and the rest of the teenagers started clapping and chanting. Up to that point it was innocent fun, but then some unruly lads decided to go wild and started ripping out seats and throwing missiles through the air; inevitably, fighting ensued. Luckily, nobody was badly hurt but, all the same, an enormous amount of damage was caused to the theatre. This particular event was the main topic of conversation in teenage circles and during the next few weeks, the same pattern was repeated. But things did gradually settle down and life eventually returned to some kind of normality. However, the 'Rock and Roll' era was here to stay ... bopping had taken on a new meaning.

Going to the pictures was a popular pastime and it was commonplace to see long queues at the cinemas every Saturday and Sunday evening. A new up and coming film actress, Marilyn Monroe was starring in films such as 'Niagra' and 'The Seven Year Itch'. She'd only recently come to stardom and was every young lad's dream ... including mine.

I had a large photograph of her pinned up in my bedroom. It was the photograph, which is still famous today. Marilyn is stood over an outside air vent with the skirt of her dress billowing up around her waist showing her undergarments.

She was my ideal ... I loved her and I used to fantasise about her, as did lots of other teenage lads.

****

It was a great time to be a teenager, as we had several good dance halls to frequent. I first went dancing down the Arcadians, better known as th'Arcs.' It was run by Sam Clegg, an ex dancer who, with his wife, had won various dancing competitions. Upon retiring they had hired a room underneath the Roxy Picture House and opened it as a rock 'n' roll venue for teenagers. It went down like a bomb and became the 'in place' for lots of us young folk. The cost of entry was two shillings, but Sam was a kind trusting kind of guy and would often waive the cost if any teenager didn't have enough. He said they could repay whenever they could ... nobody ever let him down.

To the last record of the night, teenagers smooched away to the tune of 'Sam's Song:

Here's a happy tune,

We love to croon

They call it Sam's song.

From the Arcadian's we progressed to the 'Big Band Sound. The Empress Ballroom and the Nelson Imperial were fantastic places, both of which staged live bands featuring famous stars like Cleo Lane and Johnny Dankworth, Eric Delaney's Band, Ray Ellington, Alma Cogan and many more. Every Saturday night young folk would flock to these popular places from far and wide, creating a wonderful atmosphere.

I was working at the pit and for me, like other teenagers, the weekend was the highlight of the week ... especially Saturday night. I'd meet up with my friends, Ronnie Hopkinson, David Whittaker, Pete Holroyd, Pete Fletcher, Billy Pounder and Barry Birks. All spruced up in our 'Teddy Boy' suits and our Tony Curtis hairstyles with a 'D A' at the back; we'd strut down Albion Street like bantam cocks. Our first port of call was always the Nelson Hotel where there was always a friendly rivalry. After downing a few pints and playing darts we'd make our way to the dance hall.

Once inside the dance hall the atmosphere was absolutely electrifying. Occasionally a fight would ensue; but the local bouncer, Tommy Kenny, an ex-boxer, would quickly sort things out.

The air would be pulsating with energy from hundreds of young folk; this was the ideal time for chatting up the girls and asking them for a date, especially on the dance floor. I wasn't too bad at 'Rock 'n' Roll' but when it came to the Waltz, Quickstep or Slow-Foxtrot I was hopeless, and being shy, the opportunity to chat up a girl seemed to elude me. Still, one time during a Waltz, I did finally pluck up the courage to ask a girl if she'd like to go to the pictures with me on Sunday night. The girl's name was Mary McCulloch and very nice she was too. I arranged to meet her under the clock outside the Palace Theatre. I took her to the Odeon Cinema and, so as to impress her, I bought tickets for the best seats upstairs. Afterwards I walked her home to her house on Annie Street near Burnley Football Club. I liked this girl a lot but, not being a good conversationalist, we spoke very little and sadly that was the end of what might have been a wonderful friendship.

****

The fifties were great years, especially for us teenagers ... I relished every moment. However I had a bad experience concerning our local milkman. It was quite traumatic for me and dampened my ego somewhat makin' me feel humiliated and ashamed. His name was Harold White.

He delivered milk to many household on Albion Street and his mode of transport was a horse and cart. He would often tether his horse to the gaslamp outside our house and, many a time, I would feed it a carrot.

Harry was in his early thirties and renowned for his fine physique and his reputation of having served in the Royal Marines, a commando outfit. Many a person would comment that he was as strong as an ox.

The incident happened one Saturday night after thoroughly enjoying myself dancing in the Empress Ballroom to the sound of Ted Heath and his band. All my mates had clicked, leaving me a little despondent as I made my way home.

"Not to worry," I thought, "better luck next time. Anyroad, I'm starving ... I'll just tek' myself off to the chippy for some nosh."

The Chippy was next door to the 'Coach and Horses' Pub about two hundred yards from the dancehall. As I stood in the queue waiting for my fish 'n' chips I noticed Harry in front of me.

"All reight young fella," he smiled cheerfully, "you're a Trafalgar Waller aren't you?"

"Yeah I am," I responded, "I live on Albion Street ... mi mam's one o' your customers."

"I thought I knew your face, you're the lad who feeds my horse wi' a carrot now and then. Anyroad, you look as if you've enjoyed yourself ... have you been dancing?"

"Yeah I have," I gloated, "I've been down th'Empess with some o' mi' mates ... it's an absolutely fantastic place."

"Your mates," he queried, "how come they're not here with you?"

"'Cos the lucky sods have all got fixed up ... I'm the only one who's missed out. Not to worry though, that's how the cookie crumbles ... I'll just have to settle for fish 'n' chips."

Tha' could do a lot worse lad," he grinned, at least it'll keep thi' out o' trouble eh?"

"Aye you could be right there," I mumbled as I stuffed a chip into my mouth, "but chance would o' been a fine thing. Anyroad, I'll be seeing you … so long!"

Hang on a minute young fella, it's a long way to Albion Street," he said as I attempted to pass him, "I'll give thi' a lift in mi' car if tha' wants … I'm only parked on t'other side o' road."

Aye alright, fair enough Harry," I replied not thinking anything about it, "that'll be great." I felt comfortable with the situation until we'd crossed over to the other side of the road and I couldn't see any signs of a car. He started to walk towards a large expanse of derelict ground at the back of the Odeon Cinema where large steel factory boilers were stored. As a child I'd played amongst these gigantic boilers and knew only too well that the canal ran just shortly beyond them. The spare land had no lighting and the Odeon cast a dark shadow over the area making it pitch black and eerie.

As he walked into the awesome darkness I got strong vibes telling me that something was afoot. My instinct told me that he was up to no good and common sense took over. "There's no way I'm going behind them boilers with him," I thought "I don't even think he's got a car. He more likely wants to try it on with me … no chance!"

"Are you comin' then?" he shouted from the shadows interrupting my thoughts, "my car's over yonder near the canal"

"U-umph, no way," I mumbled, "on your bike!"

"What's that? he shouted.

"Oh now't Harry," I lied through my teeth, "on second thoughts, I've decided to leg it home … it's a lovely night and I feel I need some fresh air."

Without further ado, I took my leave and walked sprightly past the dancehall towards St James' Street.

"The dirty ole' git," I kept saying to myself as I strolled through the town centre, "why doesn't he find himself a woman/"

I was just turning the corner at the bottom of Manchester Road when Harry pulled up alongside me in his car. "Well," he said, leaning out of the passenger window, "do you still want a lift or what … the offer's still on?"

I was rather taken aback … he really did have a car. I felt shamefaced for mistrusting him and my suspicions vanished. With my confidence restored I accepted the lift and got into the passenger seat. I felt relaxed as he laughed and joked whilst driving up Manchester Road; but I became uneasy when he speeded up and drove past Trafalgar Street.

"Whoa Harry!" I shouted, "You've passed Trafalgar … can you drop me off at Piccadilly Road?"

He paid no heed to me and put his foot down on the gas and sped for the outskirts of town.

"Whoa, whaddaya think you're doin'? I spluttered in panic. "Let me out … you're goin' miles out o' my way!"

"Eh don't worry about it lad," he grinned smarmily as he put his hand onto the inside of my leg caressing my thigh. "If it's a good time tha's after, I'm gonna tek' thi' to a nightclub in Rawtenstall where we can have a ball."

I was now frightened as my initial suspicions flooded back to me. The very thought of being driven by this man into the open countryside absolutely terrified me. But, despite the terror that ran through my being, I kept my wits about me … I knew I had to come up with something quick. We were fast reaching the summit traffic lights and I prayed they would be on red so that I could make a quick getaway. I was aware that the bleak expanse of "Crown Point' lay beyond the lights and I had visions of this monster having his wicked way with me. My fear intensified as my imagination saw me lying dead in a ditch on the open moors. To my utter dismay, the lights were on green and he sped through them at breakneck speed.

"Come on John, think o' something afore it's too late," I prayed. I was young, fit and strong, but I knew I was no match for this powerful man. By God's intervention it came to me that I had to play this guy at his own game. Luckily for me, there was a tiny slip road, which turned back on itself just prior to Bull and Butcher Pub.

"Harry," I said nudging him and giving him the eye, I know a great place in Padiham where we can have a fantastic time. Just turn down this snicket back onto Rossendale Road and I'll take you there." To my relief he took me at my word.

"Great," he said turning the corner on two wheels, "now you're talking!"

"Thank goodness for that," I sighed with relief, "at least it's given me some leeway."

I had to keep calm but inwardly prayed that traffic lights at Rosegrove Junction would be on red. No such luck ... they were on green and he sped through them like Stirling Moss. I began to panic again as my chances of escaping, before we reached Padiham where my bluff would be called, were fast running out.

As he accelerated towards the final main junction I geared myself up mentally to risk life and limb by jumping out of the car rather than let this evil pervert get his filthy paws on me. I was still a virgin and terrified of being sexually abused by this depraved monster; the very thought made my skin crawl. Once again I pictured myself being found dead somewhere in open countryside. The thought of my grief stricken mother and family stirred me on. I placed my hand on the car's door handle and prepared myself for the worst. But then, Lady Luck smiled down on me. A large wagon speeding down Padiham road forced Harry to slow down.

I didn't need a second chance ... in a flash I nipped out of the car and ran like a bat out of Hell ... Roger Bannister couldn't have caught me. I made my way to the nearest field and bolted over a stone wall and crouched in a corner like a frightened rabbit. I shook uncontrollably and for the life in me I daren't move. I was rooted to the spot, cold and bedraggled and I remained there until dawn. I didn't dare lift my head for fear of seeing his beady eyes bearing down on me. Gradually though I regained enough courage to scan the area in every direction, but my adrenaline was flowing and I was ready to make a bolt for it at any sign of danger. As I made my way homewards I was still on tenterhooks and constantly looked over my shoulder.

Although I came out of the ordeal unscathed bodily it affected me inasmuch as I felt ashamed. It may seem silly but, for many years to come, I never mentioned it to a living soul. If I had mentioned it to my mam she would certainly have gone to the police station. I didn't want this because I was frightened that I would get ridiculed at work with my workmates ... especially in the showers. I gave it a lot of thought and, rightly or wrongly, I decided it was one secret that I would keep to myself.

Consequently my confidence suffered somewhat. I was an innocent victim and maybe I shouldn't have felt that way, but I did. Like a lot of victims of atrocity I felt as though I was somehow to blame ... had I encouraged him in any way by giving out wrong signals? But then common sense prevailed ... clearly I hadn't, I was just a normal teenager enjoying a good night out. In my anguish my heart went out to ladies who've been the victims of sexual assault and how terribly helpless and alone they must feel.

"There but for the grace of God go I," I thought.

The secret was to remain within me until I was in my sixties. It was only when I decided to write about my memoirs that I decided to bring my ordeal into the open. Yes, I'd kept the secret to myself for fear of ridicule from my work colleagues and friends. The stigma of guilt, shame and humiliation stayed with me throughout my life. Even in adulthood I often shuddered of what might have happened.

I never set eyes on Harry again … He'd most likely absconded thinking I would report him to the police. Looking back in hindsight I should have exposed him, but I was too ashamed and lacking in confidence.

Ironically, shortly after my ordeal, I saw some graffiti on the wall of a public toilet. which read:

'HARRY WHITE THE BUMBOY.'

"U-um, "I thought, "he's obviously been trying it on elsewhere …I'm not the only one who knows about him."

****

I was a good swimmer but my mate, Peter Holroyd, who lived on Albion Street just above the railway-bridge, definitely had the edge on me both in speed and stamina. We were very competitive and every Saturday morning would go to the Central Swimming Baths. The two of us could easily swim a length underwater but Pete would always turn and swim that extra couple of yards more than me.

"I'm gonna swim two lengths o' this flamin' pool underwater if it kills me," said Pete one day.

"Yeah me too," I replied, "but I don't think it'll be for a while yet … I can just about manage a length an' half."

"I'll tell you what John … you dive in first and see how far you can get and then I'll try to beat it."

This was the course of events during the following weeks and we both gradually improved.

The length of the pool was divided into five segments by four dark lines running across the breadth. Each of us in turn would swim as far as we could, but if I swam to the third line … Pete would reach the fourth when it was his turn and so on. Neither of us smoked so we were both in peak condition and it wasn't long before Pete broke the two-length barrier. There was always a healthy competitive spirit between us and I was determined to beat him eventually. Then one day I too broke the two-length barrier … my lungs seemed near to bursting but I knew that if I was to beat Pete's record I had to carry on. Somehow I managed to turn and actually made it to the second line. Not to be outdone, Pete dove in and not only passed my mark but also carried on to the third line. That was it, I realised I could never beat him at this game. Afterwards, it became routine for us both to swim the two lengths underwater.

****

I had a good set of mates and we all knew how to enjoy life without going overboard or doing anything stupid. But like most teenagers we sometimes went a little bit over the top. We certainly enjoyed our weekends in Burnley and Nelson but we also had something else at our disposal, which was absolutely fantastic … the '4 O'clock Special'. This was a special train so called because it was laid on especially every Saturday evening and would leave Central Station at 4 o'clock, heading for Blackpool. My mates and I couldn't afford to go every week but made a pact to go at least once a month. Every week I'd scrimp and save, putting some of my spending money to one side, but it was worth every penny … when we got to Blackpool we had a 'ball'.

One Saturday afternoon after a game of football Ronnie asked me, "Whattaya doing tonight John, are you going down th'Empress?"

"Am I 'eck as like Ronnie, I'm going to Blackpool on the 4 o'clock special wi' t'other lads ... are you not coming?"

Oh aye, I forgot ... it doesn't seem two minutes since the last time we went ... time flys don't it?"

Well it's four weeks since ... I should know, I've bín skint for the last month."

Bloomin' 'eck, I'd best get mí skates on and get home to get ready."

"You'll be all right Ronnie, there's bags o' time ... it's only three o'clock and we don't have to catch the train till five past four at Barrack's Station.

Ronnie was ready with time to spare and we met up with our other mates on the platform all dressed up in our glad rags. When we boarded the train it was almost full with other excited teenagers from Nelson all raring to go. A load more boarded at Accrington and by the time we reached Blackburn the train was bursting at the seams.

"Great ... I can see the Tower," bellowed Ronnie as the train got nearer to Blackpool, "we're gonna have some fun in there tonight."

Excitement built up as we pulled into the station; many lads opened carriage doors and jumped off the train before it came to a stop, eagerly making their way to the exit.

"I'm starving," said Ronnie, "I could eat a scabby donkey."

"Aye, so am I," put in Billy, "are we going to that little chippy near to't Central pier?"

"Yeah why not," I said, "we allús enjoy our grub in there."

After a plate of fish, chips and mushy peas we all made our way to the Western Bar on the Pleasure Beach.

"It's a great atmosphere in here," David said, "I love it."

"Aye, you're reight there," said Ronnie taking a swig of beer," it's better than Uncle Tom's Cabin."

"Where we're going after here," I asked, "to the Tower or the Winter Gardens?"

"Well I think the Winter Gardens great," said Pete, "but most o' the lads on't train said they were going to the Tower 'cos Eric Delaney's playing there."

"Aye, I heard the same thing," commented Billy, "they were all sayin' it should be bouncing in there tonight."

"I'll go along with that," said David, "how about a show of hands?" The vote was unanimous in favour of the Tower.

"Right," said Billy, "now can we get down to some serious supping?"

After a few pints of beer we then cheerfully made our way along the 'Golden Mile' where hordes of youngsters were happily meandering back and forth between the Tower and the Pleasure Beach. This was a great opportunity to chat up the girls.

"Come on girls," one or other of us would quip, "get yourselves along to the Tower Ballroom it's gonna be raving in there tonight. You never know ... this may be your lucky night."

"Oh yeah, in your dreams," was the expected reply.

Not to be put off, another chat up line was, "You look gorgeous lúv ... is there any chance o' borrowing your body for a bop later on?" It was great banter and commonplace throughout the length of the promenade.

When we reached the ballroom it was packed to capacity with boys and girls standing shoulder to shoulder. We met up with Bobby Cheetham, Martin Grogan and many others from Burnley, but there were lots from other towns as far afield as Southport, Ormskirk and Liverpool, and everyone was there to enjoy themselves.

"Bloomin' 'eck Billy," I said, "you were right when you said it'd be bouncing in here tonight ... it's heaving, I can feel the floor going up and down."

The night passed very quickly and the bewitching hour to leave arrived only too soon. We had to leave before eleven o'clock as the last train for Burnley left at 11-15pm. Addresses were exchanged between boys and girls from different towns and letters would follow. All in all, the atmosphere was wonderful ... innocent and naive ... yet wonderful.

If a lad didn't make it out on the dance floor he wasn't too bothered ... there was always a good chance on the way back home on the train ... the 'Passion Wagon'. It was a single compartment train and once it left the station the fun began. Light bulbs were removed from their sockets and thrown out of the window and the 'necking' session would begin. If a lad hadn't 'clicked', as it was quaintly put, he'd risk life and limb by climbing out of a window and making his way to the next carriage. He'd edge along a narrow ledge and cling onto anything to hand. This happened frequently, but in all the times I did the trip I never heard of anyone getting hurt or killed.

"By 'eck," said Ronnie as we walked along Trafalgar after disembarking from the train, "that was a bloomin' good night weren't it?"

"It was that," answered David, "you can't beat the 4 o'clock special canya?"

"You're right there Dave," I responded, "it were well worth all the scrimping and saving ... there's now't like it. I'm looking forward to the next time if it's only to meet up with them Liverpudlians again ... they're reight characters aren't they?"

"Aye, you're not kidding" Ronnie laughed as he turned onto Derby Street, "they're a barrel o' laughs. Anyroad lads I'll see you tomorrow down the club ... adios!"

Dave, Pete and I chatted a little under the gaslamp outside our house prior to departing about 1am.

****

Sunday was a quiet day and usually, after breakfast, Dad, Jimmy, and I would go round to Peter Barrett's house on the next street for a game of cards. We'd meet up with six other blokes and then get settled down for a long session of three-card brag.

The Barretts appeared to be even poorer than us Cowells and their home was forever untidy. Mrs Barrett never threw newspapers away ... these were used as a tablecloth and even as make-do curtains. Still, the atmosphere was good and besides, Mrs Barrett baked the most delicious scones and buns. She'd mix all the ingredients in a large aluminium bowl prior to putting them into the oven. It wasn't long before tantalising smells filled the nostrils, whetting everybody's appetites.

Dad was always very particular and, being faddy, he would never eat or drink anything in anybody else's house. Nevertheless, the rest of us heartily scoffed the buns washing them down with a brew. I too was faddy but all the same, I couldn't resist Mrs Barrett's delicious buns. This went on for months, being a Sunday ritual, but then, one morning, something happened to change our minds.

It was about 11-45am and Mrs Barrett tapped Peter on the shoulder, "Nip upstairs our Peter ... the Gerry hasn't bín emptied yet." Minutes later, to everybody's horror, Peter came downstairs precariously carrying an aluminium bowl, the same bowl used for baking, with all its contents swishing about!

"Will someone open the backdoor for me," said Peter unconcerned, "so I can empty this down the lavvy!"

We all sat there in disbelief with our mouths open.

The only person to see the funny side of it was Dad as he murmured to me, "Serves thí bloody well right." He had us on for weeks after that rubbing it in at every opportunity.

However, thanks to our Mary, Dad didn't get the last laugh. He used to love Mary's baking and looked forward to her special dishes ... this was to be his downfall.

One day Mary was in Mrs. Barrett's and the kindly lady asked, "How would you like some potato pie Mary ... it's only just come out of the oven?" A delicious aroma filled the air but Mary politely declined, as she'd already heard of the aluminium bowl episode.

"No thank you Mrs Barrett, I've just had my tea." But, as an afterthought she added, "I wouldn't mind taking some home for mí supper tonight though."

"Yeah righto love, I'll just get you somét to put it in."

Mary couldn't wait to get home to prepare it for Dad along with some vegetables. Sure enough he came home at the expected time.

"I've made something different tonight Dad, a potato pie with a crust on top," she said slyly, "I hope you like it." He didn't just like it ... he loved it!

"By 'eck our Mary that were good, did you learn to make it in the cookery class at school?" Mary composed herself before dropping the bombshell. "Well no Dad, in fact, I have a little confession to make; I didn't make it at all ... Mrs Barrett did!"

"Oh, I thought it tasted different. Anyroad, who's Mrs Barrett ... is she one of your cookery teachers?"

"No Dad ... Mrs Barrett where you go playing cards every Sunday."

"**You what!**" he gasped, the awful truth dawning on him. "You mean to say it were méd in that bloody aluminium dish of hers?" he grimaced, retching. "A-ar-rgh … I feel like I'm gonna be sick!"

Mary told Jimmy and me when we got home what had happened and we both burst out laughing. Dad was not amused!

"Well Dad," quipped Jimmy, "it serves you right for laughing at us … you've got to admit it's funny."

Mary rubbed salt in the wound, chuckling as she said, "Well Dad, you can't deny you enjoyed it … it must have been some secret ingredient that Mrs Barrett used!"

****

I was seventeen when I had my first experience as a decorator. Mum never had much money and couldn't afford to pay for having the house decorated. One Saturday morning she was feeling a bit disgruntled, as the front of the house was looking very shabby. I'd always fancied having a go at painting and decorating so I raised the subject with her.

"I'll do it for you if you want Mam, I wouldn't mind having a go at painting the front o' t'house."

"How can you do that our John," she asked, "we don't have any ladders?"

"Oh it'll be all reight Mam, I'll be able to paint the upstairs window by standing on the window sill and our Barry said he'll hold the paint tin for me."

"No, you can't do that; you could fall off and hurt yourself or even be killed."

"Don't worry Mam, I'll be all reight … honest!"

She was a little reluctant but after pestering her for a while she relented. Thirty minutes later I was back from the paint shop with four tins of paint, some putty, a bottle of turpentine, some sandpaper and two paintbrushes.

"Why have you bought four tins?" asked Barry.

"Well I'm painting th'house black and white so I need two tins of undercoat and two o' gloss."

"Oh aye, I never thought o' that."

"Right," I thought, "I've never done any painting afore so I'll start on the downstairs first for a bit o' practice."

After rubbing the window frames down with sandpaper and re-puttying where necessary I started to apply the undercoat. The grey undercoat blended well with the white and I was quite impressed.

"U-um," I said to Barry, "not bad eh ... what do you think?"

"Yeah, I've got to admit it looks a lot brighter already."

"It does don't it?" I gloated feeling pleased with myself.

"I wouldn't feel too chuffed yet our John," said Barry, "that's the easy part ... you've still got to do th'upstairs' window."

"Aye, I know that, don't remind me our kid. Anyroad, I've figured a way o' doing it and I'm gonna put th'undercoat on this afternoon and the gloss tomorrow."

"I'll believe it when I see it," quipped Barry.

"Come on then I need your help this time," I said as I made my way upstairs "let's get cracking,"

"Righto ... I'm coming, I'm coming!"

"Well here goes," I said as I lifted up the lower frame of the sliding sash window until it almost touched the head lintel, and then I lowered the top frame a couple of inches. "I'm gonna climb out onto the window sill now and get started."

"Why have you lowered the top window and left the lower one a bit short of the lintel," asked Barry, "wouldn't it have been better if both of 'em were right up to the top to give thí more room to get through?"

"No Barry, I want them open a bit at the top so that I can hold onto somét."

I climbed through the window and hung on precariously with one hand whilst I did the preparation work with the other. I then climbed back into the room.

"That weren't too bad our kid," Barry said as we chatted over a brew that Mum had just made.

"That's all reight for you to say ... you weren't the one hangin' on for dear life."

"Yeah I know that, but you couldn't have managed it without my advice could you?" Barry joked.

"No I suppose not our Barry. Anyroad," I said as I clambered back out of the window, "now comes the crunch 'cos I need your help to hold the paint tin for me ... here goes."

It worked a treat. I painted the woodwork first, followed by the head lintel and then the stone jambs.

"Great!" said Barry. "All you need to do now is paint the window sill."

"Yeah, and that should be easy," I said as I climbed back into the room, "'cos I can do that from th'inside of the bedroom."

"It looks like your little plan to paint th'upstairs' window without a ladder's gonna work all right our John, you've only to put the gloss on tomorrow and that shouldn't take too long 'cos you wont have to do any more rubbing down."

"Aye, you're right there our kid, I never thought o' that. Anyroad, we'll start soon in the morning and seeing that I've now got the hang of it I'll do th'upstairs window first."

"Hey that's a good ún our John ... got the hang of it. Do you get it ... hanging on? Ha, ha, ha!"

"Ha, ha, very funny!" I quipped back.

Next morning after going to church I got started.

"Are you gonna paint th'upstairs first our John?" asked Barry "It should be a piece o' cake after yesterday."

"That's easy for you to say our kid ... you're not the one hanging on for dear life."

Once again I climbed out on to the windowsill and everything went well. By three o'clock I'd applied the finishing touch to the downstairs' window and proudly stood back in the cobbled street to admire my work.

"Bloomin' 'eck Johnny!" cracked Jack Bickle. "It looks like a Massey's House."

"A Masseys's House?" I queried. "Whattaya you talking about?"

"Well that's the colour scheme of Massey's Brewery in'it," he laughed, "all Massey's pubs are painted black and white."

"I'll have a pint o' bitter," joked Jack Smithson as he passed the house, "ha, ha, ha!"

"You can laugh all you want, but I think it looks all reight." I said a little annoyed. "Anyroad, it looks a lot better now than it did afore and a sight better than some o' t'other houses around here."

"Aye it does," said another voice from behind me, "in fact, I thinks you've made a good job of it lad." On turning I came face to face with a small slim fellow in his fifties.

"Thank you!" I said a little bewildered, "Do I know you?"

"No lad, I'm not from round here, I live o'er in Nelson. My name's Sam Sykes and I'm a self-employed decorator and I've just been pricing a job up in one o' them big houses o'er the bridge."

"Oh yeah," I replied feeling a little nonplussed as to why he was telling me this. But he soon enlightened me.

"What it is lad, I've got a lot o' work on and I could do with a good helper ... are you interested?"

I'd like to," I said, "but I can't ... I already have a job workin' down the pit."

"Oh I'm not talking about full-time; I just need someone to help me now and again. Happen you could work for me at weekends or evenings?"

"Yeah fair enough," I said, "in fact I'm on the back-shift this week so I'll be able to help you in the mornings."

"Right lad, if you bring yourself to number sixty at nine o'clock in the morning I'll find you somét to do."

"Great!" I muttered to myself, "It'll be a bit extra spending money and I'll be able to pick up a few tips on decorating at the same time." I worked with Sam for about six months. He was a good tradesman and he taught me quite a few tricks of the trade. Consequently, I did quite a lot of experimenting on Mum's house. The first time I attempted wallpapering was on the staircase and it turned out really funny. I was working with Sam one day and I asked him what he did with all the short ends of wallpaper when he'd finished a job.

"Well I throw them away, they're no good for o'wt else."

"Oh, can I have 'em then, they'll come in handy in our house?"

"You can if you want, but I don't know what you'll be able to use 'em for."

"Waste not, want not!" I thought, "I'll paper the staircase with 'em." Before going home I asked Sam if I could have a little bit of adhesive to fit them with.

"Aye take a packet o' Lapcell lad, it'll come out of your wages mind!" he said jokingly.

I took every short roll that I could, red ones, blue ones and even some nursery wallpaper with cartoons on it.

"U-um, it doesn't matter," I thought, "at least they'll brighten the place up ... it'll be better than looking at the bare plaster everytime we come down the stairs."

I did the job one weekend and was proud of it but Mum wasn't quite so impressed.

"What the 'eck's going on, what sort of wallpapering is that?"

"It's a new style Mam," I quipped, "it's what they call contemporary."

"Contemporary? I don't know about that," she replied, "all I can say is it's definitely multi-coloured ... it looks like Billy Smart's Circus."

"Well everytime you come downstairs now Mam," I joked, "It'll remind you of Joseph and his coat of many colours."

"It'll do that all right," she said trying to suppress a smile.

This was the beginning of my decorating experience. I remained interested and always kept my hand in. With lots of help and advice from Sam I became quite 'the expert'.

Sam wasn't only a good tradesman; he was also very witty and comical. He had me intrigued one day with one of his stories and really caught me on the hop. Some kids had just broken a window and Sam was re-glazing it.

"I'll tell you what," he said, I've glazed a lot o' windows in my time but I'll ne'er forget the time I glazed one for old Mrs Gorton."

"Oh aye," I said, "what happened then?"

"Well," he went on to say, "it were only a small pane o' glass so it didn't take me long to bed it into the putty, fix it with some panel pins and then smooth the putty off with mí putty knife. After that I went home for a bit o' dinner. I'd only bín in th'house ten minutes when the phone rang. It was Mrs Gorton and she said that I hadn't smoothed the putty off. I tried telling her I had but she wouldn't have it. Anyroad, sure enough, when I got back on to her house the outside putty was missing."

"So you had forgotten to do it then?" I asked.

"Well I wasn't sure, so I just re-puttied it and went back home. I'd only just taken mí coat off when the phone rang again. I couldn't believe mí ears ... guess who it was."

"Mrs Gorton?" I asked curiously.

"Aye it was and she said that I still hadn't put any putty on th'outside o' the glass. I telt her that I'd just left her house ten minutes ago but she wouldn't have it. She said she were there now and insisted there were definitely no putty on th'outside of the frame. When I got back to her house I couldn't believe it ... there were no putty in'it again. But this time I knew something was going on."

"So what did you do?" I asked intrigued.

"Well I re-glazed it again but this time I hid at th'end o' the block and waited. I could just about see the window from where I wer' standing and it was about ten minutes afore I saw it ... I couldn't believe my eyes."

"Saw it ... you saw what?" I asked more intrigued than ever.

"It wer' an animal weren't it ... a bloomin' animal!"

"An animal," I said all fired up, "what sort of an animal?"

He looked serious for a moment, then burst out laughing before coming out with the punchline, "It were a putty cat weren't it ...a bloomin' putty cat ... ha ha, ha, ha!"

I stood there for a few seconds with my mouth wide open, but then I saw the funny side and joined in the laughter. It reminded me of when my mate Ronnie had fallen for one of Bobby Cheetham's practical jokes. I liked the joke very much and was later to catch out many of my unsuspecting friends in the same way that Sam had caught me out.

****

It was after Dad had been out on another of his boozy escapades that something very amusing happened. One particular night, Mum decided that she'd just about had enough of his antics. It was turned midnight and there was no sign of him so she decided to lock the door and go to bed.

At around two o'clock, our Jimmy was awakened by Dad's voice shouting, "Winnie ... Winnie, please help me!"

Jimmy nudged me asking, "Can you hear mí dad our kid; he seems to be in bother?"

I was half-asleep and couldn't hear anything at first, but then came a kind of wailing sound, "Oh yeah, I can hear something now our Jim," I replied, "but where is it coming from?"

Then we heard a loud howling followed by an ear splitting yell as Dad cried out, "Oh come on somebody, help me please!"

By now, our Barry was awake, "Hey that sounds like mí dad," he said, "he must be in trouble, let's go down and help him."

"Yeah right," replied Jimmy, "but where is the noise coming from, I can't tell if it's from inside or outside the house?"

"No, neither can I," responded Barry, "but there's only one way to find out." All three of us crept downstairs trying not to disturb Mum and the girls, who slept in the back bedroom.

Nonetheless, we soon found out that we were left with little choice. Dad wasn't in the house and on opening the front door he wasn't outside either. Nevertheless, there was a distinctive animal like wail, which rent the night air, and it seemed to be coming from ground level and, on looking down, we saw the most hilarious sight we'd ever seen. We didn't know whether to laugh or cry, as Dad was stuck in the coal cellar chute. He'd obviously tried to get into the house via the cellar chute after finding the front door securely bolted.

"Come on you lot," he pleaded, "stop your laughing and get me outa here, it's not flamin' funny!"

"Righto Dad, don't worry about it," quipped Jimmy, "we'll have you out in a jiffy." Jimmy then started issuing orders, "Right our Barry, you stay here and help me. John, you take a chair down the cellar to stand on and try shoving him out from below whilst me and our Barry pull from here." We tried our hardest but after twenty minutes of huffing and puffing we still hadn't budged him. The trouble was that one of his arms was stuck by his side, and it seemed to wedge even more every time we tugged and shoved. We were frightened of pulling him downwards for fear of wedging him deeper; the logical thing seemed to be to pull him out the same way that he'd gone in. By this time, Mum and Mary were downstairs awakened by the commotion.

"Oh my God!" she exclaimed. "Now I've seen it all; I thought the escapade with the horse was the final straw, but now this!"

"What are we going to do Mam?" asked Barry, "Are we going to have to send for the Fire-Brigade?"

"No we're not; I've been shown up enough around here as it is. As far as I'm concerned he can stay there all night, it'll teach him a lesson."

"Oh no Winnie, you can't do that," wailed Dad, "please get me outa here!"

"It's all right Dad," put in Barry, "Mam's only joking, she wouldn't leave you like this."

"Oh yes I would if it means sending for the Fire-Brigade, he's not bringing disgrace onto this house again."

"Oh come on Winnie, do something please, I'll die if you leave me here all night!" pleaded Dad.

"You should have thought about that before you went out on your boozing spree shouldn't you?" But despite what she was saying, she encouraged us lads to try again. Nevertheless, after another ten minutes it seemed hopeless; he was completely jammed in. By now, Mary, Barbara and many of the neighbours had been aroused by the rumpus.

"Oh Mam, we're going to have to call the emergency services," said Mary, "or Dad might die."

"Yes all right, I suppose you're right," answered Mum, who was now quite concerned herself.

"Just hang on a minute before you do that," said Jimmy, "I think I have an idea that might work."

"What's that then?"

"Well, if we fill a bowl with warm soapy water and douse Dad with it, it should lubricate him, and maybe we'll be able to pull him out then."

"Hey! If you're gonna wet me through make sure the water's not cold!" protested. Dad. Jimmy ran into the house and came back with a full bowl.

Standing above the chute he said, "Right Dad, shut your eyes and put your head to one side and I'll let you have it."

"Thank you very much our Jimmy ... maybe I'll do the same for you someday. Anyway, get the flamin' thing over and done with!"

"Right Dad, here goes," replied Jimmy as he threw the water straight at the chute. I couldn't help laughing which in turn triggered off Barry and the girls. Jimmy tried his best to keep a straight face, having done the deed but without success. When we regained our composure, we got down to the serious business of trying to free Dad again. There were obvious signs of movement but he kept crying out that his arm was still jammed.

"Sorry Dad," muttered Jimmy, "but I'm going to have to douse you one more time, I think that'll do the trick."

"Aye all right but be quick about it and make it a bit warmer this time!" Jimmy went through the same routine making sure this time that he reached parts not previously soaked. After this, Dad felt himself sliding gradually downwards but once again came to a full stop. Mum knew then that there was no alternative but to call the Fire-Brigade, so reluctantly made her way to the police telephone box. When they arrived it took them about forty minutes to free him, luckily he was no worse for wear. He was as black as soot though and looked like a drowned rat; everybody had a real good hearty laugh about it including Mum. It was a late night for everyone but nobody minded; it had been a funny and yet another story for the archives.

****

Dad's lifestyle didn't change very much and one particular evening he did something very foolish, lots of people found it rather amusing but all the same it was still foolish. He was out on one of his many boozing sessions, and as per usual, the effects of the beer completely took over. But on this occasion, which happened a summer's evening, he overstepped the mark playing a silly prank that cost him the loss of his beloved horse Peggy. Two months previously, he'd actually gambled Peggy away in a silly game of cards; all the same, the man who'd won the horse had agreed to rent Peggy back to him at a nominal fee.

This particular night, Mum, our Jimmy and I were sat around the fire having a brew. It was coming up to eleven o'clock when there was a commotion on the front street. The front door opened, then there was a loud clomping noise in the lobby; all three of us wondered what on earth it could be, making such a racket. First of all, Dad popped his head around the living room door and staggered into the room drunk out of his mind; then, to our amazement, Peggy, the horse, followed him. How on earth the floor didn't collapse heaven knows; it's just as well that they were well supported by very large joists. Dad was in a rather mischievous mood and Mum was too flabbergasted to argue with him. Jimmy and I took care of Peggy, backing her out onto the front street and settling her down. Nevertheless, the damage had already been done, as Dad had been seen riding Peggy at a gallop along Trafalgar, and someone had reported the incident to the police. He hadn't been in the house very long before a police car arrived; he was arrested and kept in custody overnight. As he was taken away there were lots of people on the front street whose curiosity had been aroused by the rumpus. I had the responsibility of taking Peggy back to her stable and bedding her down for the night; little did I know that I would never see her again. I'm not quite sure whether Dad was charged with being drunk and disorderly, being in charge of a horse whilst under the influence of drink, or riding Peggy without lights, maybe all three; one thing is sure though, he got a hefty fine. It turned out that he had done it as a prank; however, the new owner was not the least bit amused, he wouldn't let Dad use her again and sold her shortly after.

Dad was at a bit of a loss at first, but not for too long, as our Jimmy came up with something. Nine months previously, he'd joined the air-force and being thrifty, had saved quite a bit of money in the Post Office.

"Why don't you buy a wagon Dad, I think it would be more practical than a horse and cart anyway?"

"Good idea our Jimmy except for one snag, where do I get the money?"

"You could buy a second-hand one Dad, I know where there's one goin' in the Mitre Area for two hundred pounds," adding, "and you'd probably get it for less than that if you bartered with 'm."

"Aye perhaps I would but like I said ... where do I get the money?"

To his surprise, Jimmy replied, "I'll lend it to you Dad, I've saved up quite a bit since I went into the forces and I reckon I could just about raise that much."

"By 'eck lad, you're a canny ún too, tha' never ceases to amaze me. Anyway, would you really lend me that much?"

"Course I would, there's no use me havin' it if I don't put it to good use is there? Mind you tha'd have to pay me back so much a week Dad with a bit of interest."

Dad shook his head a little, "That's my lad," he said, "right you're on our Jimmy, let's go and have a look at this here wagon." He did buy the wagon, and that was the end of the horse and cart era as far as he was concerned. It may well have been more practical than a horse and cart but, by 'eck, I didn't half miss our Peggy.

****

Being an early riser and an outdoor type, on Sunday mornings during the summer months, I loved to set off on my bike. I regularly did a twenty mile circular route to Bacup via Rawtenstall and Stacksteads and back to Burnley. I set off one Sunday morning unaware that I was going to find something on the return journey. I peddled up the steep incline of Manchester Road as far as the summit.

"Great" I muttered to myself, "downhill now all the way to Rawtenstall!" There were some flat bits after passing through Dunnockshaw and Crawshawbooth but it was quite easy going. On the downhill stretches I freewheeled, singing out loudly,

"Oh what a Beautiful morning,
Oh what a beautiful day.

I've got a wonderful feeling,

Everything's going my way."

This stemmed from the fact that I'd recently been to the Odeon Cinema and seen Gordon Macrae in the musical – 'Oklahoma'.

After a brief stop in Rawtenstall I headed for Bacup, cycling through Waterfoot. From there I passed through a narrow gorge which always intrigued me, then onto Stacksteads finally arriving at 14 Mowgrain View, my grandparents' home in Bacup.

"Hiya Granma," I'd say giving her a peck on her cheek.

"E-eh, look who's here, it's our Johnny fro' o'er Burnley ... come here and gimme a love."

All right Granma ... how are you?"

"All the better for seeing thí lad ... sit thasel' down and I'll mek' thí a nice cuppa tay and thá can have one o' mí buns."

"Great Granma ... what d'you think I've come all this way for?"

"Go on you cheeky young monkey!"

I laughed a little, "I'm only kiddin' Gran ... you know how much I like to see you. Mind, I do really love your buns 'cos nobody else in the world bakes 'em like you do ... I think they're smashing."

"Never mind the bleedín buns lad," put in Grandad, "how about comin' and havin' a word wí me?"

"Right Grandad, how are you feeling ... a bit better than last weekend I hope?"

"Never mind me lad ... how about thí?"

"Ah well, I've got to check up on you Grandad 'cos mí mam were a bit worried last week when I told her you weren't so well."

"Oh aye? Well think on thá tells her I'm all reight when thá gets home today ... I don't want mí lass worrying none, she's got enough on her plate as it is."

"Righto I promise. Anyroad Grandad, while I'm here, is there any chance of you telling me any more tales of when you were in the trenches during the First World War?"

"By Gum our John, you're more inquisitive than a cat ... nobody else asks me questions about the war like you do."

"Well that's 'cos you make it sound so interesting and anyway, I'm proud of you Grandad."

"Nay lad ther's now't to be proud of, we were out there 'cos we had to be. It was horrible, being bivouacked down night after night and constantly bombarded by gas bombs and shellfire. It wer' nigh impossible to sleep properly even when it wer' quiet because of smarting eyes caused by tear gas. Aye and that wer' despite wearing gas masks. And many a time we had to remove our sodden clothing not only to dry them, but because they were flea ridden. Peace wasn't forthcoming because of the constant itching ... it wer' like hell on earth." He stopped then sighing, "Anyway our John, that's enough talk about that awful war, it was terrible!"

Grandad very seldom spoke openly about the horror of the western front trenches. But when he was in this sort of mood I gleaned as much from him about that terrible war as possible.

On a previous occasion, when he was in one of his tale telling moods, he'd really opened up his heart and this he what he told me:

"Orders and counter orders were forever being received from command headquarters. Men lived in constant torment, either waiting for something to happen or all hell being let loose. We were either being attacked or on the offensive ourselves. Battalions were ordered to attack carrying full battle regalia, including grenades, gasmasks and rifle with fixed bayonet. Many men hesitated but followed others like sheep knowing only too well they may never ever see another day ... and some even thought that that would be a relief. Some even hoped

they would be injured just bad enough to be medically discharged. Bullets from machine guns whistled everywhere with many men dying instantly, others severely wounded. or pinned down. Still some managed to go forward under a barrage of artillery, enveloped in smoke. Foul smelling corpses of men and horses alike with arms and legs in pools of coagulated blood. wer' lying everywhere. Many men were unrecognisable either with burnt faces or no face at all. **It was total carnage!"** 'Forward! - Forward!' came orders shouted by senior officers. That we did, very slowly crawling on our bellies; this resulted in many more mates being killed or maimed. Many times, some men arrived at no-man's land, where they could neither go forward nor back unless under cover of smoke or darkness.

Badly injured men tried desperately to drag themselves back to the safety of the trenches moaning, 'Please help me! ... Ple ... ease don't leave me here please! ... Please! ... Ple. ease!

Stretcher-bearers courageously did their job but many died alongside the injured.

Still more orders came ... 'Onwards! ... Defend your post at all costs!'

Many men were stuck in terrible positions for days until backed up by reinforcements. Ironically, we sometimes got Jerry on the run, and took over some of their trenches, only to discover more misery, as the Germans had left many booby traps. It's a miracle that any of us survived."

At the end of his tale he'd sigh. "Aye our John, there was nothing glorious about it. Many a good lad died out yonder ... u-um, a sheer waste it was!" His face turned rather sad and his voice lowered as he added, "Aye, and many a mate o' mine has died since comin' home from that blasted war!"

I loved to catch him in this kind of mood when he'd relate to me some of the horrors of the First World War. That may seem barbaric, but I truly felt these tales needed to be told so that maybe in the future we as a nation can put an end to all these terrible happenings. Grandad, like many other soldiers who survived that terrible ordeal, was not a well man. He'd been shot through his right shoulder and could never again use it at an optimum level. And like many others he suffered also from chronic bronchitis and other disabilitating diseases.

"U-um, I know you don't always like talking about the war Grandad and I know it makes you feel really sad, but that's one of the reasons why I'm proud of you ... you went through so much."

"Aye, all reight our John, but that's enough for today ... I'm not feeling up to anymore. Mind you, I don't want you tell to tell your mam that."

At that comment I just laughed and left it at that... I loved the stories but I knew when to back off. I stayed a little while longer then bade them farewell.

"Ta-rah Gran, see you next weekend 'Please God' ... same to you Grandad."

"God bless you our John," Grandma shouted, waving to me from the doorstep, "give our love to everyone o'er in Burnley. And think on ... ték care when tha's cycling back o'er them moors,"

In spite of a two-mile steep uphill gradient passing through Weir as far as the Deerplay Pub, I always enjoyed the trek back. On reaching Deerplay I took a short respite admiring the beautiful countryside. I loved nothing more than to sit down on a grassy verge and take in all the scenery.

"Just look at this beauty all around me, as far as the eye can see," I thought taken aback by nature's wonders, "what a contrast to working down the a dusty coalmine all week." I took a long deep breathe taking in God's good fresh air to the very depths of my lungs. "By 'eck but it's good to be alive," I said to myself adding, "u-um and especially when I'm on my bike and I can free wheel it all the way back to Burnley."

Times like that always got me thinking about God's creation and especially Nature's wildlife. I just laid back on the deep luscious green grass and went into a sombre mood murmering to myself, "If wildlife disappeared then nothing else would take its place and a piece of God's plan would be missing." It got me to thinking what my dad had told me when I was a lad that we are custodians of our planet and therefore responsible for everything that lives upon it. If we don't care ... nothing else will.

"Our John," he would say, "There's nothing more wonderful than to watch wild creatures in their habitat. As I see birds in the sky or watch nature's creatures frollicking about on open moorland they open my both eyes and my heart and I am taken aback by the beauty of it all. I look up to the heavens and I am struck dumb in awe and reverence. You just cannot put a price on that type of feeling,"

I was about to go further into a nostalgic mood but a slight movement in the grass intercepted my thoughts and to my amusement I saw a baby rabbit hopping by just a few yards in front of me. I immediately became intrigued and wanted to get a bit closer to the little creature. So as not to frighten it I cautiously crouched down onto my hands and knees and started to stealthily crawl nearer. Too late ... the little rabbit spotted me and scurried off over the moor. It was then that I spotted a piece of coloured paper crumpled up amongst the tall grass.

"Can that be what I think it is?" I thought feeling a tinge of excitement. On unfolding the small scrap of paper my thoughts were confirmed ... it actually was a pound note, I was highly delighted.

"Yeah, great, fantastic … what a good do!" I whooped, "that's two week's spending money … I'm loaded!"

I niftily sat astride my bike and set off as happy as a lark singing the second chorus of my song as I free wheeled the long downhill journey home.

"There's a bright golden haze on the meadow
There's a bright golden haze on the meadow.
The corn is as high as an elephant's hide,
It looks like it's climbing clear up to the sky.
Oh what a beautiful Morning,
Oh what a beautiful day.
I've got a wonderful feeling,
Everything's going my way,
O-oh what a beau-tiful da-ay!"

On reaching home I had a sandwich and a swig of pop and couldn't wait to set off again. Before doing so I mentioned my good fortune to Mum.

"Anyroad Mam, here's ten bob here for you … it'll help you to get by till next week."

She was extremely grateful making it obvious in the way she knew best, "E-eh, I'll tell You what it is God … none of my kids have much, but whenever they have anything they like to share it with me."

I interrupted her little invocation, "Right Mam, I'm going now … I'll see you later."

"Are you off again so soon our John," she asked "you never stop in th'house for two minutes do you?"

"Not on a nice day like this Mam. We don't get many … I've gotta take advantage while I can."

"Aye, I suppose you're right there. By the way … how was my dad this week?"

"Oh he was all right Mam, he seemed much better."

"Are you sure … you're not just saying that 'cos he told you to?"

"No Mam … honest!" It was a white lie, but what else could I say? "U-um," I thought to myself as I peddled off, "she's a right wise óle bird mí mam is … she misses now't."

By the end of the day I'd covered a lot of the surrounding countryside and loved every minute. Before going into the house I looked down Albion Street and was taken aback by a beautiful sunset and a clear red sky. Even though we lived right in the very heart of the Weavers' Triangle I was still taken aback in awe. I was mesmerised by the sight of Pendle Hill in all its glory dominating the background. The lights from looming factories contrasted with the sultry hills in the distance and were testimony to the insignificance of man in comparison to the majesty of nature. I gazed in wonderment at the glory of the majestic scene and pondered over the beauty of the night. The setting sun and the beautiful red sky were a sweet contrast to the clusters of tall grimy factory chimneys and soot stained buildings. It struck me that nature makes no distinction between rich or poor … it is there for all to enjoy.

"Even amongst all the large ugly factories," I said to myself, "the beauty of God comes shining through."

****

I was always intrigued by the way the older women walked the streets dressed in clogs and shawls. Many were only in their early forties but looked much older because of their attire. They made me laugh as they clip clopped along, especially when they came out with their comical expressions:

'By gum … just hark at him'. - 'Naythen luv … Just keep tha pecker up' - 'I'm just tekkín' misél off to petty' - 'I'll go to foot of our stairs', and many more.

One day, just as our Mary had got home from a date, our Barry came out with one of these funny sayings. He wasn't too keen on the lad who Mary had been out with and vented his feelings.

"U-ugh our kid, I didn't think you'd o' gone with him ... I don't like the cut of his jib."

"U-umph, who cares what you think," she replied indignantly, "I like him and that's all that counts."

"All reight, all reight our Mary, keep your hair on... I was only tellin' you what I thought."

"Well keep your opinions to yourself ... I'll go out with whom I please. Anyroad, where did you dig that expression from ... *the cut of his jib*?"

---"Eh I don't know, it's just that I've heard loads o' people saying it. Anyroad, do you know?"

"Do I 'eck as like ... I haven't got a clue."

At that moment I happened to be parking my bike in the lobby.

"Our John's just come in," said Barry, "ask him"

I'd hardly set foot in the livingroom before she pounced on me.

"Hey our John ... d'you know where the expression, 'The cut of his jib' comes from?"

I pondered for a moment before saying, "I'm not sure but I've a sneaky feeling it comes fro' working down a pit."

"How's that then?"

"Well, the miners on the coalface use a cutting machine that has a large jib attached to it that undercuts the coal."

"How do you mean, a large jib?" Mary asked looking rather puzzled. "What's a jib?"

I thought a little before replying, "Well, the best way I can describe it is it's like the long blade of a chain saw except it's fifty times bigger. It works on the same principle and has a load of sharp tungsten bits attached, which undercuts the coal seam prior to it being fired by explosives. So you see our kid ... it's a cutting jib.

"U-um very good ... aren't you a clever clogs?"

"Oh aye, a clever clogs am I? All reight then ... where does the expression 'clever clogs' come from?"

"I don't know, but knowing you, you'll probably know Mr know it all."

"Hey don't go on at me our Mary ... it wer' you who asked me the question in the first place. Anyroad, go and mék a brew ... at least you know how to make a good cup o' tea."

Seeing the funny side, she just grinned and went to put the kettle on. We got settled around the fire with our pots of tea and some broken biscuits and the conversation continued.

"Right our John," said Mary, "now I've got one for you. Do you know where the word 'spinster' comes from?"

"I haven't a clue our kid but I've got a gut feeling I'm gonna find out."

"Too true you are ... you're not the only one with a bit of working knowledge."

"Do you really know?" put in our Barry.

"Yeah course I do ... it's to do with working in a cotton mill. Most of the spinners in the spinning department were young unmarried girls. Over the years any young girl who'd reached a certain age and was still single got tagged with the nickname spinster. ... so there."

"Very good our Mary," I quipped, "it's a good ún is that. Now who's the clever clogs ... ha, ha ha!"

****

The following Saturday afternoon, as I cycled to Bacup as usual, I decided to go via a different route directly over the moors. I was peddling up Todmorden Road when I saw our Barry and Barbara coming out of the top gates of Towneley Park.

"Where are you going our John?" asked Barry.

"I'm going o'er to my granma's and mí Aunt Katie's."

"Oh, can we come with you, I haven't seen mí gran and grandad for ages?" asked Barbara."

"And how the bloomin' 'eck can you do that?" I replied.

"Well you can ték us on the back of your bike ... you've done it loads o' times with kids on Trafalgar."

"Aye maybe I have, but don't forget they're a lot smaller than you, and another thing ... there's two of you. And besides, it's eight miles to Bacup and the first five mile stretch is steep uphill"

"Ar-gh it's not fair, I never get to go anywhere," moaned Barbara.

"Well I'm sorry, there's not a reight lot I can do about it," I replied cocking onto my bike. I'd only gone a few yards when I stopped and shouted back to them. "Come here, I've got an idea if you're willing to try it out."

"Yeah, go on then ... what is it?" they both asked impatiently.

"Well, you start walking our Barry and I'll carry our Barbara on the back of mí bike."

"No way, I'm not walking it all the way to Bacup!" he quipped.

"Hang on a minute our kid, let me finish! I'll drop Barbara off about a mile up the road and whilst she's walking I'll come back for you. Then I'll carry you until we're a mile past Barbara and so on till we reach Bacup."

"U-um, I suppose so ... we can give it a try," agreed Barry, "I'm willing if you are." So off I cycled carrying Barbara on the back of my bike as far as the Towneley Arms Pub. After a short respite I gave my little sister some brief instructions.

"Reight our Barbara, now you keep walking up Bacup Road until I pick you up again." As planned, I went back for Barry, picked him up, and started cycling furiously.

"My, our Barbara's done well," I commented as we passed the Towneley Arms, "she's way up the road in the distance."

As we passed Barbara, Barry made some kind of gesture encouraging her on, "Come on our kid, you're doing well." This time I peddled arduously up the steep gradient until we reached the brickworks.

"By 'eck our Barry that wer' bloomin' hard work," I groaned, "I'm having a breather afore I go back for our Barbara."

"Righto our John, I'll get going … I should be a long way up the road before you catch me up." It was hard going but we finally made it over the open moors reaching the Deerplay Hotel.

"Right, this is where I usually take a breather every Sunday when I'm comin' back from Bacup," I said as I pointed to the spot where I'd seen the baby rabbit and found the pound note, "so we'll have a short break here before the downhill run." It was downhill all right … over two miles to the centre of Bacup and some of it quite steep.

"Are you two ready?" I grinned. "This is going be fun 'cos this time it's gonna be three on a bike." I put our Barbara's coat over the crossbar and she sat on it. I then straddled myself behind her with one foot on the floor and the other on the pedal ready for the off. "Just make sure you keep your feet on the lower bar so you don't touch the front wheel." I warned her.

"Bloomin' 'eck, this seat's hard!" moaned Barry as he perched himself behind me and clung on to my back.

"Reighto you two," I laughed, "I'm ready when you are … let's go!"

What a ride, we sped down the road with the wind blowing in our faces thoroughly enjoying every minute.

"Yippee," shouted Barbara in sheer delight, "Bacup here we come!"

It was about five o'clock when we reached Grandmother's house and she was very surprised and a little taken aback to see the three of us.

"What the flippin' 'eck's going on," she quizzed, "what aya doing over here at this time?"

"I wer' coming over to see you on mí bike like I usually do Granma and they wanted to come as well."

"What, you mean to say our little Barbara's peddled all the way o'er from Burnley on a bike?"

"Oh no Gran, she's come on the back of mine."

"Tha's never peddled all the way o'er them moors with her on the back o' thí surely to goodness!"

"Aye I have Granma ... Gospel Truth!"

"Oh aye, and what about Barry then?"

"Yeah, I've brought him as well."

"I don't believe thí," interrupted Grandad, "it's impossible to do that trip wí three of thí on a bike."

"Oh no Grandad, there were only three of us on the bike on the downhill stretch coming into Bacup." I then went on to explain exactly what had happened.

"By 'eck, that's some feat our John ... thá must be a fit lad."

"Aye, but don't forget Grandad, I'm used to it 'cos I'm forever peddling over the Bacup Moors aren't I?"

"Aye that's reight lad, but there's a hell of a lot o' difference in doing it on tha own to what tha's just done."

"Now just hang on a minute," said Granma, "it may well o' been a mean feat but what I want to know is how long did it take you to get here?"

"About two hours Gran, but don't forget, I had to keep doubling back on myself."

"Two hours … oh dear," she mumbled with a frown on her face, "you can't set off back there tonight 'cos it'll be dark in less than two hours." She thought about it a moment longer before saying, "Right that's it, I'll mék thí somét to eat then Mat'll put all three of thí on the seven o'clock bus."

"I can't go on the bus with 'em Gran … what about mí bike?" I said

"Never mind your bike; I don't like the thought of thí peddling o'er them bleak moors at night."

"Don't worry about me Gran, I'll be all right … honest! Anyroad, if I set off twenty minutes afore the bus I'll be able to wait for 'em both at the bus station in Burnley."

"Aye I suppose so, but I'm tellin' thí now our John, I don't like it … I'll be on tenterhooks till I see thí again."

"I'll tell you what then, I'll come and see you again tomorrow morning to put your mind at rest … how's that Gran?"

"Go on then, thá could talk a bird out of a tree. Anyroad, afore thá sets off, thá can sit thásel' down and have a bite to eat wit' t'others."

I heartily scoffed the lot before setting off back to Burnley. As promised, I waited at the bus station for Barry and Barbara to make sure they arrived safely, and next morning I made my way back to Bacup.

"E-eh, I'm reight glad to see thí our John," Granma greeted me cordially, "I've bín fretting about thí e'er since thá left last níte."

"I'm sorry Granma, I didn't mean to worry you, it won't happen again."

"Oh don't ték any notice o' me," she sighed, "I wer' a bit cranky yesterday 'cos I weren't feeling too well."

"Why Gran, what's up?" I asked concerned.

"Well, I've got a swollen leg and it's bín giving mí some jip lately."

"Oh I'm sorry to hear that, I'll tell mí mam when I get home." I did tell Mum and, after that, she went over to Bacup at every available opportunity.

As it turned out, my grandmother had phlebitis in her leg and was started on a course of medication. She became very run down and contracted pneumonia, her condition deteriorated rapidly and sadly ... she died within two weeks. I was sixteen at the time and completely devastated. It seemed unreal that Granma would never again be there to greet me ever again. I just couldn't envisage what the house would be like without her.

It came as a terrible blow to everybody in our family, especially Mum. But the person most affected was Matthew, my Grandad. My grandmother, Mary, was his whole world; he'd loved her from the moment he'd first set eyes on her ... there was no consoling him. I still went over to see him on a regular basis but things were never the same. Never again did Grandad ever talk about his time spent in the trenches or anything else for that matter ... all he wanted to do was join my grandma, his beloved Mary!

****

I bought my first motorbike for five pounds and it looked like it had just come out of a museum. It was antiquated with solid forks at the front and rusty springs at the back ... a real boneshaker. Hand gears were fixed to the right side of the frame near to the petrol tank.

The first time I took to the road I got a quick lesson in what not to do. As I drove along Trafalgar I attempted to change gear without pulling in the clutch. Subsequently, I went flying over the handlebars and finished up sprawled in the middle of the road. I hurt myself a little, but I was more concerned about the state of my bike. It didn't look damaged, but I couldn't get it to start.

Not to be beaten I decided to have a word with Malcolm Davis, our next-door neighbour, who was a dab hand at mechanics.

"You must have damaged the carburettor John," he said, "you'll have to strip it down and give it a reight good cleaning."

"Clean the carburettor ... is that an easy job?" I asked.

Malcolm knelt down and pointed to the engine, "Aye, all you have to do is loosen those bolts and that fuel pipe. When you've done that, give everything a good cleaning and then swill the carburettor out with petrol afore you put it back on the bike." I carried out his instructions to the letter and, to my delight, it kicked up first time.

"Great, I'm back in business!" I mused highly delighted with myself. However, my pleasure was short-lived because I'd only gone about two-hundred yards when it started spluttering and backfiring and came to a full stop. Once again I went back to see Malcolm.

"U-um," he said stroking his chin, "it seems to me that the timing's off."

"Crikey ... how do I fix that then?"

"Well I'm afraid it's a bit trickier this time. I'll tell you what ... I'll do it for you and you can watch me for chance it happens again." Malcolm then re-set the points whilst I watched him like a hawk. After he'd finished, I tried kicking it up and once again it started straight away.

"Oh well, here goes," I said with fingers crossed, "let's see what happens this time." I did a full circular straight up Albion Street, left at Scott Park gates, down Manchester Road and back along Trafalgar. "It's great Mal," I enthused as I stopped outside his backyard, "it's running like a dream ... thanks a lot!"

Two weeks previously, our Jimmy had bought a 125 BSA Bantam and he was bursting to try it out on a long run. That weekend, Jimmy, Malcolm, Arthur Ratcliffe, Kenny Clayton, and I all set off for Blackpool.

Not to be outdone, a neighbour, Mr Daley caught us up on his motorbike and asked if he could join us. All six bikes headed off in convoy with Malcolm up front; he motored along effortlessly on his well-maintained bike. Arthur had just acquired a two-stroke Francis Barnett and he was really chuffed as he put-putted along. The other three bikes ran smoothly, whereas I chugged along after them with loads of black smoke belching from the exhaust. The others kept making fun of me but I didn't mind … that little bike got me to Blackpool and back and I thoroughly enjoyed it.

During the following months the bike was forever breaking down with one fault or another; but with perseverance and a bit of advice from Malcolm, I became quite adept at repairing it. One day though my mechanical knowledge let me down and caused a bit of a stir. I was about to go on a run with Kenny Clayton and Arthur Ratcliffe, but once again it wouldn't start.

"Let's take it into the cellar John and strip it down," suggested Arthur, "it'll be easier than working out here on the cobbles."

"Aye reighto Arthur but you'll have to give me a lift so we can do it quicker."

After a bit of a struggle we had it set up on its stand on the cellar floor ready for working on. Within an hour we'd stripped it down, cleaned the parts and reassembled it.

"That should o' done the trick," said Arthur, "get it cracked up John."

"Reight, fair enough … here goes." I stood at the side of the bike holding the handlebars with my foot on the kick-start pedal. "Are you ready lads … the moment of truth!"

I took a deep breath and then thrust my foot down as hard as I could. The bike started all right … it backfired making one almighty bang blowing out thick black smoke and some flames. It took me by surprise, spinning round in circles on its stand and whipping the handlebars from my grasp. Within seconds the cellar was filled with thick dense smoke and sparks kept belching from the exhaust.

"Bloomin' 'eck, it's gonna blow up," shouted Kenny, "we're gonna be killed!"

"Let's get outa here whilst we can still see where we're goin'!" bellowed Arthur.

Arthur was the furthest from the door but he moved so fast that he was outside on the backstreet whilst Kenny and I were still thinking about it.

I was the last to leave, as I was concerned about my bike. But I too sensed the danger and decided to follow the others.

"Oh blow this for a tale, Kenny might be right," I said to myself, "the bloomin' petrol tank might blow up!"

The bike spluttered away for a few more minutes and then ... silence. On re-entering the cellar we couldn't see the motorbike; in fact, we couldn't see anything.

"Blimey, look at all this smoke ... I can hardly see mí hands in front o' me," said Kenny.

"Aye, and it's all going up the cellar steps into the livingroom," quipped Arthur.

"A-ah flippin' 'eck, mí mam'll go mad," I panicked, "I'd better nip up and open all the windows." When I got up to the living room my worst fears were realised ... the room was full of smoke and it was making its way up to the bedrooms. After opening the front and back door and every window in the house I shouted to Kenny and Arthur.

"Quick, get yourselves up here reight away and help me to clean up this mess afore mí mam gets home ... she'll go up the wall if she finds it like this." All three of us got stuck in shaking the pegged rugs and wiping down every stick of furniture. We worked hard and did a decent job, but we couldn't get rid of the smell of smoke. When Mum got home it was evident that something had happened.

"What's been going on here then … what's been burning?"

"We've had a bit of a soot fall Mam and the chimney set afire," I said.

"Oh yes, and why can I smell petrol then?"

"Well Mam, I …"

"Never mind, well Mam, I want the truth … have you been starting that bike of yours up in the cellar?" I knew it was useless lying … Mam was too canny for that.

"Yeah, I'm sorry Mam, it won't happen again … I promise you."

"Too true it won't because you can get that bike out of the cellar right now … and keep it out!"

"Oh don't say that Mam, I can't keep it on the back-street … it'll go rusty."

"You should have thought of that before you set it off inside the cellar. Anyway, have you no more sense … you could have set the flaming house on fire."

"Hey, that's a good ún Mam … you just cracked a joke." I said trying to play down the situation.

"What are you talking about … I cracked a joke?" she asked a little puzzled.

"Set the flaming house … on fire! Get it?"

As she thought about it a little smile came to her face, "Ha ha, very funny … but don't think you're getting around me that easy."

Despite her words though, I knew she was weakening, "Oh come on Mam … I promise thí it won't happen again."

"Use the Queen's English will you for crying out loud," she corrected me "I promise you, not I promise thí!"

"All right Mam, I promise you … I promise you."

She smiled again and relented, "Right, I'll let it go this time, but it had better not happen again ... this is your last warning. Another thing, you'd best get yourself down the cellar right now and clean up the mess ... I want the floor shining like a new pin." I happily settled for that ... I knew I'd got off lightly.

Thereafter I spent many happy hours on that bike, covering much of the Lancashire countryside. But the thing I enjoyed most was riding up Albion Street, especially when there were loads of neighbours sat on their doorsteps. I was a show-off and I felt like Sir Lancelot charging forward on his trusty steed.

Motor biking was the love of my life during the next two years. The little bike finally gave up the ghost but by then I had saved £60. I'd seen a Triumph 500 speed-twin advertised in the Burnley Express for £55. Malcolm Davis from next door went with me for a bit of moral support and expertise. After some negotiation I purchased the bike for £50.

"Great," I thought highly delighted with the deal, "that leaves me enough money to tax and insure it." That bike was the best machine I ever had ... it was a good starter, good on petrol and it never once let me down.

Shortly after procuring the Triumph I put in for my driving test. On the day I was all keyed up but quietly confident. I met up with the driving assessor, a rather surly gentleman, at the Ministry of Transport Office on Nicholas Street.

"Right," he said to me, "when you set off from here I want you to drive along Grimshaw Street, turn right into Manchester Road then right again at the traffic lights. Drive through the town centre and turn right into Park Lane and right again into Grimshaw Street. Just keep driving around this circuit until I wave you down. During the drive I will test you for an emergency stop. I'm going to intermingle amongst the crowd but when I step to the kerb waving this newspaper I want you to stop as soon as you can in a safe manner. Do you understand all these instructions?"

"Yes I do," I replied edgily.

"Right then, off you go."

After the test I felt good because I thought I had driven steadily and done a good emergency stop. All I had to do now was answer questions on the Highway Code, which I did proficiently. I was shocked when the man informed me that I'd failed ... in fact, I was absolutely gutted. The official wouldn't go into any details; he just smugly handed me a slip of paper with the reasons for my failure written on it. The main reason was not glancing behind over my shoulder when signalling to turn right. I felt dejected but that made me more determined than ever to pass the test. Six weeks later I was there again ... this time I got a different assessor.

"Thank goodness for that," I thought, "this one doesn't look as grumpy as the other chap." All the same I knew I couldn't take things for granted.

He gave me the same instructions as the other official and once again I set off on the same route. I was determined this time to glance over my shoulder ... if anything, I tended to exaggerate the movement. Once again I thought I'd driven well but this time I wasn't so confident. Then came the Highway Code questions.

"Give me five instances when you can overtake on the inside of a person" "What is the difference between a road sign with a triangle above it and one with a circle above?" One question was a little tricky, "If it had been snowing and all the signs were covered in snow ... how could you tell it was a 'Halt at the Major Road' sign?" he asked

I smiled to myself, "Oh, it's shaped like a letter 'T' and the word 'HALT' stands out boldly in the top section of the sign."

"U-um," he muttered, "but what if you can't see the letters because of the snow?"

"Well, like I said, the sign has a definite 'T' shape which distinguishes it from any other sign on the road.

"Anything else?" he asked.

I faltered a little before I realised what he was getting at, "Oh yeah, it has a circle above it indicating that it's a sign that must be obeyed, unlike a triangle that gives a warning."

The official pondered for what seemed an age before saying, "Right Mr Cowell, I'm pleased to inform you that you have passed!"

Those words were like music to my ears … I could have kissed the bloke. The first thing I did was to remove the 'L' plates and then I drove up Manchester Road full of the joys of Spring, raring to give one of my brothers a ride on the pillion.

A few days later, on Saturday afternoon, a funny thing happened. Our Jimmy and I had just been to Bury on our motorbikes and on the return journey we were riding through Crawshawbooth. Dad and his friend Billy Cook had been out on the binge in the 'Black Dog' and they were both tottering at the bus stop as Jimmy and I drove through the village.

Our Jimmy saw Dad and made a gesture pointing his finger towards the bus stop.

"Bloomin' 'eck!" I thought as we slowed down, "That's mí dad and Billy Cook and they look as if they've had a reight skinful."

"Come on, let's ask 'em if they want a lift back," shouted Jimmy.

"Good idea our kid," I agreed.

"Hiya Dad … do you want a lift home?" I said pulling up near to the kerb.

"No way our John, you must be joking, I'm not gettin' on back o' that thing with you … I'm not that drunk!"

"Oh come on Dad, I'm a good driver … anyroad, you've just missed a bus so you'll have to wait ages for the next one."

At that, Billy Cook intervened, "Aye he's reight Barney … you get on the back of him and I'll get on the back o' Jimmy's bike."

"U-um, I suppose you're reight Billy." He inched forward and climbed aboard muttering, "I only hope I don't regret it later."

"All reight Dad … are you sitting comfortable?" I asked as he perched himself on the pillion. I set off in low gear as I negotiated a steep hill out of the village, keeping up a nice steady pace until we'd passed through Dunnockshaw village. But then … Jimmy came tearing past me with Billy hanging on for dear life! That was it; I put my foot down in hot pursuit, overtaking him in the open countryside prior to reaching the Waggoner's Inn.

"Whoa, slow down our John … you'll get us bloody killed!" bawled Dad, clinging on even tighter than Billy.

"Righto Dad that's it, I just wanted to show you what it could do. Not to worry though … I'll take it steady down Manchester Road." Dad and Billy may have been well canned before they got on the bikes, but they were both stone cold sober when they disembarked. Dad was fuming and he gave me a right rollicking.

"You bloody swine you're now't else, that's the last time you get me on the back of your flamin' bike!"

"Oh come on Dad, it were a bit o' fun weren't it?" put in Jimmy.

"And you can wrap up as well," growled Dad, "he probably wouldn't have gone so fast but for you trying to show off!"

"Let it go Barney," said Billy Cook, "there's no harm done … at least they got us home in one piece."

"Aye, I suppose you're reight Billy," Dad replied, "but there's one thing for sure … I'll never ride pillion with any of 'em again." Sadly, he never did.

****

I'll never forget the time that I had my first beer … it was a very memorable occasion. It was a Saturday night and I was all spruced up in my Teddy Boy suit to go dancing down the 'Arcadian's' with my mates. It was David's eighteenth birthday and he wanted to celebrate it in a pub. Billy was already eighteen but the rest of us were under age.

"How about havin' a couple o' pints down town afore going to th'Arcs'?" suggested David.

"I'm gam' if t'others are," said Barry.

"How about you John?" asked David.

"Yeah why not … it should be a bit o' fun," I answered not wanting to appear a killjoy.

"I know a good pub down the Croft called the Miller's Arms," said Billy enthusiastically, "it's a good pint and you never get any coppers calling in there."

"Aye, I've heard of it," put in David, "I know some other lads who go in that pub. Anyroad, seeing as it's my birthday I say let's go there."

Well, it was my first experience of the demon drink and what a good do it turned out to be … I really enjoyed myself. We played darts in the taproom and with every beer my confidence increased.

"Here," said David handing me a pint, "get this down you … it'll do thí good!" By the time we left the pub I'd drunk three pints of Massey's bitter and I felt on top of the world. For the first time in my life I didn't feel shy in the presence of girls. On reaching the Arcadian's I was brim-full of confidence and I openly chatted away to the opposite sex. I hardly missed a dance and my personality appeared to be second to none.

"No wonder mí dad enjoys going for a drink," I thought, "this is great … I've never felt like this in my life afore." Alas, I overdid it, as the atmosphere built up, getting warmer and warmer, I felt sick and finished up vomiting in the toilets.

"Oh 'eck David," I muttered, "I'm sorry about this, spoiling your birthday an' all."

"Don't worry about it John," he reassured me, "get it up ... you'll feel better!" When I left the Arcadian's I walked around for ages trying to sober up before going home.

"I daren't go home like this David," I groaned, "if mí mam sees me in this state she'll go up the wall." Luckily she was in bed when I arrived home.

But I didn't get away with it altogether ... I had a real ding-dong stinker of a headache the next day.

From then on we frequented pubs every Saturday night prior to making our way to the dance hall. We would go the 'Nelson' or the 'Healey Wood,' but our favourite venue was the 'Corporation' close to the Market Square where they sold Scotch bitter, a strong beer and dark in colour like a Guinness.

One incident that stands out in my mind was the time I went into the 'Big Window' with David Whittaker, Pete Fletcher and Billy Pounder. It was my round and I'd just ordered four pints at the bar when I heard a voice behind me.

"You'd better make that five lad!"

To my horror, on turning, my dad was stood there with a stern look on his face.

"Oh 'eck," I thought, "how am I gonna get outa this? I stood there speechless for a few seconds before stuttering nervously, "Well I ... I were just gonna ......"

"Never mind you were just gonna," he joked, a grin spreading across his face, "whaddaya think you're doing in here?"

"Well I ... I ......"

He cut me short again, "I know all about it our John, I haven't just come in on a banana boat ... I'm not thick so don't try and pull the wool o'er mí eyes."

"It weren't his fault, Mr Cowell," interrupted Pete, "we talked him into it."

"Oh it weren't his fault wer' it not ... has he not got a mind of his own then? Anyroad, while we're on the subject Peter Fletcher, you're even younger than he is ... how would your dad take to seeing thí in here?"

"Well I ... I'm not sure," stammered Pete thinking he'd put his foot in it.

"You're not sure are you not, well I'll tell thí what he'd do ... he'd kick your britches arse reight up to Trafalgar!" There was a stony silence for about three seconds, and then Dad started laughing. "Ha ha ha!" he roared thrusting his glass forward, "Just look at your gloomy faces, the four of you. Anyroad, I'll let it go this time so long as each one of you buys me a drink." Then on a more serious note he turned to me. "Your mam'd better not find out about this our John, she'd go mad. And while we're at it ... it'd best be the last time I catch thí in a pub until you're eighteen or you're forrít mí lad!"

****

Despite his drinking habit, Dad was a canny businessman. One particular good deal which paid dividends, in a way, came about because of our Mary.

Mary was now seventeen and a very pretty teenager she was too. It was a pleasant summer's evening and her best friend Loretta was on a date with her new boyfriend Burt Myers. Mum was out somewhere and I was playing cards with Dad and my two brothers. Subsequently, Mary was in the house feeling restless, not knowing what to do with herself.

Out of the blue, Dad said to her, "Oh dear our Mary, what a gloomy face, it's enough to stop the Town Hall Clock."

She muttered a little something or other under her breath before saying, "Well, there's nothing much to do around here is there ... it's boring?"

"Right, I'll tell thí' what cock ... get thaself ready and tha' can come out with your dad."

"Umph," she mumbled adding, "Oh yeah Dad sure, and where will you take me ... just around the pubs in Burnley I suppose?"

"That's right, have you any better ideas?"

"Don't forget Dad," she quipped, "I'm only seventeen, so I'm not allowed in pubs anyway."

"Oh righto, please yourself, I was only trying to help; but for crying out loud our Mary, straighten your face afore wind changes, or it'll stop like that."

Mary pondered about what he'd said before asking, "Do you mean it Dad, are you really serious; would you really take me 'round the pubs with you?"

"Yeah, of course I'm serious," he replied, "mind you, tha' won't be able to have a beer or the like, tha'll have to drink orange juice or something."

In a flash, Mary made her decision, "Right Dad that's it, I'll go upstairs and get changed." It took her half an hour to get ready and when she came down she was beautiful. She was wearing a royal blue dress fitted to the waist with a V-neck and short sleeves. Her light brown shoulder length hair was swept mainly to one side of her face with a quiff complimenting her blue eyes. She was wearing a pillbox hat with a white veil effect; for accessories and she had white matching high heel shoes and a handbag to match. She was always a very pretty girl with perfect features, but at this moment she looked absolutely stunning (and she knew it.)

"By èck our kid, you look really nice," I commented, and our Jimmy and Barry made similar remarks telling her how pretty she looked.

Dad was taken aback by her beauty and let her know so, "Well my love, I'm really impressed, you look like a picture and you make me feel real proud." He offered her his hand saying, "Come on then sweetheart ... let's go." She walked off down Albion Street holding his arm with her head held high; many of the neighbours, who were sat on their doorsteps, looked on in admiration. Mary was dressed smart enough for the grandest occasion but still, Dad took her into the 'Dog & Duck' and the 'White Horse,' two of the most dingy pubs in town to show her off; she obviously felt a little wary, so constantly clung to his arm for a feeling of security.

She felt uneasy as the night progressed, so let him know, "Oh Dad, is there any chance of going anywhere else, I don't feel right in here?"

"Aye all right our Mary, I'll tell thí' what, I'll tèk thí' to the Prince of Wales on Sandygate; it should be all right in there, and it's a lot closer to home." It certainly was a lot nearer, and it wasn't quite so notorious either.

On reaching there, Dad asked, "Naythen our Mary, what would you like to drink?"

"Is there any chance of me having a Babycham Dad?"

"You can have anything you want my little princess," he replied as he made his way to the bar.

He brought the drinks back and had just handed Mary the Babycham, when a rather smart gentleman tapped him on the shoulder asking, "Is there any chance of having a word in private Barney ... it's about business?"

"This is my daughter," replied, "you can discuss it here if you like."

"I'm sorry Barney but it's quite confidential, I'd rather discuss it alone with you in the tap room if you don't mind," stressing, "it is important and very good."

Dad turned to Mary saying, "I'm sorry love but do you mind coming with me for a moment?" He took her into the lounge, which was quite full with only a couple of available seats, then said, "If you just sit in here and wait for me, I promise thi' I won't be long, I have to go an' talk a bit o' business with that bloke."

"Oh Dad, don't leave me for so long please!" she protested, "I don't like being in a pub on my own."

"Aye all reight, just hang on a minute," he said and introduced her to some of his friends in the room asking if they would keep an eye on her for a short time, whilst he was in the other room. The vacant seats were directly opposite a big fat man called Pey and his wife, who was a very small lady. Mary sat down and wasn't feeling too relaxed, but then something happened.

No sooner had Dad left the room than Pey starting mouthing off in a loud voice for everyone to hear, "Don't they make you bloody laugh though, bragging and boasting." He then added sarcastically, "Aye, and bringin' in their beautiful daughter to show her off; they make me bloody sick!"

Mary was listening to all this wondering, "Is he talking about my dad?"

A silence fell over the room, then the fat man started again, "Yeah, next news, he'll be goin' home, and his wife Winnie'll be hittin' him oe'r t'head wi' fryín' pan, they're allus at it." This time, Mary was certain who he was talking about; she felt the hackles rising on the back of her neck.

She was fuming as anguished thoughts ran through her head, "Who does he think he is, talking about my mum and dad like this, and in front of so many people too?" In spite of her anger, she kept her cool; she picked up her untouched drink, and then calmly walked directly across the room to where Pey was sitting. The room went deadly quiet as she momentarily stood in front of him defiantly gazing into his eyes.

"Aye, and what can I do for thi' lass?" sneered the big fat man.

A wry smile came to Mary's face; it turned to a little snigger just before suddenly throwing the Babycham right into Pey's face, "So much for you fat man!" she rapped, then emptied his pint of beer over his head and coolly left the room.

The last words she heard were, "I'll f'fing well kill the little bitch if I get my hands on her!" There was no chance of that; Mary removed her high heel shoes and legged it down Sandygate and along Trafalgar as fast as she could.

On reaching home she blurted out to Mum what had happened adding, "Oh, mi' dad'll go mad Mam, I've really shown him up ... what am I going to do?"

"Never you mind yourself about that," put in Mum, "he'd better not start, he shouldn't have taken you there in the first place. Anyway, I think you'd best get yourself to bed before he comes home, he'll probably have forgotten all about in the morning."

"Oh please Mam! Please let me stay up till he gets home, I'd rather face him now and get it all over and done with."

"Yes all right then, please yourself; I don't want any bother mind, I'm telling you now!"

Mary didn't have to wait very long, it was just about half an hour later when she heard Dad's voice at the front door, then he came walking through the lobby. Once again, Mary was feeling defiant, standing there with her hands on her hips determined to stand her ground. She was ready for a good rollicking from Dad but instead, something quite unexpected happened.

Instead of bellowing at her, he just stuck his head around the living room door and a big toothless grin spread across his face as he enthused, "Aye, our Mary, sticking up for tha dad; I'm reight proud o' th' ... come here lass and give tha' dad a big hug."

He went on to say how everybody in the pub had turned on the fat man saying, "It serves thi' bloody well right, you were well out of order goin' on the way tha did; tha' shouldn't a bin' callin' her mum and dad in front o' lass. Aye, and they all said they were delighted to see such a young girl sticking up for herself. Mind you, I don't hold with swearing as you know, and I'd a clocked fat Pey on the snout for swearing in front o' thi' if I'd a bin' there." He then repeated proudly, "Eh ... stickin' up for tha dad, tha's a reight little good un." He never did forget it.

The following day was Sunday and Dad approached me asking, "What shift are you on this week our John?"

"I'm on nights Dad, how's that?"

"Well I was wondering, how would you like to have the week off and come working for me instead?"

I wasn't too keen on working nights, so was easily swayed, "Yeah righto Dad but what about my wage, if I don't go to work, then I don't get paid?"

"That's all right lad, I'll mék up tha' wage and happen a bit on top, depending on how well I do."

"Right Dad, fair enough, you're on. Anyroad, how come you need me Dad, have you got a good deal going?"

"I have that lad and it's all credit to our Mary."

"Our Mary, how's that then?"

"Well, but for her I'd a never a gone into Prince of Wales last night; but as it turned out, that's when I made this deal."

"Oh last night, that was great wasn't it Dad, really funny too, our Mary was telling us all about it this morning, we had a really good laugh about it."

"Yeah, me too our John, it was really funny; mind … fat Pey didn't think so." We had another good laugh about it before Dad changed the subject back to business, "Oh just one snag lad, can you lend me fifty quid till th'end o' week? I'll pay you back along with your wage."

"You must be joking Dad, I don't have that sort o' money! You'd best be asking our Jimmy rather than me." As it happened, Jimmy had just returned to camp; he was stationed at Kirkham, so that was out of the question.

"Oh not to worry," replied Dad, "I can always borrow it off Reeder." Sure enough, on Monday morning I set off in the wagon with Dad and the first place we headed for was Reeder's Scrap-yard. We both went into the office together and Dad negotiated a deal with the businessman, who then handed over fifty pounds.

"Right then our John, let's go, we've a lot of work to do."

"Fair enough Dad, but where are we going?"

"Were going to a factory reight o'er moors above Todmorden near to a place called Hepstonstall, it's a good drive from here so we'd best get our skates on." The drive there was over moorland countryside, a pleasant journey taking about one hour. On arriving at the mill, I once again accompanied Dad into the office and further negotiations took place. The deal was obviously about scrap-iron and Dad agreed to pay forty-five pounds for the lot.

Once outside, I commented, "Hey Dad, it seems a lot of money what you've just paid, how do you know how much stuff there is?"

"Don't worry about it lad, I'm not that daft, I nipped out and had a reight good look whilst you wer' having a bite to eat in the canteen."

"Oh right, I thought it wasn't like you to hand o'er money just like that."

Dad gave a little chuckle murmuring, "You'll see our John, you'll see." I saw all right, I couldn't believe my eyes; the management had been replacing some old looms, and great big heaps of scrap iron were stacked all over the factory yard.

"Bloomin' 'eck Dad, I didn't think there'd be this much, it'll ték us a month never mind a week to shift this lot."

Dad just chuckled again, "Aye you might be reight there our John; anyway, let's get cracking, we've got a busy time ahead of us." We both got stuck in, and worked very hard. Dad was only small and slight, but despite his illness he plodded on. Mind you, the fact that he'd just struck a good deal spurred him on. We got back to Reeder's Scrap-yard just after one o'clock and weighed in the first load.

Dad turned to me saying, "Come into the office with me again our John, I want you to see how things work. But don't say a word ... just keep your eyes and ears open and you'll happen learn a thing or two." For that single lorry load he got thirty-two pounds.

"You can knock that off what I owe you," said Dad, "and I'll be back with another load this afternoon." Sure enough, we did another trip that afternoon and the load was similar to the first. Not only that, we did another two trips on Tuesday and two more on Wednesday as well. I was absolutely flabbergasted, six trips in three days, which meant Dad had taken about one hundred and ninety pounds. After repaying Reeder and giving me thirty pounds, he'd still made over one hundred pounds profit. I was more than satisfied, as I'd only worked three days and my weekly wage at the pit was only about eight pounds. One hundred pounds was an enormous sum of money, even colliers working on the coal-face only earned about twenty pounds a week. I felt really proud of Dad for being so clever and astute but sadly, he didn't put the money to good use. He did give Mum about forty pounds but then he went out on the rant treating all his bosom companions. Once again I thought just how clever Dad was, yet how foolish; I would have loved to have left the pit and gone into partnership with him but never had the confidence, always feeling that Dad would let me down.

****

Sunday night was the culmination of the weekend. My mates and I would go to the Empire, Roxy, Odeon, or the Palace etc. and the film usually ended about 9-30pm. Crowds of youngsters would then walk 'The Drag' which stretched about half a mile along St. James' Street from the bottom of Manchester Road to the Cross Key's Hotel at the bottom of Sandygate. When we reached one end we'd walk right back to where we'd started from, all the time exchanging glances and greetings with girls. It was very similar to walking the 'Golden Mile' in Blackpool. This was our last chance of the weekend to chat up girls and so we'd promenade up and down several times until everyone gradually dispersed. We'd then make our way home and chat for a short while at the bottom of Albion Street before reluctantly parting.

"Bloomin' 'eck! David would comment. "Doesn't time fly when you're enjoying yourself?"

"Ah well, that's another weekend o'er with ... back to flamin' work in the morning," Pete would say.

"Yeah, back to the bloomin' grindstone," I'd reply. "Still ... there's always next weekend to look forward to."

CHAPTER 12 - TACKLE RUNNING

I really enjoyed the pit life and was especially happy tackle running for 'No 4' coalface, Jerry Dawson's team. It was hard work but the camaraderie shared between us lads and the colliers was second to none. Tackle lads always worked in pairs and my mate was Pete Neary, the lad who'd been my school friend at Towneley. We worked well together and made a formidable team ... we both felt that we had found our niche. At bait time we used to chat with Harry Allan and Terry Greenwood, two lads who ran timber to another coalface. Materials were carried into the pit in the mine-cars and it was our job to empty them and stack everything neatly in the Landing prior to transportation to the coalface. Harry, Terry, Pete and I had to regularly empty five mine-cars containing bricks, wooden props, steel girders, corrugated tin sheets, large wooden blocks and steel rings, which were roof supports shaped like giant horseshoes. There were many more heavy things including dowties, steel telescopic props, each weighing about a hundredweight. This aspect of the job took about three hours and was usually done on a Saturday morning. However, depending on demand, a mine car could arrive at any given time containing 2000 bricks and these had to be manhandled there and then. The four of us would form a chain, throwing two bricks at a time from one lad to another, which we stacked in a heap. This was no easy task as they were Accrington NORI bricks, which were notorious for being hard and heavy. In fact, they were the hardest bricks in the world ... thus the name 'Nori,' which spelt backwards is Iron.

One time, after the arduous task, Harry asked me "Do you know why they call the bricks Nori' John?

"I haven't a clue Harry, I imagine it's because they were made at NORI brickyard."

"No it's not. In fact, the brickyard got its name from the bricks, not the other way round."

"How do you mean?" I asked becoming intrigued.

"Well you do know they're the hardest bricks in the world."

"Aye I know that, and the heaviest I think. I feel that way every time we have to empty a mine car."

"Yeah you could be right there. The special quality of the bricks is because of the clay they use to make 'em, which they quarry from Hameldon Hill."

"I go along with that Harry, but what's that got to do with 'em being called NORI?"

"Well it goes back ages to when the firm was just starting up. After shaping the clay in brick shape moulds and getting them ready to be baked in a furnace they made casts and intended to call the bricks 'IRON'."

"It's a good name that because they really are like iron bricks. So anyway, why did they change their minds?

"Ah, that's just it," stressed Harry, "They didn't change their minds, it came about by accident."

"How do you mean, by accident?"

"Quite simple really. The bloke in charge of the castings got the lettering back to front. Hence, when the bricks came out, instead of reading IRON it read, NORI. The management realised this was a novel idea and so used it to their advantage.

"A nice tale that Harry. It certainly worked well because NORI bricks are exported all over the world and are renowned as the best there is."

"You're right there. They used them to lay the foundations of Blackpool Tower and also the Sellafield Nuclear Power Station. And, not to be out beaten, the Yanks used them to reinforce the foundations of the Empire State Building in New York."

Harry was quite matey with the loco driver and on occasions, for devilment, he would jump up into the driving seat and shunt a few mine cars in the Landing area. He was taking a risk and would have been up for the high jump if George Riley had seen him. But that was Harry ... work hard, play hard. Harry, like me, enjoyed timber running but one day he told me he'd given his in notice, as he'd signed up to join the army. It turned out the loco driver had convinced him that the prospects were far better than working down a coal mine.

****

During the course of a day Pete and I would make two trips to the coalface ... one before bait-time and one after. An average load consisted of steel rings, Dowties, bricks and large wooden blocks. The bogies were well constructed but even so, the wheels would buckle under the tremendous weight. The inward journey was uphill for about 700 yards, which meant a lot of hard shoving, huffing and puffing. To get the bogey rolling, we had to get well down behind it, place our feet against a sleeper and grab hold of the steel tracks. Placing our helmets against the back of the bogey we then pushed with every bit of strength we had using every muscle in our bodies. Once we'd built up a momentum we didn't stop until we got to the top of the incline for fear of not being able to get the bogey going again. As we strained with all our might sweat would drip off the end of my nose. At the top of the incline we'd have a breather before resuming the downhill run. This was quite steep in parts and so we locked the bogey's wheels with a wooden sprag in order to stop it running out of control as we held it back with a long rope.

Pete and I had already talked between ourselves about broaching the subject of' 'pey-brass' with the colliers and he agreed that I be the spokesman. On our first day as we reached the end of the track some colliers were awaiting us. Right away one of them broached the subject of us two lads carrying the tackle right up to the coalface.

I remembered the advice that John Bill Worseley had given me ... I took this as my cue to bring up the matter of pey-brass.

"U-um, I don't know about that," I said winking at Pete, "we're not allowed to go any further than th'end o' this track ... you know that."

"Oh come off it John Bill, you know only too well that t'other tackle draggers do it." moaned one of the men.

"Aye maybe they do but that's up to them isn't it ... I don't want the sack?"

"How about if we give you some pey-brass at th'end of the week ... say a shilling fro' each of us?" he said with a smirk on his face.

"You must be joking!" I retorted, "The going rate is half a dollar each ... not a shilling."

"Aye but you're only little lads and anyroad, you've only just started."

"What difference does that make? It'll be bloomin' hard work humpin' all the tackle to the face," I pointed out, "surely, if we get the job done that's all that matters to you?" The colliers soon found out that, despite my size, I wouldn't be put upon.

"Aye, reighto little John Bill, but you'll have to work a week in hand same as you did for your wage."

"No way!" I responded, "We work for you this week ... you pay us this Friday!"

"Bloody hell! I can see nobody's gonna pull the wool o'er your eyes lad." quipped another collier.

"And why should they?" I stressed, "A fair day's pay for a fair day's work, that's what I say."

Just then the main belt stopped and a lot more colliers came off the face and sat down in the main gate.

"Come on John, it looks like it's bait-time," said Pete, "let's go and squat down with 'em." The colliers, who had negotiated with me, told the others what had been said.

"You cheeky young buggers," blurted out a few in unison, "you're only apprentices ... you've got to prove yourself first!"

"Whoa, hang on a minute fellas!" put in Tommy Lowe, a union representative, "Let's give the lads a chance to see if they come up to scratch. If they don't ... they don't get paid. On t'other hand if they prove worthy ... they deserve half a dollar."

Some agreed but others didn't.

"No, I don't go along with it ... they're too inexperienced," moaned one solitary collier as he took a bite out of his jam butty, "I think it's too much!"

"Aye you would you tight swine Archie ... everybody knows you could split ha'penny in half," quipped Tommy.

"Never mind about that," he snorted, "if I'm gonna give half a dollar, I want mí money's worth!"

"Yeah we know that ... that's what we all want," stressed Tommy, "I'll tell thí what ... let's have a show of hands." Much to Pete's and my pleasure, the vote was almost unanimous in our favour ... the only dissenter was Archie. He mumbled a little but went along with the decision. Afterwards Pete and I thanked Tommy Lowe for speaking up on our behalf.

"Hey, don't thank me yet lads ... don't think I'm a soft touch. Just like Archie said ... you'll have to earn every penny o' that half-a-dollar."

This was the way of things throughout the mine … men would argue readily amongst themselves but it was always so open. There was no back-biting at all … once an agreement had been reached, that was the end of it. Overall, there was a definite affinity amongst the men … a comradeship second to none.

I loved this aspect of the pit and from then on, Pete and I regularly ate our bait sat amongst the experienced pitmen listening to their friendly squabbles.

"Great," said Pete as the colliers returned to the face, "Come on John let's get cracking, we've got to haul the bogey back to the Landing afore we can do another trip."

"Reight Pete, I hope you're feeling fit 'cos, even though it's empty, it'll be hard graft shovin' it back up that long gradient."

"Hang on, I've got an idea." said Pete, "why don't we jump onto the conveyor belt and pull it with the rope?"

"Aye, we can try it, but don't forget … we're forrit if Jerry catches us."

"It'll be reight … we'll see his spotlight coming from a mile off."

"U-um, I suppose so … come on then." It worked a treat. We had to grip the rope tightly when the bogey came to the steep parts but, on the whole, it was easier than shoving it.

Pete and I proved worthy of every pennyworth of pey-brass we got and soon earned the respect of all the face-workers. Mind you, we didn't just hump all the materials to the coalface; we actually ventured onto the face and helped the miners.

"Can we help you to shovel some o' the coal?" we'd ask.

"Aye, course you can, but we don't call it shovelling on the face," said one of the colliers, "it's called 'filling'."

Pete and I were aware, as were the men that we could be dismissed instantly for this, but it still seemed worth the risk.

Everyone, including the belt-end attendant, kept a constant vigil for the approach of a fireman or any other official. The firemen and the Safety Officer could be seen coming a mile off, as they had special spot lamps, which were very distinct from an ordinary miner's lamp. Jerry enforced the ruling about untrained youths venturing onto the coalface and was very strict about it; but all the same, although he knew what went on, he turned a blind eye to it because he knew how much timber lads depended on their pey-brass. However, woe-betide any lad who actually got caught in the act. Pete and I knew this and never once became complacent about it.

At the first sign of anyone flashing their lamp and shouting, "Spotlight! Spotlight!" Pete and I would scurry down the face and make our way back to the Landing via the bottom gate. This didn't create the problem of having to explain our whereabouts, as we frequently ran tackle on the bottom gate as well.

During the process of filling the coal the colliers put up steel roof supports every few feet and propped them up with dowties or wooden props. Large wooden chocks were also used and these had an extra special function of reinforcing the other supports. The chocks were formed from six inch square wooden blocks, each two feet in length. These blocks were then built into a square formation. This was done by laying down 2 blocks parallel to each other about 18 inches apart, and then two more on top but diagonal to them. Before a third layer was applied, a half brick was placed at each corner. More blocks were applied on top of these until the chock was roof high.

After the filling was completed the perilous job of 'striking' followed which entailed the removal of all the back supports from the coalface. This unsupported area behind the miners from where the coal had been extracted then became known as the 'Gob'. The ideal situation was for the roof to collapse in once the props were removed.

However, this sometimes took days to happen and consequently a dangerous situation was created as the hanging roof put colossal pressure onto the coalface supports ... an awesome place to be working!

One day, whilst striking, I was helping a very friendly collier called Jimmy Howarth.

"What's the idea of the chocks Jim?" I asked.

"Ah well," he stressed, "they're really important. Just shine your light into the Gob John Bill and you can see the roof hanging." I shone my light into the empty space of the Gob and could see way back. The floor looked spacious just like a ballroom until the sagging roof restricted my view.

"It's not good when the roof's hanging like that John Bill," said Jimmy, "in fact it's downright dangerous. This is the reason why we need to build chocks. When the roof hangs like it's doing right now all the weight is being pushed o'er onto the face. Without the chocks in place the weight would skirt out props like knocking o'er a set o' dominoes."

"Bloomin 'eck Jim ... does it not scare you then?" I asked feeling a bit edgy.

"Too bloody right it scares me! Sh-ssh, can you hear that creaking noise," he whispered.

"Yeah," I replied rather intrigued.

"Well we call that creaking noise 'bitting,' and it tells us that the Gob's shoving right now ... it could go at any minute."

Suddenly, the Gob roof caved in! There was a deafening roar as thousands of tons of solid sandstone rock crashed to the ground billowing up loads of dust. Jim rolled about laughing, as I nearly jumped out of my skin.

"See what I mean lad ... don't say I didn't warn thí."

Still shaking from shock I asked, "Is it safe now Jim? Flippin' 'eck, that were scary."

"Aye John Bill," he roared unable to contain his laughter, "a bloody lot safer than what it wer' afore. Reight lad, now you've got o'er the initial shock, how would you like to learn a bit about striking?" I liked this bloke and right away said I'd have a go.

"Reight, watch me first and then I'll let thí have a go at striking out one o' these chocks." I watched with interest as Jim wielded a seven-pound hammer and began to strike one of the bricks in the chock. "This is the reason why we have to use bricks lad ... otherwise we'd never get the chocks out once the weight had settled on 'em." After painstakingly knocking out all four bricks the wooden blocks came tumbling down. Jim then built another chock nearer to the coalface, before striking out the next one. He'd only knocked down a few chocks when, once again, part of the Gob roof came crashing down.

"That's better," said Jim, "that's what should happen all the time then there's not as much weight being thrown o'er onto the face."

Whilst some men were striking others were moving heavy scraper pans over into the empty space in preparation for the next batch of coal. Once the striking was completed and the scraper pans had been moved into position, the jib of a special coal-cutting machine was used to undercut the new seam of coal. Holes were drilled six feet into the coal throughout the length of the face in readiness for the shotfirer, who would fill the holes with explosives and then, using special detonators, 'fire' them. After being fired the coal was again ready to be filled. Overall, I found face-work very interesting, albeit dangerous. My experience of the hazardous life of a miner increased daily working alongside these courageous hardworking men.

****

As the months passed, Pete and I gained the respect of our seniors. The colliers held us in high esteem and willingly gave us our pey-brass. This was great for us two lads, as it fairly boosted our wage packet.

However, something happened that Pete and I didn't like ... not one little bit!

It was bait-time and one of our mates called Les, who liked attending the belt-end at the top of the face rather than tackle dragging, complained to the colliers that he should get pey-brass as well.

After discussing it, one of the colliers said, "Yeah, it's only reight, young Les is only on a little wage like t'other lads. I'll tell thí what ... why don't we give all the pey-brass to him this Friday?"

Pete didn't usually say much but on this occasion he did, "Hey hang on a minute! He doesn't do any humping like me and John Bill and anyroad, he's attending the belt-end outa choice 'cos he doesn't like hard work."

"Take no notice of 'em Pete," I interrupted, "they're having us on ... don't take the bait!"

"Never mind don't take the bait John Bill," said Archie, "we're not kiddin' ... just wait and see!"

Throughout the week, Pete and I both carried out our usual routine, humping, filling, striking, etc. But every bait-time the topic of conversation amongst the colliers was the same. Pete showed his obvious annoyance and even I began to feel irritated.

"You know somét John Bill," complained Pete, "I'll be as sick as a parrot if they give our pey-brass to Les ... I'd be in a reight mess without it 'cos I've come to rely on'it."

"Don't worry about it Pete, there's no way they'd do that. Anyroad, can you honestly see Archie handing o'er half a dollar to

Les?" Despite trying to reassure Pete I was beginning to feel edgy myself.

Finally, payday arrived. At the end of the shift Pete and I raced through the showers and, after collecting our wages, we stood outside the pay-office waiting for the colliers to hand over our hard earned pey-brass. Sure enough, as hard-faced as anything, Les came and stood at the side of us.

Pete sniggered at him, "I don't know what you're standing there for ... you haven't a cat in hell's chance o' getting any pey-brass."

Les just sniggered back, "Well, we'll just have to wait and see won't we?"

"Right Pete," I said, "we'll stand in our normal places and see what happens." It wasn't long before the colliers started filtering through. Tommy Lowe was the first one to pick up his wage packet and on opening it he approached the three of us.

"All reight John Bill, how's it goin' then?"

"All right Tommy, and you?" I replied thinking, "Aye, I knew they were only kiddin' us." But I was wrong, Tommy did the very thing I least expected ... he actually gave half-a-crown to Les!

"Hey what are you playin' at Tommy ... that's our pey-brass?" I protested.

"Listen here John Bill ... we've been telling thi' all week what we were gonna do but you obviously didn't take any notice." Pete and I were fuming!

"I don't believe this Tommy, especially from you!" I snapped.

"Don't blame me John Bill," he replied shrugging his shoulders, "this is now't personal, it was a unanimous decision ... you know how things work down a pit."

"That's all right in some instances Tommy, but in this one you're wrong," I growled, "that's mine and Pete's money you're messing about with."

"Hey, don't get cocky John Bill ... I'll gíve flamin' pey-brass to who I please. Anyroad, why don't all three of you share it between yourselves?"

"Because he hasn't done any of the humpin'," rapped Pete, "me and John Bill have done all the grafting while he's been sat on his arse all week doing now't!"

In the meantime other colliers approached and all of them did the same as Tommy Lowe. All of them that is except Jimmy Howarth.

Jimmy protested to the other miners but to no avail, "Come on fellas, I think you're taking things too far, this is beyond a joke ... these two young lads have worked their socks off for us this week." Turning to Pete and me he said, "I'm sorry about this lads but there's not a reight lot I can do about it. All I can say is here's my half-a-dollar."

"Thanks Jimmy, thanks a lot, it's not your fault. Anyroad, don't worry about it ... we'll get our pey-brass all right," I said.

"Well you won't bloody get any off me," quipped Les, "if you think I'm splitting it with thí, you've got another thing coming!" Just then, Archie, the last miner to collect his pay packet approached.

He gloated as he gave his half-a-crown to Les, "What did I tell you John Bill ... serves thí bloody well right for not taking any notice."

Pete was frantic, yelling "You bloody swine you're now't else ... after all we've done for you!" Archie just laughed and walked off.

"Just look at this John Bill," Pete moaned, "a bloody lousy one and thre'pence a piece, I feel like throwing misel' in't 'Cut'."

"Not to worry Pete! I feel as bad about it as you do but we'll sort it ... you'll see." Completely powerless for the moment we both made our way to the bus stop full of gloom.

The weekend passed and the Monday afternoon shift commenced at 2-15pm. Pete and I had discussed the matter between ourselves and decided to take action, or better still ... no action! We went about our tackle dragging in a proper manner but that's all ... we stuck implicitly to the rules. We carried all the tackle to the end of the rails, and there it stayed!

"We'll just hang around here for a while Pete," I said, "it won't be long before they're wantin' some tackle on the face."

"I hope you're reight John Bill, I couldn't do with missing out on the pey-brass again."

"No, neither could I ... anyroad, I have a gut feeling about it."

Sure enough it wasn't long before two colliers came traipsing off the face asking for some help, "Come on lads ... give us a lift, we're behind schedule!"

"You cheeky hardfaced swines you're now't else!" rapped Pete, "After what you did on Friday ... there's no chance!"

"Oh come on, it wer' only a joke ... it won't happen again."

"Too bloody true it won't!" we both said in unison, "If you want a lift, get Les to give you one."

"Please yourself," said one of them as he made his way back to the face, "but there'll be no more pey-brass for any of you anymore."

"Oh blimey, that's done it!" exclaimed Pete, "We've messed it up for good now John Bill!"

"I don't know so much Pete, they both looked nackered carrying them Dowties. Don't forget they may be used to working on the face, but they're not used to carrying tackle as well. Anyroad Pete, I just know we've got to stick to our guns ... I'm convinced that we're doing the right thing."

"I only hope you're reight John Bill ... I really do. I'll be sick as a parrot if we miss out on our peybrass again"

"Yeah so will I Pete," I grunted feeling rather dejected, but I've a gut feeling that we've just gotta stick together on this ... I can feel it in mi' bones."

"I bloody well hope soJohn Bill ... I bloody hope so!"

The day passed and the same thing happened on Tuesday. Once again Pete and I waited patiently at the end of the track. It wasn't long before a couple of colliers came to pick up some bricks ... one of these happened to be Archie.

"All right Archie, how's it goin' then?" asked Pete.

"Never mind how's it goín you little ratbags, you know bloody well how it's goin'!"

Just then the main belt stopped and all the colliers gathered in the main gate and settled down for bait. Pete and I joined them.

I sat down at the side of Jimmy Howarth, who gave me a hearty greeting, "All right John Bill, nice to see you ... keep up the good work lad, I'm proud o' thí."

"What bloody good work!" rapped Archie. "I ain't seen any bloody good work around here ... especially from them two ratbags!"

"Hang on a minute Archie!" said Tommy Lowe, "I know what Jimmy means and he's right ... we treated these here lads shabby and you know it."

"Whattaya talkin' about Tommy?"

"Come off it Archie! You know only too well what I'm talkin' about ... we've bín out of order. You wer' only saying yourself t'other week that they were the best two tackle lads in the pit. I know it all started off as a joke, but I think we took it too far."

Another collier intervened, "I'll go along wí that Tommy ... I've got to admit it's been bloody hard graft without 'em."

"Aye it has," said another, "and don't forget it's only Tuesday."

Pete and I were listening intently and lapping up every minute as the debate began to heat up a little.

Pete sniggered and whispered in my ear, "We've got 'em by the short and curlies John."

"I think you're reight there Pete, they're wavering."

Jimmy Howarth nudged me from the other side, "Well done John Bill ... keep it up and don't let 'em off the hook."

"Don't worry about that Jim," I said munching a jam butty, "there's no chance o' that."

After more discussion Tommy Lowe acted as spokesman for the colliers, "All reight lads, you've made your point ... start bringin' tackle onto the face and we'll give you your pey-brass at th'end o' the week."

"Oh yeah, and what about our pey-brass from last week?" I replied.

"You must be joking!" splurted Archie nearly choking on his coffee. "I'm just giving thí half-a-dollar ... you'll have to get rest of it from t'other lad."

I stood my ground, "No, you get it from him Archie ... you gave it to him!"

"You bloody cheeky little gít ... I'll drum your ribs if I get hold o' thí!"

"Now hang on Archie, the lads right!" a few colliers chimed in, "it's our own doing so we'll have to pay 'em."

Archie grumbled a little before replying, "Yeah go on then, I suppose you're reight ... I just don't like thoughts o' coughing up five bob."

Turning to me and Pete, Tommy Lowe said, "Reight lads, I know you've been listening to everything that's gone on ... well, you've won and we'll all give you double pey-brass on Friday. So now, how about getting' stuck in after bait and humpin' this bleedin' tackle to the face?"

"At your service Tommy, with pleasure," Pete and I answered simultaneously.

As the men made their way back to the face, Jimmy Howarth tapped us both on the shoulder, "Congratulations lads, I'm proud of you ... that were better than going to the pictures."

"Yeah and thanks to you Jim," I replied, "I don't think we could o' done it without your help."

"Oh aye you could lad, don't underestimate yourself ... I don't."

That was it, both Pete and I were elated, "We've done it ... we've done it!" bleated Pete all excited.

"Not quite," I said, "let's wait to see what happens on Friday."

On the back-shift the wage was paid out before work commenced. On Friday, Pete and I made sure we were at the pay office in plenty of time to catch everyone. One by one each collier handed over 5 shillings and then came Archie's turn. He slipped half-a-crown into Pete's hand and started to walk off.

"Come on Archie, another half-a-dollar ... you'll have to cough up like the rest of 'em," said Pete.

A grin came to Archie's face, "Oh well, you can't blame me for trying can you?" He then handed over another half-a-crown, which he already had clasped in his other hand.

Finally, Jimmy Howarth came and he too handed over five shillings.

"That's too much Jimmy ... you paid us half-a-dollar last week." I said.

"Take it lad, it's been worth every penny seeing you at work ... it wer' better than watching a pantomime."

I turned to Pete, "Great, superb, we've done it! We can really celebrate in th'Hapton Inn tonight after the shift's finished." Thirty shillings pey brass each ... we both felt like millionaires.

Pete and I were a good team and worked well together. We remained partners and good friends for nearly two years.

****

Tackle running for the colliers suited me down to the ground ... I loved every minute of it. It must have been good for me too because in those two years I grew and grew. By the time I was eighteen I'd grown to my maximum height off five-feet seven-inches and I was fit and strong with it ... nobody called me 'Little' John Bill anymore.

Eighteen years old and the time had come for me to do my coalface training. This consisted of 20 days 'coaling', 20 days 'ripping' and 20 days 'striking'. I did my coaling on 'no 4' face and my overseer was none other than 'Archie'.

"Right John Bill, you're under my wing now for the next 20 days so think on you don't step outa line ... you might well o' grown a bit but I'm still capable o' drumming your ribs!" Having worked with Archie I knew only too well that his bark was worse than his bite. We worked well together and before I knew it, I'd acquired my coaling papers, which meant I could now officially work on the face filling coal ... on collier's rate!

After completing my coaling training I worked odd days on the face earning £4 a day but this wasn't as regular as I would have liked. Most of the time I was 'dayt'ling' on normal pay, working on belt-ends, tackle running or other things.

I did my twenty days ripping training on the back-shift. When coal had been extracted and the coalface advanced the job of the rippers was to blast away stone above the coal to give height to form a roadway and lengthen the tunnel. It was an experience I won't forget in a hurry. I had to work alongside four experienced men, whose team leader was Lawrence Smith, nicknamed Loll. He was a big fellow with a baldhead, who liked to get the job done. At the time the pit was experimenting with a new shift system. This was a great incentive because, on completing a particular task, each collier could leave the pit for home and actually received a bonus into the bargain.

Loll liked to finish early and he made this quite clear to me on my first day, "Reight lad, let's get one thing streight … I'm not keen on taking on a trainee so don't expect to be pampered, you'll have to get stuck in like the rest of us."

"Righto Loll, I go along with that, I don't expect any favours … you just tell me what to do and I'll do it."

"Well first thing … the shot-firer's gonna fire the ripping so you'd best grab a bit o' bait now 'cos you won't have time to eat ow't after that."

I had barely taken a bite when there was a loud blast. Hardly had the dust settled before Loll issued orders, "That's it John Bill, if you haven't finished your bait yet, you can leave it for the rats."

As the smoke cleared I could see a mountain of shale that had been dropped by the tremendous explosion … it was nigh impossible to get from the gate onto the face.

"Come on, don't just stand there gawking at it … get hold o' that shovel and start clearing a way through!" rapped Loll.

"Righto," I replied, "I'm going … I'm going."

It took about ten minutes to form a small opening before Loll started issuing orders again.

"Reight lad that should be big enough for you to crawl through … now get your arse through there and start shovelling fro' t'other side so we can all get through."

"Bloomin' 'eck Loll, that hole's not big enough for a rat to crawl through ... never mind me!"

"I don't want any back chat; just get yourself under there ... now!"

Being very nimble I dragged myself through the gap and started shovelling. Finally the hole was big enough to allow the men through and once again Loll started giving the orders.

"Reight John Bill, we're gonna form a line and start 'backening' the shale from one man to t'other. You'll be the last in line so you'll have to build a 'pack' as we throw it to thí."

I was well-versed in pack-building ... I'd helped the colliers on number four face to build plenty. I also knew the importance of packs, as conveyed to me by my collier friend, Jimmy Howarth. Jimmy had taught me how to use larger pieces of shale to build two dry walls and then to throw the loose shale in between them to form the pack.

"U-um, I'd better make a good job o' this," I thought, knowing that packs played an all-important part in controlling the weight of the roof.

I was eager to make a good impression but my diligence soon wore off when I realised what a wet hole I was working in. Water poured in from the layers above and, to make matters worse, being blocked by the loose shale, it dammed up on the floor. We were all wearing oilskin waterproofs but these didn't help much, as the water trickled off our helmets and down our necks. It didn't take long before the water, where I was kneeling, was six inches deep and above my kneepads. I was like a drowned rat but I couldn't complain, as the other four men had to cope with the same conditions. Mind you, the thought did enter my head that they were on a lot more money than I was.

"Come on you little swine John Bill, keep going," growled Loll, "the sooner we get done the sooner we get home!"

This certainly spurred me on, "Yeah reighto Loll, I want to get finished and outa the pit as much as you do," I shouted back.

"Aye, well get your flamin' back into it and stop muckin' about!"

"Come on John lad," I mumbled to myself as the hot showers on the pit top beckoned me, "get stuck in so we can get out o' this rat-hole!" I worked furiously shovelling the shale as fast as I could, gradually forming a channel, which allowed some of the water to flow from the coalface to the gate.

Every now and again Loll would throw big flat stones, which kept landing in the water smack in front of me drenching me even more.

"He-ey, you're doing that on purpose," I moaned, "you've just splattered me full in the face with a load o' slush ... watch it!"

Loll roared laughing, "Whattaya talkin' about you little runt, we haven't got time to mess about ... just get on with it." It happened a few times, but I was never sure whether he did it on purpose or in the course of trying to get the job done.

"Oh never mind, it doesn't matter," I reassured myself, "I'm soaked to the skin as it is ... what difference does a bit more water make?"

On the first day we finished the task in less than three hours, and I actually caught the 5-40pm bus at the Hapton Inn.

On the bus home I was quite pleased, reflecting on the day, "By 'eck, I'm gonna be in th'house afore our Mary gets home from the weaving shed ... won't she be surprised!" Taking everything into account, I didn't mind working in the wet conditions if it meant finishing so early.

One day whilst working in the harsh conditions some tragic news seaped into the coal mine via the grape vine about a sporting event. It was the 6th of Febuary 1958 and Manchester United's team, 'The Busby Babes', were involved in a terrible plane crash in Munich,

392

Germany and most of the players were tragical killed. It was news that shocked the nation. It stuck in my mind because I'd just recently watched them playing against my home team at Turf Moor in a cup match. It was a memorable game because Burnley won 5-3 and I remember Tommy Taylor scoring the best goal I'd ever seen.

****

The twenty days ripping training passed quickly and, overall, I got on very well with my colleagues. I then went on to complete my final 20 days striking amongst my former colleagues on number 4 face.

I was now a qualified collier, but didn't get regular face work and had to spend many days dayt'ling on low pay. However, Jimmy Howarth was now a fireman and he always strived to find me facework whenever possible. One day all the facework was taken up, but he asked me to help the colliers to drag a heavy armoured cable down the face.

"The cutter's broken down and we need to get a cable to it urgently. I know it's hard graft John Bill," he said, "but if we get the job done I'll book you in as facework today and you'll get a bonus on top o' that." I didn't need telling twice … I loved this bloke

****

One morning, a few days before my twentieth birthday, I was on the early shift. Prior to going into the pit most colliers went across to the canteen for a brew or to buy some chewing tobacco. As the firemen had to be in the pit first to take charge they were allowed to go to the front of the queue. On this particular morning I was stood in the queue and who should walk in … no other than G T and he was no longer a fireman but an ordinary collier like me.

"By 'eck, look who's back from the gold mines in South Africa," one collier remarked.

"All right G T how's it goín'," said another, "I never expected to see thí back here again?"

I turned round and on seeing him my mind flashed back to the Bluebird days and the way that this man had made my life a misery.

"Not to worry," I thought, "that's in the past way behind me." I would have let it go at that, but then G T did something that got my back up; he actually walked right to the front of the queue as bold as brass as if he was still a fireman. What surprised me is that none of the colliers said anything to him

"Hey what do you think you're doín G T?" I yelled. "There's a queue here ... get to the flamin' back of'it!"

"And who the bloody hell are you then?" he quipped. Suddenly a look of recognition came to his eyes, "By 'eck is it little John Bill?"

"Aye that's right, but not quite so little anymore, and I'm tellin' you agén ... get to the back o' this bloody queue!"

"Oh aye ... and who's gonna mék me if I don't?"

As I looked at him my mind flashed back to when he'd literally lifted me of my feet behind the mine cars. I knew I could be asking for trouble but I was determined not to let him get away with it ... besides, by now my adrenaline was now flowing. "I'll bloody well put you there," I growled, "I'm not that little lad anymore that you pinned up against the rock wall behind the mine cars!"

He weighed me up for a while glaring at me and I could tell by his eyes that he was annoyed. "Aye, you might o' grown a bit," he growled, "but I can see you're still a fly gít!"

"It takes one to know one." I sneered, exaggerating a wry smile. I was full of foreboding and shaking a little but I didn't let him know that. However, my fear was unfounded and soon laid to rest.

G T glared at me again for what seemed an age before grunting, "Arg-gh, you're not bloody well worth it ... I didn't flamin' want ow't anyroad!" At that he stormed out of the canteen looking rather dejected ... it wasn't quite the kind of reception he'd expected. Despite a feeling of self-satisfaction, I still sighed with relief.

But I couldn't help muttering to myself, "Great ... every dog has its day!"

CHAPTER 13 - NATIONAL SERVICE

It was shortly after the G T incident that I decided to leave the pit. I'd become a little unsettled, as there had been talk of the mine closing down. Also I'd had a slight accident as I was partially buried when some shale collapsed from the roof on the coalface and it had knocked my confidence. I suffered a few cuts and bruises and finished up with a small blue mark on my cheek, a legacy of working in a coalmine. But other than that I was fine. But the main thing that swayed me was that Dad asked me once again to go into partnership with him in the scrap-iron trade.

Also, the way I saw it, the cotton industry was on the decline. By the late fifties it was reeling from the effects of cheap imports from abroad. The saying 'King Cotton' was soon to be a thing of the past. Unfair competition had taken its toll on the cotton mills and most of them were dying a slow death. One by one, many of the tall factory chimneys were being demolished, symbolising the end of the 'Great Cotton Era'. Burnley's main industry had literally hung on a thread and that thread was now wearing very thin.

I could foresee the closure of lots of other factories, which got me to thinking, "If that happens there's going to be lots of scrap iron for the taking. Yeah, I think this is a good time to go into business with Dad." So I did and we made a formidable team, as he showed me all the tricks of the trade, including introducing me to factory owners with whom he negotiated fat contracts for their scrap iron.

We worked well together; I even felt that I influenced him with my keeness and willingness to work hard, as he didn't seem to spend as much time in the pubs and concentrated more on the business. This made me feel good because our little venture was taking off and I felt that I had won Dad's respect. Yes, things were really looking good.

He still did most of the wheeling and dealing directly with the factory owners but he always took me into the office with him. But, as always, he gave me the same advice that I'd heard many times.

"Don't say a word our John, leave it all to me," he'd say. "Just look, listen and learn ... you'll soon get the hang o' things."

One day, whilst in the Salford Pub, Dad actually made a good deal with the manager of Barden Mill.

"Isn't that the mill where our Mary works?" I asked as we made our way to the factory.

"It is that our John ... why do you ask?"

"Well, I wer' thinking ... our Mary'll go mad if she knows we're collecting scrap iron from where she works."

"Hey John lad, there's no sentiment in business ... you'll learn that quick enough."

"Aye, I suppose you're right Dad ... it were just a thought."

"There's no supposing about it our John, you can get them sort o' thoughts outa your head right now ... you'll be no good in business if you don't."

We arrived at the factory about half-past twelve and it was a nice sunny day. As I started to load the wagon a few weavers were sat around outside enjoying their dinner break. I'd just climbed on the back of the wagon to sort out some of the scrap iron when I saw our Mary coming out of a shed door. As she approached us I made the mistake of letting Dad know.

"E-eh, all reight our Mary," he shouted cheerfully as she came into view, "it's your dad."

When she saw us a look of sheer horror came to her face ... for a moment she was dumbstruck.

"Oh 'eck," I thought, "she feels humiliated in front of her friends." If looks could kill I'd have dropped dead on the spot. Her face reddened as she tightened her mouth and hissed through gritted teeth. Without saying a word she turned around and walked straight back into the factory.

"What the flippin' 'eck's up with her?" asked Dad, "Who the flamin' 'eck does she think she is anyroad ... Lady Muck?"

When we got home that night Mary was in a right mood.

"What d'you think you're playing at Dad, you've really shown me up?"

"Whaddaya talkín about Lady, who d'you think you are anyroad ... I've got to mék a living just like anybody else!"

"I know you have," she screeched," but coming to the bloomin' factory where I work is a bit much in'it?"

"And what am I supposed to do then ... let a flamíin good deal slip through mí fingers?"

"I don't know but at least you could've ...."

"Never mind what I could've done, it's obvious you're ashamed o' me. I'll tell you this for now't our Mary, I'll not stop coming to that mill or any other for you or anybody else. And there's one thing for sure ... I won't ever acknowledge you anymore when I'm about mí business."

If he was expecting an apology from Mary he didn't get one ... she just tutted arrogantly and strutted out of the house. In a way I could see her point ... but I could also see Dad's.

****

Meanwhile I still frequently went over to Bacup on my motorbike to see my relatives. But the main reason was to see Grandad; he was grieving badly for Granma and his health was deteriorating rapidly. However, I also visited Aunt Katie's house and often took Michael, one of my young cousins, for a spin in the countryside on the pillion. I was nineteen and he was nine years younger than me, but despite the age gap a strong bond formed between us. I frequently took him over to Burnley and he loved every minute of it, as the many cobbled streets and high factory chimneys intrigued him.

"Bloomin' 'eck Johnny," he'd comment, "I thought we had a lot o' big chimneys o'er in Bacup but there's millions o'er here in't there?" Michael also enjoyed it because there was much more going on in Burnley than Bacup. He especially liked it when I took him home to Albion Street.

"Are you gonna ték me to see mí Auntie Winnie and mí Uncle Jack?" he'd ask.

"Aye all reight, but I know why you want to go there," I joked, "you get méd a fuss of by mí brothers and sisters … that's reight in'it?"

"Yeah, course it is," he'd answer with a cheeky grin, "wouldn't you if you were me?"

"U-um, I suppose so," I replied with a smile.

He also liked my mother because she spoilt him and often took him down town for little treats.

I occasionally took one of my other younger cousins for a ride on the back of my motorbike but more often than not it would be Michael … we just seemed to jell together.

About three and a half years after Grandma's death, the sad news came from Bacup that Grandad had died whilst sat in his armchair. Aunt Katie contacted my mother saying she had found their dad in the chair whilst visiting him. It was yet another sad time for my family, especially Mam. I was in the house with her a few days after the funeral and she sadly reflected on her younger days.

"E-eh, mí poor mam and dad, they tried their best to give us a good start in life but they didn't stand a chance. I know Dad could get a bit grumpy at times but he wer' never a well man … what with having to work out in all weathers and the war an' all. U-um, and they never got any hand-outs from the government like they do nowadays; mind you, Dad was too proud to accept anything anyway." She paused for a moment wiping a tear from her cheek before mumbling to herself, "I'll tell you what Dad ... you were a stubborn old so an' so but I'm still going to miss you."

"E-eh Mam, I'm gonna miss mi' grandad as well," I consoled her, "but at least he's not suffering or fretting anymore for Granma is he?"

"No, you're right there our John. One thing's for sure ... he certainly wanted to join her."

"He did that," I agreed as I pondered on the way he'd cut himself off from everyone since my grandmother had died.

Things were never the same now that Granma and Grandad had gone but I continued to visit Bacup frequently and often went straight after work to take young Michael for a ride on my motorbike around the Rossendale Valley.

****

Ironically, shortly after my twentieth birthday and only four months after going into business with Dad, I received my 'call up' papers conscripting me to serve two years National Service with Her Majesty's Forces. Two of my mates, Billy Pounder and David Whittaker had recently been called up to serve in the Catering Corps. Another two, Pete Holroyd and Barry Birks had signed on for nine years in the Royal Marines. Pete Fletcher and Bobby Cheetham had also received their call up papers but both had opted to sign on as regulars in the Service Corps and were serving in the Far East.

After reading my papers from the War Office I vented my feelings to Dad, "Bloomin' 'eck Dad, just my luck to get called up into th'army... just when we were geddín' started."

"Never mind lad, it's not th'end o' the world," he consoled me, "two years isn't all that long, it'll soon pass."

"Aye, I know that but it would have to happen now just when we've got a few good contracts on the go."

"Don't worry about it our John," said Dad patting me on the back, "I'll keep everything shipshape while you're away."

"I hope so Dad ... I hope so." I wasn't happy with the situation but there wasn't a lot I could do about it.

I had to go to Preston for a medical and attend a recruitment briefing. After the initial formalities I was informed that I had been placed into the Royal Army Medical Corps, where I would work as an auxiliary nurse in army hospitals. I protested strongly to the officials, asking if I could be placed into the Service or Ordnance Core. I knew if I enlisted into any of these regiments I would at least obtain a driving licence, which would be useful when I was demobbed.

A rather strict regimental officer answered, "If you want to go into the regiment of your choice my man, then sign on as a regular soldier ... if not, you go where we put you." I gave it a lot of thought but I didn't fancy signing on for three years.

"No, what if I don''t like it," I pondered, "two years doesn't seem a long while, but three ... I don't know."

After the initiation ceremony I was given a travel warrant and ordered to report to Queen Elizabeth Barracks, in Crookham, Hampshire on July 16th 1959 by four o'clock in the afternoon. I received my army number 23633183 and was officially placed into the Royal Army Medical Corps.

"Bloomin' 'eck Dad!" I moaned when I got home. "They've gone and put me in the medics working in flippin' army hospitals ... I don't fancy being a nurse, it's a woman's job. I tried to persuade 'em to put me into the Service Corps but they wouldn't wear it."

"Never mind lad, it'll be easier than workin' down the pit. Anyroad, when d'you have to go?"

"Next bloomin' Thursday. Oh, that reminds me Dad ... will you do me a favour?"

"Aye course I will our John ... what is it?"

"Could you sell my motorbike for me ... I don't like parting with it, it's the best bike I've ever had; but what else can I do?"

"Righto ... how much d'you want forrit?"

"If you get me twenty quid I'll be happy," I lamented. "Somebody's gonna get a bargain ... I give fifty quid forrit eighteen months ago and it's ne'er let me down once."

As it happened, Dad sold it to a mate of mine, Pete Abbott, for £20. Pete told me later that he ran the motorbike for two years and it was the best bike he'd ever had too.

****

As I stood waiting on Barrack's Station for the train, which was to take me directly to London, I had one great thumping hangover because Dad had arranged a farewell party the night before in the Nelson Hotel on Trafalgar. A few mates had turned up, as did my brothers and sisters and they gave me a really good send-off as they plied me with loads of drink.

"Here you are John, get this down you," said Jimmy handing me a whisky, "it'll do you good."

"Right lad, down the hatch," said Dad, "here's to the future." By the end of the night I'd had a right cocktail of drinks and did I suffer for it! As soon as I got outside into the fresh air my face turned various colours from green to grey.

"U-ugh, I want to be sick," I said making my way back inside to the pub's toilet.

Our Barry was there to console me, "You'll be all right our John … get it up, you'll feel better!" It reminded me of the night when I'd taken my first drink and David had said a similar thing … except this time I felt worse … much worse!

Hence, the grotty feeling next morning as Dad and my two brothers saw me off on the train.

During my journey I reflected on the time Mam had made the same journey to the capital nearly thirty years before. On reaching London I had to make my way via the underground to another station where I made my connection to Aldershot. Finally, later that evening, I arrived at Queen Elizabeth Barracks, to commence my training as a nursing orderly. Once again I protested about being placed into the Medical Corps, but the officials gave me the same answer that I'd been given back in Preston.

"Right, that's it," I mumbled as I resigned myself to my plight, "if I'm not going to sign on as a regular I may as well accept my lot!"

My home for the next four months was in a typical army barrack room, which I shared with about twenty other blokes in the same predicament as me. When I entered the billet all the mattresses were turned back off the bedsprings and the bedding was folded neatly at the bottom of the bed into a box formation. A soldier wearing two stripes on his sleeve, who introduced himself as Corporal Jenkins, greeted us.

"Right soldiers," he addressed us, "I'm the corporal in charge of this billet and you'll be under my charge for the duration of your training. This billet must be kept tidy at all times, and every morning the beds must be made up exactly as they are right now.

On Friday morning, we were officially kitted out with boots and full regalia. The weekend was a kind of settling-in period, allowing each one of us to get used to our new environment and also to each other; but on Monday, the serious business of rigorous training began ... this was to last for sixteen weeks. It consisted of square bashing on a large parade ground in conjunction with some arduous studying in the classroom. The classroom layout was ingenious leaving nothing to the imagination. It was like a hospital with models displaying different sections of the human body. There were many other modern teaching aids, including dummy patients and skeletons in the room. By the end of the sixteen weeks training, my comrades and I were well versed in the functions and anatomy of the human body. Having undergone a strict course in 'First-Aid' we were also competent enough to cope with an emergency situation in case of any accident or illness occurring.

Every evening in the billet room, we had to spend at least a couple of hours 'bulling' our boots to make sure they gleamed on the parade ground. The same applied to our belts, cap badges and the brass buttons on our uniforms; everything had to shine like a new pin and woe betide any soldier if they didn't. Each morning on parade, the sergeant major stomped around with a stick under his arm bellowing at the top of his voice. Anyone not passing the stringent inspection was put on a charge and ended up doing extra fatigue duties.

New intakes came into the camp every two weeks and were always known as 'squaddies' or 'sprogs'. The Army numbered each intake according to the week and year in which it had been enlisted ... therefore, our intake was 59-14. As one intake commenced training, another one, having finished their stint, would be awaiting transfer to a main camp somewhere in England. Subsequently, every fortnight, a booze-up took place to celebrate the occasion.

I met up with lads from many different walks of life. These included Jimmy Mitchinson from Wigan, Colin Hagan from Gateshead and Brian Holdsworth from Leeds. Brian was to become a lifelong friend.

The gross pay was 25 shillings a week and after one shilling stoppages we were paid out to the nearest 5 shillings, which meant that we finished up with just twenty shillings in our hand. The rest of the money went into 'credits'... a kind of saving fund. I was concerned about Mum not being able to manage whilst I was in the army, so I went to see my C O.

"Right lad, we can allow your mother an army pension of 45 shillings a week," he advised me, "but only if you're willing to contribute 7 shillings out of your own allowance."

"Bloomin' 'eck," I thought, "I'll only be left with 17 shillings, and after they've taken out the credits ... that'll only leave 15 bob."

"Well lad, come on, what do you think?" barked the C O. "We haven't got all day to mess about!"

"Oh sod it! In for a penny in for a pound," I thought, "we're all in the same boat ... another few bob isn't gonna make all that much difference." So that was it, I was left with a paltry fifteen shillings with which to buy toothpaste, razor blades, soap, etc. Even so, I still managed to be left with ten shillings ... enough to buy eight pints of beer. I could have got onto Mum and she would have sent me the seven shillings but I didn't bother.

"Anyroad," I told myself, "if I can manage on this pittance for two years, it'll put me in good stead when I'm back in Civvy Street. Another thing, I'm not into this boozing lark, so it'll give me ample opportunity to do some serious training and get myself fit."

Consequently, I trained hard during the week and on payday ... I'd join the lads for a drink and we'd have a right rave-up.

****

It was on one of these rave-ups that I had my first army fight. I only had two fights during my army days and fortunately I won them both.

The summer of 1959 was a scorcher and I was happy to take advantage of the pleasant evenings. Being determined to build myself up into peak condition I spent most of my spare time on the playing fields or on the army assault course. But most lads weren't in the same frame of mind as me and preferred drinking beer at every opportunity in the NAAFI Club.

Some of them tried to persuade me to go out on boozing sprees with them during the week but I wouldn't be tempted.

"I'm sorry lads but once a week is enough for me," I would answer. "Besides, I haven't got enough money to go out drinking every night."

"What a bloody lame excuse!" quipped Jimmy Logan, a Londoner. "You've got twenty-five bob a week the same as the rest of us."

"No I haven't," I replied, "I'm only left with fifteen bob after stoppages."

"You're a bloody liar!" he barked. "You just want to ponce about pretending to be a soldier."

I didn't rise to the bait but curtailed my natural instinct to fire back at him as I had done many times before at St. Thomas's Junior School. I didn't go into detail as to why I only received fifteen shillings, but simply replied:

"Please yourself, believe what you like … you do what you want to do and I'll do what I want to do."

That was it as far as I was concerned; I didn't think anymore about it till a few weeks later. The intake in the next billet to ours had just completed their sixteen weeks training and the entire group went out on the town to celebrate the occasion in the NAAFI Club. All the lads from our billet decided to join them and I went along too with my mates Colin Hagan and Brian Holdsworth. There was always a good-spirited rivalry amongst different billets; however, on this occasion lots of beer was consumed and as the evening progressed, tempers became rather frayed. A few insults were exchanged and the situation got out of hand. Before long two lads started fighting. The fight didn't last long, as Regimental Police became involved and they marched the two lads off to the guardroom. There was a lot of tension in the air, but on the whole, things seemed to settle down. Nevertheless, this was by no means the end of the matter ... not by a long way.

When I arrived back at the billet I decided to have a shower before going to bed. Directly on entering the barrack room there were four large red fire buckets filled with sand and four others filled with water, and next to these were two fire extinguishers. The billet was typical of any barrack room having a corridor down the middle with beds on either side. My bed was the first one on the right.

I'd just dried myself when Jimmy Logan arrived back from the NAAFI Club with some of his mates and he was in a right cantankerous mood.

"U-ugh, look who it is," he sniggered, "the keep fit boy! Where were you then when the fight started ... you didn't hang about too long did you?"

"What are you talking about?" I replied. "It was all done and dusted when I left."

"Done and dusted mí arse!" he snarled, "I noticed you didn't get involved ... you bloody coward!"

"No, you're right I didn't, I couldn't see the point," I said adding sarcastically, "Mind you, I noticed that you stepped way back into the shadows when the fight started."

This obviously infuriated him because without warning he caught me completely off guard as he took an almighty swing, catching me full in the eye with his clenched fist. I saw stars but the funny thing was I didn't feel any pain ... I was fuming. Instinctively I dived at him with fists flying.

All I could think was, "Right Logan you bastard, it's either you or me!"

Immediately, a few of the lads got in between and kept us apart as they tried to calm us down.

"Come on lads," said one of them, "we don't want any fighting amongst ourselves, we've all got to stick together."

"Stick together," I growled, "I'll kill the bastard... just let me at him!"

"Ha, ha, ha!" mocked Logan, "let the bloody weasel go ... I'll murder the little git!"

Despite trying to calm the situation the lads could see it was useless.

"Right," said Jimmy Mitchinson acting as a spokesman, "we'll all go outside onto the parade ground and form a circle and let these two settle their differences there."

"That'll do me," I snarled determined to give Logan the same as he'd given me, "I'll show him which one of us is the weasel!"

"Great ... bloody great!" mocked Logan. "I've been looking forward to this for bloody ages."

We made our way to the parade ground in two groups so as to keep Jimmy and me apart. After forming a circle they let us go. Jimmy Logan threw himself into the fight full of venom and baying for blood, but he was no match for me and I knew it. I was in peak condition, nimble and fleet footed. Besides, he had given me a reason to fight and my adrenaline was now flowing ... I had never felt so strong. We both fought like tigers using all the strength we had but gradually I overcame him. In the past, under similar circumstances, I would have let up on him but on this occasion I was determined to give him the same black eye that he had given me. After raining a few blows into his face I was happy with the outcome and that was the end of the fight.

Although I'd won I sank to my hands and knees in an exhausted state, I was absolutely shattered. Before returning to the billet Jimmy Logan offered me his open hand and we both shook on it.

"I hold my hand up John," he said wiping blood from his face, "I was wrong about you. That was a good fair fight … I didn't know you had it in you." He laughed before adding, "Perhaps we can be friends now?"

"You're on Jimmy," I said, "that suits me fine."

"Great! Mind you, you might not think so in the morning … it looks like you're gonna have a real shiner."

I just grinned and cracked back at him, "Snap … I'm not gonna be the only one by the looks o' things, you don't look so clever yourself."

"No I don't feel so clever at that … how about having a can o' beer back in the billet?"

"I go along with that," I replied with a grin, "it seems like a good idea to me."

By the time we got back to the barrack room some lads had already cracked open a few cans of ale. Both Jimmy and I had one can each and then we retired to bed … we were both in Noddy Land before our heads touched the pillow.

But this was not the end of it … our troubles were just beginning.

I woke up next morning with the most horrendous headache and could hardly lift my head off the pillow. With every little movement I felt blood throbbing in my veins. I finally managed to sit up straight but on putting one foot on the floor I felt a pool of gritty water.

"What the flamin' 'eck!" I thought. "What's happened here?" On looking around I struggled to focus my eyes on the scene that confronted me … it was unbelievable. The barrack room was in a state of complete disarray. There were pools of water everywhere intermingled with sand, and floating on top of the mess was white foam from the fire extinguishers. The eight empty fire buckets were strewn around in different parts of the billet, as were the fire extinguishers. Most of the lads were still in their beds but odd ones were beginning to stir.

"What's happened here then?" I asked puzzled as to what had gone on.

"You're joking," quipped Colin Hagan, "you mean to say you didn't hear anything last night?"

"No Colin," I replied innocently, "not a thing … honest!"

"Bloomin' 'eck John," laughed Jimmy Mitchinson, "you must be a good sleeper to sleep through all the commotion that went on in here last night … especially with thí sleeping in the first bed."

"What commotion? I don't know what you're talking about; I haven't got a clue … honest!"

"What commotion?" laughed Colin and Jimmy simultaneously. "That's a good ún … all bloody hell let loose in here last night, it were complete mayhem." Just then, to make things even funnier, Jimmy Logan moaned from the other side of the barrack room.

"O-oh my head, I've got the headache of all headaches … tell somebody to stop the room going round and let me get off." Then, just as I had done, he put one foot on the floor. "Who-oa!" What the bloody hell's happened here … there's a load o' water under my bed?"

"What, you an' all Jimmy," chuckled another lad, "you mean to say you heard nothing either?"

"What do you mean … heard ow't about what?" All the lads started laughing.

"How anyone could've slept through all the racket that went on in here last night is beyond me," said Jimmy Mitchinson, "it wer' like Bedlam in here."

"All right it wer' like Bedlam," I put in. "Now is anyone gonna enlighten us as to what happened?"

"Well," said Colin Hagan, "do you remember the fight between the two lads in the NAAFI last night?"

"Do I remember it? "quipped Jimmy Logan, "that's what got me and John fighting in the first place."

"Right," carried on Colin. "Well when you two were asleep, some of our lads went and raided the barrackroom lower down and broke a few windows."

"Crikey!" quipped Jimmy Logan, "I'll bet that got their backs up."

"You're not kidding, they were really fired up and the lot of 'em came charging up here like raging bulls."

"What ... d'you mean to say you were all battling in this billet?"

"No, but it were like a battlefield on the corridor 'cos most of our lads went to meet 'em head on," said Colin excitedly as he got psyched up about it.

"Well how come our billet's in this state?" asked Jimmy Logan.

"A-ah well," put in Johnny Church from two beds away, "some of 'em got through our barricade and they threw water and sand from the fire buckets all o'er the place."

"Cor blimey, I wish I'd bín awake ... I'd have got really stuck in. Anyway, what's all that white stuff floating on top o' the water?"

"Oh that's somét else" replied Johnny, "they triggered off the fire extinguishers as well."

"Ah, no wonder there's load's o' foam on mí bed," I said.

"Aye, and ours too," said a few of them in unison.

"How did it finish up then?" I asked becoming more intrigued.

"You might know," said Brian Holdsworth, "the Regimental Police arrived and carted a few o' the lads off to the guardhouse."

"I'm absolutely amazed," I said, "I can't believe all this happened and I slept through it all."

"No, neither can I," laughed Jimmy Logan, "if it had happened to anybody else I wouldn't have believed it."

We all started laughing about it, but then our merriment came to a sudden halt.

"Quick," shouted one of the lads, "the CSM's coming!" The warning was a bit pointless really, as there was no time to tidy things up before the company sergeant major was upon us … and he was livid. He was a man to be feared at the best of times but, at this moment, he looked absolutely nightmarish as he stomped into the barrack room splashing through the gritty water bellowing at the top of his voice, followed by two tall regimental policemen.

"Ar-rghh," he roared as he yielded a wooden baton under his arm, "by your beds the lot of you scumbags!"

Everyone scrambled to their positions at the foot of their beds and stood to attention awaiting further abuse … nobody daring to utter a word.

"Right you scruffy lot, I want the name of the culprits who did this or so help me I'll put the whole flamin' lot of you on a charge!" Everyone stood by his bed … no one uttered a word.

To his displeasure and obvious disgust, the sergeant major had to venture further into the room consequently getting his shiny boots wet. The first person he confronted was me.

"A-ahh, well at least I've got one of the culprits," he barked as he glared at my bruised face and black eye. "Right, what have you got to say for yourself soldier?"

"Nothing sir," I quivered as I felt his awesome presence draining my spirit.

"What do you mean '**nothing'?**" he screamed. "You either come up with something now or you're going to the guardhouse with them other cronies! Now I'll ask you one more time … what have you got to say for yourself?"

"Nothing sir … I still have nothing to say."

"Right," he said turning to one of the regimental police, "put this soldier under arrest!" The sergeant major then carried on around the billet until he arrived at Jimmy Logan's bed.

"A-ah, what have we got here then … another slimy creature?" he growled trying to intimidate Jimmy.

But there was no chance of that, Jimmy kind of smirked at the sergeant major and gave him the same answers that I had given. Consequently, both Jimmy and I finished up in the guardroom awaiting a charge of inciting a riot. We both had to go in front of our commanding officer the next morning and got sentenced to seven days nick inside the guardroom without privileges. Also whilst inside we didn't receive any pay. But some good came of it because after our release all the lads in the billet room rallied around and we were treated like celebrities. They even passed a hat around and every lad chipped in to make up for our loss of pay.

"Hey, this is great," laughed Jimmy, "I'm bloomin' glad we didn't blab to the sergeant major … it's were well worth doing a week in the cooler weren't it?"

"Aye, I suppose you're right Jimmy. Then again, if we had o' blabbed … our life wouldn't o' bín worth living." We both laughed readily at that.

Jimmy Logan and I became firm friends from thereon in.

****

My second fight was similar in the sense that another lad was forever trying to goad me into a fight, but other aspects of it were very different. This particular lad was called Bernard Barem and he'd just been promoted to lance corporal. Lance corporals were always hard to get on with because they were constantly striving to impress their superiors in order to get a second stripe. This attitude was commonly known amongst the soldiers as 'taping'. The name Barem always stuck out in my mind because the lads used to take the mickey out of him.

"Barem!" one of them would say. "It really suits him that name does ... I know I can't bloody well bare 'im."

I wasn't over fond of him either but I didn't want to get into any conflict and tried to play things down.

Just like the kids of my junior school days, Barem resorted to barbed comments and insulting remarks.

"Ar-rgh you bloody coward, are they all like that from your neck o' the woods?" he would say. Still, I never rose to the bait or took any notice of his scurrilous remarks. But, I had learnt from my previous experience to be on my guard.

Still, one day he took me completely by surprise. I'd just come out of the washroom and was drying my face. He came up behind and, without provocation, fisted me savagely in my back. The pain was excruciating as I fell to the floor like a stone unable to get up ... I could hardly breathe.

"You little wimp!" he mocked as he stood over me. "That'll teach you to mind your manners!" All I could do was look up into his jeering face; I couldn't even speak, as every breath was agony. My pain caused an involuntary moan. I knew I was badly hurt and needed medical attention but he thought I was just too frightened to get up and the jeering continued. As luck would have it a couple of my mates entered the room and noticed the pale drawn look on my face. After a little First Aid and assessment of the situation they called for an ambulance and I was taken to the army hospital. When Barem realised how hurt I was he started to panic. But he wasn't bothered about me ... he was only concerned for his own skin. He knew that if I reported what had really happened he would be charged and automatically lose his stripe ... but I didn't want that.

"No" I thought to myself, "I'll sort this my way, I've got to live with Barem. But there's one thing for sure, he's not going to get away with it scot free."

Consequently, when my superiors questioned me about the incident I told them I had slipped on the stone steps. As it turned out I had a pneumothorax due to fractured ribs piercing and collapsing my lung. The surgeon had to insert a tube into my chest to re-inflate my lung. Luckily I wasn't in hospital too long and I was discharged a few days later with my chest strapped up with wide Elastoplast. After a couple of weeks I had to report on parade every morning but I was put on light duties.

Barem was all right at first but it wasn't long before he started again with his snide comments. I knew in my heart that I had to put a stop to it but I wasn't anywhere near fit enough to tackle him yet ... the slightest exertion still creased me. Time passed and every day my condition improved but even after four weeks I was nowhere near peak fitness. Then one Saturday afternoon I was in the barrack room with a few of my mates. All the bed mattresses had been turned back, displaying the bare steel framework underneath, which held the metal springs together.

Things were fine until Barem entered the room and tried issuing orders. None of the lads took notice and this infuriated him.

"Get lost Barem!" a few shouted. "Are you after another tape or what?"

"Go and play toy soldiers somewhere else," Brian Holdsworth quipped. Barem never answered Brian. Mind you Brian weighed over sixteen stones and he was fit with it.

I couldn't help smirking and Barem noticed.

"Ték that smile of your face Cowell or I'll wipe it off the same as I did last time."

I wasn't fit enough to have a go at him but I still replied, "Get lost Barem, I don't want any truck with you ... at least not yet anyroad."

"What do you mean not yet you little gít ... you'll have truck with me now and like it!"

"Oh no, he's coming for me again." I thought all tensed up, "he'll murder me!" I braced myself, as I could tell by the venomous look on his face that he was going to attack me. As he came for me I plainly remember praying to God for protection. "Oh please God give me the strength to ward him off ... I don't know what I'll do if You don't."

It all happened so quickly. He came at me like a raging bull with so much venom in his eyes. I somehow managed to side-step him and he fell onto one of the beds, sprawling on his back across the steel frame. As he attempted to get up I dived instinctively on top of him. I couldn't throw any punches but I grabbed hold of the underside of the angle iron with both hands and pulled with all the strength I could muster. He couldn't move as the corner of the angle iron was firmly pinned into the arch of his back. He tried pulling my hair but I just pressed down all the more with my head and body. I kept up the pressure for what seemed an age not daring to let go for fear of reprisal; the longer I hung on to the angle irons the more laboured my breathing became. As my strength began to ebb I became agitated but didn't dare let up. Barem growled furiously at first but then the growls turned to grunts and finally to moans. I dared to lift my head but with caution, as I wasn't too sure whether or not this was another of his sly tricks. Only when I looked at his face did I realise he was not kidding ... it was deadly white and he was actually passing out. Justice or not, call it what you like ... he actually finished up with a couple of broken ribs just like me. He wasn't as badly hurt as I had been but nevertheless he was finished as far as this fight was concerned. It took about ten minutes before he was in a fit enough state to take himself off to the medical room. But before he did, I confronted him.

"Right Barem," I growled, "I've just beaten you with broken ribs so now I know you're no match for me. Anyroad I'm warning thí ... keep outa my bloody way in future or I'll rip your bloody throat out! Oh and another thing whilst we're at it, when you get to the medical room you can tell 'em exactly what happened. I've got now't to hide like you had you slimy swine!"

That was it, I'd said my piece and finally laid my ghost to rest ... I was very happy with the outcome. I'd actually won the fight without throwing a single punch. I didn't get any joy from winning the fight so much as knowing that the taunting was finished. Barem and I never did become bosom buddies, but he never bothered me again after that.

****

Once I became settled into army life I was determined to use everything at my disposal to get myself into tip-top condition. This included using the camp's gymnasium and other facilities. I loved climbing ropes and doing back flips over a wooden vaulting horse. And like my physical training teacher back at Towneley School I became quite adept at walking on my hands. I also took up jogging and every evening I did a seven-mile run. I kept this up for two months but to my dismay I suffered terribly from severe stiffness, especially in the mornings.

"I must be doing something wrong," I thought to myself, "surely I should be feeling a lot fitter by now?"

Then one day I approached one of the physical training instructors, a long-serving regular soldier called Tommy who was about forty-years old. He appeared to be in peak condition and enjoyed the full respect of all his peers. I knew that he went jogging on a regular basis and I asked if I could join him.

"Aye tha' can if tha' wants lad," he answered in a broad Lancashire accent, "but I won't hang about waiting for thí if you lag behind."

"Yeah that's fair enough," I replied, "I go along with that ... I just want to get myself into prime condition the same as you."

"I'm glad to hear it lad, there's too many young úns nowadays that just want to booze and laze about all the time. It won't be easy mind ... tha'll have to work hard at it. Anyroad, we'll set off now but think on what I said."

"Reighto, I'll keep as close on your heels as I can," I said determined to make an impression.

He didn't run very fast but kept up a steady pace non-stop for about six miles.

"We'll just have five minutes rest here and then we'll mék our way back to camp," he said taking in deep breaths of air as he soaked up the last of the evening sun.

Surprisingly, I didn't have any trouble keeping up with him; in fact, I found myself slowing down to his pace. Nonetheless, despite doing everything he did, having a shower and a rub down after the run, I still suffered from terrible stiffness. After a month of jogging with this fit older man I felt rather dejected. And so one evening whilst drying myself after having a shower I broached the subject with him once again.

"Excuse me Tommy but could I ask you something please?"

"Aye course you can lad ... fire away."

"What it is, I wer' just wondering ... how long have you been running like you do?"

"Well it's bín quite a while now since I first started; in fact I'd be about the same age as you are now. U-um that's reight, I'd be about twenty 'cos it wer' just after I joined up."

"That's interesting," I thought, "that's a bit of encouragement for me to carry on."

"Come on lad," he said intuiting my thoughts," what d'you want to know?"

"Well I was wondering whether you suffered from stiffness when you first started runnin'? And if so ... how long did it take before you overcame it?"

"Ha, ha, ha!" he bellowed from the pit of his stomach. "That's a good ún if ever I heard one."

"What's so funny?" I thought a little flustered by his reaction.

"E-eh lad," he responded seeing the bemused look on my face, "d'you really think you'll e'er get o'er being stiff if you carry on runnin' every day?"

"I don't understand," I said, "I don't know what you mean."

"You don't know what I mean?" he said laughing again. "Bloomin' 'eck lad, d'you not know you've gotta have pain for gain?"

"Whaddaya talkin' about?" I asked naively. "What d'you mean ... pain for gain?"

"I mean what I say. If you want to keep yourself in peak condition you've gotta be prepared to put up with some pain."

"Yeah I go along with that, but for how long ... that's what I want to know?"

"For as long as tha keeps runnin," he said, "does that answer your question lad?"

"What! D'you mean to say you still suffer from stiffness?"

"Aye that's reight lad … too flamin' true I do! I've bín runnin' now for over twenty years and it's always the same … especially first thing in the morning."

"Over twenty years," I asked rather surprised by his answer, "and it's still the same as when you started all them years ago?"

"Aye it is, but don't worry about it, it's somét tha' gets used to … you've gotta programme your mind to it."

"Programme mí mind be blow'd," I thought, "sod that for a lark … if that's being fit you can shove it!"

Once more Tommy noticed the look on my face. "You look a bit worried lad … I haven't put thí off have I?"

"Well actually," I replied feeling nonplussed, "in one word … yes."

"Don't fret about it lad, you'll be all reight," he said encouragingly, "you'll feel different about it in a couple o' months."

"No I'm sorry Tommy I won't," I replied, my mind made up that I would never jog again, "because I realise now this lark is not for me."

"Oh what a pity, and here's me thinking how well you were doing. It's a shame really 'cos you really need to work at it to keep tha'self in trim thá knows."

"Oh I know that Tommy and I intend to, but not by running."

"Oh aye, and what method are you gonna use then?"

"Well, I'll keep up with my antics at the gym every night and I'll do some swimming. Aye, and I'll tackle the army assault course a few times or do anything else that's interesting."

"I hope so lad, I hope so," Tommy said genuinely concerned, "I'll keep an eye on thí to watch your progress 'cos I've taken an interest in thí and I wouldn't like to see you falter at this stage."

"Thanks Tommy, I appreciate that and don't think I'm not grateful for everything you've taught me 'cos I am."

"Tha's all reight lad ... just think on what I told thí and keep at it ... that'll be thanks enough for me."

For the rest of my time on the camp Tommy and I kept in touch and despite the age gap we remained good friends.

****

I did keep up various activities and definitely benefited from them. The beauty of it was that I no longer suffered from that crippling stiffness. Of all the exercises, I enjoyed swimming the most and still frequently swam two lengths of a pool underwater as I had done back home in Burnley with my friend Pete Holroyd.

This put me in good stead one day when another physical instructor, a corporal who we nicknamed 'Smithy', took a group of us out on an arduous keep fit exercise. After an eight-mile route march at the double we cooled off by a large outdoor swimming pool. It was about half as long again as an ordinary pool. Unlike Tommy, this instructor was unfriendly and aggressive ... he was also a show-off.

"Right you toe rags!" he bellowed as we all stood around the pool in our swimming trunks. "I'm going to dive in now and swim underwater and I want to see who can get the nearest to me after I emerge."

"U-um, this should be interesting," I thought, "this is right up my street ... I can't see him being any better than Pete Holroyd."

I watched him dive in and he seemed to be going well but I got a gut feeling that he wouldn't complete a full length.

"He's not doing too bad," I murmured to myself, "but he's not deep enough in the water." I concluded this from the fact that I'd always found it easier to swim as close to the bottom of the pool as possible, almost scraping the floor with my belly, as I found that it offered less resistance.

To my surprise, lots of the lads started shouting eagerly as he reached the half way mark.

"Blimey!" quipped one of them. "He's like a bloomin' fish ... he's never gonna come up for air."

"Yeah, but he'll never make it to t'other end," remarked another.

"He should do," I thought to myself, "after all the bragging he's done. U-um, it's nowhere near as far as two lengths of the Central Baths ... and it's a straight run, he doesn't have to turn around."

My gut feeling was correct. He'd swam just over three-quarters of a length when he emerged for a breather.

"Naythen you scruffy no hopers," he bawled after a short respite, "I want you to dive in one at a time and try and match me."

He was a show-off but then again so was I. I knew for certain that I could easily outclass him and that's what I intended to do. But first, I wanted to see how the other lads fared and so I purposely stood at the back of the queue. Some were non-swimmers and had to be helped out of the pool by the aid of a long bamboo pole immediately after diving in. Others emerged after only swimming a few yards. Two lads actually reached the halfway stage but were still well short of their target.

"You feeble-hearted lot," bellowed the instructor from his position in the water, "this is what comes of smoking and boozing too much!" Then he noticed me still standing on the bank. "Right you ratbag," he yelled, "get yourself in and let's see what you can do!" This was to be my moment of glory and his downfall.

"Right you big-headed swine!" I smirked. "I'm gonna show you what a Trafalgar waller can do and bring you down a peg or two at the same time."

"Come on you bloody sprog," he shrieked, "we haven't got all day to hang about!"

"Righto," I shouted back through cupped hands, "open your legs and I'll swim through 'em!"

This created a bit of a riot as all the lads started laughing. Nevertheless, the laughing changed to cheers the nearer I got to the instructor and the cheers increased even more so when I actually passed through his legs and carried on to complete the length. I had enough in reserve to turn around and swim back through his legs the other way but I didn't bother … I'd already achieved my goal. I knew that I'd done enough to ridicule the self-centred arrogant bloke.

After that I never did hit it off with Smithy. Not to worry though, the sixteen weeks training passed quickly and we all got notice of our future postings. Along with Jimmy Mitchinson and Bill Hupboard I was posted to Crownhill Barracks, in Plymouth, Devon.

CHAPTER 14 - EMBARKATION LEAVE

Bill, Jimmy and I arrived at Plymouth Railway Station about 7 o'clock at night and had to catch a bus to our new camp, Seaton Barracks. It was stationed on the outskirts of town in the Crown Hill area on a country road leading to the expanse of Dartmoor. On entering the camp gates the guardhouse was situated directly on the left hand side and patrolled by Regimental Police. Directly facing the brig was a playing field much larger than a football pitch. The RP's were very efficient and thoroughly scrutinised our documents before allowing us onto the campsite. One of them, a very powerfully built man stood out from the rest. He was a corporal, who was in charge of the guardroom, and it became quite clear from the onset that he was a bastard. A prisoner fitted out in full battle dress happened to be under his charge and the snidy corporal was putting him through his paces. He had the soldier frog marching on the spot wearing full battle gear. Sweat oozed from the prisoner's pores as the belligerent corporal towered over him bellowing loudly.

"Now get your arse around that playing field, on the double you mingy excuse for a soldier and keep running until I tell you to stop!"

The poor bloke literally shook in his shoes as the sadistic NCO derived sheer pleasure from the fact that he had complete control over his victim.

"Blimey!" remarked Jimmy, "I wouldn't like to be in that poor bloke's shoes."

Bill Hupboard was a tough nut, but even he commented, "No neither would I, he looks a right cruel barbaric bastard!

Later on as we settled into our new regime, other soldiers enlightened us that this particular corporal thrived on putting prisoners through Hell whilst under his command in the glasshouse.

"The more his degrading reputation grows the more he likes it." stressed one bloke. "He actually loves the reputation of being renowned as a bastard because he thinks it gives him power. "Aye, and his favourite punishment is making them run about that large field in full battle gear. The evil bastard thrives on grinding down any new prisoner under his authority, and he loves it all the more when other soldiers watch on as he puts his prey through their paces."

Well, so much for our welcoming committee. We gradually settled into our new abode and it didn't take long to make more friends amongst our fellow soldiers. Time passed quickly and before I knew it Christmas was upon us. To our delight we all got a few days home leave. I caught the train at Euston Station, London and arrived at Burnley Barracks Railway Station about 7pm and happily made my way along Trafalgar. Albion Street looked different somehow, not quite as busy as it had been in the past.

"It must be me," I thought, "most of my mates are serving in the forces. Yeah, that's what it is."

Nevertheless, something was different, which I discovered on reaching home. For the first time in my life the front door was locked.

"That's funny I thought as I turned the door-handle, "I've never known this afore ... I must be at the wrong house." I pondered a moment then noticed the gas-lamp. "No this is the right house all right ... I should know, I've swung on that old gas-lamp enough times when I was a kid." After shouting through the letterbox and rattling on the door I heard a voice from above me.

"Hello there, is that Johnny Cowell?" As I looked up I saw Malcolm Davis from next-door looking out of his bedroom window.

"Hiya Malcolm ... it's me all reight. I've just got home on leave and I can't seem to get into th'house."

"Bloomin' 'eck Johnny, has nobody told thí'?" asked Malcolm.

"Told me what?"

"Well, your mam flit a couple o' days ago."

"Oh 'eck, she mustn't have had time to get in touch with me afore I left the barracks, maybe there's a letter in the post."

"I don't know about that John ... she never mentioned ow't to us about you coming home."

"No, that's because she didn't know Mal, I never told her 'cos I wanted to surprise her." I winced a little before adding, "It looks as though the shoe's on t'other foot now doesn't it ... I'm the one who's surprised."

Maybe she's trying to tell thí something," Malcolm joked.

"Aye maybe, you could be right there Mal."

"Anyroad John, if you'd like to come in for a brew and a sandwich I'll run you up there afterwards on the back of mí motorbike."

"Yeah, thanks a lot Mal ... that sounds good to me."

Malcolm's wife, Ivy, was sat in the livingroom and she gave me a warm welcome.

"Oh look who it is ... young Johnny Cowell, how are you? E-eh, but it's nice to see you."

"And it's nice to see you Mrs Davis, I hope you're keeping well."

"By 'eck, the army life must be doing you good Johnny you're looking really well and you've filled out quite a bit as well."

"Thank you Mrs Davis ... you look really good as well."

"You can dispense with the Mrs Davis and call me Ivy now you're a grown man. Anyway, sit yourself down while I put the kettle on and make you a cup of tea and something to eat."

"Thank you very much Mrs Davis."

"There you go again ... Mrs Davis."

I'm sorry, it's just that ….."

"Take no notice of me Johnny," she cut in, "I'm teasing; I know only too well how your mother brought you up to respect your elders."

As it turned out Mum had been offered the keys to a house in the Rosehill Area and she couldn't get away from Albion Street fast enough. After a brief chat I thanked Malcolm and Ivy for their hospitality and then rode pillion to my new home at 76 Moorland Road on the Rosehill Estate where I celebrated my home leave with my family. To me the house didn't have the same feeling about it as Albion Street. I couldn't pinpoint why I felt like that about Mum's new home, I just did.

Our Barry and Barbara greeted me and they made a right fuss. It turned out that this meeting was to determine our Barry's future career.

"Are you enjoying the army life our John?" he asked eagerly. "Is it òwt like you expected it to be?

"Yeah, it's all right our kid, I'm enjoying it ... especially the comradeship."

"Are they teaching you to drive ... you've allús fancied drivin' one o' them big wagons?"

"No they're not ... the thing is they've put me in the Medical Corps and I've bín working in th'army hospitals." This got Barry really interested.

"You what!" he responded, " Do you mean like a nurse?"

"U-um kind of but they don't call us nurses ... we're called nursing orderlies."

"So what do you have to do then?"

"Oh we do everything from emptying bed pans to feeding the patients who can't feed themselves."

"So it is like being a nurse then?"

"Oh yeah ... we even give medicines and injections."

"Bloomin' 'eck! That's somét I've always wanted to do."

"I didn't know that our kid ... you've never mentioned it afore."

"Yeah, I know I haven't but it's true ... honest! I've thought about going into nursing for ages but I didn't say ow't to anybody 'cos I wer' frightened o' getting the mickey took out o' me."

"Hey never mind about that ... if it's somét you want to do our Barry, go forrít!"

"Are you sure our John ... would you if you were me?"

"I'm dead sure our Barry, if that's the way you feel ... do it! Anyroad, you're a lot different from me ... with your nature you're cut out forrít."

Barry's expression changed as the excitement built up inside him, "That's it our John, I'm gonna do it ... you've convinced me ... I'm definitely gonna do it."

"Good on you our kid, go for it ... follow your dream!"

Sure enough ... the very next day he went to Burnley General Hospital and applied to do his nursing training. It was a career that was to span forty years. Little did I know then that twenty years later I too would be pursuing the same career.

****

I was determined to enjoy my home leave, but as usual I went a bit over the top and did something very stupid. During the holiday I made friends with Alan Hargreaves, a lad who was three years younger than me and lived a few doors away on Moorland Road. On Sunday night we went down town and frequented a few of the local pubs, enjoying the bright lights. By the end of the night we'd both drank a few pints and felt quite fresh.

"Bloomin' 'eck John," drawled Alan," I don't fancy that long trek back up Manchester Road ... how about catching the last bus?"

"Aye all reight Alan, but it'll have to be a Ribble 'cos the local buses stopped running at half-past ten."

"Well, what difference does it mék which bus we catch," quipped Alan, "so long as it gets us up to Moorland Road ... that's all I'm bothered about."

"That's just it," I replied, "the Ribble bus doesn't drop off at the Rose and Crown ... the first stop is the Bull and Butcher which means we'll have a long trek back."

"Oh aye I forgot about that," moaned Alan but then added as an afterthought, "anyroad we can hop off at the Summit traffic lights afore it carries on towards Rawtenstall."

"Oh yeah, and what if the lights are on green?"

"Well even if they are, the flamin' bus hasta slow down so we'll still be able to jump off it won't we."

"Right then, you're on Alan ... let's go."

So off we trotted and caught the bus from the bus station. As it sped up Manchester Road and approached the Rose and Crown, Alan and I alighted from our seats and perched ourselves precariously on the open-ended platform at the back of the bus. As it turned a slight left-hand bend the traffic lights, which were about a quarter of a mile up the road, came into view and they had just turned to amber.

"Great!" I said to Alan. "The red light's just coming on so the bus'll have to slow down." What I didn't anticipate was that they were very quick-changing traffic lights. The bus slowed down as it approached the junction but then as it got within about two-hundred yards the lights changed to green. Inevitably the bus driver put his foot down and the bus speeded up. I'd already committed myself to jump as I hung onto the steel handrail and jump I did. As I landed I tried running as fast as I could to retain my balance but I couldn't run fast enough; consequently I went crashing to the ground banging my forehead on the flagged pavement.

"Oh no John, you idiot!" I groaned as I saw the blood dripping from my head onto the stone flags, "When will you ever learn?" After wiping my brow I looked up and to my horror I saw young Alan spread-eagled face downward about fifty yards further up the road. I realised that the bus must have been going even faster when he jumped and I feared for Alan's life. "Oh please God," I mumbled, "please don't let him be dead!" As I approached him he was motionless, but I could hear him moaning.

"Thank Goodness for that!" I sighed. "At least he's alive … thank you God!" After weighing up the situation and putting my First Aid knowledge to good use I could see that, in spite of a badly swollen face and a few cuts and bruises, he was going to be all right.

"O-oh, where am I," he groaned, "what happened?"

"You might well ask Alan," I said feeling happier now, "we both jumped off the bloomin' bus like idiots."

"Oh aye, I remember now, it wer' … o-o-oh, mí bloomin' head, it feels likes it's bín run o'er with a steam roller."

"Come on Alan, I'd best get thí up to th'casualty department."

"No way," he grunted, "I'll be all reight … just get me home, I wanna go to bed."

We got home all right, but we both got a good rollicking from our mothers.

Alan and I slept well that night but we suffered for it the next day. I had a black eye and a few bruises but he looked terrible, just like a boxer after being battered over fifteen gruelling rounds. Both his eyes were almost closed and his nose was swollen and squashy.

"Bloomin' 'eck!" I thought feeling guilty, "I feel bad enough ... what must poor Alan feel like?"

From that day on nobody believed we'd jumped off a bus, especially Alan's brothers.

"Geddaway withee!" they'd say, "You've bín fighting, who are you trying to kid?"

"Well please yourself what you want to believe ... that's the honest truth," I tried to tell them.

"Ték no notice of 'em John," said Alan, "we know what happened and that's what counts."

Luckily we recovered without any adverse effects. I felt very remorseful about what had happened albeit a little wiser. I went back to camp shortly after that and Alan and I remained good friends thereafter. I put the incident down to experience and vowed never to do it again.

****

After six months service we all got a pay increase of ten shillings. Twenty-five shillings still wasn't a lot of money to get by on but it was a lot better than fifteen shillings.

Things were going well but then came a very dark shadow, which changed my whole life ... my father died! He'd recently collapsed with abdominal pains and been rushed into Burnley General Hospital for emergency surgery for a burst appendix. I was immediately granted compassionate leave and went straight to the hospital. During the critical time I, along with my brothers and sisters, spent many hours around his bed in Intensive Care. A blockage of the bowels had occurred and serious complications set in. Still, after a week on Intensive Care his condition improved and he was transferred to the main ward.

"Thank God for that," I prayed as I made my way back to Plymouth the following day. But my delight was only short-lived. I had only been back at the camp two days when I received the most distressing telephone call from my sister Maureen informing me that Dad had died. I was summoned to the commandant's office at nine o'clock on Februrary 27th where our Maureen told me the terrible news over the telephone. Before she muttered one word I knew the worst … it's hard to say why, I just knew.

"Our John," she muttered her voice trembling, "I've got something to tell …"

"Oh no our Maureen," I stopped her in mid-sentence, "it's not Dad is it? … Please don't say it's Dad!"

" I … I'm sorry our kid," she mumbled in a shaky voice trying to hold back the tears, "Dad died during the early hours of this morning."

I didn't answer … I couldn't. My whole body felt numb … it just didn't seem real.

"John … John, are you there," Maureen asked tearfully, "please answer me?"

"U-um, I'm still here our Maureen, I'm still here," I answered after a few seconds, "I just can't take it in … please say it's not true!" But even as I was saying it I knew it was true.

Maureen was over three-hundred miles away but I could still feel her sorrow over the telephone just as she could feel mine.

"I'm sorry our John that I had to be the bearer of bad news," she apologised, "but you had to be told and Mum thought it would be best coming from me."

"Yeah, I know that our kid," I said as a tear rolled down my cheek, "thanks a lot." Then as an after thought I asked, "How's Mum and t'others taking it anyroad?"

"We're all feeling the same," she replied sadly, "we all need each other at a time like this."

"Righto our Maureen, give mí mum my blessing and tell her I'll be home as quick as I can."

When I put the phone down it was obvious to everyone in the office that something was wrong. I couldn't speak at first ... I was devastated and felt numb all over. One of the lads sat me down whilst another offered me a cup of coffee and some biscuits.

The commanding officer was very good, again granting me immediate compassionate leave. Within two hours I was on the train, arriving home about ten o'clock that evening.

The next few days were very sad. My brothers and sisters and I held a constant vigil in the front room by his coffin prior to the funeral service, which took place on March 3rd at Christ the King Catholic Church. He was buried in Burnley Cemetery and afterwards a reception was held at the Co-op tearooms on Hammerton Street.

Within two days of the burial I had to return to Crownhill Barracks to continue my army service.

In the months following Dad's death I was devastated not wanting to do anything ... it seemed so unreal. Nevertheless, life has to go on; the army had been very lenient when Dad was ill but now I had to toe the line and carry out my duties like any other soldier. In a way the disciplined life was good for me and brought me back to reality. Also I had the support of my newfound friends. Six weeks after returning to camp I felt very sad. It was my 21st birthday and, although I received lots of cards from home I didn't get the one I wanted ... from my dad. However, I did receive a nice card from my Aunt Lily and she'd enclosed three pounds.

"E-eh, that's nice," I thought, "and very generous of her ... I'll have to write and thank her. Yeah, Dad would like that ... u-um, and he'd also like me to get on with my life, he wouldn't want me to be down in the dumps like I have been."

That night I went to the NAAFI Club in Plymouth where I celebrated my coming of age with big Brian. After that I settled back down to army routine and gradually started to enjoy life again.

****

During my time at Crownhill Barracks I met another lad from Burnley, Ernie Christie, who'd just completed a strenuous course with the Para-medics and loved it. I was having a shave in the washroom one morning when I heard a voice behind me.

"All reight Johnny I've ne'er seen thee here afore... whattaya doing here?"

"All reight Ernie," I replied on turning, "I could ask you the same question."

"Me? I've bín stationed here for the last ten months,"

"Aye," I said rather surprised, "then how come we've ne'er bumped into each other afore?"

"A-ah well I've bín on a paratrooper's course for the last three months up in Aldershot and now they've sent me back here."

"What, d'you mean you've bín parachuting outa planes?"

"Yeah, course I've bín parachuting fro' planes ... what the flamin' 'eck d'you think paratroopers do?"

"Bloomin' 'eck," I responded enviously, "that's somét I've allus wanted to do?"

"So have I," said Ernie proudly, "and that's why I did it."

"So you'll have a red beret now and you'll be able to wear the wings on your uniform?"

"That's reight," he said going to his locker from where he proudly produced his red beret. "Aye and the best thing is I get an extra two pounds a week on top o' mí pay. Mind thí, it were a bloomin' hard course ... you had to be as fit as a fiddle to get through it."

It was no idle boast ... Ernie really was a fit lad. He didn't drink or smoke and during our conversation he told me he went for a long cross-country run every night over Dartmoor. I didn't offer to run with him, but as I regularly went for a brisk walk over the moor myself I used to meet up with him. On warm summer evenings we would swim in one of the many streams throughout the grassland. Another thing we loved doing was trying to ride the wild ponies that lived on the moor. They appeared quite tame and would allow us to get close but when we attempted to ride them they kicked and jumped furiously like bucking broncos in a Wild West rodeo show. Ernie and I became good mates during that summer, better than we'd ever been back in our hometown.

One particular sunny day we made our way to Princetown, the place of the notorious Dartmoor Prison. It intrigued us to see a few prisoners working out in the open air in different places around the town. It turned out that, because of good behaviour, these prisoners were allowed to do menial jobs away from the confines of the prison. We actually got the chance to talk to one of them, a man in his early thirties. He informed us he was a trustee and that he'd already served ten years and was due for release in two years time. I didn't ask him what he was in prison for, but it struck me that twelve years out of his young life was such an awful waste. It seemed incomprehensible that some of these men were serving lifelong prison sentences.

On our way back to camp, Ernie made it known that his thoughts on the matter were the same as mine. "I'll tell you what John, I wouldn't like to be locked up like them poor souls, it would drive me up the wall. Just the thought of what they're missing out on makes me cringe. I can't imagine what it must be like having to live in dismal surroundings, grey walls and limited perimeters. I'd fade away and die if I had to live in confined spaces for years on end. They put me in mind o' young birds being cruelly trapped in a cage."

"Aye I know what you mean Ernie; they're missing out on all this open countryside and the wonders of nature."

"Yeah John, it makes me think about my own precious freedom and how I take things for granted." He then went into one of his nostalgic moods, "U-um, I love the touch o' the sun on my skin and to feel the wind blowing in my face. Just listen to them birds singing o'er there in that magnificent tree, it's like a concerto."

"You're right Ernie; it's marvellous how they're all syncronised as one, as if they're being conducted by a supreme being. I also love being out here in on this moor."

"Yeah, it's magic isn't it John, pure magic. I feel the same as you; I'd hate to miss out on all this fabulous countryside and its wonderful creatures. Yeah, this is the life for me."

He certainly impressed me with his natural love of nature and his simplistic look on life. We were very much alike in this respect. He was a very clean living man and didn't drink or smoke; at every opportunity he spent his time on the moor taking in God's given beauty and fresh air

"Anyway Ernie, going back on what you've just said, you're the last person in the world who takes things for granted. I don't know anyone who is more of a nature lover than you. And due to your lifestyle, it's no wonder you're in prime condition."

Trudging back over the moor we came across a slow flowing stream which cascaded over a small waterfall into a large deep gully. A formation of rocks bounding a large expanse of water made ideal diving platforms.

"Whoa, just look at that John," enthused Ernie, "How do you fancy a dip in there, it'll be a great way to cool off?"

"Ernie," I laughed, "you've just taken the words out of my mouth. I'm all for it, let's do it!"

We frolicked about in the cool refreshing water and splashed underneath the gentle cascade for two hours or more and thoroughly every minute. Afterwards we just lazed about on the grassy embankment and sunbathed ... life was good! The idyllic surroundings and the soothing climate triggered Ernie off again into a nostalgic mood.

"Just listen to the sound of that waterfall John, so relaxing! It puts me in mind of a song, 'By a babbling brook.' And just take a look around at all this green foliage. I bet it feels like Paradise to all the wild creatures that abound in this territory. One thing's for sure, there'll be loads o' rabbits on this moor."

"Aye, that's for sure - they probably live in harmony with the wild ponies and all the other creatures. I'm really glad we came out here on the moor today Ernie, it's been great, the lads back at camp don't know what they're missing."

"Talking about camp John, I think we'd better start making tracks or else we might miss out on our grub."

"Yeah, righto chum, we don't want to go hungry do we? Let's go!"

Ernie truly was in peak fitness, more so than any other person I'd ever known. This was my train of thought and he surely put it to the test a few days later. Our Sergeant Major was very stringent as far as army rules were concerned, and woe betide any soldier who broke them. A pet hate of his was skiving and he posted it on orders that any soldier returning to his barrack room during duty hours would be liable to a charge. Every day after early morning bugle call we had to wash, shave, have breakfast and be on duty parade in full regalia at 0800 hours. This is where a roll call was done and each soldier was given his task for the day. From then on no one was allowed to re-enter his barrack room before mid-day without prior consent. The barracks was a two-storey building and our billet was on the first floor. Unlike a normal terrace house the lower ground floor had a very high ceiling of about twelve feet. On this particular day, Ernie, Jimmy, Brian and I were lurking around in our billet trying to avoid latrine duty. It was a foolish thing to do, as the only exit from the room was via a flight of stone steps. This proved to be our undoing.

"What's that noise?" asked Jimmy as we stood around idling.

We all made our way to the landing and Brian peered over the banister only to see the Sergeant Major marching, into one of the downstairs barrack rooms. "Oh no," he panicked, "he doing one of his on the spot inspections."

"Come on quick, let's sneak out of here before he comes out of there," panicked Jimmy.

"No way," replied Brian, "he's gone and posted a corporal on guard at the foot o' the stairs."

We all made our back into the billet but there was no where to hide. As I glanced around the room which was likened to a long hospital ward with beds on either side, I could clearly hear the sound of studded boots marching up the stone steps.

"Bloody hell!" rapped Brian, "That's the flamin' RSM; we're all up for the high jump now - that's for sure."

"It looks to me like we've already been caught," I stuttered," 'cause the only way out of here is down those steps that he's coming up.

"That's what I thought, but Ernie had other ideas. "What are you talkin' about John," he quipped, "he's not goin' to catch me ... I'm goin' out of one of the windows. Are you coming?

"You're joking," I grimaced, "It's a fifteen foot drop. We could break both our legs or even be killed!"

"He's right," put in Brian and Jimmy in unison."

Ernie didn't take a blind bit of notice and just responded quite unconcerned as though it was like diving into the local swimming baths, "Righto lads, please yourselves, but he's not catching me." Without giving it another thought he opened one of the sliding sash windows, climbed out onto the window sill and jumped to the parade ground below, leaving all three of us staring at each other in disbelief.

A few moments later the RSM entered the billet bellowing loudly, "Right you lily livered bunch of skivers, you're all on a charge for malingering. Now get your greasy arses out of here down on to the parade ground - **now at the double!**

Knowing only too well not to argue with him, especially in this sort of mood, we all three scurried down the stone steps. To our surprise, on reaching the parade ground, Ernie was strolling around quite nonchalantly as if nothing had happened.

"See what I mean lads," he teased with a cheeky grin on his face, "I told you it was easy. it wer' child's play."

His voice was drowned out by the screeching of the RSM, "Right you three, get yourselves down to the sergeant's mess now and scrub them ablutions until they shine like a new pin. And when you've finished those, report to the officer's mess and do the same there!" As he was marching off he caught sight of Ernie and beckoned him over. At first I thought that the RSM had cottoned on to what had happened, but I couldn't have been more wrong.

"Sir!" replied Ernie coming to attention.

"Good man Private Christie," asserted the officer handing him an envelope. "Take this to the CO's office as quickly as possible please!"

Ernie took the letter and marched off, but not before glancing at us and grinning. After that he never let us forget the skirmish and rubbed it in at every opportunity.

****

Another incidence concerning Ernie was when he met up with his future wife in Taunton, a small town eighty miles north of Plymouth in the county of Somerset. An attachment, including Ernie and I was sent there to erect some army tents and set up a miniature field hospital within a territorial army campsite on the outskirts of the town. The aim of our mission was to put on a public exhibition in order to display how to cope with casualties under war conditions. It was still summer and after a hard day's work we all decided to relax by having a few drinks at the village pub along with the locals. But Ernie wasn't up for this. As he put it, he didn't want to miss out on a fine summer evening. "No way", he said, you lot relax in your way and I'll relax in mine."

"Oh come on Ernie," I asked, trying to egg him on, "I know where you're coming from because I feel like you do. But we're only up here in this village for three days and we may never get the chance again. And anyway, we've been grafting all day and I'm sure you must be gagging for a pint. I know I am."

"Yeah I know that John, but I don't want to miss out on such a gorgeous night, just look up at that beautiful blue sky."

I knew that there'd be no shifting him when he was like this. Once he made it mind up to do something that was it. Other lads tried to persuade him but he was adamant and wouldn't be swayed. "No lads," he replied politely, "thanks for asking but I'd rather do my own little thing."

That was Ernie to a tee. Nevertheless, the following night was Saturday and it turned out there was a dance being held in the village hall. Every lad was looking forward to the event, and once again we approached Ernie.

"Are you coming Ernie," we all urged him, "it should be a really good night?"

"Come on Ernie," I said stressing that I liked the open air too, but this was definitely a one off opportunity not to be missed out on.

Finally he relented. "Go on then you bunch of boozers," he laughed, "I'll come with you if it's only to get you off my back."

It must have been fate because at the dance he met the love of his life. When we arrived at the function, music was already playing and the room was typical of any other church hall. We were all rather excited as there were lots of pretty girls dancing around the floor. But, Ernie only had eyes for one ... we later learned that her name was Maureen. He'd never had a girlfriend and it became obvious that he was very shy. He didn't know how to dance, but one thing he did know ... he did like this girl. From the onset he was smitten and to my mates and me, it stood out a mile.

"Go on Ernie, ask her for a dance," we kept encouraging him, "go on, you've got nothing to lose. Don't forget, we won't ever be coming back here again."

"That's all very well," he said with a slight tremor in his voice, "but I've got butterflies in my stomach, I've never taken a lass out afore."

"We're not asking you to take her out, just ask her for a dance, that's all."

"I know that but I'm scared to death and my knees are knocking. I've never ever felt like this afore."

"That's not like you Ernie," remarked Brian, "nothing's ever scared you before."

"Aye I know, but this is different. I always feel awkward around girls."

"I'll tell you what Ernie," said Jimmy, "she keeps glancing over here and I'm sure she's looking at you."

"Yeah, I've noticed that as well," smiled Brian, "go on Ernie, go for it!"

"I don't like ......"

Brian cut him short, "Don't be a wet lettuce, the worst thing that can happen is she turns you down."

Jimmy and I tried to persuade him but it appeared fruitless and just fell onto deaf ears. One hour passed and he hadn't moved one iota. But then, out of the blue he plucked up courage and made his move. He took a deep breath, stuck out his chest and then calmly walked across the dance floor towards her. All of us looked on inquisitively wondering what would happen. Well, that was it, we never got a look in after that. Ernie and the girl both seemed totally engrossed in each other's company and he never left her side for the rest of the evening.

"Just look at him swooning," said Brian, "they seem to be getting on like a house on fire."

"Aye," joked Jimmy, "and his knees don't seem to be shaking anymore."

I couldn't resist adding, "Aye, you're right there Jimmy, and you've got to admit he's not doing too bad to say he's never had a girl before. Just look at 'em, they're chatting away together like bosom buddies." At the end of the night, Jimmy, Brian and I were stood by the exit when Ernie passed hand in hand with the young lady.

"Did you see that sly wink he gave us?" laughed Brian.

"I did that," smirked Jimmy, "we'll never hear the last of it; he'll be like a cat with two tails."

"You've got to admit it lads, she's a good looking bird," I commented.

"Oh you're right there," quipped Brian, "she's a cracker."

I couldn't help smiling to myself. "Well done Ernie, well done!"

On the way back to our billet we had a good laugh about Ernie joking that we wouldn't see him again until next morning. But we couldn't have been further from the truth. When we got back to camp, Ernie was in bed, tucked up and fast asleep. We were all amazed and couldn't wait until the following morning to quiz him about how he'd gone on.

"Great," he enthused, "the best night out I've ever had. We got on really well and I've got a date with her this afternoon."

"A date on a Sunday afternoon, and where are you going to take her?" I asked nosily.

"Well, believe it or not," he grinned, "she's into keep-fit and loves the outdoors just as much as I do. I told her I'm into cross country running and she said she'd love to do a ten mile run with me."

We all started laughing, "Trust you Ernie to come up with something like that."

But it was no laughing matter to Ernie. He was infatuated with this girl and was determined to make a good impression on his first date. It turned out well. Like Ernie, she was in peak condition and did the ten mile run as though it was a stroll in the park. They thoroughly enjoyed each other's company and decided to see each other again. He took her out one more time before we returned to Plymouth. It was the beginning of their courtship. From then onwards he hitch-hiked a hundred and sixty miles round trip from Plymouth to Taunton and back several times just to spend a few hours with her.

I realised I'd lost my outdoor mate, and we never ventured out onto the moor again together. It was rather sad, but I was glad for Ernie.

****

I began to enjoy the army life and tried to stick to the rules but, despite trying to keep out of trouble, I inevitable had to spend another week in the brig. But on this occasion it was definitely of my own doing; I actually disobeyed an order. Just days previously I'd been given three days jankers for not polishing my cap badge properly. I didn't question the decision as I was guilty of the trivial offence and felt I could do the jankers stood on my head. A condition of the charge was that I was confined to camp for three days and another was that I had to report to the orderly sergeant's office at 1700 hours. Each night I was ordered to work scrubbing piles of pots and pans in the officer's mess and then to report back to the orderly sergeant at 2300 hours. The first two nights, Monday and Tuesday, didn't bother me, but Wednesday night did. The reason for this is because Colin, a good friend of mine, was being discharged the next morning and a send off celebration was being held in the Cherry Tree, a pub near to the NAAFI Club. I'd looked forward to the event for ages and didn't want to miss out on the festivities. As it was the sergeant in charge on this particular night was Barry Smith, a lad who'd been in the same intake as me on joining the army. He was a qualified pharmacist which automatically entitled him, on enlistment, to the rank of sergeant. When I reported to him at 1700 hours I mentioned my predicament and how I'd love to join the lads to celebrate Colin's demobilisation.

"I'll tell you what Barry," I moaned, "I'm really pissed off about not being able to leave camp to give mi' mate a good send off … we've been mates ever since I landed here in Plymouth. I don't mind having to wash all the greasy grimy junk in the officer's mess but havin' to report back here at 2300 hours is a real bind."

"I understand how you feel John, but there's not a right lot I can do about it. I will say one thing though; they're having a special do tonight in the officer's mess so there's going to be a mountainous pile of pots and pans to get through. I don't think you'll finish the task in time to go anywhere. But if you do I'm willing to turn a blind eye if you don't report back to me tonight. Mind you. If anything goes wrong ... then on you own head be it!"

I didn't need telling twice; as far as I was concerned, a nod's as good as a wink.

"Great, just watch me get through this lot" I said rolling my sleeves up. For the next two hours I worked furiously until I'd cleaned every last spoon. I finished the enormous task almost on the stroke of nine and then, without giving it another thought, I ran all the way to the Cherry Tree.

Colin was glad to see me albeit rather surprised, "How have you managed it John; you're supposed to report back to the orderly sergeant at 11 o'clock tonight aren't you?"

"Not to worry Colin," I assured him, "I've sorted it."

Another voice from behind me quipped, "Hey John, what you doing here, I thought you were confined to camp." On turning it was Big Bri'.

After explaining to them both what happened we got down to some serious supping and we all finished up three sheets to the wind. Taking everything into account we had a ball.

"I hope you'll be all right John," said Colin as we made our way back to camp, "I'd hate to think you got into bother on my behalf."

"Don't worry about it Colin, Sergeant Smith said he would turn a blind eye, so I should be all right."

But I couldn't have been more wrong! As we walked through the camp gates I was singled out by the military police; and one of them happened to be the same notorious barbaric corporal that I'd experienced when I first entered the camp.

445

"What's your name and rank soldier?" he rapped towering over me.

"Cowell, Private Cowell," I answered knowing full well that I'd been tumbled.

"Private Cowell what soldier!"

"Oh, Private Cowell ... Corporal!"

"Attention," he screeched, "get your arse into the guardroom at the double you slimy little creep ... quick march, left right, left right!"

I was well aware of his notoriety for putting new prisoners through hell, and I was now under his charge. He stood over six feet tall and as he yelled through gritted teeth he looked awesome. I was well aware that he delighted in grinding men into the ground and for a moment his overbearing presence made me feel intimidated and subdued.

As soon as I entered the guardroom I saw Sergeant Smith sitting at a table looking rather sheepish and by his side sat the regimental sergeant major, who was fuming. I had to stand to attention in front of them both.

"Right Private Cowell, I'm charging you for being absent without leave," rapped the RSM.

"But Sir ….."

"No buts! I made a flying visit to the orderly sergeant's office at 23-00hours and you didn't report there, and it's come to my attention that you left the camp without permission."

I didn't say much, as I was in a catch 22 situation. It seemed fruitless to protest because, after all, Sergeant Smith had left the decision with me. I couldn't allow myself to bring his name into it; that wouldn't have been the right thing to do ... and anyway, I couldn't come up with anything that would have made a difference. So I said nothing.

"Right Private Cowell, you're on a charge and you'll appear in front of Colonel Peck at 09-00hours tomorrow morning. If you're one minute late you'll be in even more trouble than you are right now ... understand!"

"Yes Sir, understood!"

Turning to the MP he rapped, "Right, take him away, get him out of my sight!"

"Yes Sir," the smarmy bloke replied with a smirk on his face.

As the burly corporal frogmarched me towards the door I glanced at Sergeant Smith from the corner of my eye only to see him sigh with relief.

The following morning I had to go in front of the Commandant yet again, but this time on a much more serious charge than my previous one.

The orderly sergeant gave his version of events but obviously didn't mention anything about our conversation. I couldn't see any point in divulging it either; the way I saw it I was in trouble whatever I said. After listening to the RSM's statement I knew mine was a lost cause.

Colonel Peck was a fair-minded man and had been very sympathetic with me when my father died, but on this occasion he was angry ... very angry indeed.

After a severe dressing down he sentenced me to seven days incarceration with loss of pay.

The lanky corporal seemed to derive sheer pleasure from the outcome, knowing full well I would be under his power for the next week. Apprehension and fear enveloped me as he marched aggressively towards me and brought one of his heavily studded boots crashing down about two inches from my feet, halting directly in front of me. His spittle literally splattered my face as he bellowed out orders. The sheer hostility in his voice visibly shook me and an involuntary shiver ran down my spine, but despite his belligerent manner I somehow managed to keep my cool. I could tell by the snarl on his face that he sensed my fear and it was obvious that he gleaned pleasure from the power he held over me.

"Pick your feet up you scumbag," he shouted as I strutted across the camp towards the guardroom, "I'll make a soldier out of you if it's the last thing I do!" He stalked over my every movement, striving to insert fear into me with his constant bellowing and bullyboy tactics.

On many occasions I'd seen him frogmarching other prisoners at the double around the camp in the same aggressive manner and each time a shudder had run down my spine. Well this time it was my turn to be on the receiving end of this barbaric creature's abuse.

"Don't let the bastard grind you down John," I thought, "you've had to contend with bullies before."

My mind went back to my childhood when I'd had to put up with many barbed comments in the schoolyard due to the fact that my dad was a rag and bone man and had been to prison twice. Children can be very cruel and I certainly had to learn how to stick up for myself. Well now I was a young man and a strong one at that, so I certainly wasn't going to let this harsh brute dampen my spirit; from that moment I was determined to use his bullyboy tactics to my own advantage so as to turn the frustration back on him. I made it a challenge … it was either him or me and I certainly didn't intend to succumb easily. The strange thing is I actually enjoyed the next seven days of confinement; but then again I had help from above in the guise of Tommy Wilkins, an inmate … and what a character he was.

"Now get that uniform off," bellowed the MP, throwing some grey denim pants and a shirt at me, "and put these rags on!"

"This shirt's too big," I complained, "and it's moth-eaten."

"Shut your mouth you little shit," he growled as he opened the cell door, "and get in there with that animal!"

This was my first meeting with my cellmate Tommy, a rough looking character with a stubbly beard. Tommy just put two fingers up to the corporal and grunted like a chimpanzee, baring his teeth.

"Bloomin' 'eck!" I thought as the MP slammed the door shut and turned the key. "Who the hell's this …what have we got here?"

The only natural light in the cell came from a small window in the steel door and a barred window fixed high into the outer wall close to the ceiling. Other than the cell door we were enclosed within a 13-inch thick wall. The ambience of the cell appeared rather depressing, but Tommy soon changed all that.

He was five feet seven inches tall the same as me with a similar stocky frame, but other than that he was totally different, with a full shaven head like Yul Brynner, and tattoos covered his arms, back and chest. My first impression of Tommy was that he was coarse and unfriendly but I was wrong. Underneath the bravado lay an affable, warm-hearted, generous bloke with a mischievous sense of humour … we hit it off almost immediately. It soon became apparent that he had a definite rebellious approach towards authority … especially this corporal.

Tommy didn't beat about the bush, asking "What's your name and what are you in for then?"

"John," I replied and went on to tell him what had happened.

"So you're only in for a week eh … a part-timer?"

"Aye that's right … and you?"

"Just a month," he replied casually.

"Bloody hell, a month!" I spluttered, "that's a long time in'it?"

"Ha ha ha! I could do that in my sleep … the last time I did three months in Colchester."

"Blimey! What did you do then?"

"I was fighting in the NAAFI Club near the docks and I laid out a couple of sailors. The military police became involved and it took four of 'em to arrest me and bring me in."

"The MP's aren't very fond of you I take it?"

"You can say that again, especially this dickhead of a corporal ... I hate him!"

"I know what you mean; he's got a right callous streak hasn't he?"

"He has that, he's notorious all right and he loves the reputation ... he's a right sadistic bastard! I've seen many a man break down and cry because of his barbaric ways, but I personally wouldn't give him the satisfaction. Even when he's getting to me I just grin at him and it really goads him ... I love it!"

"You know something, similar thoughts went through my head as he was marching me over here stomping his feet."

"I hope you do stand up to him without flinching, it'd be great to have a bit o' backup."

"Yeah so do I; there's one thing for sure, I don't intend to bend to his will."

"We'll see," laughed Tommy, "I've heard many a bloke say that but they always cracked under the brutality of the evil git!"

"Thanks very much Tommy ... that's all I need to know."

Tommy didn't mean to be intimidating ... it was just his way. "Listen lad, I believe in getting to the point and calling a spade a spade. What's the use in pussyfooting about ... he's a right bastard and you might as well know it from the word go."

"Yeah right Tommy, I know what you mean. I've got to admit that he puts the wind up me but I still intend to stick up to him."

"Good for you. Like I said ... we'll see. Anyway, it'll be good to watch."

"We will see," I thought to myself, "I'm determined not to let the barbaric thug break my spirit." I didn't either but those seven days tested my will power to the hilt.

"Hang on a minute, that'll be the pig now," said Tommy as a key turned in the cell door, "he's probably coming back for you 'cos he enjoys putting new prisoners through their paces on their first day in the nick."

"Right you measly excuse for a man," the MP rapped as he glanced into the cell, "out here now at the double and put that on!" he hissed pointing to a large rucksack kitted out with full battle gear.

"Blimey!" I thought as I hitched it to my back, "This must be loaded with stones, it weighs a ton."

The corporal just sniggered knowing full well the rucksack was weighted down.

"Now get your arse outside you friggin' little gobshite and stand to attention till I'm ready for you!"

After standing for an hour, he marched me across to the large playing field, which lay directly facing the guardroom and ordered me to run around its perimeter until he told me to stop. By the time I'd run around it twice I was dripping wet as sweat poured from me. By now it was dinnertime and some of my mates waved encouragingly at me as they made their way to the mess hall.

The slimy MP didn't like the attention I was getting, so took over, "Quick march, quick march you scumbag," he bawled, marching me at the double back to the cooler. "That'll do for starters," he retorted, shoving me back into the cell, slamming to the steel door shut, "now get back in your rat hole where you belong with that other maggot!"

"How did you get on?" smirked Tommy sprawled out on the bed with his arms behind his head.

"To tell the truth Tommy, I enjoyed it, I got a rush of adrenaline out there ... anyway, it was better than being cooped up in this dingy place." Unbeknown to the corporal, I'd built myself into prime condition since entering the army and I thrived on physical exercise.

"That's good because making prisoners run around that field is his favourite punishment ... it really gets to most blokes."

"Well it won't get to me," I laughed, "I could put up with that all day. Anyroad Tommy, does he make you do it?"

"Does he bloody hell ... he's given up on me," he roared laughing.

A few minutes later the cell door opened again and the corporal entered carrying a tray containing two dinners. He handed one to Tommy and then turned to me.

"Get this down your throat and be quick about it!" he snarled. "And don't get yourself settled because I'll be back shortly ...there'll be loads o' washing up to do afterwards." Sure enough, he returned ten minutes later and stood there arrogantly with a self satisfied look on his face, thinking he'd got one over on me. "On your feet you little gobshite ... out here now and bring them bloody plates with you!"

"Bloomin' 'eck!" I thought. "He hasn't got a polite word in his vocabulary at all?"

Outside the cell in the main body of the guardroom were six beds where the soldiers on guard duty slept, and a small office to accommodate the MP's. At the back of the room were two toilets and a small kitchen.

"Right you moron, you can wash that lot as well," he snarled pointing to a pile of dinner plates, mugs and cutlery on a wooden table, "and you'd better not break anything!"

After I'd finished he ordered me to carry everything back to the mess hall, which stood at the far end of the camp, and then scrub a large stone floor on my hands and knees with a scrubbing brush.

That night the atmosphere within the cell felt much better because the MP's finished at 18-00hours and ordinary soldiers took over until 06-00hours the following day.

Tommy was in a rather giddy mood and wanted to lark about.

"Come on John, let's have a wrestle ... I've got a load of excess energy that I want to get rid of."

"No way! It's all right for you, you've been lounging about on your bed all day ... I'm knackered. And anyroad, I want to build up some energy to impress our friendly MP tomorrow."

But he wouldn't have it and jumped on me trying to get me into a headlock ... nevertheless, I was too slithery and soon we were grappling on the floor, all in good fun. He was very strong but so was I. As we rolled about the floor I could feel his aggressiveness and I thanked God I'd kept fit, making us well matched.

"E-eh, I enjoyed that," he gasped after about ten minutes, "it wer' great!"

After a small respite he began to feel energetic again but this time he started to frolic on his own.

"Watch this John," he laughed, "I'll bet you can't do this." The next minute he started to walk on his hands but after a few yards he tumbled to the floor.

"That's easy," I said, "and I know why you fell over ... you're doing it wrong."

"Oh aye you clever sod ... let's see you do it then."

To his amazement I stood on my hands and walked the length of the room, turned around and walked back again.

"There, what did I tell you Tommy," I smirked feeling cocky.

"Bloody hell! I've always wanted to do it like that ... come on, show me how it's done?"

"Sure why not, you've almost got the knack of it now. The trouble is you're not taking your legs far enough forward in front of your head and that's why you lose your balance."

"Go on then, show me!" he blurted excitedly.

"Right, can you see now how far forward my feet are past my head?" I asked after going into a handstand.

"Yeah I can, how come you don't fall over onto your back then?" he asked curiously.

"Well it's something that you've got to get a feel for … if I feel I'm going to topple over I just adjust my hands forward accordingly. I'll tell you what … I'll do it again but this time you take notice of what I've been saying."

He watched me enthusiastically as I pranced about the cell before spluttering excitedly, "Right, I'm with you, now get out of the way … let me have a go."

He struggled at first but with perseverance mastered it and once he got the idea there was no stopping him. It was hilarious to see him prancing around the guardroom on his hands giggling like a young schoolboy … I felt I had made a friend for life.

"Watch me John this should get a laugh," he said knocking on the cell door, requesting to go to the toilet. By the time the door opened Tommy was ready and to the amusement of the guardroom soldiers he walked past them on his hands all the way to and from the toilet, leaving them all in stitches.

"That was great," he laughed on returning to the cell, "they wondered what the bloody hell was going on … I love it I love it!"

"I've got to give it to you Tommy," I mused, "you've certainly got the hang of it now … that was a superb performance."

"Yeah it was wasn't it … thanks to you John. Anyway, how about another bout of wrestling, I'm feeling energetic."

"Oh come of it Tommy, give us a break after what our friend put me through today."

He just cracked out laughing, "All right, don't have a heart attack …I'm only kidding!"

"Thank goodness for that!" I thought settling dow+n for a good night's kip.

Next morning after a sparse breakfast the RSM did an inspection accompanied by the smug corporal.

To my surprise the RSM asked me, "Any complaints Private Cowell?"

"No Sir, thank you Sir."

"Bloomin' 'eck Tommy," I said afterwards, "how come he asked me that … am I in favour or what?"

"No way, it's obligatory."

"How d'you mean … obligatory?"

"Well it's laid down in the rulebook, he has to ask every prisoner that question … and you know what a stickler the RSM is for following the rules."

"D'you mean to say he'll ask me that question every morning?"

"That's right, you've got it in one; and not only that … he has to take any complaint seriously and follow it up."

"U-um, that's handy to know … very handy indeed."

My newfound knowledge was soon put to the test after I knocked on the cell door requesting some toothpaste, only to be greeted by the corporal.

"Oh you haven't any toothpaste have you not you scruffy little urchin." he snarled sarcastically. "Well you'll just have to scrub your teeth with soap won't you!"

"No corporal, I can't do that … I want some toothpaste please."

"Well you're not bloody well getting any … understand!"

"If you don't get me any then I'm afraid I'll have to report the matter to the RSM in the morning."

"What did you say soldier?" he spat nearly swallowing his tongue.

"I'll have to report ...."

"Shut your mouth you lippy bickering worm and get your arse out here and put that on!" he fumed pointing to the full battledress. "You think you had it hard the other day … well now I'm really going to put you through your paces."

Once again he had me running around the playing field, and just like before the sweat oozed from every pore of my body. At one point I felt downtrodden but then I thought of Tommy and it spurred me on.

After the fourth time around he stopped me and growled, "Now do you feel like changing your mind?"

There was no chance, as I was actually beginning to enjoy it. Other soldiers had yielded under this treatment but most of them were smokers, whereas I'd never touched a cigarette in my life.

"No corporal," I replied defiantly looking him straight in the eyes, "I still want some toothpaste." I knew he was ruffled because I noticed nerves twitching in his face.

"Are you taking the piss you mangy git," he cursed along with a few more choice words.

I said nothing but just stood there staring defiantly back at him. His frustration built up even more and little red blood vessels appeared to erupt in his eyes. His nose snorted as he summoned up more venom from within his big bulky frame. He towered above me and his arms tightened up like steel as he clenched his fist.

I felt like yielding, as his very presence intimidated my whole being, but somehow I managed to hold steadfast. "Stand your ground John lad," I said to myself, "don't let this coward of a man grind you down."

My tactics seemed to be working ... he began to look unsure of himself. For lack of anything better to say he screeched, "Right you little scumbag ... go on, get running until I tell you to stop ... at the double!"

As I ran around the field it came to the notice of some off-duty soldiers and they all started to cheer, encouraging me to plod on in the same way my mates had done previously. There was no need, as by now I'd recovered my second wind I felt I could go on indefinitely. By now the corporal was panicking somewhat, frightened that I might collapse or something.

"Have you had enough yet you little bastard!" he grunted frothing at the mouth.

"No corporal," I smirked once again looking him right in the eyes, "I'm enjoying this ... can I go round again?"

"No you bloody well can't," he yelled, resentment showing in his face, "get yourself over to the guardroom ... **now!**"

When I got into the cell I collapsed on my bed absolutely exhausted.

"Good lad," said Tommy, "well done. I watched you from the cell window by pulling myself up on the bars. That pig of a corporal was bloody fuming ... great!"

I didn't get any more aggravation from the corporal that day and the following morning when he did his rounds with the RSM he looked rather passive.

"Right Private Cowell," asked the RSM, "have you any complaints?"

I purposely pondered for a moment, first looking at the corporal, before replying, "No Sir, thank you Sir."

The MP sighed with relief and it clearly showed on his face. After that he relented a bit towards me; he must have thought I was another Tommy ... but I still didn't get any toothpaste.

The friendship between Tommy and me made the time spent in the cell more bearable, especially when something happened that I found hilarious.

Tommy was lovesick, having a girlfriend in Plymouth who hadn't visited him since his incarceration.

"I've tried writing to her but I'm bloody hopeless with letters, I haven't got a clue where to start," he moaned, "I'm no good at words."

"Just put down what you feel about her," I said as though I was the expert, "girls like to hear nice things you know."

"Hey, hang on a minute; you seem to know a bit about it ... you write a letter for me!"

"Get lost Tommy, I can't do that. Anyroad, she'd know in a crack that it wasn't your handwriting."

"All right then, just write down anything that comes into your head and I'll copy it."

"Aye, go on then, anything for a bit of piece and quiet," I replied feeling a bit mischievous.

I scribbled down something like this on a piece of paper:

My dearest darling Helena, with all my heart I'd like to express my undying love for you but my imagination cannot capture the reality of your being. Your beauty is far beyond words or pen, the elegance of the sun, the stars or anything in the entire universe, and my feeling for you goes far deeper than the deepest ocean. The flowers, the trees, the birds ... everything in nature that is beautiful reminds me of you.

It carried on in this vein.

I was only joking but he literally copied everything I'd jotted down, more or less, word for word. I couldn't believe it next morning when he told me he'd posted the letter.

"Come off it Tommy, you haven't written down what I said have you?"

"Too bloody true I have, it brought tears to my eyes before I sealed it up. If that doesn't do the trick I don't know what will."

"Crikey!" I cringed as I scratched my head, "I hope so Tommy, I really do."

Well, nobody was more surprised than me by what happened next. Helena received the letter and it worked a treat; the following evening she came to visit him and the meeting was all 'lovey dovey, kissy kissy'.

"Success!" I thought, feeling happy for Tommy.

"Thanks mate," he smirked after Helena had left, "that was great, I owe you one ... she's well in love with me again." For the remainder of that night he was as happy as a lark.

The remaining days in the cooler passed quickly and, although I didn't relish being locked up my time spent there was very memorable. All the same, I was glad to be released.

****

During the next few months an arduous regime continued and, my army mates and I spent many hours, on the bleak expanse of Dartmoor, setting up makeshift field hospitals. Other times we did long route marches with full battle regalia on our backs over the vast grasslands, which were criss-crossed with muddy tank tracks. I found it very fatiguing trying to negotiate soft peaty soil covered in thick ferns, heather, bracken and moss. On many occasions, after footslogging until sunset we just bivouacked down for the night in the middle of nowhere. On one occasion we had to traipse through a swamp that, to me, looked like the Straight of Gibraltar .Despite being out in the open, I still slept well that night. Other days, still fully dressed in battle regalia, we spent hours on an army assault course specially designed to test the fittest of men. We'd to climb high hanging nets and scale six-foot walls prior to crawling through muddy pipes on our bellies and negotiating many other obstacles. Hence, were all in prime peak condition, up and ready to be sent anywhere in the world at short notice.

****

On reflection, the main reason why I wanted to go into the Service Corps was so I could learn to drive.

However, after serving a few months it got me got to thinking, "I'm glad now that I got placed in the Medics; I really enjoy working as a nursing orderly in the field hospitals. Yeah, when I get demobbed I might even apply to work as a nurse at Burnley General Hospital like our Barry. But it would be an added bonus if I got my driving licence as well … I wonder how I can do that?"

I racked my brains trying to think of something but to no avail. Then one Saturday afternoon whilst walking along Union Street in Plymouth I passed a British School Of Motoring centre. There was an advertisement in the window that read:

A COURSE OF LESSONS WITH US GUARANTEES A 90% PASS RATE.
COME IN AND ASK FOR A QUOTE.

"Why not?" I thought, "I may as well find out how much it'll cost me … I've got now't to lose."

"Six shillings a lesson," said the receptionist, "and we recommend that you take at least two lessons a week for a period of six weeks."

"U-um, that's twelve bob a week," I pondered, ""that'll only leave me with thirteen bob." I knew I'd struggle but I felt a tinge of excitement building up in my stomach. "Oh blow it! I've bín skint afore ... a few more weeks isn't gonna mék that much difference."

I started my lessons with enthusiasm but things didn't go too well and after eight lessons the school informed me that I would need to take at least another ten to come up to scratch. And then there was the added cost of a few pounds for the driving test. I became rather despondent as negative thoughts ran through my head.

"Oh 'eck, what if I don't pass the test the first time, that'll mean more expense ... I just can't do it!" I was feeling rather dejected but then I came up with an idea that paid dividends. I went to see my C O Colonel Peck, and asked for an advance on my future pay.

"And what's so important that you need this money now?" he asked.

I explained the reason, emphasising that my driving licence would come in handy during my army career. "During emergencies I would be able to drive ambulances, stretcher Rovers or any other vehicle for that matter sir." To my surprise he was intrigued and came up with something to my advantage.

"Private Cowell, I've got to say that I'm highly impressed with your enterprising scheme ... I only wish I had more men under my command who thought like you. Yes indeed, anyone who would spend so much out of his meagre pay deserves some encouragement."

"Encouragement!" I thought. "This sounds interesting."

To my delight he then said as he handed me a chit of paper, "As from this moment you don't have to spend another penny out of your own pocket ... take this form to the Service Corps Depot and give it to one of the officers." He looked at me with a pleasant smile on his face and asked, "Do you know what this is?"

"No sir?"

Well, it's an authorisation slip requesting the officer in charge of vehicles to arrange a full course of driving lessons and a driving test for you. I think it's a good idea what you've come up with and from now on I'm going to arrange for every man in my regiment to undergo driving instructions." He muttered to himself as he stroked his chin, "Yes indeed, it should prove very useful to them and the corps during their spell in the army ... especially driving the stretcher Rovers." Turning his attention back to me he said, "Right Private Cowell, seeing as you came up with the idea I think it only fair that you should be the first to do it along with another lad. So, starting from Monday morning you will be excused normal duties ... how does that sound to you?"

"Very good sir," I stammered obviously delighted, "thank you very much sir!"

"Just one more thing before you go, have you anyone in mind who'd you'd like to join you?"

"Yes sir I have," I replied hardly able to believe my luck. "Private Brian Holdsworth, he's in the same billet as me."

"Yes I'm quite aware of where he's stationed thank you. I'll make arrangements for him to be excused duties as well."

I couldn't wait to get back to tell my mate Brian. He was as excited as I was and went eagerly with me to the Service depot.

"Right," muttered the officer in charge after reading the slip of paper, "report to me the pair of you on Monday morning directly after inspection parade and I'll get one of the corporals to take you out in a Land Rover."

That was it ... Brian and I couldn't believe our luck.

"Great!" laughed Brian expressing his obvious delight, "no more fatigue duties for a few weeks and a chance o' geddín our driving licences in the bargain ... absolutely great!"

For the next three weeks, Brian and I thoroughly enjoyed ourselves getting to know Plymouth and all the surrounding countryside very well. Our driving instructor was Corporal Gallagher, a regular soldier. We had our first driving lesson on an old disused aerodrome prior to taking to the roads of Dartmoor, driving through Princetown and other neighbouring villages. But we did most of our driving course around Plymouth city centre, driving past the docks, Plymouth Hoe, Union Street, and the Drake Cinema near to the NAAFI Club.

Things were going great and then something happened in West Africa, which almost put an end to our good fortune. There had recently been an uprising in the Belgian Congo, West Africa and now the British Cameroon was fighting for its independence. A state of emergency was called throughout the camp and all leave and special privileges were cancelled forthwith.

"Oh no, what lousy timing!" moaned Brian, "We'd o' bin' going in for our test in two weeks ... now this has blown it."

I was disappointed as Brian, but then I came up with an idea. "I don't know so much Brian, all's not lost yet. How about us going to see the Service Corps' officer and asking him if he'll test us today?"

"Oh sure, and how do we get excused duties after th'inspection parade?"

"We'll just tell the sergeant major that everything's bin arranged with the Service Corps."

"What, just like that? He'll have our guts for garters if he checks it out... we'll be thrown in't cooler quicker than we can blink."

"Oh come on Brian, we've got loads to gain from it ... I'm gam' if you are."

"Aye OK John, I suppose you're reight, it'd be a shame to give up at this stage."

So we took a risk, by playing one officer off against the other. First we'd to get past our own sergeant major.

"What?" he screamed, his handlebar moustache twitching as air gushed out of his mouth, "I haven't been told anything about it!"

"Yes sir, it's right," I said lying as I stared him in the eyes, "the officer in charge of transport said we had to get there as quickly as possible." Luckily for us he didn't double check on it as he had other things on his mind. He just grunted and growled once more, then let us go.

When we reached the vehicle depot the officer in charge was just as puzzled, "I'm afraid I don't know anything about it … have you got an authorisation slip?"

Feeling flustered, I had to think fast, "Well no sir, but the sergeant major sent us down here to see if you could test us this morning. "He said it would be handy to have at least two drivers amongst the medics when we go abroad."

To our relief he didn't question it further, "Righto then, you come with me," he said pointing to Brian, "I'll take you first."

By the end of that morning both Brian and I had passed … we were elated. We were also relieved, we'd taken a risk and got away with it; no cross-checking was done, as everybody seemed too involved with the emergency situation.

"Congratulations," said the officer as he handed us both an authorisation slip, "well done!

Looking down at the little slip of paper in my hand, I gloated in sheer delight, "Ye-eah … I've done it … I've done it!"

****

Only the powers that be knew where our destinies lie and in our case it happened to be West Africa. Just a couple of days later we were all informed that our regiment was being posted to the British

Cameroons. I was quite pleased in a way because at least I would get to see another part of the world. My mate Ernie was rather taken aback because he wasn't being drafted abroad alongside us.

"Bloomin' 'eck John, just my luck," he moaned, they won't take me because I've only got another two months to serve."

"You'll just have to sign on for another three years Ernie as a regular," I joked, "they'll take you then, that's for sure."

"You know something John, I've thought about that but, because I've just met Maureen, I can't do it."

"Eh, I'm sorry about that my mate, I'm going to miss you."

"Yeah, me too, we could have had a ball out there in Africa. Anyway John, good luck and I'll see you again back in Burnley sometime." I felt sad for Ernie. It turned out to be our last meeting under army life.

Talk of an uprising in Cameroons against Nigerian Authority spread through the barracks and within twenty-four hours the entire camp was put on emergency standby. All leave was cancelled until further notice. Standing orders notified us that we had to report in batches to the medical centre in order to be inoculated against foreign diseases. A bit of scare mongering went on amongst the lads, as rumour had it that during the First World War, the Cameroons was referred to as *'The white man's grave'*. This came about because many men had died due to numerous diseases prominent in that part of the world. The Cameroon climate is one of the most humid in the world and the English soldier was very prone to tropical diseases and open to infection. Because of the circumstances, a law has since been passed in Parliament and now, under no circumstances, can any British soldier serve more than nine months in that harsh environment.

"Bloomin' 'eck, I'm not looking forward to this!" I moaned as I stood in line waiting to be inoculated by dreaded needles." No neither am I" whined Rob, "why do we have to have them anyway?"

"Because you wouldn't last two minutes in Africa without 'em, that's why you bloody dimwit," rapped a corporal who was standing directly behind us. "Especially when you go out on patrol in the jungle over there."

"I take it you've been somewhere like this before?" I asked

"Well I've never been to the Cameroons, but I have served in a tropical climate twice before in the Far East. But even I have to top up my immune system because there are so many different diseases that we are not immune to."

"How many pricks do we have to have?" asked a rather nervous looking lad. I can't stand needles, does it hurt?"

If he was looking for sympathy he didn't get it. In fact the corporal just sneered and teased him, "Yeah, you're not kidding it bloody well hurts and the sadistic bastards give you three, using the bloody longest needles they can find."

The poor lad turned as white as a sheet and his distress increased even more as another bloke mocked him, "I've heard the vaccine for yellow fever is thick like treacle and it kills when it's going in."

"Yeah, and it throbs for hours afterwards and it numbs all your fingers, sneered the corporal. "And if you think that's bad, the one for smallpox is even worse."

Others joined in ribbing the poor lad and he started to shake like an aspen leaf on a windy day.

Mind you, he wasn't the only one. I could feel my legs trembling, but I didn't let on to anyone ... no way. If I had have done, they'd have ribbed me as well.

Ironically, fate took a hand. What happened next reminded me of something my dad had said to me when I was a young lad. "What goes around our John, comes around. Do anybody a bad turn in this life and somewhere along the way it will rebound back onto to you."

Well it certainly did in this case. The nervous lad had all his injections without any adverse effects, whereas the corporal came over all faint and had to be sat down on a chair. As for the other soldier, who had been ribbing him, he flaked out completely and had to be laid on a bed. The rest of us got a right laugh when the nervous lad went up to the NCO asking, "Are you all right corporal, is there anything I can do for you?"

After the ordeal, I was all right, but quite a few other lads had slight reactions and retired to their bunks.

To our delight, Colonel Peck, our commanding officer, granted us all ten days embarkation leave. But he made it abundantly clear that, should the need be, we would have to report back to camp at short notice. After collecting railway warrants for the homeward and return journey we all made our way to the railway station. I'd been on home leave before but this time it felt different, much different. I knew that on returning back to barracks, I wouldn't see my family for quite a spell afterwards. Also, the daunting aspect kept crossing my mind that I may never ever see them again. For this very reason, I became determined to enjoy every moment at home amongst my loved ones. It was during this short spell that I met up with my future wife at a Saturday night dance in the Empress Ballroom.

When I arrived home I was feeling at a loose end, as most of my friends were serving abroad in the Forces; however I was determined to enjoy my last Saturday night in England before I too was shipped out of the country. As it happened I'd been down town that afternoon and bumped into another mate of mine, Martin Grogan, who came out with some intriguing news.

"All reight Johnny," he greeted me, "how's it going?"

"Oh not so bad Martin, an' you," I asked, "are you still playing football nowadays?"

"Aye I am, but not in Civvy Street, I'm in th'army now doing mí National Service."

"Bloomin' 'eck Martin, so am I; what regiment are you with?"

"I'm in th'infantry serving with the King's Own Borderers and I'm stationed at Barnard Castle up in Durham ... which regiment are you with?"

"I'm in the Medics and I'm stationed in Plymouth in Devon. I weren't keen on th'idea at first but it's all reight now; in fact, I'm quite enjoying it."

"Yeah, you will be you lucky bugger," he joked, "it's just like thí to get a cushy number."

"You wouldn't say that Martin if you knew where I wer' going next week."

"How's that then, where are you off to?"

"To a place called the Cameroons somewhere in West Africa near to the Belgium Congo."

"You're joking!" he laughed. "That's incredible, I don't believe it."

"Why not, what's so funny about that Martin... soldiers are geddin' posted abroad all the time?"-

"Oh I know that John," he laughed, "but the thing is ... I'm geddin' posted there as well."

"You're joking!" I said responding as he did, "You mean to say you're on embarkation leave too?"

"I am that and I get shipped out next Thursday on the Devonshire, a large troopship from Southampton."

"Flamin' emma, this is geddin' more uncanny by the minute," I grinned, "that's the same boat as I'm going on … you never know, we'll be sharing the same bunk next."

"Bloomin' 'eck that's great John!" he said excitedly. "We're gonna have to do somét about it … how about a celebration toníte?"

"I'm all for that Martin … have you ow't planned?"

"Aye, I have as a matter o' fact … I've bín told it's a great night o'er in Rawtenstall at the Astoria Ballroom … what d'you think?"

"Aye, why not, it sounds good to me … what bus d'you wanna catch?"

"Well, I'll catch the seven o'clock bus from th'end ó Trafalgar … how about you?"

"Yeah fair enough, I'll catch it further up Manchester Road outside the Rose and Crown."

"Sounds good enough to me," said Martin, "I'll see thí later then … think on, don't forget."

"There's no danger o' that," I grinned, "I'm lookin' forward to it as much as you are."

The bus was on schedule and as arranged we arrived in Rawtenstall around half-past seven.

"How about having a couple o' pints in the Queens?" asked Martin. "It's usually packed in there and a good atmosphere?"

"Yeah, I'm with you there Martin," I replied, "it's the same pub I've always gone in with mí mates Pete Holly and Dave Whittaker."

We entered the pub full of enthusiasm but to our disappointment there were only a few people stood around the bar.

"Bloomin' 'eck John, it's flamin' dead in here," moaned Martin, "I wonder what's goin' on … I've never known it this empty afore?"

"No, neither have I, it's usually jam packed by this time. Still, give it another half an hour … things may buck up."

However, before we'd finished our first pint, Martin became a little edgy, realising something was wrong.

"Bloomin' 'eck John," he whined again, "whose flamin' idea wer' it to come to this pub?"

"Well, if I remember rightly Martin it wer' …."

"Aye I know it wer' me," he laughed, "don't remind me. Still, I wonder where everybody is … I can't weigh it up."

"No, neither can I. Anyroad, I don't know about you, but I'm bursting … I'll have to nip to the loo."

"Aye, me too," quipped Martin, "I'll join thi"

We both made our way to the gents where we got talking to another lad from Burnley, Joe Franklands.

"All reight Joe," said Martin, "it's flamin' dead in here tonight in'it?"

"Aye I know it is," replied Joe, "and I know why too. I've just found out that most people have gone down the Nelson Imp 'cos Johnny Dankworth and Cleo Laine are playin' there toníte. It'll be no good goin' to th'Astoria, it'll be as dead as a dodo in there."

"Charming," retorted Martin, "flamin' charming! We've come all the way o'er here to have a rave-up and everybody's back o'er in our neck o' the woods."

"Blast it," I moaned, "that's put the tin hat on'it! What are we gonna do now?"

"There's not much we can do," replied Martin looking at his watch, "by the time we caught the bus back to Burnley and then to Nelson it'd all be o'er bar the shouting. We'll just have to mék the best of a bad thing."

"P-p-pth," I pouted, "just our flamin' luck, and on our last Saturday night out in England for ages."

"Not to worry lads," put in Joe with a grin on his face, "if you want to go down th'Imp I'll ték you there."

"How d'you mean Joe," asked Martin, "how canya do that?"

"Well I've got a van outside; I only bought it two days ago. It's only an old banger but it gets me fro' A to B and that's all I'm bothered about."

"Oh great! enthused Martin. "That'll do us ... as long as it gets us down th'Imp that's all we're bothered about as well."

I was as keen as Martin to get to the Nelson Imperial and so after quickly downing our pints we clambered onto the back of Joe's rickety old van and headed back up Burnley Road. It was a bumpy ride but we arrived at the Nelson Imperial about ten o'clock and it was absolutely packed to the doors.

"Yeah!" exclaimed Martin excitedly, "this is more like it, the place is buzzing."

"You're not kidding," I agreed, "I've never seen it as packed as this afore ... it's absolutely heaving in'it?"

It was a great atmosphere all right ... you could feel the dance floor moving up and down with the sheer weight of all the young folk doing their own thing. Little did Martin and I know that we were to meet two girls that night, who were to become our future wives. Shortly after arriving there I lost Martin in the crowd and didn't see him again that night. In fact, the next time I was to see him was when we were sailing to Africa together on the Devonshire where the conversation went as follows.

"What happened to you Martin when we got to th'Imp ... I lost you once we'd got into the ballroom."

"Aye. No bloomin' wonder John in that crowd ... it were superb weren't it? Anyroad, the first person I saw on entering the ballroom was a girl called Mary Smith, who was dancing with her sister. We clicked right away and after dancing with her all night I made a date with her."

"Bloomin' 'eck Martin, somét similar happened to me. After losing you I spotted a girl who I've fancied for ages ... they call her Edna Simpson. I've seen her loads o' times down th'Empress Ballroom but I was always too scared to ask her for a dance. When I saw her this time though I plucked up the courage. I thought blow it, what have I got to lose, I won't be coming home again for at least a year."

"Aye, and what happened then?"

"Well, I asked her onto the floor and everything just flowed ... I found her dead easy to get on with. We had a couple of bops during the rock 'n' roll session and I even attempted a quickstep. I took her on the floor for the last waltz and then asked if I could take her home. We chatted easily and so I made a date to see her the on Sunday night. I met her under the clock outside the Palace and we went for a drink in the Hall Inn and the Coach and Horses. We had a really good night and decided to swap addresses so we could write to each other whilst I'm away in Africa.

****

My embarkation leave soon passed and the day arrived when I had to make my way back to the barracks in Plymouth. It was quite a sad affair as I waved Mum farewell as she stood by the garden gate. As I made my way along Moorland Road I was full of nostalgia ... everything about my life seemed to be changing so quickly.

My grandparents and Dad had died, my Albion Street days had come to an end and now I was being shipped off to the Cameroons in West Africa ... it might as well have been the other side of the moon!

Before making my way to the railway station I decided to call in at no 14 Albion for a last look. My old home was still vacant and the front door remained locked. However, not to be put off I walked around the back and entered the house via the fourteen stone cellar steps. As I walked through the lobby the house seemed to come alive as nostalgic memories flooded through my head.

My mind flashed back to my childhood days: My Uncle Ted, the Workhouse, Mum's stories, my schooldays, playing on the frontstreet, working down the pit, all my fond teenage memories of Sandygate Youth Club and finally, my home leave from the army.

"Well John lad," I lamented sighing deeply, "I've spent a lot of happy times here, a lot of hard ones mind, but happy times all the same." I looked at the flag floors and the old cast-iron fireplace, which triggered off even more memories within me as I saw all my brothers and sisters' happy smiling faces and I could hear all their laughter. The old gas-lamp was still hanging from the ceiling, covered in dust, never to be lit by me again.

And then I saw Dad in one of his frivolous moods dancing a kind of Irish jig in front of the fire with his trousers folded above the knees. He looked so funny as he danced on the old pegged rug … his legs were so skinny, just like picking sticks. I saw myself laughing at how I used to think there was more meat on a ginny spinner's legs. The laughter turned to chuckles as I remembered the time he'd brought Peggy, our horse, into the living room when he was drunk, and the time he was equally drunk, when he got stuck in the coal-chute, trying to get into the house after Mum had locked him out.

"Aye Dad," I murmured to myself, my eyes welling up, "when you were like that you were great … absolutely great, I wouldn't o' swapped thi' for any other dad in the world! Anyroad, I'm going now Dad but I'll never forget you, you'll always be in my thoughts and my prayers wherever I go … and I know I'll gain strength from that."

I then walked upstairs and glanced for the last time over the rooftops of all the other streets. The distant hills of Cliviger and the Bacup hills beyond reminded me of my cycling days.

In the chimney alcove nearest to the window I smiled noticing the pencil marks that my two brothers and I had scribbled there over the years, depicting the progress of our growth. By the side of the marks were excited comments by whoever had grown the most.

The cracks in the ceiling were still apparent and my imagination still conjured up many different shapes as I recalled the happy hours we'd spent playing 'I spy with my little eye'. The bare wood floors, my secret hiding place, looked so sparse and yet all I could think of were the good times I'd spent there. The hours we'd played about with candles, hanging up pillowcases on Christmas Eve in preference to stockings … I even pictured our Jimmy playing there happy and contented with his bag of dried peas spread all over the wooden boards pretending they were regiments of soldiers. Finally I looked at the place where my bed had been and where I'd prayed every night alongside my two brothers before going to sleep. I thanked God that we had all come through it safely, and asked Him to keep His holy light shining around my family and me and to guide us on our way throughout the rest of our lives. And especially so whilst I was out in Africa.

At that I got down on my knees and said my last prayer in that humble house.

I was brought back to reality as I heard the Town Hall Clock and Watt's Clock chiming simultaneously on the hour as I'd heard them so many times in the past.

I smiled to myself and sighed at the same time, "A-ah well I'd better be off … let's see what life holds in store for me in the Cameroons."

I descended the multi-coloured staircase and finally walked through the lobby. I unbolted the front door and closed it for the last time, leaving it unlocked as it had always been throughout my young life. On reaching the bottom of Albion Street I took my last look at the humble abode and, taking a deep breath, made my way to the Barracks' Station.

I felt rather sad as I meandered along Trafalgar passing all the familiar cobbled streets, Rowley Street, Whitaker Street, Derby Street, Sandygate, Mile Street and finally Lord Street where the Pawnshop, sporting the three balls above its shop window, still stood on the corner. Memories of all the poor folk, who had pledged heirlooms and other valuable objects just to make ends meet, flooded through my head; I could picture them as plain as day bartering with the smug Pawnbroker. Mrs Thompson's happy smiling face sprang readily to mind.

Before leaving Lord Street my thoughts were on my young friend Derek Ratcliffe, who was tragically killed on Trafalgar whilst riding a butcher's bike at the age of sixteen.

"My how time flys," I thought, "that's over five years ago. "May God bless you Derek ... I know I'll never forget you and I'll keep you in my prayers."

As I passed the Alhambra picture House I reflected on the Saturday afternoon matinees and the times I'd spent there with my friends, David Whittaker, Ronnie Hopkinson, Kenny Clayton and Bobby Cheetham. Also the time David and I had sneaked in the side door and been copped by Bella, David's mum. And finally, just before reaching the Mitre Junction, I stopped at the Ribble bus-stop at the side of Mullen and Durkin's Builder's Yard.

"U-um," I thought, "many are the time that I've caught the Accrington bus here during my working days timber running at Thorney

Bank Colliery." I lingered a while longer reflecting on all the nostalgic memories ... I even smiled when the dreaded 'Bluebird' came to mind. Taking a deep breathe I then tried to compose myself, "A-ah well never mind John," I mused, "it all seems rather sad but still, look on the bright side ... you've made a lot of new friends in the army and most of 'em are going off to West Africa with you." At that moment my thoughts were interrupted by a voice from behind me; as I turned there stood Jack Lofthouse.

"All reight Johnny Cowell," he said as bright and cheerful as always, "where are you goin' in that army uniform?"

"Oh hiya Jack, how's it going ... it's a long time no see?"

"It is that too, long gone are the days when we used to raid the Paper Mill. By 'eck, but they were good days weren't they Johnny?"

"They were that Jack ... we fairly got into some scrapes didn't we?"

"We did that, it were really good fun. Anyroad you still haven't told me where you're off to."

"Well, believe it or not Jack, I'm making my way back to Plymouth on a train and as from next week I'm being shipped off to the Cameroons in West Africa."

"You lucky so and so you're now't else ... I wish I were comin' abroad with you 'cos there's now't round here worth stoppin' for anymore. Anyroad," he added as he walked off, "let me know if ther's any good papermills o'er yonder, ha, ha, ha!" Then on a more serious note, at least for Jack, he called, "All the best Johnny... go and show 'em what the Trafalgar wallers are made off!"

"What the 'eck!" I thought, "I'm just turned twenty-one and as fit as a fiddle. The world's my oyster ... come on John lad go for it!"

I smiled, threw out my chest and walked on with a spring in my step as I entered this new chapter in my life!

EPILOGUE

I spent the remainder of my army service working as a nursing orderly in army field hospitals in West Africa. After a two week Atlantic journey on the 'Devonshire,' a large troop ship' I was posted forty miles inland to Kumba, a small village in the middle of a thick tropical jungle. During this time I made many friends working alongside local natives. I had known poverty, but these deprived people were poor beyond believe. My upbringing held me in good stead.

THE YOUNG MINER

I left school at fifteen years of age,
To go down the pit was all the rage.
I left for work with head held high,
And wanted to show the whole world why.
I worked very hard in every way,
And can honestly say I deserved my pay.

My first task was as a tackle lad,
Taking from me all the strength I had.
Steel girders and props I had to carry,
For every Tom, Dick and Harry.
The colliers were a happy lot,
So long as I was on the dot.
But woe betide if I was late,
Getting tackle to the bottom gate.

The gate was likened to a tunnel,
Running from the coalface like a funnel.
Throughout the tunnel ran a conveyor belt,
Onto which the coal was spilt.
Alongside this ran a small steel track,
To help carry the tackle right to the pack.
The pack consisted of shale and stone,
To help sustain the weight in that lower zone.
Tackle lads always worked as a pair,
T'was better as far as wear and tear.
Working as hard as on can,
The boy very soon became the man.
The weekly wage was just a fiver,
No one could be called a skiver.

A bonus which helped boost this cash,
Each collier gave us some 'pey-brass'.
For carrying all those props and bricks,

Each miner handed over 'two and six'.
Till the age of eighteen I kept up this pace,
Then commenced training on the coalface.
Seven yards of rubble I had to haul,
In order to shift sixteen tons of coal.

Water leaked in from the layers above,
One could say ours was an act of love.
Working in conditions that were wet and dusty,
It's little wonder ... one's knees were rusty.

Toiling in seams only eighteen inches high,
Many a back felt broken ... no one wondered why.
Seven and half hours we had to strive,
In order to keep our hopes alive.
An extra bonus given to shift the lot,
An incentive to keep us on the dot.
Colliers and tackle lads worked as a team,
Their goal ... to completely strip the seam.
Because of the friendship we were seldom beat,
Working together we completed this special feat.
At the time I often wondered why,
Those men always appeared so home and dry.
Looking back over my own life's span,
I know the miner is a special kind of man.

Working deep down in the bowels of the earth,
With a deep commitment for all his worth.
Beneath the ground ... each one like a brother,
The life of each one ... dependant on the other.
Since then I've worked everywhere you can name,
But the camaraderie had never been the same.

JUNIOR SCHOOL

St. Thomas's was the name of our school,
All the kids were poor but ever so cool.
Wearing steel bottom clogs that made a great sound,
Creating bright sparks by kicking the ground.
At nine on the dot into single file we fell,
Then marched into class to the sound of the bell.
Paraded like soldiers dressed in our togs,
Clip clop, clip clop, went the sound of our clogs.

At playtime we used to play in the yard,
i soon learnt I hadd to be hard.
The yard was concrete, and much to my plight,
In that very yard, I had my first fight.
Sparks from clogs, shouts and jeers,
Left many a black eye filled with tears.
'Twas a hard life, but not quite so cruel,
No kicking, no biting! One stuck to the rule.
Life is quite strange, and through all this strife,
Lots of us kids became friends for life.

.